384.5540941 SEN

UNIVERSITY OF WESTMINSTER

✔ KU-249-734

HARROW COLLEGE LIBRARY

3 8022 00025097 7

INDEPENDENT
TELEVISION
IN BRITAIN

Volume 1

Origin and Foundation, 1946–62

Forthcoming volumes in the same work by the same author

Volume 2   EXPANSION AND CHANGE, 1958–68

Volume 3   RECOGNITION AND RESPONSIBILITY, 1968–80

TELEVISION SITUATION

The original of this cartoon was presented by Sir David Low to Mr Norman Collins, who has kindly made the photograph available. It appeared in the *Manchester Guardian* on 22 September 1954, and refers to a flurry of indignation amongst Conservative politicians, and expressed in some newspapers, at the appointment of a former Socialist, Sir Robert Fraser, as Director General of the Independent Television Authority. (Published by permission of the Low Trustees and the *Standard*)

INDEPENDENT
TELEVISION
IN BRITAIN

Volume 1
Origin and Foundation, 1946–62

BERNARD SENDALL

© Independent Broadcasting Authority and
Independent Television Companies Association 1982

All rights reserved. No part of this publication may be
reproduced or transmitted, in any form or by any means,
without permission

First published 1982 by
THE MACMILLAN PRESS LTD
London and Basingstoke
Companies and representatives
throughout the world

ISBN 0 333 30941 3

Printed in Great Britain by
PITMAN PRESS LTD
Bath

HARROW COLLEGE OF

HIGHER EDUCATION LIBRARY

To Robert Fraser
Architect of Independent Television

CONTENTS

PREFACE AND
ACKNOWLEDGEMENTS

I embarked upon this history because I was asked to do so by the Independent Television Companies Association with the agreement of the Independent Broadcasting Authority. It was a flattering invitation to receive after twenty-two years' involvement in ITV. There were to be no strings saving those imposed by the requirements of publishing. Such archives as I sought to consult would be made available. I was to remain my own man, and this is the first volume of a history of events viewed by one who played some part in them in the public authority sector of the system. Those who had experience elsewhere in ITV may well have seen these events in quite a different light.

I began work in the autumn of 1978, shortly after the publication of the Labour Government's White Paper of July 1978.[1] This made clear what, so far as television was concerned, would be the main item in Labour's legislation about broadcasting in 1979, namely the introduction of a third force in the shape of an Open Broadcasting Authority. But the reception of it at Westminster also showed that if within the next year or so a Conservative Government came to power then this legislation would make provision for a second Independent Television service planned in conjunction with the first. In either event Independent Television would in some degree be plunged back into the turmoil of politics out of which it had been born in 1954. It appeared to be a good time to begin to record the growth of this unique feature in the social history of the past quarter of a century. This is the first of three volumes which will between them trace the story of Independent Television from its origins through to the new Broadcasting Act and the franchise decisions of 1980.

From both the Annan Committee on the Future of Broadcasting, which reported in March 1977, and the Labour Government, had come words which unequivocally established that the story of Independent Television had been not only of crucial importance in the history of British broadcasting but also beyond question a success story. The Annan Report said:

> in our judgment – and we believe the public's – the greatest of all changes in the nation's broadcasting system took place when commercial television was born in 1955. The new system has been successful because it introduced *regulated* competition into what was until then a monopoly.[2]

and

> At a time when the art of governance in Britain – the reconciliation of public interest with initiative, productivity, and satisfaction in one's job – has fallen into some disrepute, the achievement and success of the British system of organising commercial broadcasting ought not to go unrecorded.[3]

The Labour Government said:

> The Government welcomes the opportunity of this White Paper to associate itself with the Annan Committee's general praise of the performance of the IBA.[4]

These favourable verdicts came after Independent Television had been operating for more than twenty years. The report of the Pilkington Committee in 1962 had had vastly different things to say. For example: 'The disquiet about and dissatisfaction with television are, in our view, justly attributed very largely to the service of independent television'.[5] How these judgements, separated by a space of fifteen years, came to differ so greatly will emerge in this history.

Independent Television today is a complex organisation in which the individual enterprise of fifteen separate programme companies is knit together under the Independent Broadcasting Authority to produce a kind of unity in diversity, providing what the Annan Report called 'regulated competition'. The new Channel Four is being planned to include programmes from other producers not directly under contract to the IBA. The amount of regulation that prevailed in 1960–2 when the Pilkington Committee was deliberating was markedly less than it was between 1974 and 1977 when the Annan Committee was at work. As Annan was not slow to perceive, the pendulum had, if anything, swung rather too far in some respects towards regulation. However, to see the story of Independent

Television in terms of how something bad eventually became good would be to see it in a distorting mirror. The most far-reaching decisions of the Authority itself were those taken in the very first year of its existence in 1954/5. It was then rather than in the sixties that the seeds of success were planted.

This first volume dwells extensively on political issues and on problems of structure, finance and organisation. It was organisational change which created Independent Television in 1954 and it was this too which principally determined the character of ITV in the sixties and seventies. But I accept the argument of which Lord Windlesham has reminded us in *Broadcasting in a Free Society*[6] that it is on the values of the programme makers rather than on organisational factors that the standards of British broadcasting ultimately depend, and I have paid attention to programme developments, particularly in Parts III and V.

In 1961 there appeared unobtrusively a timely book. Its title was *British Broadcasting in Transition*, and it described developments in radio and television, but especially the latter, since the BBC monopoly ended in 1954. Its author was Burton Paulu, Director of the Department of Radio and Television Broadcasting at the University of Minnesota.[7] Dr Paulu was by no means unknown in British broadcasting, for he had earlier published *British Broadcasting: Radio and Television in the United Kingdom* to which the further book was a sequel.[8]

British Broadcasting in Transition was a lucid, scrupulously fair, brief but scholarly assessment of the impact of competition on television over more than five years of BBC–ITV competition. Had it been made required reading for members of the Pilkington Committee, whose cerebrations will be described in Volume II, and had it been decreed that all who volunteered evidence to that Committee should first have read it, much confusion, misunderstanding, and prejudice laced with large measures of ignorance, would have been avoided. Other published works I have found especially helpful were later in date. One is *The Mirror in the Corner: People's Television* by Peter Black.[9] This lively book, written in 1972 by a journalist at the height of his powers and after twenty years of observing television, remains a source of enlightenment for those who wish to understand what, in the British context, competition in broadcasting meant. Another is *Factual Television* by Norman Swallow[10], published in 1966. Here was a book by someone who had himself worked as a writer, producer and director for both BBC and ITV for sixteen years and had reached the peak of his profession.

Whilst the present volume was in preparation there was published a story of television advertising, entitled *The Tuppenny Punch and Judy Show* by Jo

Gable.[11] Limitations of time and space have led me to rule out attempting, as ideally I should have done, to provide the advertising counterpart to the programme story told in Part v, and I am glad that this entertaining book has filled the gap.

Publications without which, as one says, this history could not have been written have stemmed from Her Majesty's Stationery Office; reports, White Papers and, last but not least, the oft-ignored Hansard itself. For his massive reading of the Parliamentary Debates I am indebted, as for much else, to Joseph Weltman OBE. It was my great good fortune to find him available to join me early in 1979, nominally as a research assistant. He was an old colleague and friend, who had come to the ITA in 1963 as its first Education Officer after previous experience both in radio and television with the BBC and with Granada Television. Various parts of the book rely heavily on Joe Weltman's patient studies. I am glad to declare my dependence on his collaboration and to place on record my immense gratitude to him.

So far I have consulted fewer people than perhaps I might have done and they are not 'too numerous to mention'. I must express my gratitude to three men whom I came to regard as my 'professorial board'. By a typically informal decision of the ITCA and IBA they assumed the task of looking after my interests. Their convenor has been Sir Denis Forman, Chairman of Granada Television, who has worked in ITV since its inception. The other two have been Lord Windlesham, Chairman and Managing Director of ATV Network until December 1981, who came to Independent Television in 1957 but left it temporarily between 1970 and 1974 when he was a member of the Government, and Sir Brian Young, Director General of the IBA, who came to ITV from outside the industry in 1970. All three gave up time to guide and steer me, but never to control me.

In this first volume in particular, I owe a special debt to my old friend Norman Collins, both for the information he gave me and for his advice on typescript, based as much upon his experience as an author as on the influential part he played in many of the events I have described. I am also much indebted to Sir Geoffrey Cox, to the late Cecil Bernstein and to Howard Thomas.

I must gratefully acknowledge the help in relation to Part v given to me by Bernard Davies, who has since died. He wrote critically about television programmes for nearly twenty-five years, first for *Television Mail* and then for its successor, *Broadcast*. He was an ideal 'informed outsider'.

Finally, there is Sir Robert Fraser who might fairly be described as the architect and master builder of Independent Television. Throughout his sixteen years as Director General, Fraser wrote and spoke *living history*. I have drawn heavily on his writings, some of them published, but most in the form of internal correspondence and memoranda, never written with a view to publication. The extent of my obligation to him will be readily understood by everyone with whom he worked during the early years of Independent Television.

I have been blest by the help of Miss Joan Shilston MBE, my secretary in former times, who, by the courtesy of the IBA, has spared me approximately one day a week. Nobody could have been better qualified to hunt out documents and help me assemble a mass of information into some sort of order. Another part-timer, Mrs Tina Hampson, has given me sterling service. Preparation of typescripts has been in the skilful hands of Heather Laughton. I hope I may be forgiven for not naming particular individuals who belong to the parts of the infrastructure of the IBA which have been at my disposal: the secretariat, the library, the registry and information services. To a smaller extent I have also drawn upon the services of the ITCA, always readily given. However, in a personal capacity the IBA's librarian, Barrie MacDonald, has done me the signal service of compiling the index.

In relation to this volume I have further sought and gratefully received information and advice from the following people:

Lord Aylestone
Professor Michael Balfour
The late Lord Barnetson
Gillian Braithwaite-Exley
James Bredin
Frank Brown
Mark Chapman-Walker
Lord Clark
Arthur Clifford
George Cooper
James Coltart
Frank Copplestone
Frank Coven
Aidan Crawley
Anthony Curbishley
Lord Derby
Lyn Evans
Cyril Francis
Brian Henry

Lord Hill
Peter Hunt
Penry Jones
Joan Kemp-Welch
John McMillan
Alex Mair
James O'Connor
Peter Paine
Laurence Parker
Anthony Pragnell
Sir John Rodgers
Sir William Ryland
Anthony Seldon
Leslie Thornby
Professor George Wedell
Sir John Spencer Wills
David Wilson and
Alan Wolstencroft

Lastly I would like to take the opportunity of acknowledging my debt, self-evident at various stages of this volume, to the audience research and measurement organisations, notably the A. C. Nielsen Company, Television Audience Measurement Ltd, and Social Surveys (Gallup Poll) Ltd.

B. S.

ABBREVIATIONS

AAC	Advertising Advisory Committee
ABDC	Associated Broadcasting Development Corporation
ABPC	Associated British Picture Corporation
ABS	Association of Broadcasting Staff
ACTT	Association of Cinematograph Television and Allied Technicians (formerly ACT)
A-R	Associated-Rediffusion
ATV	Associated Television
BBC	British Broadcasting Corporation
BET	British Electric Traction Company
BMA	British Medical Association
CAC	Children's Advisory Committee
CRAC	Central Religious Advisory Committee
ETV	Educational Television
ETU	Electrical Trades Union
HMSO	Her Majesty's Stationery Office
IBA	Independent Broadcasting Authority
IPA	Institute of Practitioners in Advertising
ISBA	Incorporated Society of British Advertisers
ITA	Independent Television Authority
ITCA	Independent Television Companies Association
ITP	Incorporated Television Programme Company
ITV	Independent Television
NATKE	National Association of Theatrical and Kine Employees
NTC	National Television Council
NUT	National Union of Teachers
PMG	Postmaster-General
PTA	Popular Television Association
SCC	Standing Consultative Committee

STV	Scottish Television
TAC	Television Advisory Committee
TAD	Television Advertising Duty
TAM	Television Audience Measurement Ltd
TWW	Television Wales and West of England
UHF	Ultra High Frequency
VHF	Very High Frequency
VTR	Video Tape Recorder

Part I

BREAKING THE MONOPOLY

I should like to think that new ideas always spring fully armed from the collective brain of Her Majesty's Ministers. That would be pleasantly flattering to one who has spent fourteen out of the last twenty years as one of them. The truth is . . . that the origin and genesis of each change is not simple. It is complex, complicated, sometimes long in gestation, and sometimes, thanks to the vigilance of the Opposition, extremely painful in parturition. Many things contribute. There is the germination of an idea; the growth of a conviction; the forming of public opinion, all adding up to a high tide in the affairs of men.

(The Rt. Hon. Viscount Kilmuir, GCVO
House of Lords, 9 May 1962, col. 326)

In my sleepless hours the other night . . . I thought I found myself in the camp of Israel, when their Assembly was debating the suitability of erecting a golden calf in addition to the established Church of the time. The Government of the day was in favour of the proposal on the ground that the calf was only a little one. They said: 'Of course, we all admire Jehovah and think Jehovah did a very good job of work in getting us out of the land of Egypt; but a little golden calf will provide just that element of healthy competition'.

(The Rt. Hon. Viscount Hailsham, QC
House of Lords, 25 November 1953, col. 517)

I

BEVERIDGE

It is a testimony to the strength of democratic tradition in Britain that so much of the discussion about public service broadcasting has concerned itself with the problems of monopoly. Commercial interests certainly played an important part in the events which led to the first Television Act, but their role was mainly to provide the means whereby the political will to end the BBC monopoly could be made effective. Initially concern was felt not so much over the dangers of monopoly as over monopoly control by certain groups or sections of society. Soon after the creation of the British Broadcasting Company in 1922, the Sykes Committee of 1923 recorded its view that 'the control of such a potential power over public opinion and the life of the nation ought to remain with the state'. But this committee did not actually recommend a public monopoly and left open the possibility of more than one provider.

Later committees of enquiry, starting as soon as 1926 with the Crawford Committee (on whose recommendation the Government bought up the privately held shares in the infant Broadcasting Company in order to create the Broadcasting Corporation under Royal Charter) showed themselves aware that there could also be dangers in too much state control. 'We think it essential,' said Crawford, 'that the Commission should not be subject to continuing Ministerial guidance and direction.' The first BBC Charter and Licence of 1927 made it clear that the Corporation was to be independent of government in respect of its day-to-day programming operations, even though ultimate power to control policy or to issue directives in certain specified matters was retained.

The Governors and staff of the BBC were deemed to be deeply aware of the grave responsibility thus laid upon them; to be whole-heartedly and unreservedly committed to service of the public interest and to be justifiably confident – under the leadership of John Reith and his successors – that in serving this public they knew what was best.

3

Although the Selsdon Committee of 1934, which had considered the future of television alone, did think that further consideration might be given to the possibility that some of the much heavier costs of the visual medium might be met by a modicum of screen advertisements, the Ullswater Committee of 1935 confirmed the BBC's position, recommending also that the conduct of television services should be added to their responsibilities. Yet Lord Elton, who had been a member of that committee, was to say in a House of Lords debate on broadcasting some ten years later that the one outstanding omission from its deliberations had been its failure to examine 'the fundamental question' of monopoly and its justification.

It is undeniable that in their use of the monopoly the BBC served Britain well, displaying an awareness of the obligations of privilege in accordance with the highest principles of *noblesse oblige*. Moreover their wartime achievements both in overseas and domestic broadcasting earned them world-wide admiration, not only for their programmes as such, but also for the exemplary demonstration they offered of the workings of that unique British constitutional invention, the public corporation.

Yet doubts and worries remained. The very idea of a single public corporation, enjoying unchallenged monopoly control over a channel for the communication of information and ideas, seemed wrong to many thinking people. This undercurrent of doubt and criticism became strongly vocal in Parliament itself, soon after the end of the war. As Professor Wilson remarks in *Pressure Group*,[1] the corporation's very wartime achievements, involving unavoidable close contacts and co-operation between broadcasters and government, 'may have contributed to the genuine concern of those who in 1946 pressed for a re-examination of the Corporation's role'. The BBC had after all formally agreed that they would accept the direction of government in all matters affecting the war effort.

Early in 1946 the new Labour Government made known its decision not to set up another committee of enquiry before renewing the BBC's charter and licence. This decision was sharply criticised on both sides of the House; and doubts about the future of the monopoly as well as fears of political control were expressed. Admittedly among critics of the monopoly at this stage there appeared little common understanding of what might be the most desirable, or practical, alternative. Nevertheless, the debates that followed during that year can justifiably be regarded as the point of departure for the campaign that ended with the creation of Independent Television.

The Labour Government's decision had been announced in January. By 26 June a motion on the Order Paper in the name of Winston Churchill calling for the matter to be referred to a Joint Select Committee of both Houses was able to attract no fewer than 211 signatures. There was also a debate in the Lords in which concern about monopoly and the arguments for commercial broadcasting as an alternative, were more clearly defined. Nevertheless the White Paper on broadcasting policy which appeared in July, while reaffirming the Government's belief that no change from the existing broadcasting system was desirable, rejected an enquiry on the grounds that time would be needed for the corporation to reorganise their operations from a wartime to a peacetime basis. A five-year extension of the charter was proposed, after which there would be a committee of enquiry. The criticisms that were voiced in the Commons during the debate that followed publication of the White Paper were not noticeably on party lines. These cross-party divisions of opinion about monopoly and the merits of commercial broadcasting persisted until the passage of the first Television Bill into law, and in the case of some individuals, well after that date.

By the time the promised committee of enquiry held its first meeting in June 1949 under its chairman, Lord Beveridge, there had been built up within the Conservative Party a group of influential back-benchers with the aim of getting accepted as their party's official policy the termination of the BBC's monopoly and the creation of a second competing commercial service. But the imputation that they were largely moved by expectations of pecuniary gain has been rightly denied, most notably by the Lord Chancellor, Viscount Kilmuir (formerly Sir David Maxwell Fyfe) in a debate introduced by Lord Reith in May 1962 on the subject of Professor Wilson's book. A mere recital of the names of some of the political figures influentially involved should of itself be sufficient to scotch the myth that sees the origins of ITV in the machinations of a profit-seeking pressure group. After the 1950 election, there was, for instance, and that pre-eminently, the so-called 'One Nation Group', a semi-official association of some of the more able new Conservative politicians, all of whom were destined to make their mark and all of whom were united in their opposition on principle to monopolies of whatever kind. Their opposition was not limited to monopoly in broadcasting, although they were naturally deeply aware of its special dangers in a medium of public information. They included men like Robert Carr, Edward Heath, Iain Macleod, Angus Maude, Enoch Powell and John Rodgers.

Development of the television service had been stopped by the war at a time when it was still only available to the London audience. The White Paper of July 1946 records (para. 68) that 'The London television service was re-opened on the 7 June 1946 and urgent consideration is being given to the difficult problems involved in extending it to the Provinces'. By November 1949 a five-year plan was announced to open a Midlands transmitter and to build a further eight so as to serve all main centres of the Kingdom with a potential audience of 80 per cent of the population. This expansion of the BBC's television services could not help but reinforce the doubts of those who saw in the monopoly too great a concentration of 'media power'.

The Beveridge Report[2] was the first truly thorough and critically analytical examination of the problems relating to the organisation of British broadcasting. The contrast in scale between the labours of earlier committees and those of Lord Beveridge's is striking. Whereas Sykes saw 32 witnesses, Crawford 22 and Ullswater heard from 28 groups or individuals, Beveridge received and digested 368 memoranda and other papers from a wide variety of interested individuals and groups, to say nothing of the many face-to-face interviews. Doubtless the difference reflects growing public awareness of the social importance of the broadcast media. But it must surely also be attributable in part at least to the energetic and lucid mind of the Committee's chairman, whatever his supposed failings of character. He was not without enemies, not least in the BBC, which would have been happier had the Government's original choice of chairman – Lord Radcliffe – not been cancelled by his becoming a Lord of Appeal. Within three days of his own appointment Beveridge summoned his committee to their first meeting. They held sixty-two in all. For the first time a largely successful effort was to be made to bring order and clarity into a debate that had been characterised by much well-intentioned but confused thinking.

As often happens in discussion where prejudice intervenes, concepts and principles that have no necessary logical connection had repeatedly been assumed to be inseparably linked. For many people the issues had been over-simplified into a straight choice between Corporation monopoly on the one hand and a competitive system, subject to the unbridled excesses of commercialism, on the other. But a careful reader of Beveridge could not help but realise that there was not – and never had been – any necessary correlation between public service and monopoly, whether or not under state control. There was no overriding reason why competitive services could not also be conducted in the public interest; the Minister of Information, Brendan Bracken, in 1945, and a former BBC Director General, Sir Frederick Ogilvie, in a famous letter to The Times on 26 January 1946, had made this very point. Nor, on the other hand, did revenue from advertising necessarily involve a competitive system: a state-supervised monopoly could just as readily carry advertisements as could a commercial competitor, as had been argued by a pamphlet from the British Institute of Practitioners in Advertising in 1946. Moreover, if, for practical reasons of cost, competitive systems had to seek advertising money, it did not follow that the public interest could not still be served. To be more general, there was no necessary conflict between commerce on the one hand and culture or things of the mind on the other; nor was there any evidence from which to conclude that the pursuit of profit *per se* inevitably suffocated all moral or artistic aspirations. Evidence on all these matters and on particular aspects of them, was received and considered by the committee. A whole chapter of the report was devoted to arguments for and against monopoly because 'we have felt it incumbent upon us to probe more deeply than our predecessors on this main issue'.

Of the many groups submitting evidence, among them the Labour Party, the TUC, and BBC Advisory Bodies for the Regions, for Education and for Religion, the majority recommended continuance of the monopoly, although some introduced criticisms and suggestions for improvement. Most of the outside bodies representing the interests of creative contributors to broadcasting such as the writers, the actors, the musicians and the concert artistes saw serious disadvantages in the monopoly, and in most cases recommended that it should be broken. Research groups from the Liberal Party and the Fabian Society both wanted the monopoly to end and the television service to be made independent, the Liberals adding that there should be a 'carefully regulated element' of commercially sponsored programmes. There was no submission from the Conservative Party, as such, probably because, at this stage, there was insufficient consensus within the party to permit a collective view.

In the end an eminent Conservative member of the committee, Mr Selwyn Lloyd MP produced a personal minority report in which he declared downright opposition to the principle of monopoly, and recommended the establishment of independent competing agencies for radio and television to be financed by carefully regulated advertising from programme sponsors. It is not clear from Selwyn Lloyd's minority report whether he fully recognised what later became the crucially important distinction between sponsorship and 'spot' advertising. However, there are passages in the body of the report which suggest that the committee was as a whole indeed aware of that distinction. While rejecting (para. 196) the idea of finance by commercial sponsors the report goes on: 'this does not itself settle the issue against any advertisement at all'; and (para. 360) 'it is unfortunate that little attention has been paid to the difference in the form which commercial broadcasting may take . . . spot announcements are like advertisements mixed with reading matter in newspapers'.[3]

In fact, although the Beveridge Report records the committee's majority view that the monopoly should continue and that advertising should not be permitted, an appended special note (signed by the chairman himself as well as Lady Megan Lloyd George and Mrs Mary Stocks) suggested that the ban on advertising might well be reconsidered. 'Is there any decisive reason why the most persuasive of all means of communication should not be used for this legitimate purpose?' they asked. And they concluded by saying 'we regret that the issue raised by our note has never been explored seriously in this country'. In the years that followed it was to be explored if not always seriously, certainly at great length and with much heat.

2

BEYOND BEVERIDGE

The Beveridge Report was published in January 1951. With that infinite capacity for delay generally displayed by British Governments when they have to make decisions about broadcasting, the Labour administration did not announce its proposals until a White Paper appeared in July. It was generally assumed that, apart from minor matters of detail, all the Beveridge recommendations had been accepted. In the parliamentary debates that followed, Lord Beveridge in the Lords vehemently protested that this was not so: for instance, important proposals for devolution within the BBC, involving the establishment of separate authorities appointed by the Government (not the Corporation) in the three national regions had been set aside. Apart from critical speeches from a handful of members, the Conservative opposition did not reveal any clear and consistent party line. But these were already the dying days of the Labour Government. In September the Prime Minister, Mr Attlee, announced that there would be a general election on 25 October. Labour were defeated at the polls and, with the BBC charter due to expire at the end of December, it was left to the incoming Conservative administration to make up its mind.

A Cabinet committee was set up under the chairmanship of Lord Salisbury to formulate a policy; and the announcement of an extension of the BBC charter until 30 June 1952 gave them six months in which to do so. As well as the Home Secretary, Sir David Maxwell Fyfe, and James Stuart, Secretary of State for Scotland, this Cabinet Committee included Lord Woolton, who replaced Salisbury as Chairman when the latter became Secretary of State for Commonwealth Relations in March 1952.

The White Paper debates of 1951 had revealed that a small number of Conservative back-benchers were determined advocates of change. Some of them, though by no means all, had outside business interests in the electronics industry (Ian Orr-Ewing) or advertising (John Rodgers). They had been active members since early 1950 of the various successive party groups that had been discussing broadcasting policy. Proponents of free enterprise and enemies of monopoly as much from principle as from interest, these members were typical of one important section of a political party which then, as now, was an alliance between representatives of aristocratic traditions personified by Salisbury and men from the world of industry and commerce, of which Woolton was a good example. But most other members of the Conservative party group set up in February 1951 by the Chief Whip to advise on 'the party's policy on broadcast services', had no apparent commercial interest in broadcasting or advertising. They included for example Duncan Sandys, Ralph Assheton, Brendan Bracken, Geoffrey Lloyd, Kenneth Pickthorn, as well as, naturally, Selwyn Lloyd. Still it was surely highly relevant to what was to happen that in the October 1951 election so many of the successful Conservative candidates were new members drawn from the world of free enterprise; and that the party's overall success was largely and readily attributed to the efforts of Woolton himself to refashion (he said 'democratise') the party machine after his appointment as Party chairman of the party in 1946. In *Sound and Vision*, Asa Briggs writes of there being at least a hundred Conservative 'Libertarians' on the back benches. Harman Grisewood, then in charge of the BBC Third Programme before becoming Director of the Spoken Word in May 1952, was quickly convinced after talking to Conservative MPs not associated with commercial television in any way that there was a current of feeling that the BBC was self-righteous and arrogant.[1] It may also be, as Professor Wilson suggests, that the Government's small majority (of sixteen) gave a cohesive group of backbencher 'Libertarians' greater influence than they might otherwise have had.

The 'campaign' that led to the breaking of the BBC monopoly and the creation of Independent Television took place largely within the ranks of the majority party in Parliament, and was aimed at bringing that party's leadership to acceptance of a policy about which they were at first unconvinced, if not actually hostile. Of crucial importance to securing the support of this leadership was the bargain struck between Woolton and members of the One Nation Group. This was to concentrate on television and leave radio out of the reckoning. The leadership, including Woolton himself, still thought radio by far the more important of the two; and it was in radio that the BBC had made their reputation. A fundamental change in the arrangements for television presented fewer difficulties within the Cabinet. Apart from the Parliamentarians, and other would-be leaders and formers of opinion, the many millions of the broadcast audience on whose behalf all this was to be done were not effectively involved. Their chance did not come until the existence of a second television service finally gave them the freedom to choose. For, as the Pilkington Committee was to observe in 1962, it is not possible to say what the man in the street prefers until you offer him alternatives between which to decide.

3

WHITE PAPER, 1952

The Conservative Party's group on broadcasting policy was reconstituted shortly after the October election victory, some of its former members having become ministers. But it still included Ian Orr-Ewing (now Lord Orr-Ewing), John Rodgers and John Profumo, all of whom had spoken in the July 1951 debate on the Labour Government's abortive White Paper. In its new form this Conservative Party Broadcasting Study Group included also Anthony Fell, an employee of Pye Radio, Captain L. P. S. Orr, a member of the Executive Council of British Chambers of Commerce and Sir Wavell Wakefield, who, besides being vice-president of the National Union of Manufacturers, was a director of Broadcast Relay Service (Overseas) and Rediffusion Limited. Another member of the group was Kenneth Pickthorn, an academic whose dislike of Beveridge, of the BBC and of all monopolies, especially in ideas, combined with a rare gift for acid phraseology to make him a most able advocate of the cause. Encouraged by the response of the Postmaster-General, Lord De La Warr, when they met him at dinner just before Christmas 1951, the group prepared a paper setting out their views on 'The Future of British Broadcasting' for presentation to the Cabinet. It was arranged that the group's relatively modest and cautiously worded proposals should be discussed at a meeting of the Party's uniquely influential '1922 Committee' in February 1952, at which both Salisbury and Woolton of the Cabinet's Broadcasting Policy Committee would be present. Repeating most of the criticisms that had been heard in the past, (concentration of power, risks of government control, top heavy and over rigid bureaucracy, slowness – in the absence of competition – of technical progress etc.) the group were most emphatic that the monopoly should be broken. They believed they had over 90 per cent of the Parliamentary Party with them and at least 50 per cent of the general public. They pointed to the likelihood of increasing uncontrolled commercial broadcasting aimed at this country from abroad and therefore suggested that it would be better to develop competitive systems of our own which could be 'developed according to our traditions and approved by Parliament'.

Salisbury does not seem to have been persuaded that more would be gained than lost by change. He agreed about the drawbacks of monopoly and that it was in principle contrary to Conservative doctrine, but he saw threats to standards in the introduction of competition, especially in the form of commercially sponsored services. He did not believe there was in fact a widespread public demand for commercial broadcasting. However, the group remained undeterred and continued with their persistent efforts to convert hesitant ministers.

Events moved in their favour when in March 1952 Woolton took over the chairmanship of the Cabinet's Broadcasting Policy Committee and struck his bargain with the One Nation Group. When the promised White Paper appeared in May, it included a cautiously worded sentence, which was to herald the start of a new era in British broadcasting. 'The present government have come to the conclusion that in the expanding field of television provision should be made to permit some element of competition.'[1] But, as if to dampen any feelings of triumph felt by the anti-monopolists the following words were added ' . . . when the calls on capital resources at present needed for purposes of greater national importance make this feasible'. A later paragraph seemed to indicate that such 'purposes of greater national importance' included the completion by the BBC of its building programme of new transmitters for television and VHF radio.

Altogether the White Paper bore signs of having been produced to meet an approaching deadline for a Government that was hesitantly and reluctantly making up its mind to introduce the most important change in British broadcasting since 1927. Before the competitive service could start Parliament should first be given an opportunity of considering 'the terms and conditions under which competitive television should operate': also 'it would be necessary to introduce safeguards against possible abuses and a controlling body would be required'.[2] Neither political nor religious programmes should be permitted. But, while proposing that the BBC Charter should be renewed for a period of ten years and reaffirming that the Corporation should continue to be the only broadcasting organisation with a claim on licence revenue, the White Paper said nothing specific about the financing of the competing television service. There was a subheading which read 'The Questions of Monopoly and Sponsored Broadcasting'; and there was a sentence which recorded the Government's unwillingness to contemplate a change in the BBC's policy towards sponsoring or accepting advertisements. That is all.

Clearly, before any substance could be given to the qualified commitment to a second competitive television service, serious consideration would have to be given to what Beveridge called 'the differences in the forms which commercial broadcasting may take'.

As seen in Chapter 2, the proposal was to end the monopoly only in respect of television. This concession by the anti-monopolists in their discussions with the party leadership was tactically wise, for the majority of those who were reluctant to accept an end to BBC monopoly were certainly basing their judgement on the achievements and prestige of the Corporation as an internationally admired radio service. The television record was as yet less distinguished, and many of those establishment figures who wanted things to stay as they were had most probably watched very little. Part of the anti-monopolist case (which was hard to refute) relied on the allegedly unadventurous and hesitant way in which the Corporation was planning to develop its television service.

One man who influenced MPs in this sense was Norman Collins, who had been Controller of BBC Television from December 1947 until October 1950 when he resigned after being informed that George Barnes, Director of the Spoken Word and Controller of the Third Programme, was to be appointed over his head to the new post of Director of Television. Collins had already written in the BBC's own quarterly that television was the medium of the future, in competition with which radio was bound to decline in importance. This was an opinion manifestly not shared by the Director General, Sir William Haley. Collins saw in the appointment of Barnes a clear indication that the Corporation's 'vested interest is sound broadcasting' would continue to hamper the development of the infant new medium. 'The principle at stake' he was reported as saying, 'is whether the new medium shall be allowed to develop . . . along its own lines and by its own methods or whether it shall be merged into the colossus of sound broadcasting and be forced to adapt itself to the slower tempo and routine administration of the Corporation as a whole.'

He had been in touch with the Conservative Party broadcasting group as early as 1951, soon after his resignation. In the years between the White Paper of May 1952 and the enactment of the first Television Bill he was to play a key role; and he probably did more than any other single man to achieve the creation of ITV. Lord Simon of Wythenshawe, Chairman of the BBC Governors at the time, said later 'if we hadn't fired Collins there would be no commercial television now'. In fact nobody fired him. He resigned.

There was still little general realisation that there were other more acceptable ways of providing a commercial broadcasting service than by use of programmes provided by sponsors. To judge from statements made at the time, 'sponsorship' was rapidly becoming a 'bogey' word. For many people, among them not a few leading Conservatives, a competitive commercial system involved sponsorship, and the prospect of a public service for which the programmes were provided in this way filled them with dismay. They had learned about the system as operated in the United States – sometimes maybe at second or third hand – and they did not like what they had heard.

This was amply demonstrated when the White Paper proposals came to be debated in the Lords on 22 and 26 May on a motion put forward by the father of the BBC, Lord Reith. 'Have the Government any other means in mind?' he asked. 'If not why is sponsoring not mentioned?' Lord Samuel hinted that the Government might be feeling some shame about doing so. The principle of sponsored broadcasting 'must be opposed now'. Several other peers expressed themselves in similar terms, notably Lord Hailsham who saw in the proposal to introduce sponsored television 'an attempt . . . to kill the BBC'; and Lord Halifax who was 'profoundly sorry that it should be the Party with whom I have been associated who have made themselves responsible for it'. In reply, De La Warr made a conciliatory speech, denying that there was the slightest intention to 'scuttle' the BBC. But, he suggested, we have to make up our minds which should be given more weight, the dangers inherent in monopoly or our distaste for commercial sponsorship. He even suggested that the competitive service might be provided by other, non commercial, bodies such as universities for example. In any case, he emphasised, 'competition against the BBC will not start until that organisation is at least well on the way to supplying the whole country'. Although the motion was withdrawn and the House did not divide, neither the Commons back-benchers in the broadcasting group nor the Government can have drawn much encouragement from the debate. Twelve peers (including the two Government spokesmen) spoke in favour of the White Paper proposal and seventeen against, including highly respected figures such as Lord Halifax, Lord Brand, Lord Samuel, Viscount Waverley and Lord Radcliffe.[3]

In advance of the Commons debate on 11 June, the Conservative Party broadcasting group conveyed to the Assistant PMG their strong objection to the proposed delay until the BBC had achieved national coverage. This made it possible, they pointed out, for the Corporation virtually to dictate when commercial TV might start.

When Maxwell Fyfe opened the debate in the Commons he started with the customary tribute to the achievements and unsurpassed reputation of the BBC but then went on, in moving renewal of the Charter for ten years, 'the Government do not propose to ask Parliament to commit itself to continuation throughout the next ten years of the BBC's exclusive privilege of broadcasting'. He was rather less vague than the PMG had been over the timing of competition, saying that competitors would have to wait until the BBC had been 'allotted the resources' to carry out their station-building programme and to make 'reasonable progress' with the development of VHF Radio. He declared firm commitment to a service that would rely on 'advertisements and sponsored programmes for their income'. He did not think this would lead to debasement of standards or Americanisation. 'Is it really suggested that such a people as ours are unfit to decide what they want to see?'

The debate followed party lines. For the Labour opposition, Herbert Morrison asserted that the Government did not have public opinion with them. 'This proposed development is totally against the British temperament, the British way of life and the best or even reasonably good British traditions.' An able speech was made by John Profumo, Chairman of the broadcasting group. He criticised Government vagueness over timing. He and his colleagues wanted competitive television to be given the go-ahead at the earliest possible moment. He was scornful of the intellectuals who wanted to protect the public from being 'culturally corrupted by a service that might put entertainment before uplift. We are not a nation of intellectuals.'

The Assistant PMG did his best to reassure the group and others who were demanding a firm commitment. The decision to allow the BBC to go ahead with its building programme did not mean that 'competitive television must wait until the BBC extension is complete in all respects . . . The Government are in earnest, not only over breaking the BBC monopoly but also in permitting sponsored television.'

There was a three-line whip and the Government motion was carried by 297–269 votes. It was obvious, however, that the Government had not at this stage any clear idea of the way in which an additional, competitive television service might be organised; nor could they draw any final assurance from these two Parliamentary debates that they were proposing to do 'the right thing' in the public interest.[4]

4

INTERLUDE: 1952/3

Over the months ahead conflicting voices sought to make themselves heard in public places outside the political arena in an attempt to indicate to government where the public interest in this matter truly lay. But there is a marked lack of evidence that the mass of listeners and viewers were ever seriously involved. What emerged was rather a succession of statements from members (or adherents) of two opposing special interest groups, describing their respective attitudes towards the BBC monopoly, competitive television and advertising; and their reasoning was as much based on value judgements about what would be good (or bad) for the general public as on factual knowledge. This encounter between special interests was not simply one involving the men of money pursuing a prospect of profit on the one hand and the disinterested upholders of cultural values and standards of taste and morality on the other. It would be nearer the truth to say that it was a prolongation of the age-old argument between two groups within that section of society which, for want of a better term, might be called 'the communicators'.

Broadly speaking there were on one side those primarily concerned with the content of communication (i.e. the churchmen, the educators, the moralists, the ideological politicians and some journalists); and on the other many whose professional preoccupation was mainly with the distribution of communication content (i.e. many performers, some script writers, the makers of receiving and transmitting equipment, advertisers of consumer goods, market researchers, pragmatic politicians and some journalists). Even that is broadly speaking. Some obvious 'distributors' such as the West End theatre managers, newspapers, film companies and cinema chains were ambivalent: anti-monopoly they may be, but should they support a potentially dangerous rival or seek the advantages of alliance and participation? Granada theatres for example had said to Beveridge that the right of access through broadcasting to millions of homes ought not to be in private hands. The Associated British Picture Corporation, for a time at least, gave material support to the opponents of competitive television. Generally speaking the newspapers, except for the *Mirror* group and the *Financial Times*, were hostile to commercial broadcasting, either editorially on grounds of principle – *The Times*, the *Observer*, the *Manchester Guardian* – or managerially towards a competing advertising medium. Nor was the advertising industry itself committed as a whole to one side. Before the war they had campaigned actively for advertising on the air in Britain. But this was for the acceptance of advertising by the BBC, in the face of a growing audience for commercial radio based in Luxembourg and Normandy. Once the possibility of a competitive service, financed by advertisers' money, had become practical politics, the Institute of Incorporated Practitioners in Advertising adopted a policy of more or less benevolent neutrality. Some of the smaller agencies were in fact hostile to a development which they rightly foresaw would favour their larger rivals.

Crucial to the eventual success of the campaign was the fact that individuals from two or three of the larger agencies (such as J. Walter Thompson and S. H. Benson) organised themselves to give a better understanding of the different ways in which television advertising might be introduced. The public memorandum *Television: The Viewer and the Advertiser* which the IPA jointly with the ISBA (The Incorporated Society of British Advertisers) presented to the PMG in April 1953 largely achieved this purpose and significantly influenced the decisions that were ultimately to be taken. It was no mean achievement on the part of those concerned to have produced a booklet under the imprimatur of these bodies within whose ranks there were conflicting views and some serious hesitations.

The radio industry was understandably in favour of an extension of television broadcasting and the introduction of a second channel. But their collective view as expressed by the Radio Industry Council was non-committal on the question of how, and by whom, the additional service should be run. The Chairman of Thorn Electrical Industries was a declared opponent of commercial television. But there were also individuals connected with the industry who thought differently. Apart from Ian Orr-Ewing MP, C. O. Stanley of Pye and his friend Sir Robert Renwick, an industrialist with wide interests in the electrical industry and the financial world (as well as influential connections in the Conservative Party, notably with Woolton), were vehement supporters of a commercially-financed competitive service. Stanley and Renwick had formed an alliance with Collins shortly after his resignation from the BBC and the role played by these three together was an increasingly powerful one. They were tireless in their efforts to influence members of the Conservative and Liberal Parties and indeed anyone who would listen, in favour of commercial television. The unpalatable fact they and their fellow campaigners had to face was that opposition was by no means limited to the Labour Party.

The BBC had been quietly but effectively encouraging their admirers to come together in their defence against the threat of competition. They had demonstrated by their superb coverage of the Coronation – and to the delight of their supporters – that their standards in television were no less distinguished than those they had achieved in radio. This was a great fillip to their cause. On 5 June 1953 the *Financial Times* was constrained to point out: 'The case for commercial television has not been altered or weakened. It was never based on any contempt for the abilities of the BBC.'

The many eminent people among the opinion formers who still felt dismay at the prospect of the introduction into Britain of the vulgarities of commercial broadcasting had been greatly strengthened in their conviction by the undignified way in which some American commercial stations were reported to have handled their presentation of the BBC's coverage. The appearance of a chimpanzee called J. Fred Muggs in one of the accompanying commercials was felt to be outstandingly, but characteristically, lacking in taste. Christopher Mayhew, a Labour politician and frequent broadcaster, made much of it, and it featured in a gladiatorial debate with Collins at the Oxford Union. Mayhew had written during the Spring of 1953 a pamphlet called *Dear Viewer* in which he argued the case for the maintenance of public service television within the BBC monopoly. He had shown the draft to the Chairman of the Governors, Lord Simon, and to senior BBC officials. In its final form it incorporated some of their suggestions and amendments. Immediately after the Coronation there appeared in *The Times* on 4 June a letter announcing the intention to form a National Television Council 'to resist the introduction of commercial television, into this country'. The letter was signed by Lady Violet Bonham Carter, Lord Brand, Lord Halifax, Lord Waverley and the Labour MP Tom O'Brien, who was also Secretary of the National Association of Theatrical and Kine Employees and current Chairman of the TUC. The moving spirit behind the Council was undoubtedly Mayhew. In the months ahead, throughout the summer and autumn, the Council campaigned actively, writing letters to the Press, supplying speakers for existing groups and organising meetings up and down the country, and distributing pamphlets to people of influence, including the members of both Houses of Parliament. They made much play with the Council's all-party composition and with the support they were receiving from the leaders of religious, cultural, educational, professional and trade union organisations. They were out to impress the Government with the weight of authority in their support from all sections of the community, and to demonstrate, as a *Sunday Times* leader put it on 5 July, that there was 'a very large body of opinion in the country, not least among Conservative supporters, that is strongly opposed to television or radio advertising'.

By the end of June members of the Conservative broadcasting group began to feel that the Government were weakening in their resolve. The NTC campaign was forging ahead, and Mayhew's *Dear Viewer* was said to have sold 60,000 copies. He had the advantage of being a television personality well known to BBC viewers: his Conservative opponents were prone to call him 'the honourable member for Lime Grove'. Into this defence in depth such isolated attacks as an article by Collins in the *Observer* on 21 June (which the paper published with reluctance) could achieve little penetration. Apprehension was intensified rather than allayed when it was announced in Parliament on 2 July that a White Paper was to be published in the autumn outlining the conditions under which 'competitive television might be permitted to operate'. The use of the auxiliary looked to some like a prescription for lengthy delay.

If it was indeed the case that ministers were being impressed by the weight and standing of those hostile to commercial broadcasting, then steps had to be taken to persuade them that public and party support for their proposals was also substantial. The Collins–Renwick–Stanley triumvirate, together with the merchant banker, Lord Bessborough, Lord Derby and Mark Chapman-Walker (who had been appointed Conservative Party Director of Publicity by Woolton) decided to set up the Popular Television Association, as a rival to the Mayhew Television Council. A letter to *The Times* of 29 July referred to the dangers of monopoly and the aim of the PTA to have competitive television brought to the British public as soon as possible. This organisation, like its rival, embarked on a national campaign of public meetings, articles and letters in the national and financial newspapers, distribution of leaflets and wide showing of specially-shot filmed interviews with celebrities. It had Lord Derby as Chairman and its tireless chief executive was Ronald Simms, later Director of Publicity at the Conservative Central Office in succession to Chapman-Walker. Among their supporters were numbered, *inter alia*, Alec Bedser, Joan Griffiths, Labour MP David Hardman, Rex Harrison (brother-in-law of Maxwell Fyfe), Ted Kavanagh (of ITMA fame), Somerset Maugham, Maurice Winnick, Malcolm Muggeridge, Viscount Nuffield, Gillie Potter and A. J. P. Taylor.

Throughout this campaign, which was actively assisted both officially and unofficially by the Conservative Central Office, two main themes were repeatedly hammered home: the evils inherent in monopoly and the certainty that British advertising would conform to British taste and eschew the alleged vulgarity of the American version.

If in July there was still 'a very large body of opinion . . . ' in the Conservative Party strongly opposed to commercial television, little of it was in evidence among the delegates to the Party Conference when they met at Margate in October. Of five resolutions dealing with television four supported the Government's intention to provide a competitive television service financed by advertising. Only one asked for a free vote in the House, the course that had been advocated by the NTC and which appealed not only to many members of the opposition but to the Prime Minister himself. Such comments as Churchill made in private were usually on those lines. For example, a letter to Lord Woolton dated 15 August 1955 quoted in Anthony Seldon's recent account of the final Churchill administration said: 'It is difficult to see what good the Conservative Party can get out of this machine-made and to some extent interested agitation by members of the 1922 Committee. It could lose us support at critical by-elections coming up. I am sure the only solution would be the free vote, and that I understand from Butler, is what he is working for.'[1]

However, the difference between the two 'Umbrella Groups', as they would be termed today, was that the NTC included several distinguished elder statesmen, whereas the PTA contained none, let alone any members of the Government. Did *their* resolve need boosting? The Conservative Party broadcasting group sought an answer, and this was given by the Chancellor of the Exchequer, R. A. Butler, in a talk to the 1922 Committee on 9 July. Yes, the Government firmly intended to press ahead with its plan, and a new official Radio and Television Committee would be set up under the chairmanship of Walter Elliot. So it was; and it is also evident that some members of the Government took the opportunity of the August recess to give their minds to the issue.

For, after all, it was not so much a question of what headway the rival campaigners were making on public opinion but which way the Government cat would jump. To change the metaphor, it might still have beaten a retreat without too much loss of face. Woolton had not been well, and nobody could be sure that the Prime Minister would not press his personal reservations upon a Cabinet of which some members were decidedly lukewarm. The outcome – the real irrevocable commitment – was signalled by a speech by De La Warr at Mottram, Cheshire on 29 August.

> What we do want to do is to provide alternative programmes and because
> we distrust monopoly from however good a source it may come, and
> especially in the realm of ideas, we want them to be provided by people
> other than the BBC. And so far as we can see the only practical way of
> financing them is by advertisements. Here we come up against the snag
> that surely you will say this must mean at least in part the American
> system of sponsoring. But this is not so at all.
>
> There is a world of difference between accepting advertisements and
> sponsoring. The press accepts advertisements but they remain responsible
> for their own news and editorial columns. The cinema shows advertise-
> ments in the interval, but their programmes are not sponsored by
> advertisers. The Government has made it clear that they envisage a
> system whereby the station and not the advertiser is responsible for the
> programmes.
>
> The system proposed, therefore, in this country differs from the
> American system, first in that the BBC remains as it is and that nobody
> need look at anything else if they don't want to, and secondly, in that
> advertisers will be no more responsible for the actual alternative
> programmes than they are for the news that you read in the press or for the
> pictures that you see in the cinema.

This speech gave the cue to IPA and ISBA to intervene much more
decisively than they had hitherto done. They rapidly produced a pamphlet
entitled 'Open letter to the Postmaster-General', printing an extract from
his speech and giving it a warm welcome. 'Your authoritative statement
should make it quite clear that sponsorship is not synonymous with
advertising, and any future attack on competitive television which is based
on the idea of sponsorship would be knowingly misdirected.' In part the
Open Letter was also a plea for relieving the future television companies of a
controlling authority. 'There is no necessity to impose more legislative or
administrative restrictions on competitive television than on newspapers or
any other medium.' This was misjudgement. People closer to the political
scene were already aware that a controlling authority was the price that had
to be paid for securing sufficient support in Parliament for commercial
television.

5

WHITE PAPER, 1953

It must have been a close-run thing in Cabinet and just how Woolton and James Stuart played their cards awaits the disclosure of the documents. However, when the White Paper Memorandum on Television Policy[1] was presented to Parliament by the PMG on 13 November it was apparent that the Government had taken decisive steps towards a position on the basis of which practicable legislation could be framed. Neither of the rival campaigning groups had succeeded in enlisting any genuine mass support. Attendance at public meetings was negligible. If anything, however, there had been some signs in the opinion polls that many Labour voters probably favoured the idea of commercial television.

The Government as a whole believed it right on principle to end the monopoly, but was worried lest the practical means for supporting a competing service would constitute a serious threat to broadcasting standards. The issue had too often been presented, sometimes even by proponents of change, as a straight choice between monopoly (which was bad) and sponsorship (which was also bad). By mid 1953 the falsity of that dichotomy had been exposed. *Television: the Viewer and the Advertiser* had set out in simple terms the case (supported by figures for estimated revenue) for a financially viable system based on spot advertising i.e. one in which the station had responsibility for the creation and standards of its own programmes, but agreeing, in return for appropriate payment, to the insertion of advertisements by the advertisers or their agents. The authors had then proposed a list of no fewer than thirteen regulations for the control to be exercised by the station over programme standards e.g. no nudity or obscene features, no statements likely to cause public alarm, nothing disrespectful to the Royal Family or any other Head of State and so on; and, in special additional proposals for children's programmes, no material that tends to create lack of respect by children for their parents, no film classified by the British Board of Film Censors as 'Horrific'. Stories must present their heroes 'as intelligent and morally courageous'.

Clarification of the sponsorship issue formed the substance of para. 6 of the White Paper, and it exactly followed the lines of De La Warr's Mottram speech. It added: 'The Government has consulted representative advertising bodies . . . and is satisfied that separation of advertisements from the programmes would not prejudice the financial success of the new television service.'

The controlling body that had been originally proposed in the White Paper of 1952 was to be strengthened by making it a 'public corporation' which would own and operate the transmitters, charging the programme stations a fee for the broadcast distribution facilities thus provided. In order to permit the 'controlling body' to exercise its gate-keeper function effectively, regulating all advertisements and forbidding classes of programme material if it thought that desirable, programme companies would be required to produce programme schedules and scripts in advance. The illogical ban on politics and religion proposed in the earlier White Paper was to be withdrawn, provided that – as with BBC programmes – religious programmes were subject to approval by a Central Religious Advisory Committee and that political topics would be dealt with impartially. In order to finance its initial capital expenditure, the controlling body would receive an advance from the Treasury on which interest would be payable and which would be repayable in due course from the fees received from programme companies for the broadcast transmission of their programmes.

The proposed policy was stated to have three objectives: to introduce an element of competition and to enable private enterprise to play a fuller part; to reduce the financial commitments of the State to a minimum; and to proceed with caution to safeguard against abuse and 'the lowering of standards'. The controlling body 'with Directors appointed by the Government and free from risk of outside pressure . . . will be basically responsible (to the Postmaster-General, and through him to Parliament) for the standard of new programmes to be shown . . . in our homes'. These proposals attracted criticism on just those two main points which the Government thought would commend them to the public as 'a typically British approach', namely 'effective control on the one hand and greater freedom on the other'. Opponents deplored the complete dependence of the programme-makers on advertising revenue. Proponents did not like the prospect of what appeared to be excessive censorship powers in the controlling body. The risk was that if the Government tried to please everybody they would end up by pleasing nobody.

6

FIELD DAYS IN PARLIAMENT: 1953

The proposals were debated in the Lords on 25/6 November and in the Commons on 14/5 December 1953. The Lords debate was on a motion tabled by Lord Halifax asking the House to disapprove of the White Paper proposals. With his consent the National Television Council had written to all peers asking them to attend the debate and support the motion. The Government responded by issuing a two-line Whip. Clement Attlee speaking at a miners' rally the previous June had hinted that Labour would repeal the proposed measure when they were next returned to power. This effectively made it a party issue, excluding the possibility of a free vote.

The attendance at the Lords' debate was said to have been greater than it had been for at least a generation. Said Lord Ammon: 'Some noble Lords who are now present I have never seen before.' The Archbishop of Canterbury interrupted his holiday in order to be present. Feelings ran high. Many speeches betrayed strong undercurrents of emotion. In the closing stages scarcely a single speaker was free from interruption. Halifax was ill and in his absence it fell to Hailsham both to open and to close.

Towards the end of the two days Salisbury remarked on the atmosphere of near hysterical moral indignation, resembling calls to a Holy War, encouraged by opponents of the White Paper. Something of this was already present in Hailsham's display, in his opening speech, of those vituperative talents enjoyed by his fans among listeners and viewers of the BBC's *Argument* and *In the News*. As did several later speakers, he wanted a second TV channel but not a competitive one and above all not one carrying advertising. In some fields of public service, he asserted, monopoly is necessity – a view shared by, among others, the Earl of Listowel and Lord Samuel. 'There are monopolies and monopolies,' said the latter. Other peers were for competition but were equally convinced that advertising finance would lower standards, requiring programmes that appealed to the lowest common denominator. They refused to acknowledge the distinction, emphasised by the Government, between sponsorship and spot advertisements. But Lord Layton, with first hand experience of newspaper management (and better knowledge than most of American commercial broadcasting), contradicted them. Differing from his Liberal colleagues, he welcomed proposals that would increase freedom of choice for viewers, pointing out that a recent Gallup poll, taken in October before publication of the White Paper, already showed that 48 per cent of those questioned (57 per cent of those with television receivers) favoured a second, commercial, channel.

The Archbishop of Canterbury tried to take the heat out of the controversy remarking 'this is one of many matters in which starting from common principles, Christians may come to different conclusions'. This conciliatory approach was reflected in the rest of his speech. For himself he doubted whether more television would be good for the nation. But if others felt more was wanted, it should be paid for in other ways, by an increased licence fee for example. Speaking for himself he did not want advertising in any form. It was never a good idea 'to mix advancement of culture and the increase of commercial sales'. But again, if others thought advertising was acceptable, then let the money be pooled with licence money to pay for both the BBC and the new service rather than have one of them totally dependent on commerce. There were other ways than those proposed for achieving the Government's purposes. They should be explored.

The general line taken by Government spokesmen and supporters was straightforward. They were committed to ending the monopoly. Competition would mean freedom of choice for viewers and it could be paid for by spot advertising without any of the dire consequences predicted. These predictions were an insult to the good taste, integrity and sense of public service of British business. The British viewer could in any case be trusted to choose sensibly without 'grandmotherly' protection. Moreover any threats to standards that might arise would be safeguarded against by the powers of control proposed for the controlling body of the competitive service. Altogether, as Salisbury remarked in his able, moderately-worded contribution, the White Paper's opponents had no consistent common approach. Some wanted to preserve BBC monopoly; others welcomed the prospect of competition but disagreed over the means of achieving it. Had any constructive proposals been put forward, he said, the Government would have been happy to consider them. Helpful suggestions made by the Archbishop and Lord Waverley in particular would be given further study. A note of acerbity, symptomatic of the generally heightened emotional atmosphere was, however, introduced when both the Lord Chancellor and

Hailsham had to protest against imputations that, as lawyers, they were playing their familiar advocate's role, speaking to a brief rather than sincerely expressing their true minds. The Lord Chancellor had been attacked in this sense in a Sunday newspaper by Reith whom he felt constrained to describe as 'one of those unfortunates who is incapable of believing that anyone who disagrees with him can possibly be sincere, much less right'. With the Whips on, the vote was a foregone conclusion. The motion against the Government was lost by 87 votes to 157.[1]

There was strong feeling in the Commons too. Even before David Gammans could start his opening speech several points of order had to be taken on the status of members with advertising interests. And before he had finished speaking he had been interrupted more than thirty times. Members seem to have approached the debate with attitudes of deeply-felt commitment similar to those they customarily display towards issues involving ethical or religious principle, transcending normal party divisions. Perhaps this was because by the 1950s, broadcasting had already become such a deeply interwoven strand in the British way of life. It was, said Herbert Morrison, 'one of the – if not the – most important debates since the war . . . On it depends the future thinking of our people and our standards of culture.' In an outburst of Celtic fervour the former Labour PMG, Ness Edwards, appealed to the Home Secretary, who also had responsibility for Welsh Affairs 'not to let TV decline to the status of a music room in a pub. If he does that, Wales will never forgive him.'

The debate itself added little new thought to what had been said in the Lords. As Clement Davies remarked in one of the few mercifully short speeches 'it was unlikely that at this stage any new arguments would be forthcoming'. Gammans reiterated the Government's readiness to consider any constructive suggestions for practicable alternative ways of carrying out their firm intention of ending the monopoly, a step they were taking, he insisted, on grounds of principle and not under pressure from back-benchers with commercial interests. But – a point emphasised by later Government spokesmen – there was, as the White Paper made clear, not the slightest intention of abolishing or curtailing the BBC: it would remain the main instrument of broadcasting in the United Kingdom. The Government had some sympathy with the view that the new public corporation that would run the new service should not be totally dependent on advertising revenue, though he believed the danger of advertisers influencing the programme had been greatly exaggerated, especially under the system of 'spot' advertising now proposed. The new public corporation would be required to draw up a Code for advertisers for Post Office approval and its Members, appointed in the same way as BBC Governors, would have ample powers. Initially the new service would be available in the London, Birmingham and Manchester areas, reaching some 50 per cent of the population; a Government loan would cover initial capital costs.

Morrison, in his reply, accepted the desirability of a second service – as did most other opposition speakers – but he did not see the need for wasteful competition, least of all when supported by advertising money. He and all his party colleagues continued to assert the necessary conflict between public service and commercial enterprise. It would be better to have a second service on BBC lines, he urged. But not all other Labour spokesmen seem to have thought the second service should also be run from Broadcasting House. There was considerable confusion, and consequent argument, about the estimated costs of the second TV service, until the Home Secretary was able to explain to members that their belief in a less costly alternative supported from licence fees was erroneously based on BBC estimates for a second service of their own in four to five years time, starting with one hour a day and assuming no deductions from licence revenue by either the Post Office or Treasury. It did not represent the cost of a second genuinely alternative and independent service. Although Morrison (as did other later Opposition speakers) continued to deny any significant advantage in the change from a sponsorship to 'spot' advertising he nevertheless appeared to have modified Attlee's blunt threat of a future repeal of the intended measure. He made what he described as his 'peace offer' calling for a free vote to be followed by an all-party round table discussion about the future development of British television. Both these suggestions were put forward repeatedly by Government opponents throughout the two days of the debate.

Selwyn Lloyd, since 1951 Minister of State for Foreign Affairs, responded to the Morrison peace offer by signifying government acceptance subject to two basic conditions: (i) an end to the monopoly; and (ii) financing of the new system, at least in part, by advertising, leaving the BBC to continue to be supported as hitherto from licence revenue. He did not believe his colleagues on the Beveridge Committee had allowed themselves to face the logical consequences of their own approach to the monopoly question. And, on advertising, he was not the only speaker in the debate to quote the words of the Beveridge–Megan Lloyd George–Mary Stocks question 'Is there any decisive reason why the most persuasive of all means of communication should not be used for this legitimate purpose?' On the supposed baneful influence of advertising, Walter Elliot reminded the House that Lord Simon of Wythenshawe, a former BBC Chairman, because of a reference in his book *The BBC from Within*[2] to commercial broadcasting in the West Indies as 'sensational and demoralising' had faced a High Court libel action, had agreed to pay damages and to apologize, saying he had been 'misinformed'. Elliot also noted that Reith himself had been first appointed by a commercial company and had done an outstanding job. Why, he asked, should we not assume that there are other mute inglorious Reiths still awaiting discovery by commercial enterprise?

But Mayhew, the chief architect and campaigner of the National Television Council, stayed convinced that the crux of the matter was 'the extent to which advertisers will control the programmes'. It was not so much that public taste would be debased, he said, but rather that there would be no place for programmes of minority interest, not all of which (snooker or table tennis for example) were highbrow. This concern was shared by Jo Grimond who otherwise welcomed the prospect of competition. He felt it would be achieved successfully in popular light entertainment (which he liked) but that there would be little time for minority or unpopular issues (Scottish or Welsh Nationalists, Humanists, Marxists) which neither ICI nor Unilever, for example, would be interested in 'sponsoring'. Perhaps the solution would be to subsidise the new 'corporation' either from licence money or from a special levy on advertisers so that it could itself provide the programmes of serious minority appeal. Anthony Wedgwood Benn was also concerned about minorities, believing that advertisers would not be over-interested in broadcasting beyond the main centres of population. He would welcome the break up of the BBC's over-centralised, monolithic monopoly, and seemed to be arguing for a number of smaller BBC's regionally based, on lines that Beveridge had advocated. A few members apprehended that competition between rival services would be more likely to lead to similarities, if not virtual identity, between the two rather than a genuine choice for the viewer between alternatives.

There was an interesting contrast between two Government supporters. Anthony Fell, probably the most extreme of the free enterprise proponents, expressed dismay at the powers of control proposed for the new governing body. It was essential to allow a strong and virile programme industry to develop in Britain without too many irksome inhibitions such as, for example, controls on broadcasting hours. The financial risks for the programme companies would be formidable: it could be up to five years before they showed a profit. They should be given maximum freedom. For himself, speaking philosophically, he would much prefer the possible evils of freedom, from which people could learn, to the evils of authoritarian dictation. John Rodgers, on the other hand, a former member of the BBC's

General Advisory Council and an advertising agent, while confidently asserting that advertising fulfils a positive social function (otherwise he would not be in it), nevertheless expressed doubts whether the powers proposed for the new public corporation would be sufficient to ensure proper programme balance. He put forward a scheme which substantially foreshadowed the Pilkington Committee's proposals of 1962. The corporation should itself do the overall programme planning. It should itself sell the commercial time; and with the money thus earned be able to commission suitable programmes from the producers. British broadcasting would have nothing to fear from an alliance with commerce, he was certain, but it would be well to ensure that it had no influence over the programmes.

The winding up speech by the Home Secretary was never completed. He started by answering a number of questions: on the cost of a second independent service; the impartiality of news bulletins (to be guaranteed as in the case of the BBC); the proposed advertising code; the frequencies that would certainly be available for a BBC 2 even after the new service had been accommodated; the debarment of advertising agencies from having an interest in programme companies; and the degree of day-to-day Parliamentary control. He was about to give his response to Morrison's suggestion of a round table discussion when he was interrupted by the clock. It was either ten o' clock or two minutes to ten. Opinions – and clocks – apparently differed. There were angry exchanges and questions whether, under the rules of the House, the closure could be moved. When he was finally able to make himself heard, Mr Speaker ruled that the debate should be resumed on the following day, after 10 p.m. When that occasion came along, Morrison and the Government Chief Whip rose more or less simultaneously. In spite of Morrison's protests that he still wanted to hear what the Home Secretary intended saying in response to his 'peace offer', the Speaker ruled that the closure had been moved and the House divided. The motion approving the White Paper proposals was carried by 302 votes to 280.[3]

7

THE TELEVISION BILL

As related by Asa Briggs[1] the BBC management began to consider likely effects on themselves soon after the White Paper of May 1952 had made known the Government's intention to introduce 'an element of competition' in television. 'Our aims' (to inform, educate and entertain) 'cannot be fulfilled unless we retain the attention of the mass audience, as well as of important minorities.' They would have to learn to compete.

Moreover, both BBC management and Governers, whilst actively supporting the National Television Council in its public campaign for maintenance of the status quo, declared themselves ready to offer advice to the Government on how its intentions might be realised. The Director General, Sir Ian Jacob, provided a paper for the Governors on 'Possible Broadcasting Systems'. Three of the four plans he examined involved revenue from advertising and one of them, even, acceptance of advertising by the BBC. Governors and management were clearly of the opinion that, besides being 'the main instrument of broadcasting in the United Kingdom', they were also the main source of knowledge and practical experience in development of broadcasting policy. They thought it right therefore 'to place their experience at the Government's disposal'. An *aide-mémoire* was presented to the Government on 12 January 1953 and a further meeting with Ministers took place one week later during which programme matters such as the place of religious and educational programmes in the proposed commercial service, were discussed. Later, in April, after publication of the Television Bill, the Governors sent a note of comments and criticisms on its text.

Meanwhile the National Television Council soldiered on. They distributed leaflets emphasising once again – but now as their principal argument – the inevitable fall in standards that would result from financial dependence on advertising. In the last week of January 1954 they sent a deputation, made up of Lady Violet Bonham Carter, Lord Waverley, Lord

Beveridge and Mayhew, to a meeting with Woolton, Maxwell Fyfe, De La Warr and Gammans. But they came away with little more than reassurances about the powers of control that would be given to the new corporation.

When the Television Bill was published on 4 March 1954, however, one important additional concession to the critics had been made. It had been proposed in the White Paper that the governing body of the new service should receive a government loan of up to £1 million to cover initial capital and running costs. The Bill now had an additional financial proposal for an annual grant to the 'Independent Television Authority', for up to ten years, of £750,000 from public funds, thus following up one of the suggestions made in the Lords by the Archbishop. Moreover, the original proposed Exchequer loan of up to £1 million had now become 'advances up to £2m'. How soon these advances would be repaid could not be estimated; but there was also a provision whereby any revenue surplus should be paid into the Exchequer.

The Bill was the first published document to use the title 'Independent Television Authority'. This title which was to be the target for much sniping in subsequent debates was first suggested by Norman Collins in conversation with Mark Chapman-Walker. 'Mark and I met in the Reform Club to see if we could give shape to Mark's idea of the Governmental agency. I suggested we could match an *Authority* against the BBC's *Corporation*, and I further suggested that it should be called the Independent Television Authority.'[2]

The text of the Bill reflected in many ways the attitude already adopted by Government spokesmen during the two White Paper debates. In the structures and organisation outlined for the competitive service efforts had clearly been made to build in potential safeguards and responsibilities to allay the fears of critics and doubters. But all this remained dependent on two essential pre-conditions put forward by Selwyn Lloyd in his response to Morrison's 'peace offer': the breaking of the monopoly and the financing of the new service in part, if not wholly, by advertising. If all-party discussions had indeed been held on those conditions it is difficult to believe that the Bill that emerged would have been substantially different.

The proposal for a £750,000 annual grant to the Authority to reduce dependence on advertising was one of the safeguards. The Members of the Authority would be appointed by the Crown and chosen from a wide spread of personal backgrounds – industry, commerce, administration, education, entertainment and the arts. Three of them would be concerned respectively with the interests of Scotland, Wales and Northern Ireland. The programmes would be provided not by the Authority but by programme contractors independent of each other as to control and finance; and it would be a duty of the Authority to ensure competition to supply programmes between them. But the Authority would still be free to provide programmes (or programme items) itself, should that be thought necessary to ensure a balanced output. It would also be the duty of the Authority to ensure 'so far as possible' that programmes were predominantly British in 'tone and style'; that they did not offend against good taste or decency, incite to crime or disorder, or be offensive to public feeling; that accuracy and 'due impartiality' be observed in the presentation of all news and in particular in any items dealing with matters of political or industrial controversy; and that no expression of their own opinion on such matters be allowed from any of their Members or officers, or of any director or officer of a programme contractor. Although no matter designed to serve the interest of any political party was to be included, this was not to be taken to exclude relay of the whole series of the so-called 'party political broadcasts' shown by the BBC, nor the presentation of properly balanced discussions. As for religion, the Authority was to appoint, or arrange for the assistance of, a religious advisory committee representative of the main streams of religious thought in the United Kingdom. There would be strict separation between programme contractors and advertising interests; and, in relation to sponsorship, nothing was to be included in any broadcast that suggested or implied that any programme (or part of a programme) had been supplied or suggested by an advertiser. Arrangements would also be required to avoid exclusivity in the broadcasting of important events or sporting occasions of general national interest.

A second schedule to the Bill contained seven more detailed rules about the advertisements. They were to be clearly distinguishable from the programmes; not so frequent as to detract from the value of the programmes as a medium of 'entertainment, instruction and information' and placed only between programmes or in natural breaks within them. There would be no discrimination against or in favour of any particular advertiser; and no advertisements directed to political or religious ends. Under a third Schedule the Authority would be required to include in its contracts with the programme companies provisions enabling it to demand advance sight of scripts and of recordings of both programmes and advertisements; and to have reserve powers to forbid the broadcasting of any matter or category of subject matter. Ministers would be entitled to require broadcasts on specified matters related to their ministerial concerns, and the PMG, besides being able to prescribe the hours of broadcasting, would also be able to place a ban on programmes on specifed matters.

It is too facile an interpretation to see this Bill, with its safeguards, as an uncomfortable attempt at compromise between the pressures of commercialism on the one hand and the pressures from those concerned to keep intact the British traditions of public service broadcasting on the other. Rather was it that since, as all parties to the debates seemed to accept, television broadcasting was a uniquely powerful means of influencing minds, then any person or persons granted the privilege of using that power should, in the public interest, be made subject to proper restraints. Thus in the debates that followed, Government spokesmen repeatedly asserted a willingness – provided the two prerequisites of competition and advertising finance, stayed untouched – to consider, possibly to adopt, any reasonable measures to dissipate whatever grounds or justification there might be for the fears of the Bill's opponents. They themselves, and certainly their most vocal supporters, regarded such fears as illusory, at best melodramatically exaggerated. For that reason they made it clear that the safeguards should in the main be framed as reserve and optional powers, rather than mandatory ones for the Authority and the PMG. Whether by the time the Bill became law the ultimate powers of government over British broadcasting had been increased and strengthened, as Asa Briggs suggests,[3] is arguable. Only time would show whether politicians' concern over the risks of commercial influence had weakened the long-established tradition of non-interference.

The really important new issue to be introduced by the creation of Independent Television concerned not the relationship between government and broadcasting, but whether a statutory concept of private enterprise under public control offered a beneficial alternative to the exclusive continuance of a single large public monopoly established by Royal Charter. This history will study how power was initially divided and subsequently distributed within ITV, the changes over the years in its distribution and the extent to which all concerned – Authority, companies and those who worked for them – succeeded in establishing a synthesis which could become a model for broadcasting institutions throughout the free world. A subsidiary question is whether the BBC became more or less of a public service once it was opposed by the brute force of competition instead of sustained by the brute force of monopoly.[4]

The final parliamentary battle was long drawn out. It lasted – with breaks for such other matters as Atomic Energy, National Health, Judges' remuneration and of course the Budget – just over four months. The start was with the second reading of the Bill on 25 March 1954. The goal was reached with the Royal Assent to the first Television Act on 30 July. By the third reading on 22 June, according to Gammans, more words had been spoken on the subject in Parliament than in the whole Old Testament. A reading through the hundreds of columns in Hansard devoted to those repetitious debates brings forcibly to mind the comment in *David Copperfield*: 'Night after night I record predictions that never come to pass, professions that are never fulfilled, explanations that are only meant to mystify – I wallow in words.'

8

PASSAGE OF THE BILL: 1954

So it was a long and stormy passage. The ministers in charge in the Commons were Gammans and Maxwell Fyfe. The main burden naturally fell on the former. If anyone deserves the title of hero of the enterprise, it must surely be he. Or perhaps martyr would be a more appropriate term. Throughout the debates he was subjected to a running fire of gibes, moralistically superior sneers not to say insults, from Labour speakers. He may perhaps not always have been the intellectual equal of some of his front bench opponents, but the fact that he managed to keep his temper throughout is certainly a testimony to his character. If at times, under the sniping, he appeared confused, even to have contradicted himself – and he did – that is entirely understandable. Even so, it was Maxwell Fyfe who had the commanding role in Parliament. He was at the height of his reputation and displayed at all times a cool, articulate competence.

He introduced the Bill in a moderately-worded speech. He drew attention specifically to provisions designed to deal with issues that had already been (and in the years ahead would continue to be) matters of dispute: the degree to which the Authority should be a producer (or provider) of programmes and should be therefore appropriately equipped; how competition in the supply of programmes was to be assured; the sanctions to be imposed on programme companies in breach of contract; the rules for control of advertisements; those governing programmes, with particular reference to 'high quality' and 'proper balance' in subject matter; the conditions for the inclusion of programmes of religion and current affairs; the problem of 'exclusivity' in coverage of important sporting and other national events.

As we have seen members were not all of one mind with their party colleagues in the nature and degree of their opposition to – or support for – the Bill. Leading Labour spokesmen like Morrison and Ness Edwards were for maintenance of the status quo, with a planned expansion and eventual duplication of the television services under a continuing BBC monopoly. This attitude was shared by some Tory peers such as Waverley and Halifax, to say nothing of Hailsham as well as the Liberal, Samuel. But some Labour members like Wedgwood Benn and George Darling also favoured an end to the monopoly, and in this they were at one with other former BBC employees in the Tory ranks, like Orr-Ewing. Only on the central issue of programme finance from commercial advertising were the two main parties steadfastly divided in the Commons. In the Lords this issue also divided the Conservative Peers.

The two-tier structure and many of the prescriptive and proscriptive provisions of the Bill had been largely designed to meet the misgivings of respected Government supporters and leaders of opinion, both inside and outside Parliament about the introduction of private enterprise and the profit motive into broadcasting. Some Conservatives certainly thought the proposed safeguards excessive and likely to jeopardise the success of the scheme. Some Labour members too felt, or rather hoped, this would be so. Eric Fletcher, Labour member for Islington, who was destined to play an important role in the early days of Independent Television, said that the system was almost certain to fail if the contractors were made to observe all the proposed programme safeguards. It was on this question of finding the right balance between safeguards and freedom to compete that the Government felt most tentative and, consequently, vulnerable. Whether any such questions of right balance between freedom and restraint could ever be settled categorically by legislation rather than by administrative method was indeed doubtful. In the event the Government were constrained, notwithstanding the gibes from the Opposition, to leave them largely to the Authority.

However, it soon became apparent that the Labour leadership were determined to exploit the situation for maximum Government embarass-ment and political advantage to themselves, even if they could not succeed in blocking the Bill. Herbert Morrison opened his attack by moving that the Bill be read 'upon this day six months',[1] that is to say, never. In his reply to the Home Secretary he pandered to the familiar left-wing addiction to 'conspiracy theory', shedding crocodile tears over the damage to democracy done by a Conservative Party that had sunk to 'such depths' that some twenty back-benchers – 'a band of buccaneers' – could push a reluctant Cabinet into this stupid and offensive Bill. Yet, like the skilled political tactician that he was, he was careful to re-state in cautiously qualified form Labour's threat to repeal when they next returned to power. Should there be a general election and Labour win it before this scheme was working –

they would, he said, scrap it. But if it was already working, they would seek
to maintain and enforce the safeguards. If it had proved unworkable, 'we
shall certainly not scrap the safeguards, but must reserve the right to modify,
or indeed, abandon the entire scheme and this may well include the
complete elimination of . . . advertising'.[2] It seemed that the Labour
leadership, in spite of loud proclamation of outraged principle, were already
forseeing a need to retire to prepared positions.

Until the Committee stage was half way through its course, the
Opposition's determination to delay and, if possible, wreck the Bill was most
evident. They put forward amendments not only to abolish the proposed
annual grant of £750,000 to the Authority – introduced, as Gammans
reminded them, to sustain the public service element – but a bewildering
group of contradictory ones. Some of these would have provided for delay in
the implementation of the scheme for periods between twelve and twenty-
four months. Others would have introduced a requirement that it should
start at the latest within one year. After the Committee had spent close on
two hours disputing whether 'independent' was the right adjective to
describe the Authority (because it might imply the BBC was not) ribald
laughter greeted Ness Edwards' bland assertion: 'I do not think that there
has been any waste of words about the matter'.[3]

Government moves to introduce a 'guillotine motion' became virtually
inevitable when Margaret Herbison finally blew the gaff. 'If we could get
the Minister to accept every one of these amendments, the Bill would come
to naught (laughter). I say it quite openly.' But, whatever the Opposition's
intentions, the Government were fully determined to get their Bill into law,
and that before the summer recess.

The second Committee Day ended just after midnight in the first few
minutes of 6 May. When the decision to adjourn was taken, the House had
just divided on an Opposition amendment to insert a specific requirement
for Advisory Committees for Scotland, Wales and Northern Ireland, instead
of leaving it to the Authority; and the Government majority had fallen to
three.

Later that day the Lord Privy Seal, Harry Crookshank, when announcing Parliamentary business for the following week, said the Government
would be introducing a Timetable Motion for the Television Bill.
('Outrageous' protested Attlee.) When that motion came to be debated on
11 May, the Home Secretary was able to point out that already thirteen and
a quarter hours had been spent on the first three (out of eleven) subsections
of Clause One of the Bill. 'A fair period of trial,' he said, 'has shown that it is
the intention of the Opposition unreasonably to delay this Bill.'[4] He went on

to propose a timetable of five more days, making it seven in all, for completion of the Committee Stage plus another two for Report and Third Reading. After another six- to seven-hour debate this proposal was approved, as it was bound to be. In the meantime Morrison had made yet one more unsuccessful offer of all-party talks and George Thomson had claimed that a Bill raising an issue 'at least equal to and, it seems to me, possibly of greater importance than – the death penalty'[5] obviously needed more time. Thomson had arrived at Westminster in 1952 after winning a by-election in Dundee. He was opposed to the introduction of the Guillotine and to the issue being argued on party lines. He strongly favoured a free vote and believed that it was unseemly to rush through a decision on such a major matter of social policy. He is now, as Lord Thomson of Monifieth, Chairman of the Independent Broadcasting Authority.

Given that the question had already been under discussion both inside and outside Parliament for two and a half years and that nine Parliamentary debates in both Houses had been devoted to it, the allotment of time could hardly be called unreasonable. However, although the Government had given substance to their firm intent by this Guillotine motion in the Commons (and later in the Lords by insisting that elderly Peers continued in session long past their customary bedtime) it would be wrong to conclude that the well over 200 amendments put forward by their opponents were of no value: or that the discussions they occasioned had no influence at all on the final form of the Bill. Indeed in the sessions after the passage of the timetable motion discussions were noticeably more practical, more rational and above all better informed. One has only to compare the text of the Bill in its first version with the Act as it appeared in the statute book and both of these with the White Paper of November 1953 to realise that Parliament had done a workmanlike job on this controversial and innovatory measure. Whatever their failings and occasional absurdities the Parliamentary proceedings that culminated on 30 July 1954 represented the fullest and most conscientious examination of broadcasting policy by the elected representatives of the British people that has taken place at any time before or since.

One of the more significant amendments to the Bill was in the wording of parts of Section 2, those dealing with the powers of the Authority to participate in the business of programme-making itself. By this, the power 'to provide and equip studios and other premises' was changed to read 'to arrange for the provision and equipment of, or if need be themselves to provide studios etc' (Section 2 (1) (b)). In the Bill it was stated that the Authority may themselves provide parts of programmes which in their opinion are necessary for securing a proper balance 'and cannot, or cannot as suitably, be provided by programme contractors' (Section 2 (2) (a)). And in the following subsection the Authority was to be empowered additionally 'to provide' programmes in cases where no suitable programme contractor was available. In both these cases also 'provide' was changed to 'arrange for the provision of'.

At first glance these small verbal changes may appear to have been, if anything, a concession to those who wished to have as full a field as possible for private enterprise in the competitive service. They served after all to emphasise the reserve, or facultative, nature of the Authority's powers in this respect. It is necessary to go back to the debates in both Houses, both on the White Paper and the Bill, in order to see how far they form part of a Government reaction which reflected a genuine desire to take into account reasonable argument from both sides, aimed at achieving a satisfactory marriage between private enterprise and public service. Of central relevance to this area of discussion was of course also the provision under which the PMG was empowered subject to Treasury consent to pay the Authority £750,000 in any one year.

The more extreme supporters of private enterprise television had claimed that all the proposed legislation was both unnecessary and redundant. All that was needed, they said, was for the PMG to exercise his existing powers to grant broadcasting licences to suitable applicants. Any controls and safeguards, in so far as these were held to be at all necessary, could be introduced quite simply as terms and conditions in the licences when issued. Whether or not they were right in this is, however, irrelevant. The Government were far too conscious of two important issues, both of which had to be aired in Parliament. One was the organisation of the competitive system in such a way as to ensure responsible supervision of its actions without breaking with the established British tradition of avoiding direct government control or interference in the day-to-day work of the broadcasters – a principle all the more important in the context of a competitive, free enterprise. The other, newer problem was how to pay for the service out of advertising income without conceding too dominant a role to the advertisers.

There were undoubtedly still feelings of uncertainty about the proposed association between advertisers and programme producers, between sales-men and the 'creative' people. Indeed the general rejection of sponsorship by almost everyone concerned was based mainly on the assumption that it implied far too close a relationship between these two sides. The question that was exercising the minds of doubters was whether the substitution of 'spot' advertising would ensure a sufficiently 'arm's length' relationship. These doubters did not of course accept the extreme views of those opposition spokesmen who held that commerce, however circumscribed, would, because of its profit-seeking motivation, always exercise a harmful influence. But they did feel that there might well be something in the argument that programme makers should be motivated solely by the urge to make good and effective programmes and not by the aim, secondary and indirect though it may be, of selling goods. No doubt this was over-simplified thinking, and a consequently distorted view of reality. No man, however disinterested his aspirations, has unmixed motives. We know now, in the light of experience, that the committed programme maker in whatever field of broadcasting shows little or no concern about the advertising material that will eventually accompany the programme when it goes on the air. This is not to say, as the BBC were to discover, that the size of audience is a matter of indifference to programme makers.

As the root and branch opponents saw it the only escape from the supposed problem was to have no advertising money at all: to operate the service wholly on public funds. Others, for whom buying and selling did not seem of themselves unworthy activities, sought a solution in one of two ways. One of these was to create a parallel to the planned division between transmitting and production responsibilities by having a similar organis-ational division between the collectors of advertising income on the one hand and the programme producers on the other. It was the device put forward originally by Rodgers in the White Paper debate, and subsequently to be taken over by Mayhew and adopted by the Pilkington Committee as one of its main recommendations. It would mean that the Authority would sell the advertising time and use the money to commission programmes from producers (or production companies) whose sole unmixed preoccupation would be the making of good programmes. The idea was also put forward in a slightly different form in the House of Lords by the Archbishop. This, he most ingeniously pointed out, could be brought about very simply by changing the word 'to' to the word 'by' in Section 2(2) so that the contractors would not *pay* rentals but would receive payment for their programmes from an authority which had itself collected the advertising revenue.

As has been seen the Archbishop and others were anxious to make the new service less than totally dependent on advertising revenue. The logic behind that position was that financial dependence entails influence and total dependence overwhelming influence. It was a line of reasoning which had for long been consistently rejected in the case of the BBC with its ultimate total dependence on government's decisions about allotment of a share of licence revenue. But it was certainly the reason why the decision to provide for an annual subsidy of £750,000 was seen by men like the Archbishop and Beveridge as a step in the right direction.

The Opposition in the Commons showed little gratitude and less logic. On the one hand they argued that the grant was being filched from BBC licence revenue to subsidise their competitors and that the proposal should therefore be withdrawn. On the other hand, they said, it reflected a tacit admission that the programme contractors could not be relied upon to do 'the decent things', which would consequently have to be provided out of public funds; and that to do that £750,000 would not be anything like enough. Gammans, in rebutting these arguments, said he was confident that there were potential programme contractors of high standing who would be prepared to operate the system without cost to the Exchequer; but he added they would not be subject to anything like the same control without the Authority's ability to call on the £750,000. To withdraw it would not destroy commercial television, he said, but it would make the service 'more commercial and less of a public service character'.

Nevertheless, the proposal did place the Government in more than one uncomfortable dilemma, not least with their own supporters. In the case of the BBC finances it could always be argued, with some show of plausibility that, in the last resort, the money came not from government but from actual users of the service, viewers and listeners in the general public; no one bought a licence if he did not want to view or listen and that the term 'public service broadcasting' was therefore no misnomer. It was not 'state broadcasting'. But could the same be said of the £750,000? If this was represented as government money, did not that imply a substitution of government influence for advertisers' influence? And was that not an incongruous element in a system calling itself 'independent' and ostensibly devised to break a monopoly in the noble cause of freedom of thought and communication? It was, said Woolton, 'a very considerable alteration in the original plan' that 'met with little favour in the minds of some who wanted this new private enterprise corporation to be entirely independent of public funds'.[6] The incongruity might, in part at least, have been eased if it could be openly conceded that the grant also came out of licence fees. But that was something that Government spokesmen were at all times most unwilling to concede. On the contrary it was stoutly affirmed that the licence fee was money paid by the public for the right to own and operate a radio or television receiver and not to pay for the programmes broadcast by the BBC. Unhappily that merely laid the Government open to the secondary charge that the grant would be coming out of the pockets of the general body of tax payers irrespective of whether they wished or were able to view commercial television programmes, 'a monstrous thing'[7] argued Mayhew. The money would be used to reduce the costs of the programme contractors and hence their charges to the advertisers. The latter would thus be indirectly subsidised out of public funds.

The dilemma was one from which the Government never succeeded in extricating itself completely. Indeed the ambiguities of the situation were emphasised even more when Parliament came to discuss, in more detail, to what programme uses the £750,000 was likely to be applied. Early in the proceedings during the Committee discussion of the Bill's money proposals, Gammans tried to spell out the purpose of the grant and its possible use as follows:

> We are laying on this Authority certain definite obligations of impartiality in the presentation of religious matters, in the presentation of the news and in other directions. It is no use doing that if we are not prepared to give it the money to carry out those obligations. There are two objectives. The first is to maintain a proper balance in the programmes . . . The second objective is to put on programmes with which we should not want advertising to be associated, such as state occasions and Royal events. . . . Another item with which possibly we should not want advertising associated is the news . . . and maybe even the children's hour.[8]

For the reassurance of free enterprise spokesmen on the Government benches who feared the emergence of the ITA as a 'second BBC' he added:

> It may well be that those programme companies . . . may put on such broadcasts. That is why we made it optional. . . . I do not envisage that the Authority will use this money to equip its own studios or to maintain its own outside broadcasting organisation. I think it is far more likely to use the money if it wishes to commission from some programme company or from some specialised organisation.[9]

Furthermore, when the Opposition moved successive amendments to make the Authority and not the contractors responsible for the production of children's programmes, educational programmes, religious programmes, coverage of Royal occasions, news and current affairs, they were all firmly resisted because they all tended 'to extend the scope of the Authority at the expense of the programme contractors. . . . We do not share this philosophy.'[10]

The Conservative 'philosophy' was nicely summed up by the back-bencher Captain Orr, speaking about the provision of news. 'The proper way is to put an obligation on the contractor to provide . . . I agree that it would probably put a burden upon them, but I am confident that any programme contractor would say that it was money well spent . . . ' His concluding words foreshadowed fairly accurately what was to happen: 'I was thinking that some of the programme contractors might have that obligation put upon them that they should get together and form a joint agency for the presentation of news.'[11]

The Authority's freedom itself to provide those programmes without which the service could not conform with the requirements of the law was therefore to be qualified and circumscribed. Only as a last resort when other sources were for whatever reasons ruled out would it be expected to ask for the £750,000 with which to pay for such programmes. This could be interpreted either way, as a weakening or a strengthening of the Authority's position; to impose upon it a statutory obligation to provide certain programmes, as the Opposition suggested, would make it less than master in its own house, whatever the proposal might do for the public service principle. On the other hand, to leave it to the Authority to judge for itself whether the programmes needed were either not available or unsatisfactory and that a call should therefore be made on the £750,000 was to give it a decisive responsibility and power. Yet the power was at the same time significantly watered down by the amendment qualifying its freedom to have its own studios and programme staff. The ITA would have been spared much frustration if the provision had never been devised.

Two further amendments, however, may have served to reassure those who feared that the public service imperatives were being weakened. The inclusion in the Act of a new Section 8, instead of Section 3 [3] (dealing with the appointment of advisory committees) added to a general optional power a mandatory requirement to appoint a religious committee; a committee advising on the standards to be observed in advertisements (especially those for medical and surgical goods and services); and a committee to advise on all programmes intended for children and young people. More important still in relation to two of the programme categories which the £750,000 grant was intended to support, was the duty placed on the Authority by this new Section 8 'to comply and secure compliance with the recommendations of the said committees'. And, as if to reinforce the intention in respect of religion, a new Section 3[4] provided that no religious service or 'any propaganda relating to matters of a religious nature' may be broadcast without previous Authority approval.

The Government, having abandoned its earlier doubts about the inclusion of any religious programming at all, had throughout shown itself sensitive to the views of religious interests and had always intended that there should be a representative religious advisory body. There had been consultations with the British Council of Churches, and Ministers repeatedly voiced the hope that the Central Religious Advisory Committee, which advised the BBC, would also be the advisory body for commercial television. The addition of Children's and Advertising Advisory Committees was new; and so was the requirement that it was the Authority's duty to comply with any advice from the three committees (subject only to such 'exceptions or modifications' as may arise from other Authority duties prescribed under the Act). Both these additions can be traced back to amendments moved in Committee by Labour members, even though the form in which they were proposed was at the time not accepted by the Government.[12] They were incorporated in a Government amendment moved at the beginning of the Report Stage on 21 June.[13]

Previously Gammans agreed with the view expressed by the lawyer J.E.Simon on an Opposition amendment to require the Authority to conform with the advice of recommendations of its advisers. 'Informed opinion is valuable, but what would be quite fatal would be to turn an advisory committee into an executive committee . . . As soon as we indicate that the Authority must "conform" . . . it ceases to be an advisory committee and the responsibility devolves on the committee itself.'[14] In spite of the Minister's agreement with this comment, the requirement found its way into the Act and was to prove a considerable embarassment in later years, not least to the members of the Children's Committee. It was not until the Pilkington Committee had once again drawn attention to the anomaly of an advisory body with mandatory and virtually executive powers, that legislative action was taken to remove it. This was yet another example of the way in which an ill-thought-out attempt to strengthen the public service requirements of the Bill tended to weaken rather than reinforce the powers and responsibilities of the body whose overall duty it was to ensure and sustain the public service character of Independent Television.

However, another amendment moved by Sir Robert Grimston and immediately accepted by Gammans very considerably strengthened those powers. In the Bill, Section 3 (powers and duties of the Authority in relation to programmes) said it was 'the duty of the Authority *to secure that*, so far as possible, the programmes . . . comply with the following requirements

. . . '. The amendment changed the wording so that it would be 'the duty of the Authority *to satisfy themselves* that so far as possible the programmes . . . comply'. For the Opposition, Edward Shackleton criticised this change as a 'whittling away' of the Authority's powers. This was roundly contradicted by J. E. Simon who, here again, showed himself far-sighted. He pointed out that the amendment in no way reduced the Authority's powers: on the contrary. 'What the amendment does is to withdraw the determination of the way the Authority is fulfilling its duty from the scrutiny of the courts and leave it purely a matter for the discretion of the Authority.'[15] Although Simon thought that in the present case the new form of words was justified, he considered the device of 'administrative discretion' to be objectionable when applied to the rights of an individual citizen faced with a public authority.

As Parliamentary discussion proceeded, it must have become increasingly apparent to those members concerned to make the plan work to the public interest that success would largely depend on the powers and status of the Authority and the way these were defined. This would not mean, however, a marked increase or strengthening in details of the Authority's prescribed duties and responsibilities. Rather the contrary. Good television programmes are not produced, any more than good pictures are painted or good books written, by virtue of statute or regulation. Such measures would not enhance the standing of the Authority *vis-à-vis* the contractors, nor make it any easier for it to ensure adequate competition between suppliers of programmes and stimulate that freshness and variety of approach which the ending of monopoly was designed to do. As Philip Bell (Bolton) remarked, it would inhibit rather than encourage development in the still young television medium if we were to have 'two Aunties' instead of one. The Opposition were placing themselves in something of a dilemma too when they argued in the Committee stage debate on Section 3 for a higher degree of ministerial and hence parliamentary control than that provided for in the Bill[16]. To have that might well increase the danger of political control, especially since one of the reasons they adduced was the need to correct an unconscious right-wing bias in the men of commerce. The device of the statutory public corporation in charge of a nation-wide public service was one by no means unfamiliar to Labour members, least of all Morrison. Its adaptation to the circumstances of broadcasting had been successfully achieved in the case of the BBC. Ministers repeatedly insisted on the analogy between the BBC's Board of Governors and the Independent Television Authority: they would be the same sort of people with a similar role to play.

But the Opposition found it difficult to see how to adapt the device to a new situation where the actual providers of the service were not the employers or servants of the public authority but independent, private enterprise contractors. How could they square the need they had come to accept in the case of the BBC – some more reluctantly than others – for maximum freedom from day-to-day supervision and interference in the programme planning and production process with what they saw as the imperative need to supervise and control the commercial operators? The answer had to be to give the Authority very wide powers of control which, on paper at least, were much greater than any that had so far been exercised *de facto* by the BBC Governors over their programme service heads. Yet at the same time – and here was the sticking point – the Authority, thus armed with such powers, had to be given the widest possible discretion as to when and how far it should make use of them. If the Authority's job was to be above all the monitoring and maintenance of broadcasting standards then it would need to do more than apply controls on the commercial operators, prescribing the amount, nature and distribution of the advertising. It would also have to find ways of influencing the work of programme planners and programme creators.

Thus, in addition to owning and operating the transmitting stations, there were to be three areas where the Authority would need to be in a position to exercise influential control; the advertising, the arrangement and management of the programme output, and the planning and production of the programmes themselves. It was on advertising that the Government retained most scope for ministerial supervision and intervention, thus limiting the Authority's own freedom of decision. As we have seen, the Advertising Advisory Committee was to be enabled to tender advice which it was the Authority's duty to observe, and very special stress was laid on the inclusion of qualified medical advisers in relation to the advertising of patent medicines. There was to be a continuing obligation on the Authority to produce and publish an advertising Code on the advice of that Committee and to consult with the PMG from time to time about the rules in that Code and particularly about the classes of goods and services for which advertisements could or could not be permitted. Any prolonged period without such consultation, said the Home Secretary, would be regarded as a failure on the part of the Authority to carry out its statutory duty. Indeed an amendment to relieve the Authority of this obligation was rejected, with a comment from Gammans to the effect that the decision about what advertisements should not be permitted was not a matter for the Authority alone.[17] Nevertheless, the Government was equally firm in saying that the detailed rules on what advertising was acceptable (alcohol, gambling,

tobacco, money lenders, for example) were not to be specified in an Act of
Parliament but should be in the first place a matter for the Authority in
consultation with its Committee; and it should be for the Authority to
choose and appoint the members of that Committee. There were explicit
pledges (committing the Authority in advance) that no advertisements
would be associated with religious services or with items featuring members
of the Royal Family. Some Government sympathy was expressed with
Opposition arguments that commercials in children's programmes should
be banned, but this again was to be left to the Authority to decide in the light
of qualified advice. So was the amount, timing and distribution of the
commercials, although on more than one occasion it was broadly hinted
that six minutes in the hour, the average amount eventually adopted by the
Authority, would be about right.

In the arrangement and management of programme output more latitude
was left for the Authority's own discretionary judgement. Practically the
only rights to be reserved to government were the PMG's power to dictate the
hours and times of broadcasting; and, as had long been the case with the BBC,
both the rights of Ministers of the Crown to make 'on air' announcements in
relation to their ministerial functions and the PMG's reserve power to direct
the broadcasters to refrain from transmitting such items as he decided were
unsuitable. In this last case, it was emphasised that the power would be very
much an emergency reserve power. It was to be left to the Authority to
decide, without ministerial assistance, how the contracts with the companies
were to be drawn up in order to ensure that the purposes of the programme
and other provisions of the Bill were complied with.[18] Financial penalties
would be imposed for breaches of the contractual agreements, but only after
the Authority's claim that a breach had occurred (or had been justifiably
apprehended) had been confirmed by arbitration. This condition seemed to
several members a serious weakening of the Authority's position: on
Opposition insistence, an additional amendment moved in the Lords by
Lord Ogmore[19] and accepted by the Government, spelled out the
Authority's undisputed right to terminate forthwith in the event of a breach
going 'to the root' of the contract. It was further provided that the Authority
should have the right to advance information as to a programme
contractor's programme intentions in the form of scripts and other forms of
evidence if it felt it had good grounds to apprehend a breach.

This provision was reinforced by a late amendment moved in the Lords
by Lord Silkin and promptly accepted by the Government on 13 July
(Section 5 [5]) giving the Authority the optional right to require documents

and such other information as it might consider 'necessary or advisable' for the purpose of ensuring compliance with the Act.[20]

Among the prime duties of the Authority was that of ensuring competition in the supply of programmes between a number of contractors independent of each other both as to finance and as to control. There is nothing in any of the Parliamentary debates, however, to indicate that the Government had any very clear idea how this was to be achieved. Since there were to be initially only three stations (London, Midlands, the North) each with only one Band III channel, it was not easy to see how this might be brought about. If there were to be only one contractor responsible for the service in each of these places, this would mean three local monopolies, pointed out the Opposition. The Government could only reply that it would still mean competition with the BBC – which was not what the relevant clause of the Bill seemed to be about. At that time ministers and their supporters took it almost for granted that this situation was a temporary one and that more channels would become available, facilitating direct competition between programme contractors in each area. Darling in the Commons and Hailsham and Jowitt in the Lords reverted to the criticism that what was needed was not so much a 'competitive' service as an alternative one. Competition could well lead, they suggested, not so much to wider choice as to duplication. Jowitt cited the example of as many as eight stations in the same town in the United States all showing the same ball game. But this criticism overlooked the significance of the statement in Clause 1 of the Bill as to the very *raison d'être* of the ITA. It was 'to provide . . . television broadcasting services *additional* to those of the BBC'. If the choice of the adjective meant anything at all, it surely reflected an intention that the new service should not be inhibited from doing those things the BBC were already doing, so long as those responsible believed they could do them better.

It was the perceptive, not to say prophetic, Captain Orr who put forward a possible solution to the 'adequate competition' problem very close to the one eventually adopted by the Authority. Genuine competition *in the supply* of programmes could be achieved, he said, even though each transmitter was allotted to the output of only one company, provided each company made up its weekly schedule by selecting from those on offer from the productions of all three.[21] A fuller development of this plan and an analysis of its consequences was prepared in the Conservative Central Office by Mark Chapman-Walker for the benefit of Walter Elliot, now Chairman of the Party's official Radio and Television Committee. Orr, like other

Conservative speakers, however, also looked forward to the day when there would be more than one competing contractor for each region.

In the event the Government was content to add this problem to those which it felt would be better left to the Authority to cope with. It would be for the Authority, thought Gammans, to find the right compromise between the demands of competition and those of efficiency, given the limited outlets for the time being available. 'Adequate competition' was as far as the Government were prepared to go in defining their objective, added De La Warr. Some further guidance for the Authority might be desirable, he agreed; and he even expressed a personal preference for a set-up with two or three companies sharing time on the whole network, but with local contractors providing supplementary local programmes in the regions. This was in fact a scheme that had been propounded by the Television Committee of the ISBA in a note dated 5 February 1954 and handed to Post Office officials at a meeting with them and representatives of IPA on 9 February 1954. His conclusion was, however, that it would be better to leave matters flexible, free for the Authority's decisions after discussion with the new companies.[22]

But there was still the no less important need to ensure a 'proper balance' in the subject matter of the programmes provided. However, as we have seen, the Government were gradually persuaded that the objections to making the ITA into a programme provider in its own right were of greater weight than the risks that the companies would not include such 'non-commercial' programmes in their output. And so, although the idea was not abandoned, the various and often conflicting Government statements came to emphasise that Authority intervention to provide so called 'balance programmes' would occur only when, in the Authority's own judgement, other steps to ensure a balanced output had proved ineffective. It was left to the Authority to decide. There would be no point in using public money if the job could be done by private enterprise.

Attempts by the Opposition to get written into the Bill a statutory requirement to include a prescribed quota of named programme categories were rejected. This was so even in the area of religious programmes where ministers had shown themselves most sensitive to pressure, in spite of the tempting suggestion from one Welsh MP that there should be a quota for religious services including Welsh services because it will 'do people in . . . other parts of the British Isles all the good in the world to hear Welsh preaching – in Welsh'. The Government stubbornly insisted that the Authority in consultation with its advisers should decide.

A similar conclusion was reached in the discussions about the permitted proportions of non-British material. This was an important issue for the Bill's opponents for two main reasons. One was the knowledge that the main source of non-British programme material would be recordings from the much derided commercial TV stations in America. The other was a desire to protect the jobs of British programme makers against unfair foreign (i.e. American) competition. There was a third, related, reason which they shared with Government supporters, namely the desire to stimulate the growth of a flourishing British programme-making industry, capable of significant export earnings in the English-speaking world. The original clumsy formulation in the Bill that the 'tone and style' of the programmes should be 'predominantly British' had been deservedly mocked at by speakers on both sides of both Houses. What about Mozart's 'Marriage of Figaro'? asked one Tory Member: an Austrian composer's score for the Italian adaptation of a French dramatist's play about a Spanish nobleman and his servants. But in spite of efforts by members with experience of the related problems of the film industry, to establish a statutory quota for foreign imports of 25 per cent, the amendment which was embodied in the Act spoke in general terms of 'proper proportions' of matter of 'British origin and performance'. Interpretation and application was to be left to the judgement of the Authority. 'A proper proportion is what a responsible Authority regards as proper proportion,' said Gammans.[23]

There was no Opposition criticism of the Government amendment, moved in the third Committee day in the Commons, to add to the programme requirements in Section 3 a provision that each station should include in its output a 'suitable proportion of matter calculated to appeal specially to the tastes and outlook of persons served by the station'.[24] The amendment was agreed without debate or division. Presumably they felt that 'suitable' was not as vague or meaningless an adjective as they had claimed 'proper' was; and that it was therefore proper to leave its interpretation to the ITA. Be that as it may, the amendment was crucial: it determined what was to become the most distinctive feature of ITV.

One amendment relating to the arrangements for obtaining programme material, dealt with a problem which over the years has never ceased to be a matter of concern and some dispute in public discussions on broadcasting policy. It was the question of exclusive rights to broadcast coverage of major events (mainly sporting) of wide national interest. The problem was one that the Government found difficult to deal with by statutory regulation. There was for instance the situation that had obtained for a good many years in which BBC radio had regarded itself as free as any other news medium to report an event such as the Cup Final, a national boxing championship or a

Test Match for little, if any, greater payment than the costs of the seats occupied by its reporters; and yet broadcast coverage of such events, especially if it was simultaneous, was bound to affect the 'gate'. The advent of a commercial competitor seemed to offer to the promoters of sporting events the prospect of turning the right to broadcast coverage into a saleable franchise. This thought gave rise in other minds to genuine apprehensions that wealthy commercial interests might outbid the BBC and, by virtue of exclusive agreements with the promoters, deprive BBC viewers of events they expected to see on the 'national' service.

On the other hand, to place a ban on exclusive agreements would be unfairly damaging to the legitimate business interests of promoters. In the original text of the Bill, it was provided that for certain events, to be determined in consultation with the PMG, the Authority should aim to secure 'reasonable facilities' for their broadcast coverage 'on reasonable terms' by all television broadcasting stations in the United Kingdom. But the Government clearly did not consider this satisfactory. At the Committee stage in the Lords, De La Warr virtually threw himself on the mercy of the House, asking for advice on the handling of this 'extremely difficult and complicated problem'. 'I am not giving any secrets away when I say that the Government draftsman produced something like ten drafts on this subject; it has been the most difficult problem in the Bill.'[25] He proposed that the matter should be best left to voluntary arrangements; but that, as an interim measure, and subject to the advice of his Peers, the existing provision be removed and consideration given to an amendment which would give the PMG a reserve power to nominate a limited number of events – subject to Parliamentary approval – on which the three parties (BBC, ITV company, promoter) would be expected to negotiate and, if unable to reach agreement, be compelled to go to arbitration. He assured the House that this proposal – which would be acted on only if it proved necessary – had been discussed and agreed with both the BBC and the sporting promoters. The noble Earl was able to say that the BBC Governors were 'strongly in favour of the principle of non-exclusivity' and that he was making this statement with their knowledge and agreement.[26]

There was no division of opinion between the two main parties in the Lords on this issue. At the Report stage one week later, Earl Jowitt moved a clause[27] which eventually found its way into the Act as a reserve power for the PMG to make regulations (a draft of which should be first submitted for approval by both Houses of Parliament) to deal with the question should this prove necessary. In other words the matter was to be left in the first instance to be settled by voluntary agreement between promoters and broadcasting authorities. So it has remained. Dissatisfaction with the results sometimes achieved has encountered continuing reluctance by the responsible Minister to exercise the reserve powers and abandon the principle of voluntary agreement.

It was inevitably in the area of programme planning and production that the Authority would need to have the greatest scope and freedom for the exercise of discretionary judgement. In the area of taste (even perhaps moral and aesthetic values), it is not merely a question of closing the gap between incomplete evidence and confident assertion, but of embracing a broad and unstable spectrum within which individual and social factors, mood, emotion, prejudice and habit all play a part. Here judgement needs to be free to move within widely-placed limits, which are themselves contingent on time, place and circumstance. Parliament was not at its best when discussing such matters, but at least Orr-Ewing injected a strain of realism into the debate when he said:

> The suggestion has been made that people will work for the programme companies with their eye on the profit motive . . . I do not believe artists work only for money. An awful lot of people – writers, painters, film makers, broadcasters work for the joy of doing a good job in their own medium.[28]

Already several hundred people, he added, many of them from the BBC, had approached Norman Collins because they were 'anxious to work in this new television experiment'.

The quality of such people's work cannot easily be influenced in any positive sense by statute or by administrative regulation. When the Earl of Listowel moved an amendment to include in the text of the Bill a provision obliging the companies to observe the rules governing programmes (in Section 3), in addition to the one requiring the Authority to secure compliance with them 'so far as possible', the Government rejected it. When other Opposition spokesmen asked for more precise definitions than those provided by the ambiguous terms 'high quality', 'good taste', 'due impartiality', 'due accuracy', 'offensive to public feeling', and suggested that a qualifying phrase like 'so far as possible' should be deleted because it merely served to reinforce the ambiguity, they were reminded by Viscount Swinton that these were matters outside the sphere of 'exact science'.[29] They could be dealt with only by the Authority exercising its judgement on particular cases in its day-to-day dealings with the companies.

Much to the irritation of the Opposition, Ministers repeatedly returned on one issue after another to the same regular refrain: 'that is something better left to the Authority to decide, once it is appointed'. The Opposition's complaint was summed up by Douglas Houghton in the final stages of the Bill when he said that so far the refuge of Gammans on all questions about definition had been:

> what is proper is what the Independent Television Authority considers to be proper; what is suitable is what the Independent Television Authority considers to be suitable; what is due impartiality is what the Independent Television Authority considers to be due impartiality; what is good taste is what the Independent Television Authority considers to be good taste.[30]

Such continuous withdrawal from precise definition seemed to the Opposition a weakening, not to say elimination of all the promised safeguards and controls. It was turning the controlling body of the commercial service, said G. R. Mitchinson, into a 'toothless, aimless, purposeless and hopeless object'. Strange that, shrewd lawyer that he was, he did not seem to appreciate that the Authority could well be not less but more powerful the freer it was to make up its own mind and reach its own unfettered decisions about the applicability to specific cases of those provisions of the law which had been deliberately left vague and undefined. It was Maxwell Fyfe who reminded Members 'that the Common Law of England, under which we have existed in tolerable security and comfort for hundreds of years, is based on one conception: the reasonable man, and what it is reasonable to do. That is, broadly, the conception we have here.'[31]

Yet the power of the Authority to control the new system was, it must be concluded, no more than potential. Much would depend on the extent to which the Members – appointed within a few days of the Royal assent to the Bill – chose to use those powers; and on the working relationship they thereby established with their programme contractors. How far and how effectively and in what ways they did so will emerge in subsequent chapters.

There was a case, which the Bill's opponents had not been slow to argue, for saying that the Authority, however wise and widely experienced its Members, would be faced with an impossible task if it had to rely too much on its own acts of lonely judgement and on the willing concurrence of the contractors rather than on unambiguous requirements of the law. 'So long as the ITA is satisfied, everybody else has to be satisfied,' said Ness Edwards.[32] That was one way of putting it; and nineteen years later the Master of the Rolls (Lord Denning) did not put it very differently when in a famous judgement in the Court of Appeal (McWhirter v. Independent Broadcasting Authority on 5 February 1973) he recounted the steps taken by the Authority to satisfy itself that a programme entitled *Warhol* was acceptable for transmission. As recorded in *The Times* Law Report, Lord Denning, in giving judgement, said: 'The Authority were the people who mattered. They were the censors. The courts had no right whatever – and, his Lordship would add, no desire whatever – to interfere with their decisions so long as they reached them in accordance with law.'

Part II

THE BEGINNING: 1954/5

9

THE FIRST AUTHORITY

The Act reached the Statute Book on 30 July 1954. Five days later – on 4 August – the Independent Television Authority held its first meeting at the headquarters of the General Post Office in St. Martins-le-Grand. Over the following year it held thirty-five formal meetings mostly at the Arts Council in St. James's Square. Its first offices were in a temporary structure in Woods Mews off Park Lane and it was not until August 1955 that it moved to 14 Princes Gate which was to be its elegant abode for the next six years. This had been the residence of the American Ambassadors, and nowadays it is marked with a plaque recalling that the late John F. Kennedy had lived there.

Behind Princes Gate was a delightful garden shared between the residents, amongst whom, at number 16, was the Iranian Ambassador. His children, as once did those of Ambassador Kennedy, frequently played in it. Twenty-five years later that garden was the scene of very different happenings, when the cameras of Independent Television News covered the 'siege of Princes Gate' for more than 800 million viewers throughout the world.[1]

The fifty-seven weeks from 4 August 1954 to 22 September 1955, when the independent service began in London, is a story on its own. There never was to be another year like it: decisions were taken which have established the shape and structure of Independent Television for a quarter of a century.

Although, as has been seen, the Act itself set out in some detail the kind of system which in the end Parliament had decided upon, there was a range of different ways in which, within the Act's provisions, that system could be devised. To Sir Kenneth Clark (now Lord Clark), then fifty-two and already Chairman of the Arts Council after being Director of the National Gallery from 1934–45, to his nine colleagues and to Sir Robert Fraser, the man they chose as Director General, generations of broadcasting professionals, not to mention the viewing community, owe a debt of which, today, few are conscious. In the main Part II of this volume tells the story of what they did. Certainly they avoided pitfalls which might easily have been lethal for ITV; and it was in no small measure due to the decisions made in this first year that the service took on the shape and character which ensured its successful survival during twenty-five years of great political and economic upheaval. It must however be admitted that there were to be times when survival seemed uncertain and the future shape of things in doubt.

With the exception of Kenneth Clark and Dilys Powell, the film critic, the Members of the first Authority – all part-timers – were virtually unknown to professional broadcasters. In this respect they did not differ significantly from the Governors of the BBC or from later Members of the Authority. For most of them, their term of membership was just one job amongst several others in busy public lives.

Nobody quite knew what to make of the appointment of Clark. The association of such an eminent man of culture with founding a commercial enterprise of such controversial origins seemed to lack credibility. Few remembered that at the age of thirty-five he had been seconded from the National Gallery to occupy one of the hottest seats in the wartime Government service, that of Controller of Home Publicity in the much-harassed Ministry of Information from 1939–41. He has himself described how Earl De La Warr invited him to be a Member of the Authority and then, next day, rang up to say 'You might as well hang for a sheep as a lamb. Will you be Chairman? . . . I saw a number of ways in which the Authority could intervene and prevent the vulgarity of commercialism from having things all its own way.'[2] He describes himself as a 'pseudo-intellectual' who came to believe that 'commercial television might add some element of vital vulgarity which is not without its value'. The idea of inviting Clark may owe something to Sir David and Lady Maxwell Fyfe (later Lord and Lady Kilmuir) who were close friends of De La Warr, but all that can be said with certainty is that the idea emerged out of informal talks which De La Warr had with close colleagues and associates.

After the resignation of Sir Charles Colston (Chapter 11 (iv)) as Deputy Chairman and his replacement by Sir Ronald Matthews, the Members worked together harmoniously, although in some important matters they had their differences. Inevitably in the first year it was the establishment of an entirely new public enterprise on a sound business and financial footing which forced itself on the Authority's attention; and Clark needed colleagues with wide business experience to help him in making some of the decisions for which his own background had not conspicuously prepared him.

Colston had clearly been appointed to 'complement' Clark. He had just retired from being Chairman since 1937 and Managing Director since 1928 of Hoover Ltd. He was, *par excellence*, the practical man. After distinguished service in the First World War, he joined Hoover in 1919 and introduced the vacuum cleaner to the British housewife. He had made a £20,000 Hoover business into a £12 million empire. His successor, Matthews, was a Yorkshireman and Chairman and Managing Director of Turton Bros and Matthews, tool steel manufacturers of Sheffield. He had been Chairman of the London and North Eastern Railway from 1938–48. A brisk and lively Member was Sir Henry Hinchliffe, a businessman from Market Drayton in Staffordshire, who was sixty-two. Banking was his main occupation but he was, or had been, president of the Association of British Chambers of Commerce, a member of the Court of Governors of Manchester University and on the Advisory Council of the Department of Scientific and Industrial Research. Completing the trio was Lord Layton, then seventy-one, Deputy Chairman of *The Economist*, a director of Reuters and Vice-Chairman of Daily News Ltd. He had served in the Ministry of Munitions in the First World War and the Ministry of Supply in the Second World War. He had been editor of *The Economist* from 1922–38. An eminent Liberal, he was Deputy Leader of the Party in the House of Lords from 1952–5. These three provided the nucleus of creative business acumen.

Fraser was fifty years old. He was an Australian, born in Adelaide, who had graduated at Melbourne University and come to Britain in the twenties to study at the London School of Economics, at that period widely regarded as a breeding ground of left wing socialism. Subsequently, on the advice of Professor Harold Laski, he became leader writer for the *Daily Herald* and might have made a political career had he succeeded in 1935 in being elected to Parliament as a Labour member. He joined the wartime Ministry of Information, where, as head of the Publications Division, he was responsible for the enormously successful series of MOI booklets about major aspects of the war. When the war ended he elected to remain in the Civil Service and abandoned his political interests. In 1947 he became Director General of the Central Office of Information. He did not spontaneously seek to become Director General of the ITA, but he was urged by his friend Norman Collins to do so and was eventually persuaded by Clark to offer himself as a candidate.

Fraser was chosen on 14 September from a short list of five candidates, two of whom were Generals and one an Air Chief Marshal. The fifth was Sir Gerald Barry, formerly Director General of the Festival of Britain 1951, and obviously a strong candidate. Fraser took up his appointment at once, for there was not a moment to lose; but he did so in an atmosphere of quite vitriolic hostility in the Tory press, because of his Socialist antecedents.

Lastly, there was the first Secretary of the Authority, Alan Wolstencroft, a civil servant, seconded from the Post Office. He had been head of the Broadcasting Division, a post which in normal times would have been quiet and undemanding. But the White Paper of 1952 changed that. From then on, he was increasingly involved in developments leading to the enactment of the Television Bill. His secondment to the Authority was crucial; for here was a quiet, unobtrusive but highly intelligent and lucid administrator who, for well over a year, had done little else save explore how the new element of competitive commercial television could be made to work. His value to Clark and Fraser was immense. He returned to the Post Office on promotion in July 1955 and was succeeded by the author, who became Deputy Director General.

IO

COMPETITION

Section 5[2] of the Act enjoined the Authority to do all it could 'to secure
that there is adequate competition to supply programmes between a
number of programme contractors. The first Annual Report recorded:
'No problem exercised the Authority more than this need to secure
competition, since its initial decisions here would clearly be far-reaching
and would set the pattern of the new television system for years to come.'[1]
Competition to supply programmes, the report went on,

> can be obtained fully only when viewers have at all times a choice of
> two or more programmes, or in other words when there are at least two
> stations covering each area. This the Authority hopes ultimately to
> bring about. It could not do so in the first phase of its existence since, all
> other considerations apart, more frequencies would have been needed
> than the two allotted to it. The Authority therefore had to provide
> 'adequate competition' with only one station in any one·area.

It never entered the heads of the Members of the Authority
that successive governments would so allocate frequencies as to preclude all
freedom for the ITA to cover the country with more than one station in any
area. Monopoly had at last been broken: they can hardly be blamed, in
view of all that had been said, for assuming that it was to be succeeded by
genuine plurality and not by mere duopoly. They were not to know that
in later years the notion of competition, except in terms of competition
between BBC and ITV, would lose favour; and that even between these two
organisations competition, as distinct from planned co-existence, would
come to be increasingly deprecated.

Although Parliament had made it clear that the Authority would be
expected to cover the country as soon as possible, or as much of it as was
practicable, there was nothing in the Act itself which specifically

precluded it from starting off with two competing services in London. It never regarded this as practical politics, but neither did it believe that a second ITV service could only come about following some new and weighty decision of government and Parliament. 'What is appearing among us,' wrote Fraser on the eve of the first programme transmissions, 'is the beginning of a system of free television. When I use the word free in this sentence, I mean what everyone means when they speak of a free press.'[2] He went on to envisage (assuming an allocation to the Authority of six channels out of a total of eight in Band III) about fifty separate ITV stations (not just transmitters) affording direct competition between two ITV stations and two ITV networks over much the greater part of the country. He reminded his readers that a choice of three programmes was already a commonplace in the United States and that Australia was beginning with a three-programme system. As it seemed to the Authority, the brute force of monopoly had gone for good in television, as surely it would soon go in radio, and what was to take its place – beside the BBC – was a system of free competition under public control. Only certain technical limitations stood temporarily in the way.

What to do, given its initial limitation to two channels in Band III, was the Authority's first major preoccupation and the issue came to a head in October 1954. That there should be three stations initially, one in London, one in the Midlands and one in the North (thus covering some 60 per cent of the population) was not questioned. The problem was twofold: first, how to get the stations built and equipped by the earliest possible date and to procure from the Post Office the radio or cable links which would join these stations together and enable them to operate as a network; and secondly, how to share this initial service between a number of competing contractors.

At first it did not seem that there was any alternative to allocating a single networked programme between perhaps three contractors, either horizontally or vertically. Such words had been used in the debates.

By 'horizontal' we meant dividing the programme into layers of time, one company, say, producing all the morning programmes, the next the women's programmes, the third the children's programmes, a fourth the news and topical programmes in the early evening and a fifth the entertainment programmes of the middle and later evening, these programmes to go out from all stations; an automatic network. By 'vertical' we meant that the lines of division would run not across from day to day, but downwards dividing one day from another; an automatic network again, but this time there would be a Monday–Tuesday company, and maybe a Saturday–Sunday company. We even talked of one equitable rotation of days, the company having Monday–Tuesday one week, having Wednesday–Thursday the next week and so on in mechanical yet dizzy routine. These seemed to exhaust the possible forms of organisation.[3]

The Authority decided upon none of these forms of organisation. It realised that they would be, as Fraser put it 'cages in which we would be caught forever'. It met on 14 October and chose to have for the three major areas of London, the Midlands and the North one or two companies appointed to each station to operate a 'competitive optional network'. If there were two companies at a station, the division should be vertical not horizontal. By this means the Authority thought that a true element of competition could be introduced into the system, since the companies would be competing with each other to get their programmes on the network. It could see no other way (nor indeed was there) of securing genuine competition in the absence of two companies providing a simultaneous choice of programmes in each area, and for that the extra frequencies were not available. The Authority made one proviso which seems to have been entirely forgotten when the time to observe it came along some years later; it was that there should be a 'reasonably small network quota, to which the regional stations would have a right for an experimental period of, say, one year'.[4]

The dominant anxiety was to introduce competition between the contractors, as the Act required, but the ultimate significance of the decision was different. For what was established was the framework around which new companies operating in new areas could readily fit, and within which there was ample scope for serving local 'tastes and outlook' in accordance with the Act. This aspect was not entirely ignored at the time of the decision, for Fraser pointed out that it was the system which seemed to cater best for the additional stations that would be opened in the future.[5]

Fraser always attributed the devising of the plan for the competitive optional network to the Authority collectively – to the interplay of ideas between the Chairman and the Members. The early Minutes of its meetings confirm that this was not just the language of diplomacy. But Fraser's fertile and original mind was the principal source of the policy which the Authority adopted. From the moment when, in the second half of August, Clark and he came to an understanding that, subject to the formal decision of the Authority after considering other candidates and to his securing his release from the Civil Service, he would become Director General, his mind seems to have dwelt on little else but the initial problems of founding Independent Television.

It was on 27 September, less than two weeks after his official appointment, that he wrote the memorandum to Clark which laid the foundations of ITV. In the course of it he said:

> Although I want the system to be vertical in *control*, I want to see it largely horizontal *in operation*, in the *movement of programmes* – that is, I want a network connection technically capable of giving an unlimited introduction of programmes from any one region into either of the others. I want London to be in full competition with the Midlands in selling programmes to Northern, Midlands with Northern in selling to London, Northern with London in selling to the Midlands. Each will be eager to sell, each eager to buy. It will save each of them vast sums. Viewers will have the best possible programmes. This will be competition with a vengeance, and with all its fruits. The network must be optional – or it is not competition but cartel or market-sharing. I would expect London to be the big exporter, but it should do some importing too. We must not despair of non-London stations succeeding as exporters. I think the Authority might put a percentage in the contract, to be reduced if it was satisfied that sufficiently good programmes were not being cross-offered.
>
> I would like to see the Authority insist that each producer company should secure a proportion of its own original programmes from sub-contractors. I do not see why this should not be fixed as a percentage, either. This would give competition at another level. Sub-contractors would be in competition with one another, and the main contractors would be competing with one another for the best programmes of the sub-contractors. (If the network were compulsory, there would be only one buyer for sub-contractors to approach.)[6]

The reality of what later came to be called the 'carve-up' never conformed to this vision of a state of perfect competition. Tendencies to monopoly in Independent Television soon began to disclose themselves. It was to prove necessary for the Authority itself to assume powers and undertake functions to an extent which would have horrified Fraser in those days. Through a protracted course of circumstances Independent Television was destined to emerge after twenty-five years as a semimonopolistic system under powerful public control. The very success of the two-tiered system (public authority and private companies) eventually so diminished the appeal of the ideals of competition which prevailed in 1954–5 that competition in television, saving in the form that exists between BBC and IBA, fell out of favour; and, ironically enough, one forlorn attempt by the 1977 Annan Committee to revive it in a somewhat unconvincing form was squashed by the incoming Conservative administration of 1979 after having been supported by the previous Labour one.

THE NETWORK COMPANIES

(i) APPOINTMENTS IN PRINCIPLE

Invitations to those interested in becoming programme contractors to get in touch with the Authority and submit an outline of their plans had been published in the press on 25 August. In all, twenty-five applications of widely varying degrees of detail and precision were received. The interviews began on 28 September and ended on 20 October.

Less than a week later, on 26 October, the Authority decided upon the following allocation of the contracts:

London station
  Monday to Friday
	Broadcast Relay Service/Associated
	  Newspapers

London station
  Saturday and Sunday
Midlands station
  Monday to Friday
	} Associated Broadcasting Development Co.
	Ltd

Midlands station
  Saturday and Sunday
Northern station
  Saturday and Sunday
	} Kemsley–Winnick Group

Northern station Monday to Friday	Granada (TV Network) Ltd

Offers of contracts in principle were made, and by 6 November all had been accepted. And so there came about within three months of the Authority's appointment the ingenious network mosaic which was to last until 1968. Three stations split vertically in a ratio of 5 to 2: six parts between four companies, so contrived that each had concessions, so far as could be seen, of approximately similar value measured in terms of time on the air and population coverage. At any rate the risk that any one company would totally dominate the others was avoided, and, above all, no single company was allowed, by virtue of being the sole London contractor, to become the Titan of Independent Television. In October 1954 the Authority did as hard a month's work as it has ever done, and, of course a major part of that work was choosing the winners from amongst the applications received for these programme contracts.

Persuading all four of the groups to accept their allotted pieces of the mosaic was subsequently described by Fraser as 'a delicate and laborious task'.[1] The whole process was, however, extremely rapid, extremely informal and, it must be noted, left much detail to be settled over the months ahead. In respect of two of the four chosen companies acute problems arose, which were in one case ultimately resolved and in the other case never resolved. Fraser wrote:

> Although we worked so rapidly I do not suppose the Authority would have reached different decisions, however laborious we had made the work. We made – it would seem to me – one mistake and it proved a bad one. We were not sufficiently inquisitive about the details of ownership, actual or proposed, of the applicant groups, or about the extent to which they were sure of their money, not merely hopeful of it.[2]

(ii) NEWSPAPER INTERESTS IN ITV

The difficulties which arose in respect of two of the four companies are described below, but we look first at the political criticism which exploded when the appointments became known. It started in the *Daily Mirror* on 23 October and rapidly gathered force, reaching the floor of the House of Commons on 3 November when a question about the prospects for a second BBC Television Service was being asked. 'Are they (the Government) holding up the BBC' asked Morrison, 'in order that they may give preference to their friends, the Kemsley Press and the *Daily Mail*?' On 1 November the Authority had been forced to make a press announcement stressing that it had received no applications from any national newspapers other than those represented in the Broadcast Relay Service/Associated Newspapers and the Kemsley–Winnick Groups; that it was a non-political body, and that one of the main reasons for its existence was to ensure that the complete political impartiality required by the Television Act was observed. A hoped-for application from the *Manchester Guardian* had not materialised. On 3 November, however, Morrison was saying in Parliament: 'Of course we are making a charge of political partiality . . . The charge is against the Government and it may be the case that it is against the Television Authority.'[3]

Before the storm blew itself out there was on 23 November what amounted to a motion of censure, with Morrison moving: 'That this House expresses its alarm at the manner in which the Television Act is operating; and requests Her Majesty's Government to bring forward legislation to amend or repeal the Act'.[4] The motion went to a division and was defeated by 300 votes to 268.

That same day *The Times* published a letter by the five signatories who had in earlier days launched the National Television Council; and its own leading article said: 'The essence of the case to be made by the Opposition in the debate on the television motion in the House of Commons this evening is that the Government having started out with Milton have had to end up with Lords Kemsley and Rothermere'. This remark can hardly have pleased Sidney Bernstein of Granada. He had long been, and still was, a fully paid-up member of the Labour Party – a fact which the Government spokesmen on the motion did not fail to mention.

In a breezy, knockabout speech Morrison spoke of a 'shock to the nation, namely the inclusion of newspaper proprietors in the programme contracts'. He ranged far and wide. He kept saying that he was not censuring the Authority but the Government, and yet it was the Authority, not the Government, which had taken the action to offer contracts to two groups in which Conservative newspaper interests were prominent. He made as much mileage as he could of the one passage in the report of the Royal Commission on the Press 1949 which was of conceivable relevance viz: . . . 'we think that the scale and significance of any future combination of newspaper ownership with control of either news films or news broadcasting ought to be carefully examined'.[5] He managed to throw doubt on the propriety of the continued membership of the Authority of Dilys Powell because of her employment by Kemsley newspapers as a film critic, took a swipe at Sir Robert Renwick of ABDC, because of his alleged political connection with the Government and insinuated that the ramifications of Mr Harley Drayton's many activities (see Chapter 28) which included both Broadcast Relay Service and a Provincial Newspaper group had sinister implications. But his central argument was unmistakable.

Our objections to newspapers coming into this business are based, first, on the principle of the Royal Commission's objection; second, on opposition to the further concentration, in the hands of a few men, of power in the formation of opinion and of public taste.[6]

What was important about the debate was that it opened up for the first time the issue of newspaper financial interest in television (or for that matter television financial interest in newspapers) which has attracted the attention of every enquiry into broadcasting since then and which was to become the subject of legislation when the Act was amended in 1963. Speaking for the Government, Gammans referred back to the debates on the Television Bill and said:

at no time in those long and weary discussions we had in this House was the question of the Press raised at all. If the Opposition felt that the Press should be excluded, the least they could have done was to put down an amendment. I would suggest that it is very difficult to think of a system of independent television which does exclude newspapers.[7]

The debate openly disclosed the fact that the Authority had gone fishing for participation by newspapers of differing political persuasions. It had already announced that it received no applications from any national newspapers other than Associated Newspapers and the Kemsley. Group. Said Gammans:

The Authority then took what I regard as most exceptional steps to discover whether some of these newspapers, especially non-Conservative newspapers, had not submitted application because of a misunderstanding. The ITA therefore approached Odhams, the *Manchester Guardian* and the *News Chronicle* to see whether the absence of their applications was due to a deliberate decision on their part or was due to a misapprehension . . . The *Daily Mirror* was not approached in this way, because exactly the same point had been made perfectly clear to it by letter as late as 23 July this year.[8]

This letter had been written (before the Authority had been set up) by the PMG. If these approaches had met with any success, subsequent events concerned with ABDC would have taken a different course.

The proprietor of the *Daily Mirror*, Mr Cecil King, had made approaches to De La Warr before the Act reached the Statute Book. But he did not care for the idea of a supervisory Authority on which the Act was eventually based. On 8 November the *Mirror* said that they had not pursued their application because 'fantastic restrictions had been introduced – under pressure from Lord Halifax and the Bishops – which hacked the original TV Bill to shreds'. This by itself would not have deterred King. 'I was in favour of commercial television from the start as the only way of putting some life into BBC television' he wrote on 1 April 1979. 'I told my people we would come in after the second bankruptcy, as I foresaw a large expenditure before any possible return.'9

The main burden of all this canvassing of the Press fell on the shoulders of Fraser. He also took it upon himself to defuse so far as he could the political crisis over the Authority's appointments. As he wrote subsequently:

> The work of pacifying parts of the press and preventing the extension of attacks on the Authority and of getting our point of view understood proved very laborious in the two weeks that followed the outburst in the *Daily Mirror*. And now of course it proved imperative to leave nothing undone to try to prevent the Labour Party from committing itself to take destructive action against Independent Television if it were returned to power.10

A General Election could not take place later than 1956 and might well be sooner – before ITV was on the air. In fact it occurred in the summer of 1955, and resulted in a Conservative victory. If Labour had won they could have repealed or drastically amended the Television Act before their supporters had had a chance to see and enjoy the programmes. Whether they would have done is a different matter.

'This debate is a backwash of the summer debates,' declared Crookshank, the Lord Privy Seal, in summing up for the Government. No doubt he was right, and there was certainly nothing in Morrison's speech to suggest he wanted to do more than twist a few tails and pay off a few parliamentary scores. He had been at the top of a visiting list through which both Clark and Fraser had assiduously worked during the fortnight preceding the debate. Fraser, in particular, was worried lest the backwash prove more powerful than the as yet insecure foundations of Independent Television could withstand. The whole episode was an anxious one for the ITA and the companies, and it was as well that Parliament got it out of the way so quickly. For other developments within the system were about to material-ise which would have greatly exacerbated the issues that had been debated.

(iii) ASSOCIATED-REDIFFUSION AND GRANADA

Of the two contractors, Broadcast Relay Service/Associated Newspapers soon to be christened Associated-Rediffusion and Granada (TV Network) Ltd, there is little that need be said at this juncture. Despite the issue of newspaper involvement in television in the case of the former, both groups seemed to the Authority well qualified in their different ways to be contractors and also to have the necessary resources for the task. That the Granada company was a wholly-owned subsidiary of Granada Theatres Ltd was in no way thought a drawback – quite the reverse, for the reputation of the Bernsteins in the cinema and the theatrical world stood high. Their wish to become more active on the creative side of entertainment was evident and wholly understandable. For their part Broadcast Relay Service already operated broadcasting stations in Canada and various colonies. In John Spencer Wills and his associates on the one hand and Sidney and Cecil Bernstein and theirs on the other the Authority believed they had thoroughly competent people who could be relied upon to bring enterprising television companies into existence. It had no hesitation in offering them the contracts which had been allocated and the companies seemed to have had no hesitation in accepting them.

In offering the contracts, and almost as if it were an afterthought, the Authority spelt out one proviso which proved to be of great significance for the future of Independent Television; namely that it was reserving for a separate company 'the news and newsreel period'.[11]

(iv) ABDC/ATV

One leading applicant group which had been brought into being as early as 1952 for the express purpose of providing private enterprise television was the Associated Broadcasting Development Co. Ltd. The word 'Development' was used because the Board of Trade would not allow 'Broadcasting' without qualification, since the BBC enjoyed exclusive rights in broadcasting. Its leaders, Norman Collins, Robert Renwick and C. O. Stanley had, as has been seen in Part I, been associated from the outset with the campaign which eventually led to the passage of the Television Act. In their own eyes and those of many others, not least the Authority itself, they seemed an automatic choice for one of the first contracts. Their official application was, however, deficient in one important respect – it failed to disclose the source of their finance, which might without too much exaggeration be described as Pye in the sky. Nevertheless, the Authority regarded them as an indispensable part of its 'mosaic' and it made strenuous efforts to persuade them to regard Saturdays and Sundays in London and Mondays to Fridays in the Midlands as a suitable allocation. In the end it succeeded in doing so, despite the company's longing for a larger slice of the London service. They had banked on getting all seven days in London and had probably sought, if not secured, their original financial backing on this basis. The actual offer (which two years later revealed itself to be a goldmine) seemed less attractive in terms both of prestige and financial prospects. Cautious financiers would have noted the Labour Party's warning that the Act might well be repealed after the next election. Hoping to stifle ITV at birth if he could, Morrison had said in Parliament some months before: 'In any circumstances the Government's plans provide a most insecure and unpromising field for investment on the part of programme contractors . . .'.[12]

The written offer on the part of the Authority was a letter from Fraser dated 5 November, which fastened at once on the near fatal flaw in the company's application:

We have been quite happy to deal with Associated Broadcasting Development Co. Ltd as a rather special case on the financial side. While the other programme companies have provided us in confidence with an account of the arrangements they have made, or were proposing to make, so that we could see both the financial structure and where the control would lie, we have appreciated your reasons for wishing to leave your financial arrangements for completion only when an offer had been made to you . . .

You explained to us that you had in mind . . . a financial structure in which there would be about 'ten members', each of them with a holding that would be, perhaps, 10 per cent and not higher than 15 per cent and in which the contribution from each would be of the order of £250,000 – say, something between £200,000 and £300,000.

Though your public announcement of a few days ago did not of course go into figures, you reaffirmed that this would be the financial basis of the operation. In the course of conversations you had mentioned to us Odhams Press and the *Daily Mirror* as two organisations with which you had been in touch and whose response, you felt, had been encouraging. Other names were not, I think, mentioned except that it has within the last few days been confirmed that similar contact had been established with the *News of the World*. . . . If you have any cause to doubt whether you can complete the arrangements on your suggested basis, the Authority feels that it would wish to reconsider the situation with you in a friendly spirit.[13]

A reply came from Renwick in a letter dated 8 November:

We would like to say without being specific that the general terms outlined in your letter are in line with our intentions. We would prefer, for example, that *News Chronicle* were substituted for *Daily Mirror* in the penultimate paragraph of your letter. This is an example of the kind of thing we mean when we say 'without being specific'.[14]

The company's failure to line up its financial backing in advance of accepting the offer of a contract in principle, and the Authority's tolerance of this failure, were bad mistakes. The period between early November 1954 and the announcement on 11 March 1955 of the formation of a new company formed jointly between Associated Broadcasting Development Co. Ltd and Incorporated Television Programme Co. Ltd under the Chairmanship of Mr Prince Littler – a company first called Associated Broadcasting Company Ltd and subsequently Associated Television Ltd – was a delicate one in the relations between the Authority and the group to which a contract had already been offered, albeit only 'in principle'.

The story is anything but straightforward. Both the parties had put themselves in very awkward positions, and there was an abundance of argument and counter-argument between them, in conversations between different people, some of which were recorded and some of which were not, and some of which were recalled subsequently, sometimes in one way and sometimes in another. Wide differences of outlook were most marked. Essentially the clash was one between free enterprise in its conventional sense and free enterprise subject to public control; and the outcome was to establish that, given the system created by the Television Act, public control was bound to emerge the winner. When Fraser spoke, as he often did at this time, about 'free television to be put beside a free press', he was minimising the Authority's role. Parliament had seen to it that free enterprise television was not really to be the name of the game; but Fraser, the voice of the Authority, preferred at that time to encourage the belief that it was. The wish was father to the thought: had he been in politics he would probably have been found in the ranks of the 'libertarians'.

Correspondence between the Authority and the company continued throughout November and December and there were also oral discussions to which the correspondence related. Little solid progress towards a resolution of the difference and difficulties was, however, being made, and by the middle of December the Authority, while remaining polite, was finding it necessary to become decidedly explicit. In a letter written to Renwick on 17 December Clark had this to say:

> The Authority, subject to contract, offered the appointment of your company as a programme contractor on the basis of your statement that it would be made up of members drawn from existing companies and from other interests including one or more newspapers. The only newspapers or newspaper organisations you said you were in contact with during the whole time that the application was being considered was Odhams Press, the *News Chronicle* and the *Daily Mirror* . . . You are now proposing a very different kind of company. Certain newspapers which at an early stage you gave the Authority every reason to believe would join you, have not done so, and other newspapers have come upon the scene. Neither the *News of the World* nor the *Daily Express* were mentioned at all in your application, not even orally . . .
>
> You must see that to introduce these two national Conservative newspapers alters the character of your original proposal. If papers of such standing as the *Daily Express* or the *News of the World* had wished to take some part in the first stage of the scheme, either they could have applied direct to us, or they should have entered into firm negotiations with you prior to your application, in which case you would have informed us of it . . .
>
> It is true that the inclusion of the Littler Group and the two Birmingham newspaper groups also varies your first proposal; but we are prepared to accept it, partly because both Littler and the *Birmingham Mail* were among the original applicants for contracts. That is the limit to which we can go.
>
> The Authority has no objection in principle to any particular newspaper, but having regard to the balance of the scheme in its first stage, feels that it would be contrary to the public interest, and above all contrary to the maintenance of public confidence in the scheme, to have any further representation of the Conservative national press at this stage.[15]

In brief, whereas the participation of Conservative newspapers in ABDC Ltd at this juncture was going to be ruled out by the Authority, that of Littler's Incorporated Television Programme Company was going to be allowed, not to say encouraged. It is not difficult to understand ABDC's chagrin and it is possible to sympathise with them in their predicament. They were no longer free to secure the financial backing for their company from the sources they preferred. Events had overtaken them.

Nor is it difficult to understand why the Authority felt bound to be so intransigent. It could not, however much it valued its independence, brush aside political implications. The whole future of Independent Television could be jeopardised if further Conservative national newspaper interests became involved at this stage. The presence of Associated Newspapers and Kemsley Newspapers in two other contractors had provoked a political storm; the arrival of the *Daily Express* and the *News of the World* in the structure of a third company *after* that company had been offered a contract might well have caused a tornado in which Independent Television would have found itself engulfed. The mere fact that other newspaper groups like Odhams, the *Daily Mirror* and the *News Chronicle* had been given an opportunity to join in but had not chosen to avail themselves of it would have been no protection.

But the negotiations rumbled along through January, with the need to settle matters becoming increasingly imperative. Eventually, on 1 February Clark reported to the Authority that it seemed that the formation of ABC was assured on the basis previously contemplated, namely a third of the finance would be in the hands of the Littler Group, a third held by Birmingham interests (including the Westminster Press) and the remaining third held by the original associates of ABDC. The main point still under discussion was to what extent and in what way the Authority was to keep future changes of shareholding under its control. It had been accepted in principle that the Authority must keep 'control of control'.

At the height of its difficulties with ABDC the Authority lost its first Deputy Chairman, Sir Charles Colston. On 9 December he tendered his resignation to the PMG 'for urgent and private reasons'. It seems he had warned the Minister at the time of his appointment that this might happen and so there was no question of his resignation not being accepted. His decision came as a surprise to his colleagues[16] but they were content to accept his assurance that it had nothing to do with the affairs of the ITA. The fact remains that Sir Charles was out of sympathy with the attitude taken by the rest of the Authority towards the desires of ABDC in respect of the composition of the Company. At a meeting of the Authority on 7 December he said that Renwick had been given the impression by the PMG (*sic*) that, provided he approached Odhams, the *News Chronicle* and the *Daily Mirror*, as well as the *News of the World* and the *Daily Express*, it would be open to him to accept the Conservative newspaper in the event that the others had turned down the opportunity.[17] This meeting went on to state 'The Authority confirmed its opinion that it did not wish any national Conservative newspaper to participate'. Colston then informed his colleagues of his intention to resign forthwith.

As they were both fund raisers for the Conservative Party Colston's relationship with Renwick appeared embarrassingly close. He was a free enterprise man, first and foremost, and he does not seem to have shared the view of his colleagues as to the role of the Authority in determining the composition of the programme companies. To the rest of them the requirements of the Act were clear: the internal structure of the companies and the nature of their control were matters that were indisputably the business of the Authority. If Colston was unable to accept that this was so then there was a fundamental cleavage between him and his colleagues which was bound sooner or later to make his position either as Deputy Chairman or Member untenable. But it was an awkward time for such a happening to occur and it might well have rocked the boat much more than in the event it did. Given his background, his appointment had surely been a political gaffe.

The ABDC episode, though some aspects of it were distasteful, was far from being a disaster for ITV. The reason why a powerful and talented group headed by Prince Littler was there waiting in the wings to join forces with ABDC can be readily explained.

In August 1954 there was in formation the Incorporated Television Co. Ltd, bringing together a large number of interests in the field of entertainment. These included Moss Empires Ltd and Howard and Wyndham Ltd, the Grade Organisation, the leading talent agency; and, on the financial side Messrs S. G. Warburg and Co. Ltd. The company was designed to cover practically every aspect of live and film entertainment. It had ample resources. In the eyes of most observers, both well disposed and otherwise, they seemed to have just the characteristics which could be expected to be found in a 'commercial' television company on the model of those existing elsewhere. In all probability it was for that very reason that their application to the Authority for a programme contract was not successful. They did not conform to the Authority's own notion of the breadth of interests which Independent Television companies should possess. What was perhaps more important was that they seemed to have all the characteristics of a great show-business monopoly, and, thought the Authority, it surely would not do for them to be given the chance to swallow up Independent Television right from the outset. At any rate they were not included amongst the four groups to which contracts were offered. But if they were not among the chosen few, it was still envisaged that they would play some part in some way in the programme output of ITV. To their chagrin and amazement the Authority thought of them as potential 'sub-contractors'. The main contractors would need to turn to them to provide some notable and substantial programmes. Such was their predominance in Britain's light entertainment industry that their services were virtually indispensable. If the front door had been closed to them, the side door stood invitingly open. They were anything but grateful for the role thus informally assigned to them. As it turned out, however, they were called into the front line before the battle began. They provided the Chairman of the jointly-formed company (Littler) and they also in due course provided the Managing Director (Val Parnell). They were, right from the outset, the dominant element in ABC (soon to become ATV); and their emergence had many characteristics of a takeover. Collins became, and remained, the Deputy Chairman, and at a later date Renwick took over the chair. But in most respects day-to-day management was firmly in the hands of the Littler Group, first in the person of Val Parnell and later of Lew Grade (now Lord Grade).

The financial rewards reaped by the founder members of ATV proved to be immense. One man who shared in them was Collins. But the merger of the two companies much diminished his scope for effective leadership, although he continued in a wide variety of ways to put his brilliant talents at the disposal of Independent Television as a whole. Writing to the author in February 1979 he said, 'As regards the merger with Prince, Val and Co., I personally never regarded this as being imposed on us. If you said "suggested" this would correctly convey the spirit of the merger because we welcomed the obvious advantages of the entertainment world connection.' Whether he found in the years to come the complete satisfaction to which his unique contribution to the introduction of the new broadcasting system entitled him is open to doubt. Although he never displayed rancour towards the Authority, the failure to incorporate a national newspaper in the group that had originally been offered a contract in principle disappointed him deeply. However, by the time a year had passed the position in this respect was transformed by the arrival of the *Daily Mirror* group as subscribers of £750,000 of new capital to ATV, with two nominees on the Board.

(v) KEMSLEY–WINNICK

The application from the Kemsley–Winnick Group included a number of what in later years became the copy book ingredients of a programme contract proposal; it made dutiful bows in every conceivable direction in order to establish the high-minded character of the group. Types of programmes listed included News, Documentaries, Discussion, Drama, Music (including ballet), Education and Daytime Programmes devoted to the special interests of women and children.[18] Brief descriptions of specimen programmes under all those heads were appended. It was the first of the 'classic' applications, in the drafting of which the hand of John McMillan (whose later career in ITV was to be a distinguished one) can readily be detected. An offer of the contract for the Northern and Midland Weekends was made in principle on 20 October and accepted in principle on 5 November. The Authority had been given to understand that Lord Kemsley, or companies under his control, would own about a third of the shares, Mr Isaac Wolfson, head of Great Universal Stores, another third and the remaining third from various interests independent of the two major shareholders. It also believed that the leadership of the group was to be provided by the Kemsley interest, and probably by Lord Kemsley personally.

By 3 January 1955, the Director General was writing to Lord Nathan (of Oppenheimers), in terms which revealed some anxiety, asking if it could not now be confirmed that these financial plans had not materially altered and if 'a little more' could not now be said about the composition of the 'neutral' third. In reply he was informed that the position was still that the Kemsley and Wolfson interests respectively were each proposing to take not more than 30 per cent of the issued share capital and that the position as regards the remaining 40 per cent was at the moment 'rather fluid' but that no part of it would be in the hands of either Kemsley or the Wolfson interests.[19] The Authority's anxiety at this stage clearly derived from its experience with ABDC and its desire to ensure that nothing comparable arose in regard to any other group to which a contract had been offered.

News was reaching the Authority from various sources during February that there were troubles within the Kemsley–Winnick Group but it was only on 1 March that it learnt from a meeting between Nathan and Fraser that Kemsley had withdrawn from leadership of the group some weeks earlier and had notified Winnick by letter on 11 February of his decision to reduce his interest to taking up shares to the amount of £50,000. It was learnt that even earlier than this Wolfson had decided to withdraw his entire interest, apparently as a result of a disagreement with Winnick. Fraser at once affirmed that it would be the Authority's view that the group to which it had offered a contract had disintegrated, that the 'slate was wiped clean' and that any proposals by Winnick to reconstitute the group with the help of different interests would have to form the basis of a fresh application. Following a meeting of the Authority on 9 March, Fraser said in writing to Nathan:

> I was asked to confirm to you that the Authority feels that the changes in the group have already gone a long way past the point at which it could be said that it is no longer effectively the same group as it was in October and November, and in consequence both the application and the offer may be said to have lapsed. We must therefore start afresh and await any proposals that those now interested may have it in mind to make.[20]

If, in addition to withdrawing from the television group, Kemsley had not also withdrawn from London to Portugal, some of the confused comings and goings of early March might have been avoided. By the time of his return about the middle of the month he appeared to be in a different frame of mind and we find Clark writing to him on 23 March:

> At the Authority's meeting yesterday evening I reported the news that there was still hope of your taking the same sort of interest in the programme contractorship which in the first instance we had understood you were likely to take. I need not tell you how relieved and delighted the Members of the Authority were by this news. As you know, the contract was offered to the original Kemsley–Winnick Group entirely because of our confidence in you and your organisation and the news of your withdrawal was a great blow to us.[21]

What Kemsley does not seem to have bargained for were the complications within his group generated by his defection back in February. He seems to have hoped that they would just go away. The enthusiasts within Kemsley Newspapers were Denis Hamilton, Kemsley's personal assistant, and Ghislaine Alexander, his step-daughter. It was largely they who pushed him into the Winnick enterprise, but there is little to show that he had any ardour for it himself. The Authority waited hopefully for a satisfactory outcome, but none was forthcoming. In May it was being alleged that the Authority's own uncertainty about the readiness of the transmitting stations in the Northern area were adding to Kemsley's difficulties in completing his financial arrangements and it was indicated that he might be unable to proceed any further. Information about any progress became scarcer and scarcer, but there was always just enough to keep the Authority hoping that all would be well. By 21 June it was being reported unofficially that the

Board of the company had now been finally settled, and that three-quarters of the equity shareholding was already available. Three days later, on 24 June, Kemsley informed Clark by letter that his difficulties were such as to lead him to feel that he was no longer able to proceed. On 29 June he confirmed orally that this did indeed mean that he intended to have nothing more to do with television.

Only poor Winnick, who had shown little capacity for winning friends and influencing people, was left to argue that the contract could still survive. He wrote describing plans to re-establish the group, with the *Daily Express* taking the place of Kemsley Newspapers. But sympathy for Winnick in his disappointment was not enough. The Authority decided on 5 July that it had no option but to re-advertise the contract – applications to be received not later than 13 August. Nobody could say that it had not waited long enough for the Kemsley–Winnick Group to materialise.

There can be no doubt that Kemsley behaved very badly, even irresponsibly. For no really compelling reason, he had been treated by the Authority right from the outset with great deference and respect and this attitude persisted long after he had ceased to deserve it. The personal association of an eminent press baron, proprietor of the *Sunday Times*, in the new television enterprise may have been potentially good for its standing and reputation, but, in restrospect, the Authority seems to have leaned too far backwards in efforts to retain it.

(vi) ABPC AND ABC TELEVISION

Sir Philip Warter, Chairman of the Associated British Picture Corporation, had displayed a marked interest in joining Independent Television well before the Act was on the Statute Book. The General Post Office note of a discussion with the PMG and others on 26 February 1954 (at which Howard Thomas accompanied Sir Philip) records the impression that 'the Associated British Picture Corporation was genuinely interested in the possibility of forming a programme company and that they had adequate resources, both financial and material, to undertake this development'. Their subsequent application to the Authority bore this out; they had everything going for them – modern premises at Elstree, all the technical resources of film production, a subsidiary called Associated British Pathé, widely experienced in covering public events and making newsfilm, documentaries, educational films and specialised films of all sorts and descriptions. In charge of Pathé production was Howard Thomas, who was intended to be the chief executive in charge of the television programme operation. 'It will be seen' they said, 'that Associated British has the facilities, the experience, the equipment and some of the manpower to service television programmes.'[22] Their modest aspiration was 'to operate a programme service on a national scale for two complete days a week'. It was really too modest to be true.

Howard Thomas, the designated chief executive, had been a BBC staff producer during the war and responsible for many famous wartime radio programmes, not least *The Brains Trust* (his own invention) and *Sincerely Yours*, with Vera Lynn. Afterwards he became Producer-in-Chief of Associated British Pathé, responsible for Pathé news, documentaries and children's feature films. For Pathé he produced a superb colour film of The Queen's Coronation in 1953.

'Half-hearted' was the description applied by the Authority to their application after they had been interviewed. Did the Authority get it wrong? The staff had pointed out to it that in terms of studios available and entertainment experience they could be considered the strongest applicant. Howard Thomas has since made it clear enough that there were forces within ABPC against participation in Independent Television. They centred around Dr Eric Fletcher, a solicitor, who, as a Labour MP, had opposed the passage of the Television Bill. (He also voted for the Morrison motion of censure on 23 November.) Warter was eventually deterred from adopting Thomas's bluff film industry doctrine 'if you can't beat 'em, join 'em'.[23] The 1955 Annual Report of ABPC claimed that the Corporation had been invited to become a programme contractor (one wonders by whom) and then went on to say: 'It was, however, felt that the re-equipment and modernisation of the cinemas demanded much of the resources in manpower and money and the Board decided not to take part for the time being.'

So ABPC fell out of the running, and the Authority was right at that juncture to disregard them. Howard Thomas had to decide whether to stay with them and so remain out of television, or respond to offers which came to him from other contractors and also, it seems, from the BBC. 'I knew I was going into commercial television, somewhere,' he wrote, 'and mentally I began to clear my desk at Associated British Pathé.'[24] Fortunately for him the turn of events which opened the door to his being Managing Director of the fourth original contractor ensured that he joined ITV in the best possible way for his future success.

Fraser did not feel that the emergence of a group capable of filling at a late stage the gap left by Kemsley–Winnick could be left to chance. It is understandable that his main hope should have centred on ABPC and he decided to make a personal effort to persuade Warter to bring his company forward again, this time in a positive and convincing manner. He seemed to be making little headway until one day, waiting to see Sir Philip for a further effort at persuasion, he sat in the outer office where the door happened to be open. He caught sight in the corridor of C. J. Latta, Managing Director of the company and a nominee of Warner Brothers who had a $37\frac{1}{2}$ per cent interest in it. On impulse he asked Latta to spare a few minutes for a chat, and here, at last, he got the response he wanted. Thomas had already persuaded Latta of the potential value of a television contract, but it was the conversation with Fraser which induced Latta to take action. He moved fast and secured the backing of the Warner Brothers executives in America. Fletcher was a member of their Board and he had no option but to go along with their decision which, once taken, he dutifully supported. Consequently, the ABPC Board also swung round in favour; ABC Television was formed as a subsidiary company with Thomas as Managing Director; their application to the Authority was accepted on 21 September 1955, the day before the official opening of Independent Television in London. The network mosaic was at last securely formed. The Authority's principal task in its first year had been accomplished at the eleventh hour and Independent Television was off the ground.

12

BIRTH OF INDEPENDENT
TELEVISION NEWS

When the Authority first addressed its mind to the provision of news, which was early in that crowded month of October 1954, it was thinking of three aspects of news and three possible ways of providing it. It saw the three aspects as spoken news and newsreel, news commentary and 'balanced' discussions. Section 3(1)(c) of the Television Act had placed upon the ITA the duty of satisfying itself 'that any news given in the programme (in whatever form) is presented with due accuracy and impartiality', but had said nothing about the arrangements for the procurement of news, nor, of course, what was meant by the little word 'due'. It seemed that only the Authority could decide that.

The possible ways of providing news that had been canvassed in discussions with potential programme contractors were (a) by separate arrangements with the press – in effect PA/Reuters *or* (b) with a film newsreel group *or* (c) with a group specially formed by the programme contractors and including possibly the Authority itself. This last proposal had been put forward by Captain Orr in the Commons Committee Stage on 20 May 1954. The first discussion on 5 October got to the point of tentatively opting for an independent news and newsreel company working under a committee of the contractors which might include representatives of the Authority. The matter was to be further considered, and the offers of contracts in principle were to reserve for separate arrangements the news and newsreel periods. A further discussion a month later defined the aim as 'to achieve a system under which the Authority retained effective control of the editorial function without itself participating in the day-to-day provision of news, finance being provided by the four programme contractors in common. There should be separate provision for purely regional news.'[1]

The collective opinion of the four companies was unequivocal. At a meeting with Clark and Fraser on 18 November they said, as the minutes record: 'News bulletins and newsreels should . . . in their view be the responsibility of a special body created by the four programme contractors, the ITA being associated in some way with editorial control.'[2]

However, some Members of the Authority still liked the idea of handing the whole job over to PA/Reuters and lengthy discussion took place with that organisation which showed much interest but grew increasingly coy about taking on the task. In the meantime, however, the Authority was being pushed towards the solution favoured by the companies by the concern that arose out of the complaints about Conservative bias in the companies. In debates on 23 November Crookshank was enabled to say, 'What I understand is likely to happen is that there would be a news company, a sort of federation of the four programme companies and all other interests, working on a basis approved by the Authority and with the Authority taking responsibility for its objectivity and impartiality.'[3] It was this arrangement which finally emerged as the chosen instrument for presenting national and international news on Independent Television.

The plan which received the Authority's approval on 18 January 1955 had, following discussion with John Spencer Wills, been set down by Fraser in a note to Clark dated 13 January:

The four programme companies will collectively create a specialist subsidiary in which each will take a quarter share. The governing board will have eight members, two from each of the companies. The working head of the organisation – that is to say, the editor-in-chief will be appointed only after consultation with the Authority and with its prior approval. If this approval is withdrawn, the appointment will lapse, and a new editor be found. The Authority will have the right to appoint a senior adviser to the company. I am given to understand that his advice would be welcome over the whole range of the news problem, but of course his real function will be to watch the operation of the news through the eyes of the Act.[4]

The plan described by Fraser was in its essentials one evolved by a committee appointed to make recommendations to the four companies. Members of it were Philip Dorté from ABDC, Gerald Sanger from A-R, Victor Peers from Granada and John McMillan from Kemsley–Winnick. *Inter alia*, its report envisaged news bulletins running for thirteen and a half minutes, *delivered in vision by 'personality newsreaders'* (my italics).

Negotiations went smoothly and by the middle of March everything was settled. The news company was to be initially owned and operated by the four contractors: and there was agreement in principle that new contractors would be able to join it. The chief editor was not to be appointed without the Authority's prior approval. A senior member of the staff of the Authority was to act as adviser to the company and attend meetings of its board: in practice the role came to be discharged by the Director General in person, although this did not prevent him delegating day-to-day relations with the company to subordinates.

The Independent Television News Limited was incorporated on 4 May 1955, and Captain Tom Brownrigg RN, General Manager of A-R, was elected as its first Chairman. Fraser attended a meeting of its Board on 14 June as representative of the ITA, when the Editor-in-Chief gave an exposé of his proposals for the make-up and presentation of the news bulletins and newsreel.

The appointment of the Editor-in-Chief had been announced on 8 February. The choice had fallen on Aidan Crawley and had been approved by the Authority on 1 February. Crawley had become well-known to television through his BBC public affairs programme *View Finder* and a whole range of special programme series such as *India's Challenge* and *The Edge of Success*. Piloting a Hurricane in 1941 he was shot down in Africa and spent four years as a prisoner of war in Germany. He entered Parliament as a Labour member in 1945 and held his seat until 1951. He served part of his time as Under Secretary of State for Air. Writing to Clark on 28 January Fraser had said:

> For myself I regard the proposal as wonderfully good, although it is not in fact consistent with my first prescription that the occupant of the post must be entirely without political associations . . . In so far as an appointment could do it for us, I should have thought that his was the perfect answer to our initial problem.[5]

This story of the origins of Independent Television News affords no corroboration of any individual claims to parentage; as Peter Black has reminded us, success has a hundred fathers.

13

THE PROGRAMME CONTRACTS

During the whole of the time from the end of October 1954 to May 1955, whilst the events that have been described were occurring, continuous negotiations were taking place about the provisions of the contracts between the Authority and the first four companies. Fraser wrote on 1 May:

> We had nothing to guide us – except the Act, of course. No one had ever made this sort of contract before: there was no precedent, nothing to look up. The job was one of creative legal thinking and of skilful negotiation. Our final document is of course much better than our first draft: it has been very salutary for us to have to argue things out with the contractors, even if the multilateral nature of the negotiations has made progress seem sometimes tediously slow.[1]

A fundamental issue on which there was much division of opinion both within the Authority itself and between the Authority and the contractors arose out of Section 10 of the Act which required the Authority so to conduct its affairs as to secure that its revenue became at the earliest possible date, and thereafter continued, at least sufficient to meet all sums properly chargeable to revenue account and to make provision as soon as practicable for necessary capital expenditure.

This gave no answer to the question whether the Authority's income should be related simply and solely to its needs or whether it should plan to take its share in the profits of the system over and above its needs. The companies were in no doubt; unanimously and emphatically they said that, since the Authority was not to be a risk-bearer, it should not be a profit-taker. The Authority on the other hand was in real doubt; it debated the pros and cons at immense length and in the end made up its mind by majority decision. Of course, nobody doubted that it had to guarantee itself at least the minimum income necessary to pay for its development programme; that is to say it had to secure each year such a surplus as would enable it, having paid tax, to meet all the capital costs of building its transmitting stations, and to own these, free of all debt, at the end of its life. (Even within this axiomatic requirement was involved the question whether uneconomic stations in sparsely populated areas should be subsidised out of higher rentals charged to contractors in more densely populated areas.) Although, at the insistence of those Members who felt strongly in favour of securing a royalty, notably Lord Layton and Sir Henry Hinchliffe, the Authority sought to persuade the companies to agree to one of 5 per cent, the eventual conclusion, painfully reached, was that arguable as it was that public profit could and should properly be derived from renting the use of publicly-owned transmitting stations, the Authority would be better able to do its job if it stood aside from money-making considerations. The monopoly ownership of the transmitting stations, on which such profits would depend was purely incidental to its essential purpose, which was to provide policy leadership for Independent Television.

Whilst a majority of Members of the Authority, including the Chairman, believed the decision to be the right one, the companies could feel well satisfied with their negotiating skill and collective determination. In return for the Authority's agreement to drop its claim to charge a royalty on advertising revenue they were willing to concede that the Authority should have the right to increase rentals by 20 per cent after 31 March 1959 in its absolute discretion.

Once and for all this crucial decision kept the Authority clear of the responsibility for imposing on the television companies a form of taxation over and above that required by the normal functions of the Inland Revenue. When the time came to milk the companies of profits which were widely regarded as in excess of what was decent, the decision was made by Parliament and not by an Authority acting under pressure from a Government operating behind the scenes. The discussion on this issue within Independent Television in March 1955 was no more than a prelude to much more protracted debates at Westminster some years later.

Apart from the financial clauses of the contract, the ones which received microscopic scrutiny were those governing what came to be known as the 'control of control'. The Authority had to ensure that the companies to which contracts were originally given did not substantially change their character without its consent. The Act itself did no more than lay down that no contract was assignable without the Authority's previous consent, but the developments within ABDC Ltd, and subsequently Kemsley–Winnick, demonstrated clearly that this was not enough. Legal provisions in the contracts to secure control of control were carefully drawn up by Allen and Overy, the Authority's solicitors, and were agreed with the contractors. They were to be invoked and further modified on several occasions in the years ahead.

Much importance was attached – and rightly – to the clauses, formulated at the suggestion of the companies, establishing the Standing Consultative Committee, which became, and remained, the principal forum for the discussion of all matters of policy between the Authority and the contractors. Its decisions were not binding either on the Authority or the companies themselves, but it was foreseen that this body would be extremely influential and that in practice much power of decision would be delegated to it. So it proved. It met for the first time in June 1955.

In its discussions about the contracts the Authority did not attempt to conceal its belief that full implementation of the Act's requirement for adequate competition could only be achieved when it became possible to have more than one ITV service operating simultaneously at any rate in the main areas. In the meantime the only competition obtainable was by means of dividing the week between two contractors in each area. If the companies had to accept this arrangement, as they did, it was natural that they should seek some assurance about their position should the Authority succeed in introducing other companies competing with them in the areas in which they were operating. For it was reserving to itself the right to make arrangements which would greatly reduce the value of the contracts it was offering, and in respect of which these companies were taking all the initial risks.

The Authority agreed that, on the opening of second stations in the London, Midland and Northern areas, the four existing companies serving these areas would be given the first refusal of seven-day contracts there, subject to its reserving the right to require any company granted a seven-day contract to abandon any days it might have on another station under its original programme contract. The 'mosaic' would thus give place to a new system which would allow the introduction of new contractors into the three central areas, whilst safeguarding the position of the original four.

This assurance, which was not mentioned in the first two annual reports, did not become a formal agreement until 1956/7.[2] In all the circumstances it gave no undue privilege to the original four. This did not prevent the 'option agreement' as it was called, being widely regarded as some kind of secret sell-out to the Big Four. The Authority would have been wise to make the assurance public as soon as it had been given. In the event, the mosaic remained intact until the new contracts of 1968.

The companies negotiated skilfully. They obtained nine-year contracts, which were much longer than the Authority had at first intended. They avoided a royalty payment, and even obtained a special letter from the ITA's Chairman undertaking not to exact rental in excess of its own foreseeable needs without there being further discussion. They secured their 'options'. They obtained, contrary to the contract as originally drafted, the very valuable exclusive right of publication of advance programme details. They were the initiators of the Standing Consultative Committee. The identity they had established was decidedly not that of servants to a master. Fraser liked to call them 'partners'. But it was not always as cosy a relationship as critics of ITV have been apt to claim.

14

THE TRANSMITTER CRISIS

Greatly complicating and confusing the problems which beset the Authority and the companies was the stark fact that the transmitting intentions with which the Authority began had to be abandoned as unworkable after the lapse of several months, and replaced by a wholly different policy which had to be worked out from scratch. On the best available engineering advice, and following much exploratory work done in the Post Office, the Authority had hoped to reach an agreement with the BBC for its transmitters to be installed beside theirs and for its aerial arrays to be accommodated on their masts. Months of negotiation with the BBC ensued. It was only in December 1954 that it was revealed by discussions between the engineers of both sides that the BBC's masts were structurally incapable of accommodating the types of aerials which the Authority needed in order to carry the power necessary to provide coverage in Band III equivalent to that already being obtained by the BBC in Band I.

This calamitous discovery was fortunately not material to the plans for opening transmissions in London in September 1955. As the new London transmitting station being built by the BBC at Crystal Palace could not be ready until 1956 the Authority had decided to build a temporary station of its own six miles away on Beulah Hill in Upper Norwood. This project went forward according to plan and began its test transmissions on 13 September. But it had also been hoped that not many months would elapse before programmes could go on the air as well in the Midlands and the North, by using masts of the BBC stations at Sutton Coldfield and Holme Moss respectively. The collapse of this proposal threw the whole ITV plan into disarray. It was essential to the viability of the enterprise that the lapse of time between starting in London and starting in the Midlands and the North should be kept to a minimum. As soon as the major snag became evident at the end of 1954, the Authority's engineers began to examine the possibility of building its own separate stations where it could erect its own masts. But in the meantime the possibility of overcoming the difficulty that had revealed itself at the BBC stations had still to be painstakingly examined. This examination proved abortive. Eventually it became possible to obtain decisions on the locations of two new stations: the first near Lichfield in the Midlands and the second on Winter Hill near Bolton. Construction at the former began in July 1955 and at the latter in September 1955.

The predicted service area of Lichfield corresponded closely with that of the BBC's Midlands station at Sutton Coldfield. But Winter Hill, which was on the west of the Pennines, was designed to serve Lancashire, Cheshire and parts of Staffordshire, and it left the serving of Yorkshire to another station – still to be found – on the east of the Pennines. This was at once a difficult and a highly significant decision, and it came about because it was established that an ITA counterpart to the BBC's Holme Moss – straddling the Pennines and throwing signals down into both Lancashire and Yorkshire – could not be brought into service in less than two years. To quote the Authority's Annual Report for 1955/6:

> The Authority could not contemplate the postponement of programmes for the twelve million or so people living in the vital Northern area for this length of time. Furthermore, it felt strongly that the Lancashire and Yorkshire areas should if possible be treated in such a way that their respective regional interests could receive expression in the programmes. It seemed that the engineering problem, the time factor and regional considerations all pointed towards the construction of two separate stations on either side of the Pennines, each having a lower (and hence more practicable) power, a more accessible site and a lower mast. In this way it would be feasible to have a station for the Lancashire area in operation by May 1956 and to follow it by a separate station for Yorkshire opening in the late Autumn in 1956.

After sixteen different sites had been examined the choice for the Yorkshire station was Emley Moor, some seven miles south west of Huddersfield.

Splitting the coverage of the North between Winter Hill and Emley Moor proved in the end to be a masterstroke. For one thing it probably increased by as much as two million the population inside the primary service of the Northern area for which Granada and ABC had the contracts, and for another it enabled programmes to get going a good year sooner than would have been possible had the Authority persisted with a policy of constructing a single station on the Pennines. In the longer term it afforded the possibility of a greater element of plurality in the system as a whole and enabled provision to be made for programmes specially designed for the Lancashire/ Cheshire area on the one hand and the Yorkshire area on the other. The idea of creating a new Yorkshire contract area was mooted even at this early stage. A note of an informal meeting of the four companies on 24 January records a collective decision to press the ITA to abandon it.

In the stresses and strains of 1955/6 all the advantages of the Pennines split were not so self-evident – at any rate not to Granada Television. No argument adduced by the Authority could prevent Sidney Bernstein from feeling deprived of a facility he felt he had initially been led to expect, namely a single powerful transmitter up on the Pennines, providing for ITV a powerful and penetrating signal both west and east, at least as effective as that provided by the BBC's station at Holme Moss, and operative from around the end of 1955. His sense of grievance in this matter disturbed the smooth working relationship between his company and the Authority well into 1956. It was, of course, true that the breakdown of the plans for sharing BBC masts meant that programme transmission in the North in the winter of 1955/6 ceased to be possible and that Granada were unable to make a start on the Lancashire side until 3 May 1956 and on the Yorkshire side until 3 November. These were bad dates on which to begin to attract business from still sceptical advertisers. But the obstacles to an earlier start for Granada's programme service were not all on this one front: in March 1956 the studio equipment they had been awaiting from Marconis had still to be delivered and they were admitting that they would have considerable difficulties in being ready even by 3 May. It can now be seen that this air date was a remarkable achievement by both the Authority and the company.

15

TELEVISION HOURS

A note by Fraser on 16 March 1955 was cosily entitled 'Hours: A Problem out of the Way' and then paradoxically went on to describe the agreement that had been reached and why it did no more than provide a temporary solution which by no means disposed of the problem of hours of television. On Mondays to Fridays there was to be a maximum of 35 hours actual broadcasting, transmittable between 9 a.m. and 11 p.m., with a maximum of 8 hours in any one day. There was to be a closed period between 6 p.m. and 7 p.m. (the 'toddlers truce' to get the children off to bed). On Saturdays and Sundays there was to be a maximum of 15 hours for the two days, with a maximum 8 hours on Saturday and 7¾ hours on Sunday. Television on Sunday was permissible between 2 p.m. and 11 p.m., subject to a closed period from 6.15 p.m. to 7.30 p.m. (the 'God-slot' to protect evensong) and change of programme at 7.45 p.m. Any broadcasting between 2 p.m. and 4 p.m. was to be designed for adults so that children would not be tempted to stay away from Sunday School. Religious services or analogous religious programmes and live outside broadcasts of special importance and public interest were, it was agreed, exempt from these rules.

The rules were equally applicable to the BBC. Section 9(3) of the Television Act had reserved to the Postmaster-General the power to fix the hours of television and the Government believed that there were good social and economic reasons for keeping the amount of television available to the public within prescribed limits. Furthermore the BBC did not want ITV to be allowed to broadcast for longer hours than they saw fit, or felt they could afford, to broadcast themselves. Over the ensuing years the Authority together with the companies, unaided and usually opposed by the BBC, struggled for freedom from these controls, but succeeded only in nibbling away at them until on 19 January 1972, seventeen years later, the then Minister of Posts and Telecommunications, Christopher Chataway, finally agreed to tear them up.

Fraser's note of March 1955 was uncannily prescient:

At long last, an agreement has been reached about television hours, and thus one major problem is out of the wáy. This accomplishment has proved such a labour as you would never believe – an object lesson in the sort of difficulties that lie concealed in the Act. We got away to a good start at a meeting last November with the Postmaster-General in the chair. His senior advisers were present, and so was our own Chairman. But then the troubles began. In the four months since the first meeting, there has not been a week, and in some weeks there has not been a day, and on some days it seems that there has not been an hour, during which negotiations have not proved necessary between ourselves, the programme companies, the Post Office at both Ministerial and official levels, and the BBC. The bureaucratic overheads that result from a preference for detailed regulation rather than broad control (let alone freedom) can really be terrifying.

. . . I am sure we shall fairly soon come to regard this first agreement as a quaint antiquity; it could more accurately be classed at the moment as a major act of liberalisation. Present BBC hours average about five a day. Also, the new agreement allows television at important periods during which it is at present prohibited or withheld as an act of policy.

We have of course not finished with the problem of hours or anything like it. Just as soon as their programme resources allow, we may be sure that the programme companies will occupy the last minute of the time allowed them, and they will then ask for more. They will do so for two reasons. Firstly, the companies will stand to gain financially from an extension of hours. They may have to drop their average advertising rates, but the reduction of overheads and average programme costs will more than compensate. Secondly, they are not inhibited by any feeling that television is a drug which the patient should be allowed only in prescribed quantities. It is their life, and they will want to live it to the full.

I should guess that the first dam against which they will wash is the evening break. As soon as they feel their strength, they will find this a maddening interruption in the continuity of their programmes, and they already know perfectly well that it is an hour rich in potential advertising revenue . . . They will all the time ask why they should not be allowed to provide as much television as experience shows the public would like to have.

The trouble is that a lot of responsible people do not see it this way at all, but on the contrary believe either that it is a pity that television was ever invented or else that television programmes should in the public interest be limited in quantity. The Postmaster-General makes no bones about his adherence to this second school of thought.[1]

The PMG was, of course, Dr Charles Hill. Written in 1955 these were revolutionary words, and even today it is not difficult to find 'responsible people' who believe that the total amount of allowable television should be rationed by government in the interests of the community at large.

16

THE STATUTORY COMMITTEES

(i) ADVERTISING

Today, when commercial sponsorship of all entertainment save television and radio is accepted with equanimity in Britain, the anxieties of twenty-five years ago about television financed by advertising are hard to understand. They were but a part of the great debate about the power and influence of mass communications which had been proceeding for a century or more and which was bound up inextricably with fundamental beliefs about the nature of liberty in a free, democratic society. For what distinguished radio and television services from the theatre, the opera house or the tennis court was that they were a medium of information and opinion. Parliament found it necessary to ensure in the Television Act that so far as possible commercial television was insulated from control by commercial interests over the information supplied and opinions expressed in its programmes. Those who thought that the degree of public control need not exceed that prevailing in America were a distinct minority.

That television advertising need not involve the sponsorship of programmes was, as has been seen, largely brushed aside during the discussions that went on between the publication of the Beveridge Report in 1951 and the passage of the Television Act in 1954. Even after the Act was on the Statute Book and the Authority had been established, public confusion on this matter was extensive. As it was necessary to say in the Annual Report:

It cannot be stressed too often in view of the amount of misunderstanding which has existed on this subject that the system brought into being by the Television Act makes impossible the 'sponsoring' of programmes by advertisers as practised in the USA and elsewhere. . . . The programmes will not in any circumstances be provided by or adopted by advertisers and will be the sole responsibility of the programme contractors. The advertisements will be inserted at the beginning or the end of the programme items, or in natural breaks within them, in much the same way as they appear in the columns of a newspaper, or are shown between films in the cinema.[1]

The report might have gone on to say that what Section 4(6) of the Act expressly precluded was the *appearance* of sponsorship, whether sponsorship was being exercised or not. In a special proviso to this clause, sponsored documentary films were allowable even if the name of the sponsor, say, Shell Petroleum, was mentioned, so long as the Authority was satisfied that such items were 'proper for inclusion by reason of their intrinsic interest or instructiveness and do not comprise an undue element of advertisement'.

The peculiar wording of this clause was to give the Authority a few headaches in the years ahead, but for the time.being it involved no problems. Nobody wanted sponsorship, certainly not the programme contractors, nor, by and large, the advertisers or their agents. It was losing ground in America to 'spot' advertising. All concerned happily settled down to doing without it; and so they continued with relatively little aggravation for the next twenty-five years. The Annual Report for 1955/6 had this to say: 'Of all the many apprehensions which have been expressed concerning a system of free enterprise television in Britain, none has proved so illusory, having regard to the terms of the Act, as those concerning the influence of advertising interests over the content of programmes.'[2] The Authority was able to point out to the Pilkington Committee in 1960 that the complete and manifest distinction between the programmes and the advertisements made British Independent Television unique among all the large systems of self-supporting television to be found in the world.

The Second Schedule of the Act said that 'the amount of time given to advertising in the programmes shall not be so great as to detract from the value of the programmes as a medium of entertainment, instruction and information'. This placed the ball well and truly in the Authority's court and, to nobody's surprise, it decided to go for 10 per cent, i.e. the time given over to 'spot' advertising should not exceed an average of six minutes an hour. This was the proportion which Barnett of the Post Office had plucked out of the air in order to assist Gammans during the progress of the Bill. The Authority also decided that the number of periods given over to advertisements should not exceed six an hour on the average. These decisions were ratified by the PMG, as the Act required. Although experience showed the need for various subsequent refinements and amplifications of these two basic rules, the average amount of six minutes an hour proved to be a very shrewd guess and it survived the passage of time and the scrutiny of several committees of enquiry.

During the debates on the Bill it was envisaged that, in addition to spot advertising, there might be a separate form of advertising described as 'shoppers guides' which might last for fifteen minutes or so. The notion was that these would be a form of advertising which would have sufficient interest to hold an audience on their own. The Authority followed up this idea and decided to allow 'advertising magazines'. It did not foresee a need to ration this particular form of advertising, nor did it believe that they would blur the distinction between advertisements and programmes, however popular their appeal turned out to be. This form of advertising was destined to death by execution at the hands of the Pilkington Committee and the Government, but in the early years it certainly seemed to provide a welcome service to the public and it helped to boost revenue at a time when it was most needed. It gave rise to increasing difficulties as time went by and there were those who saw this activity as, apart from all other considerations, an intrusion into programme time that, under the controls over hours of television, was already in short supply.

Even today there is a national consensus in favour of keeping advertising in its place. Most people would be affronted if advertising found its way into the churches or was allowed to decorate formal, set-piece royal occasions like Trooping the Colour. In May 1955 it was agreed that advertisements should be kept away for a period of at least two minutes from televised religious services, formal royal ceremonies or occasions and even from appearances of The Queen or members of the Royal Family in televised coverage of other occasions, be they racing at Ascot or variety shows at the Palladium. The substance of these rules has survived to the present time; and other classes of programme, like television programmes for schools, have been added to the list.

Nervous, not to say hostile, members of the European Broadcasting Union, whose governments (excepting Luxembourg and Monaco) were uniformly opposed to broadcast advertising, were to refuse to accept any ITV contributions to Eurovision unless they were 'clean feeds' protected from advertising by what they called a '*cordon sanitaire*' of at least three minutes.

There was also the requirement that advertisements should not be inserted otherwise than in 'natural breaks' in programmes. In 1954/5 before a service had begun, there was nothing that the Authority could do to enlighten the companies as to how to live with it. In due course ways and means of doing so were found, and the critics eventually grew tired of twisting ITV's tail about its alleged failures to comply with the law of the land. The meaning of the term 'natural break' has never been tested in the Courts. It was, however, a provision of vital significance for the whole character of Independent Television. If advertising had been allowable only between programmes and never within them, it is difficult to see how ITV could ever have paid its way, save by devising all, or nearly all, its programmes to have running times of stultifyingly short duration. There were many conflicting views about what was 'natural' but in the end the people most prone to suffer frustration and inconvenience from the breaks have been the writers of television drama and dramatised documentaries who have been to some extent regimented to follow predetermined patterns.

That highly influential pamphlet *Television: The Viewer and the Advertiser* to which reference has been made in Part I was much in the minds of some of the members of the Authority's Advertising Advisory Committee when it was appointed in January 1955 and settled down to produce in a remarkably short time the statement of 'Principles for Television Advertising'. Membership of this commmittee included representatives of the Advertising Association, the IPA and the ISBA; all bodies 'concerned with standards of conduct in the advertising of goods and services'. There were representatives also of the Ministry of Health, the British Medical Association, the British Dental Association, the Pharmaceutical Society and the British Code of Standards Committee (a body concerned with the voluntary control of medical advertising in media other than television). A representative too of the Retail Trading Standards Association, a national association of retail traders and manufacturers that was concerned to bring influence to bear against manufacturers or trades whose advertisements or selling methods or descriptions of merchandise were misleading to the public. The Committee was, in the Authority's opinion, a well-balanced mixture of professional and consumer interests, adequately fulfilling hopes expressed in Parliament during debates on the Bill. Its Acting Chairman was a man of much distinction in advertising affairs – R. A. Bevan OBE, a member of the Council of the IPA and Chairman of the firm of S. H. Benson Ltd, advertising agents.

The Principles for Television Advertising, after receiving the necessary approvals from the Authority and the PMG, were published on 2 June 1955. They took the form of a general code with two appendices containing detailed rules about specific classes of advertising and methods of advertising and the advertising of medicines and treatments. Full account was taken of the voluntary codes by which advertising was governed in other media and much of these were incorporated in the television code. 'All television advertising should be legal, clean, honest and truthful.' So ran the Preamble to the Principles. The main subjects covered were the legal requirements; the prevention of misleading advertisements; disparaging references; testimonials; guarantees; competitions and advertising in children's programmes. Appendix 2 was in fact a reprint of the British Code of Standards in relation to the Advertising of Medicines and Treatments, a code which was generally observed in other advertising media.

At the insistence of the Authority, the Committee gave much attention to the question of betting and football pools advertisements, but decided to defer its advice about them until more was known of the form and content of the coming television programmes, and that in the meantime there should be no betting advertisements. The Pools Promoters Association had itself decided that its members would not book advertising time in the initial stages. The members of the Committee and the Authority were well aware that here was a hot potato lying around and were relieved that for the moment they did not have to pick it up. Subsequently they could not escape handling it, but managed not to burn their fingers.

Given all the anxieties that were prevailing about television advertising, the document as a whole can only be described as a boldly liberal one, even though it excluded from television some products or treatments, or advertising methods, that were acceptable in other media. Money lenders, matrimonial agencies and fortune tellers were among the ones that were shown the door. Smoking cures were banned but cigarettes were not. Products for the treatment of alcoholism were also banned but the Committee, bless its British heart, recommended to the Authority at its very first meeting that there should be no prohibition of any kind on the advertising of alcohol – advice to which neither the Authority nor the PMG saw reason to demur.

The publication of the Principles was a triumph for the Advertising Advisory Committee, whose work in the first half of 1955 was a priceless boon to Independent Television. Never again did the ITA secure a body of advisers which saw its task so clearly and accomplished it so effectively and expeditiously. This Committee remained in being and had some knotty problems to resolve on occasions over the years, but it never quite attained again the clear incisiveness of those early days.

Meantime, of course, the companies due to begin programme transmissions in London in September were establishing their sales departments and determining their tariffs of rates. This they had to do with very little knowledge of the direction which television advertising would take. What rates they should charge was entirely their own affair but, under the Act, it was necessary that the tariffs should be 'drawn up in such detail and published in such form and manner as the Authority may determine'. They were also enjoined in paragraph 4 of the Second Schedule to ensure that 'in the acceptance of advertisements there must be no unreasonable discrimination either against or in favour of any particular advertiser'. This business of procuring, distributing and presenting the advertisements came under almost ceaseless public scrutiny in the years ahead.

(ii) RELIGION

This was another subject in relation to which the Authority was required to appoint a committee under the terms of Section 8(2) of the Television Act. It had to be 'representative of the main streams of religious thought in the United Kingdom, the Isle of Man and the Channel Islands'. A separate provision of the Act, Section 3(4)(a), had ruled that 'any religious service or any propaganda relating to matters of a religious nature' should not be broadcast except with the previous approval of the Authority. This provision was seen as placing upon the ITA a special responsibility as regards religion, and, in consequence, the amount of time initially spent at its meetings discussing arrangements for this category of programmes was disproportionately large.

Having regard to the debates on the Bill, it was in the minds of some Members of the Authority, and certainly of its Chairman, that, given the Authority's special responsibility, here was an area of programmes which could, under Section 11, be financed out of the £750,000 grant. It seemed to Clark that if the Authority was to make its mark on the programme output of ITV here was a field in which it could most easily start. What preoccupied him in the first place was the nature of the advisory committee it should appoint. He recalled that, during the debates on the Bill, it had been strongly advocated that the Authority, rather than appoint a new committee, should arrange for the assistance of the Central Religious Advisory Committee of the BBC. But, whilst recognising the desirability of avoiding rivalry between separate committees of churchmen, neither the ITA nor the companies were much impressed by the prospect of tagging on to a large BBC-oriented body which met only twice a year. A compromise was tried out by which the Authority drew the membership of its own Committee from the membership of the larger BBC committee, but this proved unsatisfactory since the membership became nervous about 'divided loyalties' whilst the Authority could not help feeling that it was making do with nothing more than a sub-committee of a BBC committee. Reluctantly it came to the conclusion that it should, with the BBC's agreement, make use of the full, existing body. This, it was envisaged, would take care of issues of principle; for the more day-to-day business of giving advice to the programme makers it hit upon the happy device of appointing a trio of consultants, one Anglican, one Free Churchman and one Roman Catholic who would be answerable on broad issues to the 'CRAC'.

While these solemn issues were being thrashed out, Clark decided that he would like to have a Religious Programmes Officer on the staff in order to underline and safeguard the ITA's own special responsibility in this area of programme making. In the event, however, no appointment was made, partly because the notion aroused a flurry of objection from two company members of the Standing Consultative Committee. One of them, Victor Peers of Granada, described such an appointment as 'a first step towards dictatorship'.[3] Curiously, the objections came from the weekday companies: the weekend companies, who were to be more regularly involved in religious broadcasting, took quite a different view. As it turned out, the very talented Panel of Three (Canon Eric Heaton, The Revd Dr John Marsh and Monsignor G. A. Tomlinson), working closely with myself as DDG, proved to be fully capable of looking after the Authority's interests without the aid of specialist staff, and its three members unanimously recommended that no such staff should be appointed – advice which Clark accepted with good grace. Not until 1964, following the new Television Act, was the first Religious Programmes Officer appointed.

Out of these confused beginnings the advisory arrangements proved a great success and survived without any fundamental change for the next twenty-five years. When it came to the point, the majestic and in some respects Reithian Central Religious Advisory Committee took a puckish delight in treating Independent Television as of equal standing and importance with the BBC. Indeed, when in due course CRAC was confronted by the advice of the Pilkington Committee, backed by the strong wish of the BBC, to withdraw its services from ITV, it refused to do so.

(iii) 'MATTER INTENDED FOR CHILDREN'

The third committee which the Authority was enjoined to set up by the terms of Section 8(2) had to be 'representative of organisations, authorities and persons having experience of and special interest in the welfare and education of children and young persons' and its function was to advise the Authority 'as to the principles to be followed in connection with the broadcasting . . . of matter intended for children or young persons'. This committee was a novelty; no counterpart to it was to be found amongst the BBC's list of committees, and the latter's Schools Broadcasting Council had no responsibility for non-educational programmes. The Authority decided to cast its net as widely as possible, whilst aiming at a committee comprising about a dozen people. Although it sought nominations from various bodies it did not commit itself to allowing standing representation of any particular interest or organisation. This was a policy which the Authority came to adopt as a matter of course as the need for other advisory committees came along in later years; it always reckoned to appoint *persons* – not designated spokesmen of particular bodies or organised interest groups. No difficulty was found in getting a committee together by the time it was needed, that is shortly after programme transmissions had begun. Perhaps inevitably, it was heavily weighted on the educational side, but it did have members drawn from the Mothers' Union, the National Council of Women and the Boy Scouts Association. As will be seen in Chapter 31 (iii) its services in regard to programmes for schools came to be needed sooner than anyone at the outset could have foreseen.

17

'PROPER PROPORTIONS' OF BRITISH MATERIAL

Despite the rush of developments during the year following its appointment, the Authority was mulling over in its mind the responsibilities it would in due course have to exercise as regards the programmes themselves under the terms of Section 3(1) of the Act. There were two particular provisions which could not be left until transmissions began; first the presentation of any news with 'due accuracy and impartiality' and secondly the presence in the output of 'proper proportions' of the recorded and other matter that were of 'British origin and British performance'. The first was one of the reasons for establishing Independent Television News and the second called for negotiation and agreement with the programme contractors and no less than fourteen different organisations[1] concerned with the employment of British citizens in one or other capacity in Independent Telivision.

Fortunately, all the fourteen organisations combined for the purpose of this negotiation – incidentally for the first time in the history of the entertainment profession – and it fell to the Secretary of the British Actors' Equity Association, Gordon Sandison, to act as their principal spokesman. Their demands were presented to the PMG on 18 February 1954 shortly before the Television Bill was published. These were in the main, first that not less than 80 per cent of the programmes transmitted by any television station should be British, this quota being applied separately to peak and off-peak periods and separately to live and recorded material, and secondly that there should be no transmission of films which had already been publicly exhibited at home or abroad before the date of the first licence. This second demand drew no distinction between British and foreign films, and its aim was simply to prevent contractors from starting off with schedules containing a surfeit of old films.

The case for the 80 : 20 quota was later pressed by the Opposition during the debates on the Bill, but as we saw in Chapter 8, all the amendments designed to write it into the Act were defeated, the Government taking the line that it was unnecessary to be so specific. A deputation to the Chairman and Director General of the Authority on 2 December 1954 returned to the attack and it was evident that the Authority would have to consult with the companies and see what could be done.

The idea of having to administer such a quota, with all its potential for bureaucratic chaos, was anathema to the companies and the Authority alike. What real grounds, they asked themselves, were there for anxiety on the part of the fourteen, other than the possibility of an undue use of imported American films? A private conversation between Fraser and Sandison, who had formed a good relationship, disclosed that this approach might well be the germ of a solution to the problem. Sidney Bernstein, who had been made chairman of a sub-committee of the companies on this subject, got together with Fraser and Sandison, and they concocted a plan which was the first foundation of the so-called Gentleman's Agreement.

The programme contractors embraced this plan with relief. On the basis of fifty hours a week of total transmission time ten hours a week of foreign films could be shown, seven on the weekdays and three on Saturdays and Sundays: these ten to be divided as to five hours in the evenings and five in the afternoons. The figure of ten hours per week could be calculated as an average figure over quarterly periods, but in no one week should there be more than seven hours in the evenings or fourteen during the week as a whole.

But the plan had still to run the gamut of scrutiny by the fourteen organisations and it soon became apparent that they found it too tolerant. Either the ten hours a week must, they thought, be related to programme material of all kinds or, if the control was confined to foreign films only, then seven should be the magic figure not ten. Twenty per cent would have to become fourteen per cent. A period of delicate negotiation ensued, with the contracting companies for their part searching for terms on which the reduction to seven hours could be made tolerable to them. They knew that the Authority's support for adherence to the Bernstein–Fraser–Sandison plan could not be counted on and that it was in the mood for compromise. Victor Peers – a long-standing aide of Sidney Bernstein at Granada and a most able and experienced negotiator – looked after the companies' case, Sandison continued to act for the unions and Fraser, adroit and ingenious as ever, represented the Authority.

The document that finally emerged in time to be brought into force on 22 September was indeed ingenious, and all sides were able to draw satisfaction from it. It was agreed that it should remain a Gentleman's Agreement and not be published. Although it was intended to run for a year in the first instance, it was never actually revised, and all subsequent arrangements have been an evocation of the spirit of it. Although it provided for arbitration in questions of doubt about classification, no arbitrator ever had to be appointed. But it hardly fulfilled the hope that it would create few bureaucratic chores. As ITV grew larger and more complex, so also grew the tedium of administering the foreign material control fairly. It also threw up problems of classification which involved some finely balanced judgements of Solomon on the part of the Authority. Nevertheless, it was a good agreement and a triumph for commonsense. It was brief and workmanlike and its terms were as follows:

1 The use of foreign filmed programmes should on the average not exceed seven hours a week of which not more than four on the average shall be included in the evening programmes.
2 The test whether films made in this country primarily for American or other foreign television use should be classed as foreign or British should lie not in the first intended use, but in the character of the product as revealed by such factors as labour costs, scripts, stars and director.
3 Films made in non-British territories by British companies should be treated as British unless it can be shown that there was no good and natural reason connected with the subject matter why they should have been made abroad, or that the employment of British nationals was not substantial.
4 Films made by British companies in any territory of the Commonwealth should lie outside the restriction, though films made in these territories under foreign direction and with the motive of securing a British classification should lie inside it.
5 Questions of doubt about the classification of cases under 2 above should be referred to a committee of an equal number of representatives of the programme companies and the trade unions, with an agreed independent chairman to take the final decision in the event of disagreement.
6 The restriction will apply to a full week's programmes, and will not be divided between the weekdays and the weekends.
7 The arrangements should operate for a period of one year, this period to run, in the case of the first four programme companies, from the inception of their programmes.
8 The figure of seven hours a week will be calculated as an average figure over periods of three months, subject to a maximum of ten hours in any single week.
9 The figure of seven hours will be related to a total programme output of fifty regular hours' broadcasting a week and within the period of the

agreement shall vary pro rata in so far as regular hours are less or more than fifty.

The Gentleman's Agreement became a sort of shibboleth over the next two decades. It was more often talked about than read, and it gave Fraser and his staff much room for manoeuvre. For those who enjoyed practising the art of the possible, it possessed a peculiar fascination.

18

LABOUR RELATIONS

Conspicuous absentees from the list of fourteen unions with which the ITA negotiated were the BBC Staff Association – conspicuous because, after all, they were the only union so far recognised by the BBC as representative of television workers, as well as those in radio, since 1946. An attempt had been made in 1952 by those in the union who could foresee a possible end of the monopoly to secure a change of name, but the proposal did not receive sufficient support. In the event a change in title to the Association of Broadcasting Staff became imperative early in 1956; indeed it was overdue because by this time they were well on the way to losing the foothold they had established in the companies.

At first, despite the embarrassment of their name, the association made good headway in Independent Television. For the ITA itself, whose technical staff was drawn almost entirely from the BBC, relations with a BBC staff union seemed in no way incongruous. More remarkable was the progress they made with the companies. The first development was with A-R and by 21 February we find Brownrigg, the General Manager, reporting to one of the companies' informal meetings that a final settlement had been reached between his company, the BBC Staff Association and the National Union of General and Municipal Workers on the terms of 'recognition'. Copies of this agreement were handed in confidence to the other companies. Two further unions received similar recognition, namely the Electrical Trades Union and the National Association of Theatrical and Kine Employees. The other companies seem to have followed the lead taken by A-R without much further consideration.

A year or so later the Association of Broadcasting Staff, as they started to call themselves in February 1956, had been ousted from the programme companies (though not the ITA) and replaced by the Association of Cinematograph and Allied Technicians (ACT), soon to be called the Association of Cinematograph Television and Allied Technicians (ACTT). Undoubtedly this development was of great importance in the history of ITV.

Under their urbane and congenial General Secretary, Leslie Littlewood –
a man who liked to be liked – the BBC Staff Association had been anything
but militant. In this they faithfully reflected the views of most of their
members. As Littlewood put it in a talk he gave in 1950, 'Staff of the
Corporation, whether or not they are members of this Association, regard
the broadcasting service as one which, above all, should be free from
interruption by disputes.'[1] They had not applied for affiliation to the TUC,
and they were not at all popular with other unions. 'The general view was
that the Association's membership was dominated by establishment
orientated middle class individuals who had no notion of "real" unionism
because their predominant loyalty was to the employer.'[2] It is not difficult to
appreciate how this utterly respectable association found favour with
Brownrigg who had had no previous experience or knowledge of trade
unionism.

There then occurred a course of events which was destined to alter the
whole character of ITV's labour relations. It is well recorded in issues of the
Cine Technician (the journal of the ACT) and principally in vol. 21, no. 124,
for May 1955. More recently it has been recounted in Peter Seglow's book
Trade Unionism in Television.[3] A-R planned to film a television play at their
Shepperton Studios in April 1955. In March they received a peremptory
letter from the ACT organiser saying that his union expected the company to
negotiate the rates and conditions for the technicians through them; and in
reply the company merely referred the ACT to the two unions they had
already recognised. ACT at once proceeded to demand immediate
withdrawal of this reply or otherwise their members would be advised not to
work on the production.

This strike began on 12 April. After three days Brownrigg, who must by
this time have been pining for the old days of 'good order and naval
discipline', informed George Elvin, the ACT's General Secretary, that the
agreement with the BBC Staff Association did not preclude the participation
of other unions in the television industry, withdrew his previous letter and
offered to recommend to the other contractors that they should meet
representatives of the union 'to hear your views on this problem of union
recognition'. A series of talks took place and it was eventually settled on 20
September that, pending a formal agreement, the companies would employ
ACT members 'under terms which are not less favourable than such staff
would have enjoyed if they had been employed under the terms of the
Agreement between ACT and the British Film Producers Association'. It was
not Brownrigg alone who learnt from this episode that commercial
television was going to be exceptionally vulnerable to industrial action.

19

THE AUTHORITY AND THE PROGRAMMES

By the early summer of 1955 the Authority felt that it could no longer refrain from considering in broad terms its own future role in regard to the programmes of ITV. It was possible to adopt, and find reasons for justifying, two quite different points of view. On the one hand the very existence of the ITA as a public authority with the function under Section 1 of the Act of providing television services 'additional to those of the British Broadcasting Corporation and of high quality' could be taken as implying a positive programme responsibility which would not be abrogated. On the other hand it could be said that commercial television was founded on a belief in free enterprise which could only find expression if the contractors were allowed the utmost freedom within the law; the provisions of the Act did not really go further than make the Authority the landlord and the companies the tenants. As Clark put it, 'The Act, on this point, is as ambiguous as the Elizabethan prayer-book, and it is really for the Authority to interpret its rulings bearing in mind (a) the intentions of Parliament as expressed in the debates and negotiations which preceded the Act and (b) the practical working of the system.'[1]

In his paper Clark went on to expound some of the pros and cons. He drew attention to Section 3(1)(b) which, as already noted, called for 'a proper balance' in the subject matter of the programmes and reminded his colleagues that it was in relation to this particular duty that, although it did not say so, Section 11 empowered the PMG to pay to the Authority 'sums not exceeding £750,000 in any one financial year'. It appeared from the debates that this money was intended for use in preventing deterioration in programme standards, and for ensuring the presence in the output of programmes which might not otherwise be there. Moreover, he put it to his colleagues that they might all feel a personal responsibility for seeing that the new service was used in a 'civilising and life-enhancing manner'.

Turning to the other side of the coin he stressed the importance of the companies being made to feel that they had the Authority's confidence. 'They are setting out with honourable intentions, and would be justifiably resentful if from the first we implied by our interference that their programmes would need civilising.'[2]

Concluding his review and, as some might well think, rather against the weight of his own argument, Clark said:

I am confident that in the minds of those who framed the Act free competition weighed more heavily than control . . . Any attempt we made at an extended interference in programmes would be resented as unwarranted and unfair, and I am inclined to think that if, in a dispute on this point, an appeal were made to Her Majesty's Government the decision would go against us.[3]

To all of which the Authority's collective response was 'let's wait and see'. The Chairman was content with this conclusion, but declared himself as not too optimistic about the future, believing that the Authority might feel the need to intervene quite soon, as the programmes might tend to be uniformly 'popular'.[4]

Some years later Clark was to say to the Pilkington Committee:

Personally I think that the Independent Television Authority could have done more with the companies if they had tried. But admittedly the 'balance' clause is a feeble clause, and I think the new Act should give them something a little sterner to use on occasion. You will remember that such a clause was deliberately omitted from the original Act, to satisfy those who were afraid that the Independent Television Authority would become a second BBC.[5]

Kenneth Clark was a kind of Jekyll and Hyde in television affairs. There was the Jekyll who launched ITV and saw it through its initial difficulties with brilliant success. He was tolerant and considerate and displayed infinite resource. He withdrew after three years, to the universal disappointment of his ITV friends. He states that he was not asked to stay on[6] and hated leaving. There was the Hyde who subsequently presented disparaging and destructive evidence to the Pilkington Committee. He was an aesthete and an intellectual, and yet in his dealings with the whole range of Independent Television from the tycoons to the bureaucrats he showed no hint of condescension. 'Much of my pleasure in founding the Independent Television Authority,' he wrote, 'was due to the fact that I was working with a man (Robert Fraser) in whom I had complete confidence.' Yet the respective outlooks of the two men were vastly different. Whether, had Clark stayed for two further years, the Authority would have 'done more' with the companies is just speculation; but the probability is that it would.

20

GETTING READY

The staid language of the Authority's second annual report for 1955/6 recorded that, 'The vigour and enterprise of the programme companies in making themselves ready from scratch for the provision of up to fifty hours a week of television programmes in the extremely short time at their disposal deserve the highest praise.'[1] Each of the four had different tasks, different problems and different deadlines. The two London companies, with a starting date within a year of being offered contracts, had to perform miracles of improvisation, and so did Independent Television News. But all had studios to provide and equip, all needed outside broadcast resources, all had staff to find and recruit and all had programmes to plan and film to acquire. And they had to learn how to work together, not only in dealings with the ITA but in order to make a reality of the concept of a competitive optional network. From April 1955 a Television Programme Contractors Association was in being and even before that, from December 1954, the original companies had been holding informal meetings. From June 1955 they were also meeting formally with the ITA in the Standing Consultative Committee.

Most of the business of that committee in its early months was concerned with the immediate problems connected with starting transmissions in September. The provision by the Post Office of sound and vision links between studios and transmitters and between city terminal points in London, the Midlands and the North was one such subject. These were of vital importance and it was essential that the Post Office Engineering Department should move in step with the Authority as regards the transmitters and with the companies as regards the studios. Another and, at the time, highly contentious matter was the content of the so-called trade test transmissions, which provided sound and picture when programmes themselves were not being transmitted, in order to assist dealers when installing and lining up television sets capable of receiving both BBC and ITV. The PMG was determined not to allow these necessary transmissions to be turned into a *de facto* service of programmes and advertisements, capable of attracting and holding an audience, or even to be used to promote or 'trail' forthcoming programmes. He got his way, but the companies – and the Authority too – considered he was unnecessarily holding back the development of an enterprise which depended for its success on building up an audience as fast as possible.

To turn from the formation of policy, with which Part II has so far been mainly concerned, to the events which were taking place 'out on the ranch' is to move into a totally different world. As has been seen, offers of contracts in principle were made to four companies early in November 1954. For the two companies appointed in London, A-R and ATV (initially called ABC) little more than ten months elapsed before they went on air on 22 September 1955. The speed and scale of their preparations were almost miraculous.

(i) ASSOCIATED-REDIFFUSION IN LONDON

In command of the Associated-Rediffusion operation was Captain Tom Brownrigg RN, the General Manager. He was a remarkable chief executive of a remarkable company; for none of their high command had previous experience of television or film production, although those directors who came from Broadcast Relay Service (Rediffusion) had wide commercial radio interests which were already extending into television in some places. One of them, Paul Adorian, was an expert in electronics. They soon acquired as ITV's first programme controller a man possessing the experience they themselves lacked. He was Roland Gillett, who, after working in films both in Britain and Hollywood, had become one of the leading television producers in the United States. BET had acquired their interest in BRS as far back as 1947 and their own Managing Director, John Spencer Wills, also became Chairman and Managing Director of this new interest.

What Brownrigg knew initially about television and advertising amounted, as Arthur Groocock, the company's secretary, put it, 'to fractionally more than nil'. He had made his first contact with Broadcast Relay Service in his capacity as General Manager of Bracknell New Town Development Corporation. Formerly he had experienced a classically successful career in the Royal Navy, but he made enemies and the decision to pass him over for promotion and place him on the retired list as Captain did not completely surprise his fellow officers. He was certainly not all things to all men. His idiosyncracies were such that the latest Brownrigg story went the rounds of ITV much as they circulated around the wardrooms of the Navy in earlier days. Wrote Groocock on his death in 1967, ' "Never baffled", is the phrase with which we shall always associate Captain Brownrigg.' He was said to have commanded A-R as if it were a battleship. Quite possibly the company were none the worse for it.

Meanwhile the ship had to be built, complete its trials and become operational within the space of ten months. In reality it was more a squadron than a single ship that had to be ready by September 1955. Adastral House in Kingsway – vacated by the Air Ministry – became Television House, the flagship, incorporating studios 7 and 8, as well as being the administration headquarters, and at the same time accommodating the processing, cutting, dubbing, newsrooms and studio of ITN, together with temporary accommodation for the staff of the weekend company. The ninth studio, for audience participation programmes, to be located in the basement of Television House, was due to join the squadron in November. The other six were at Wembley (four), the Granville Theatre, Walham Green and the Viking Film Studios. Peter Black wrote in the *Daily Mail* on 13 September of 'four different miracles' and 'the most sustained pieces of hustling ever undertaken by a commercial undertaking in Britain'.

On that day the national newspapers, whose correspondents had been given a conducted tour, were filled with detailed stories of the hustle. They were all impressed. For instance, the relatively sober *Times*:

> Three hundred workmen are engaged on the work, which goes on night and day. The whole Adastral House is being gutted with the help of batteries of pneumatic drills; already many massive walls have been removed; and the rubble so far amounts to about 4000 tons.
>
> The staff of Associated-Rediffusion, who have been in the building since work began in May, have often to stop work while materials are hoisted in through the office windows. Amid the dust and rubble of reconstruction television workers, builders and electricians mingle on each of the ten floors, and although the general impression is one of confusion, the contractors, Messrs Bovis Ltd, are certain that the work will be completed by the right time. They have a special organisation for work at high speed. Already, in spite of the threat of labour trouble, the parts of the building essential for programme production are ready.

More than 1000 staff were recruited during those hectic months. It is safe to say that not one of them alive today lacks memories of incidents and experiences that lose nothing in the telling. Collected up, they could fill a book at least as large as this one. With Brownrigg in supreme command, it was a masterpiece of rapid planning and execution reminiscent of the Second World War. Appropriately enough, Peter Trench, Managing Director of Bovis Ltd, had been a planning staff officer with Mountbatten's Combined Operations HQ and later on Montgomery's planning staff for D-Day.

(ii) ATV IN LONDON

ATV had advantages in the preparatory phase which A-R did not enjoy, although these were obviously offset by the prolonged delay in establishing the final structure of the company and by the lateness of the inclusion of ITP in the group (Chapter 11(iv)). The original Associated Broadcasting Development Company, which had been in existence since 1952 had, through their association with High Definition Films, a studio at Highbury, which had for some time been making films for television. They had a small nucleus of senior staff under the leadership of the man who had been Controller of BBC Television from 1947 to 1950, Norman Collins. They had been in a position to show filmed programmes to Members of the ITA as early as 16 September 1954. ITP were also able to bring into the company from the outset the considerable resources at the disposal of its various directors. These included control of the Theatre Royal, Drury Lane, the London Palladium, the London Coliseum and the London Hippodrome, as well as many provincial theatres and music halls, through Prince Littler, Val Parnell and Stewart Cruikshank; film production through Philip and Sid Hyams; and also, through Harry Alan Towers, Managing Director of Towers of London Ltd, the resources of the largest international organisation for the production and distribution of recorded television programmes. Lew and Leslie Grade were jointly in command of the largest theatrical agency in Europe covering every aspect of the entertainment industry, as well as being producers and presenters of plays, musicals, revues and pantomimes.

By September 1955 the company had in working order a television control centre in Foley Street and its own theatre at Wood Green, as well as having available to it film studios at Elstree, Nettlefold and Highbury. Last but not least it had two fine outside broadcast units, thus enabling the first Sunday Night at the London Palladium to be transmitted on 25 September, hosted by Tommy Trinder, with Gracie Fields at the top of the bill. In 1955 the standard outside broadcast unit consisted of three cameras, an eight-channel sound mixer and precious little else, and mounting a spectacular such as the Palladium show made an excessive demand on its capabilities. Four or five cameras and up to twenty-four sound mixing inputs were more like what was required. One of the techniques adopted at the Palladium was to put another sub-sound mixer inside the theatre. This made it possible to mix several microphones and only occupy one of the faders in the outside broadcast unit; and also to anticipate the moves on the stage and fade up the appropriate microphone at the right moment. Later on a separate sound mixing vehicle was added to the conventional outside broadcast unit.

Some two hundred production, engineering and administrative staff had been recruited for the London weekend operation. The main brunt of the programme preparation was borne by the ubiquitous Towers and the launch of their sales operation came under the command of Richard Meyer, formerly Towers' chief in Radio Normandy, whose experience of the commercial aspects of broadcasting was second to none. There was never a man more totally dedicated than Meyer to the principle of private enterprise broadcasting, whether in radio or television and whether in Fécamp, London or Douglas, Isle of Man.

(iii) ATV AND ABC IN THE MIDLANDS

By November 1955 the ITA was in a position to commit itself to opening the Lichfield Station on half power for programme service on 17 February 1956, and so the attention of ATV to the weekday service from Birmingham in conjunction with the weekend service from the newly appointed ABC Television was by then first priority. With time pressing on both of them the two companies were, as Howard Thomas put it, 'thrust into partnership'.[2] Thomas and Parnell had already resolved to share the same studios on a 5-day: 2-day basis and to establish a joint company, Alpha Television, for the purpose of operating them.

The time factor alone precluded their constructing an entirely new studio complex such as Granada had embarked upon in Manchester. The best proposition proved to be an old theatre built in the last decade of the nineteenth century and taken over for use as an ABC cinema: this was the New Theatre at Aston Cross. Its conversion in three months, in time for the first programme transmissions on 17 February, was a makeshift business if ever there was one, but it was achieved, even if it had to be supported by an outside broadcast unit stationed in the backyard. Alpha Studios were never to be a genuine programme company base but they were efficient and economical in their operations. Both the programme companies were separate entities in competition with one another for advertising revenue, and their Midland Studios were a servicing unit run by a group of technicians under the management of Bernard Greenhead, who had belonged to a team of brilliant engineers who worked with High Definition Films at Highbury. Each of the two programme companies had other interests elsewhere, ATV in London and ABC in Manchester, and their producers and directors came and went to Alpha as occasion required. Neither company took root in the Midlands in the first phase of Independent Television; and it was not until ATV were relieved of their London responsibility and became the seven-day contractor for the Midlands in 1968 that this sprawling area with a population of nearly six millions really began to receive the individual attention which its size demanded. The principal significance of 17 February was that this was the date when ITV ceased to be a service for London alone and became a network.

Before leaving ATV and ABC it is worth recording that Greenhead went on to become Technical Controller of ABC, then Controller, Studios and Engineering and, after 1968, Director of Studios and Engineering at Thames Television. The Technical Controller of ATV was Terence Macnamara, a legendary figure in British broadcasting. Both had come together after 1950 in High Definition Films under the aegis of Norman Collins, forming a research and development team which included such figures as Dr Walter Kemp, Gerry Kaye, Fred Becker and Stuart Sansom who subsequently provided the nucleus of ITV's engineering expertise.

Macnamara had joined the British Broadcasting Company in 1922, moved to Marconis and then back to the BBC (by this time the Corporation) as Head of the Planning and Installation Department. He became associated with television in 1935 bridging the transition from the Baird to the Marconi–EMI systems. He was responsible for both the studios and the transmitter at Alexandra Palace. He possessed what Collins has described as the 'rare combination of technical achievement and sheer practicality and common sense'. 'Mac' was probably the first to have recognised late in 1954 that the sharing of the BBC masts would not work and he promptly alerted P.A.T. (Pat) Bevan, the ITA's Chief Engineer, who had been his protégé at the BBC, to this fact.[3] Bevan had been Design Engineer, Studios and Transmitting Stations, at the BBC from 1934–46 and, following an interlude during the Second World War when he was deeply involved in the development of radar, Chief Planning Engineer 1950–54. He served the ITA from 1954–67 and his successor, Howard Steele, came from Greenhead's stable at ABC, starting as Assistant Engineer-in-Charge at Alpha studios in 1957/8. Steele is now Managing Director, Sony Broadcast Ltd, after ceasing to be Director of Engineering at the IBA in 1978.

(iv) GRANADA IN THE NORTH

'We wish to become exclusive Programme Contractors for the Manchester–Liverpool Station for seven days a week.' So wrote Sidney Bernstein to the ITA on 20 September 1954. This is what Granada eventually came to be, but not until 1968. In the meantime the piece of the mosaic they were offered and accepted covered both Lancashire and Yorkshire from Mondays to Fridays. Offered in principle early in November 1954, the contract was signed in May 1955. Transmissions in Lancashire began on 3 May 1956 and in Yorkshire on 3 November 1956. The company transmitted 1807 hours of programmes in its first operating year, of which 345 hours were programmes devised and produced from an entirely new Manchester TV Centre and their mobile Travelling Eye units.

As is recorded in their publication *Year One*, Granada TV at the time the contract was signed,

> consisted of little more than a general idea of what the new television service should seek to attain. There were no tools with which to carry out this idea, no studio, no electronic equipment, not a single camera; no directors, electricians, camera-men, sound and vision mixers, typists, or designers. The craftsmen, technologists, administrative and creative workers who were to create Granada Television were working at other jobs in Manchester, Toronto, London, Liverpool and New York, many of them unaware that their future lay in television. Just a year after the contract was signed, the first Granada transmission went on the air from the most modern television centre in Europe – a building which in eight months had risen on a waste plot of ground in Quay Street, Manchester, the first building in Britain expressly designed for television.

This 4½-acre site in Quay Street adjacent to the Manchester end of George Stephenson's Manchester–Liverpool railway was acquired in May 1955 and it was decided to take half an acre of it to build, as the first stage of a more extensive development which would come later, a self-contained Centre comprising studios, workshops and offices. The winter of 1955/6 was decidedly one of Britain's wetter ones, as the ITA learnt to its cost when building the Winter Hill transmitter, and a remorseless pressure had to be kept up by architect Ralph Tubbs and others in order to fulfil the schedule. As architect of the Dome of Discovery at the 1951 South Bank exhibition, Tubbs had little to learn about meeting deadlines in foul weather. Meantime staff had to be recruited and an adjacent warehouse was taken over and turned into temporary offices.

The Travelling Eye units were an integral part of Granada's plan: two units were specially designed and built – studios on wheels, capable of being serviced by mobile power generators and with sound and vision links direct to the transmitter. Training courses for both types of studio had to be provided.

Since May 1956 was some seven months after the start of transmissions in London and two months after the start in Birmingham, Granada had more time than the others for preparation but on the other hand that much more was expected of them in terms of initial polish and accomplishment. Clark was to write in 1958, 'We did not quite foresee how much Granada would develop a character which distinguishes it most markedly from the other programme companies and from the BBC.'[4]

(v) ABC IN THE NORTH

Although they had fewer transmission days than the other three companies, ABC covered the widest area and the largest population. When, with the opening of Emley Moor on 3 November 1956, the ITA's service for London, the Midlands and the North was completed, ABC had a population of some 18 million people within their reach. We have seen how they scrambled into service in the Midlands: their arrangements for the North were a good deal more substantial. If he had to operate outside London, Manchester was the place which Howard Thomas preferred. 'I felt I knew the place and I understood the people better than I ever grew to understand the people of Birmingham and the Midlands.'[5]

The choice of a studio base fastened on one of ABC's largest cinemas, the Capitol at Didsbury, Manchester. It was in fact a combined cinema and theatre, possessing an ample stage as well as a huge auditorium, together with dressing rooms and other facilities. Its car park was more than adequate for housing the three outside broadcast units and supporting paraphernalia which had been ordered. One large television studio was constructed out of the auditorium and a smaller one at balcony level. The first was to be used for major light entertainment shows and drama and the second for the less ambitious programmes and the advertising magazines. It was from Didsbury that the first of the Armchair Theatre productions was transmitted in July 1956, and then on a regular weekly basis from September. They were, of course, live, rehearsed initially in London and then transmitted from Manchester after just one day in the studio.

(vi) THE NEW LOOK IN TELEVISION NEWS

The experience of Independent Television News in the months before D-Day was truly the biggest adventure of all. Distinctive as they were from the outset, the general ITV programmes were not complete innovations; with the possible exceptions of Sunday Night at the Palladium and the 'Give-away' shows, they might have been made, albeit in a different style, by the BBC. What ITN set out to prepare for was a style of news presentation which the BBC had not dreamed of attempting. BBC Television, inheriting the tradition of sound radio, had moved cautiously into the field of news. At first they had the news read by a reader who was not in vision, flanked by a cinema-type news reel. Only a few weeks before competition confronted them did they bring their news readers into vision, and mingle some filmed stories with the spoken reports. But the news reader remained unnamed, to ensure that no element of subjectivity in presentation might impair the objectivity which was the pride of BBC news.

Aidan Crawley, who was familiar with the more personalised form of news presentation used in America, had come to the same view as that of the *ad hoc* committee about the value of personalities (see Chapter 12), and decided to break away from tradition and go in for 'newscasts', in the preparation of which the presenters would take part and inject something of their own personalities and character. Without straying from the legal requirements of due accuracy and impartiality, the ITN news was to be a performance in its own right. By comparison with later years, the orchestration of this performance was rudimentary, but it was nevertheless totally different from any news presentation viewers in Britain had seen before.

They began their life in Ingersoll House, which was across the way from Television House in which they only took up residence shortly before the first transmission. Perhaps 'residence' is hardly the word for, with their newsroom on the second floor and the studio on the eighth and a lift system that was notoriously unreliable, the fitness of Christopher Chataway as a runner was on occasion all that made possible their getting on the air on time. Together with Robin Day, Chataway had spent the preceding weeks rehearsing dummy bulletins extracted from the newspapers in a bare room at Ingersoll House. The newscaster would deliver his pieces into a wooden frame in the shape of a television screen, with film or inserts run through a 16 mm camera on to an adjacent wall. Twice a day, the entire staff were instructed by Crawley to gather round to watch, comment and criticise. Meantime the news editor, Arthur Clifford, and his small team of reporters which included Lynne Reid Banks and Barbara Mandell, were making their preparations. Clifford was the originator of 'vox pop' – that irresistible stock-in-trade of every news bulletin and news magazine for the ensuing twenty-five years.

Recalling these events nearly twenty-four years later, Clifford wrote to the author:

> The enthusiasm was enormous. But it all seemed strangely unreal and a long way from proper broadcast journalism. And even to the most optimistic, this infant ITN looked and felt ludicrously inadequate to compete with the might of the BBC News Division . . . Nevertheless during the late August and early September, ITN's dry-run operation started to resemble the real thing. Each day reporters and camera-teams would disappear through the Kingsway traffic to cover stories as if for transmission that night. Politicians, union chiefs, Churchmen and sports stars gave earnest interviews that would never see the light of day. Though the editorial set-up was still minute, though closed-circuit facilities were still awaited and test film was still being screened on the newsroom wall, the founder-members of ITN were steadily learning their jobs.

Robin (now Sir Robin) Day was a young barrister whom Crawley had personally selected for the job. Some people at the time thought it a rather eccentric choice. Day has published his own account of his early experiences in *Day By Day*.[6] After twenty-five years in television and radio journalism he is the acknowledged leader of his profession in Britain.

21

PUBLICATIONS

'There are five publications or types of publication', wrote Fraser on 7 March 1955, 'which might spring from the soil of the new television programmes. They are: (a) a programme journal (b) a popular television weekly (c) trade and technical journals (d) a serious review (e) a reference handbook.'[1]

It was his own view that responsibility for ITV's counterpart to the *Radio Times* ought to rest with the companies, because its main purpose would be to attract an audience to the programmes. In any case, as he reminded the Authority, it had, in the give and take of the contract discussions, agreed to leave the copyright entirely in the hands of the companies, provided that satisfactory assurances were forthcoming that any programme journal would be edited with political impartiality. Such assurances had been given. 'I am afraid the position is, therefore, that we have surrendered the right to publish any such journal.'[2]

As regards the other types of publication, Fraser saw a television weekly as eminently something to be left to the periodical publishers; a trade and technical journal as a job for private enterprise; a serious review as a probable flop but in any case something completely independent – independent even of the ITA; and only in the case of a reference handbook did he see an appropriate enterprise for the Authority. The Members rather reluctantly accepted Fraser's advice, and he undertook to pursue the idea of a reference manual. In the event the first ITA handbook (as distinct from the annual reports), did not emerge until 1963.

The Authority was reluctant because it apprehended the mushrooming under the aegis of various companies of a number of indifferent programme journals rather than the production of one first-class publication with regionalised editions. This is precisely what came about; and it was not until the mid-sixties that the opportunity occurred to put the matter right. However, thanks to the initiative of Associated Newspapers and in particular to Stuart McClean, one journal – *TV Times* – got off to a flying start under the proprietorship of A-R, and it always dwarfed the other journals that sprang up later in different parts of the country. Even the *TV Times* had many faults; for, unfortunately, it was so easy to make any programme journal profitable that there was no adequate incentive to achieve excellence.

However, the early story of *TV Times* was to be described, without too much exaggeration, as 'a record unparallelled in the history of modern publishing'.[3] The nucleus of the editorial team started life in June 1955 in cramped quarters in Gough Square, behind Fleet Street. The first issue was on the streets in good time for the opening on 22 September: 300,000 copies were produced and sold.

A year later, when distribution had extended to the Midlands and the North, *TV Times* could announce its first million circulation. But it had no monopoly outside London and the North and had to rely on skilful business negotiation to secure a circulation elsewhere. But first of all in the Midlands, and later in Scotland, Wales, Northern Ireland and the North-East, other journals were established. All were successful, *TV World* in the Midlands securing a larger circulation than had *TV Times* when it was serving London alone. None of them brought esteem to Independent Television at all commensurate with their revenue. Twelve years later it took all the driving force of Lord Hill to ensure that ITV should in future be served by one journal with regional editions, produced by a company which was a wholly owned subsidiary of all the programme contractors in the United Kingdom. *The Channel Viewer* survived in the Channel Islands as a reminder of the early rash of local journals.

It is unfortunate that the remorseless pressure of events precluded the planning and execution of a comprehensive publications policy at the start of Independent Television. As is now recognised, television has been more of a stimulus than an obstacle to reading and writing. Over time the marked affinity between the making and broadcasting of television programmes and the writing and distribution of books and journals has been discovered in fragmentary and piecemeal stages. Fraser's memorandum shows that, if he had had nothing else to distract him, he would in all probability have advanced the fertile relationship between broadcasting and publishing by anything up to twenty years.

22

CURTAIN UP

A-R took the lead in planning and arranging the gala opening of Independent Television, and the operation was placed under the command of Captain Brownrigg. It was accomplished with the skill and attention to detail worthy of the best traditions of the Royal Navy. The venue finally chosen was Guildhall in the City of London. 'It would be singularly appropriate,' wrote Clark to the Lord Mayor of London, 'if it (the opening ceremony) could link the traditional commercial centre of the Empire with this new commercial enterprise.' There was a banquet attended by guests from Government and Parliament, from Mayors of the Metropolitan Boroughs, from the world of the Arts and Entertainment and from the Press, together with a wide-ranging group of people called 'public and business celebrities'.

Invitations in this last category included the Chairman, Director General, and the most senior staff of the BBC, all of whom initially declined. At a meeting of the Authority on 13 September, Clark reported that he had pressed Sir Alexander Cadogan (the BBC's Chairman) to reconsider this decision but had been unsuccessful. He sought the Authority's approval to write formally to Cadogan and this was given.[1] He wrote:

> I need hardly remind you that the ITA is a public body set up under Act of Parliament in order to see that commercial television discharges its functions with a due sense of responsibility . . . In the day-to-day programmes there must of course be competition, but we have never conceived that this competition with the actual programme contractors could be taken as the basis for an affront to the Authority.

There is no trace in ITA records of any reply, but both Cadogan and Jacob, the Director General, were eventually present on the night. In *Governing the*

BBC, Asa Briggs records that at the first meeting of the Board after the start of Independent Television Cadogan found it necessary to explain to the members why he and Jacob had accepted an invitation to the ITA's formal dinner at Guildhall.[2] Strangely enough, one finds that on 30 September – only eight days after the opening – Jacob was not only attending a meeting of the Television Programme Contractors Association, but actually taking the chair.[3]

A menu proposed by Ring and Brymer, the traditional caterers for Guildhall, was referred for Clark's consideration. It consisted of smoked salmon, turtle soup, lobster chablis, baron of beef, sorbet, roast grouse or partridge, pear melba and dessert, together with white burgundy, punch, madeira, Rhine wine, champagne, claret, port and brandy. The price for all this was to be £5 a head! By joint agreement between Clark and Brownrigg, the baron of beef and the sorbet were deleted and there were also some subtle changes in the wines. The meal remained what could be described as good value for money. Although invitations had been issued in the name of the ITA the cost of the whole function was borne by the two London programme companies.

At 7.15 p.m. on Thursday 22 September, the cameras on Channel 9, after a preliminary scanning of the face of London on film, fixed upon the arrival of guests at Guildhall. At 7.30 p.m. the Hallé Orchestra, conducted by Sir John Barbirolli, struck up – what else? – Elgar's 'Cockaigne' overture followed by the National Anthem. Then at 7.45 p.m. the Lord Mayor of London, Sir Seymour Howard, the Postmaster-General and the Chairman of the ITA made the inaugural speeches. Thereafter viewers at home were offered an evening programme, provided by both the London companies and ITN, which started with a forty-minute variety show transmitted from the Wood Green Empire, television theatre of ABC (later ATV) and produced by their one and only Bill Ward and compered by Jack Jackson. The first break for commercials – greeted with applause by the guests – came at 8.12 p.m. with advertisements for toothpaste, drinking chocolate and margarine in that order. A general account of the whole evening's viewing and of its reception by critics and others has been given by Asa Briggs in *Sound and Vision*.[4]

Five hundred guests were present at Guildhall. There were other ancillary functions – a vast reception at the Mayfair Hotel for 900 guests mainly from the field of the arts and entertainment and a party for lesser mortals at the Authority's new headquaters in Princes Gate.

It was intended that the proceeds of this first evening should be devoted to a charity or charities nominated by the Lord Mayor of London. It had been expected that these might amount to some £10,000 in view of the premium rates charged for the commercials, but later it was discovered – to the embarrassment of all – that there were no proceeds but only a loss. There was indeed some rather painful confusion after the event as to whether it was 'revenue' or 'proceeds' which had been offered. Some advertisers had also thought that the 50 per cent premium they had agreed to pay was destined for charity. Since the Lord Mayor had nominated no less than twelve charities, each were eventually sent a donation of 100 guineas by the two companies jointly.

There were also a number of disappointed advertisers who had been led to believe they had a firm booking, but who in the event were crowded out. Somebody had overestimated the amount of time which would be made available for commercials on this special night. The advertising manager of Fords of Dagenham telegraphed in these terms: 'Rediffusion continue to refer to first night being merely preview stop We do not agree . . . stop Any suggestion of preview not acceptable stop As in marriage there can be only one first night stop With best wishes for success over future hurdles and regrets that we have bumped at Beechers Brook.'

The speeches were brief and to the point. Said the Lord Mayor of London, 'There are many who have felt that competitive commercial television would open the floodgates to a rapid decline in the standards of national entertainment, but I think you will agree in due course that there is no truth in this assertion.' The PMG spoke about 'the known and the unknown, the famous elder child and the lively youngster'. Clark remarked that it had been said it would take two years to get going but that it had taken nine months. Hitherto television had been controlled by a public corporation. 'Ten minutes ago that weapon was placed in the hands of companies who are hardly controlled at all.' He went on to use words which had an echo in the Annan Report twenty-two years later in a sentence quoted in the Preface. 'The ITA,' said Clark, 'is an experiment in the art of Government – an attempt to solve one of the chief problems of democracy; how to combine a maximum of freedom with an ultimate direction.'

Ironically enough, the PMG, before whom Clark took excessive pains to minimise the controlling power of the Authority, became the Chairman of the ITA who in the sixties saw to it that the Authority exercised that power to a degree which would have astonished and even dismayed the founding fathers of Independent Television. As has been seen in Part I, some Ministerial statements during the passage of the Television Bill seemed to justify Clark's modest interpretation of the Authority's role. Hill, in his turn, could not fail to heed the decision of a later Conservative Government which in 1962, with the subsequent approval of Parliament, stated: 'In future . . . the Authority, suitably equipped, will take a commanding position in the affairs of independent television'.[5]

Part III

IN AND OUT OF THE RED

23

THE LONDON AUDIENCE

Of all that was said and written about Independent Television during the first hectic weeks of programme transmissions nothing gave greater satisfaction at management levels of the ITA and the two companies than an article in *The Times* of 21 October 1955 and the weekly articles by the television critics of the *Sunday Times* and the *Observer* – all newspapers serving the educated middle classes. There had never been much reason to doubt that ITV programmes would be popular in those working class homes equipped to receive them. After all, the audience for Radio Luxembourg had been steadily rising at the expense of the audiences of the three BBC sound programmes, and that showed no aversion amongst the great mass of listeners towards broadcast advertising. The opposition to the Television Bill had in large part been found amongst the educated middle classes, where advertising was often thought vulgar or worse. What these three articles showed only a month after programmes began was tacit acceptance of ITV as worthy of comment by three cultivated middle class critics whose standards of taste were unquestionable. In two of the three articles advertisements were explicitly brought within the area of acceptance. The extent to which the ITV programmes were praised or criticised did not matter: the point is that they were recognised as deserving attention, and Maurice Wiggin of the *Sunday Times* saw what that implied when he wrote that the time had come for some words to be eaten.

At much the same date there were in existence four research organisations available to supply information about television audiences. One was the BBC's Audience Research Department and the others were private enterprise companies – the Gallup Poll (which carried out only irregular surveys), Nielsen's, which was American controlled, and Television Audience Measurement. The last two companies issued regular reports giving minute-by-minute charts of how the potential audience was split between BBC and ITV, together with fifteen minute averages. The record was attained by means of meters attached to television sets in homes included in the sample. These were the 'ratings', on which advertisers and their agents based decisions and on the altar of which ITV soon came to be accused of sacrificing their programme standards. There was a very high degree of correspondence between the results of each organisation, both of which automatically metered the viewing behaviour of a comparatively small statistical sample of viewers. The BBC's measurements used the technique known as 'aided recall'; they were based on personal interviews of people who claimed to have seen television – BBC or ITV – the previous day. They gave for each programme the respective percentages for BBC and ITV audiences.

The results obtained from the two methods were not strictly comparable. In the first place, Nielsen and TAM calculated the *number of sets* switched on at any one time and the BBC assessed the *number of people* who claimed to have seen a programme, or at least half of it. A simple adjustment of the Nielsen and TAM figures by reference to the average audience per set had only limited validity, because viewers per set varied significantly with different programmes.

Furthermore, whereas Nielsen and TAM had as their samples households which could receive both services well, the BBC included in their sample all who admitted to having seen ITV programmes, whether in the ITV area or not. Thus some of the sample were unlikely to be receiving ITV programmes sufficiently well to establish regular viewing habits. The numbers of viewers in the Nielsen and TAM sample did not vary from day to day but the number of ITV viewers in the BBC sample did. They interviewed 700 people per day in the very large London area and it could happen that only a small percentage of that number saw an ITV programme on a particular occasion. The size of the estimated audience for ITV at any one time depended, in the case of Nielsen and TAM, on an accurate assessment of the number of sets capable of receiving the programme, and households outside the recognised ITV area were not included. In the case of the BBC the total population sampled in their London Region was fairly accurately known (11,400,000), but the size of the daily sample was very small in relation to it.

Over the first month the Nielsen and TAM services showed that, in the evening, something between two out of three and three out of four homes with sets converted to receive both BBC and ITV watched the main ITV programmes. The figure did not, of course, measure anything more than the attractiveness of one sequence of programmes relative to the alternative available on the other channel. It was estimated that homes capable of receiving the first transmissions numbered some 188,000 out of 4 million homes licensed for television in the country as a whole. The revelation of this miniscule number caused alarm and despondency in the companies. Even Richard Meyer fell prey to doubts about the prospects of success. But by the end of 1955 the number had risen to 495,000, and by the end of 1956, when ITV were fully operating in the Midlands and the North as well as in London, the number was 2,656,000.

The higher share of homes served by ITV in the first month might well have been explained, at any rate to some extent, as novelty appeal. However, in February 1956 – four to five months after the start – the BBC's own figures were recording a 63 per cent share for ITV in the London homes able to choose and the Nielsen figure was slightly lower at 60 per cent. The number of homes involved had risen to 584,000, a growth which, taken together with the shares of homes viewing the programmes, was providing an audience rather more than double what it had been in October. A different kind of measurement involving value judgement, provided by a Gallup Poll in March, produced the following figures:

	London	Birmingham
Prefer ITV	60	58
Prefer BBC	16	16
No choice	19	20
Don't know	5	7

The service in Birmingham had been operating barely a month when the measurement was taken.

Like it or not, the British newspaper readers were forced to live with weekly, sometimes daily, publicity about ratings. The appetite of the press for publishing the so-called 'top ten', described, quite erroneously, as the ten most popular (rather than the most widely watched) programmes of the week, proved insatiable. To the ITV companies and their advertisers, ratings were important for valid business reasons. But they were publicised as if they were the one and only measure of competitive success in programme terms. It would have been better if from the outset as much prominence had been given to measurements of 'audience appreciation' as to those of audience size.

It would also have been better if from the outset all interested parties – ITV, BBC, the advertisers and their agents – could have agreed on a method of audience measurement capable of serving all their respective requirements. At a meeting of the Television Programme Contractors Association on 30 September 1954 (the one at which Jacob of the BBC took the chair), Sidney Bernstein proposed the establishment of a TV Research Company with equal shareholdings by the BBC and the contractors. This company 'would decide what information both parties wanted and would then commission the BBC research organisation to obtain it for the information of their staff and for distribution at a fee to advertisers through the IPA and ISBA. This would replace rival organisations advancing conflicting figures.'¹ However, at a later meeting on 13 October, it was reported that the BBC were unable to accept this proposal.

For the next twenty-five years, rival claims based upon conflicting figures became a commonplace. There were nearly always statistically valid explanations for these disparities well known within the television industry, but about which most viewers remained ignorant. A collective determination by the parties involved either to remove these disparities or to explain them in language capable of being widely understood was sadly lacking until the mid seventies when pressure of outside criticism led to attempts – eventually successful – to rationalise and consolidate the audience measurement services.

From the very beginning ITV offered something that large numbers of people wanted and were prepared to pay for in the cost of new sets and new aerials. It was believed by many people that the object of the BBC was to improve the viewer; and feelings of alienation, however unjustified, were certainly widespread. Along came ITV with their brash new programmes seeking the 'mass audience', and challenging the accepted standards of broadcasting in much the same way as Northcliffe had 'betrayed' established standards of journalism when he launched the *Daily Mail*. ITV set out to be popular – to achieve the common touch; and, as an advertising medium, their natural ambience was the market place.

Fraser had no misgivings, at any rate at the outset. For him this was 'people's television'. He believed passionately in the judgement and good sense of ordinary people. As Anthony Sampson remarked, he regarded himself as a 'liberal with a small "l"' and saw himself as a Benthamite, believing in democratic choice, in contrast to the Platonic ideals of the BBC.² He nurtured the new service with as much mastery as Reith had moulded the BBC. But his style could not have been more different. In *The Other Half* Clark writes of having been approached by Lord Reith with an offer of services, which he regarded as unthinkable.³ It had been said of Reith (by Mary Agnes Hamilton) that he believed in democratic aim but not democratic method.⁴ Fraser believed in both, and yet, before many months had passed, he was to find himself totting up the total of 'serious programmes' on ITV and endeavouring to show that in the matter of programme balance there was little to choose between BBC and ITV.

It was mainly the streak of earthy vulgarity in ITV which got the switches turning from Channel 1 to Channel 9. But, of course, the Television Act and the contracts required that the programmes maintain a proper balance in their subject matter and a high general standard of quality, and that nothing should be included in them which offended against good taste or decency or was likely to be offensive to public feeling. Problems relating to these requirements began to crowd in upon the Authority and the companies during the first tumultuous year of ITV's programme life.

24

PROBLEMS OF BALANCE

The first schedules of the London companies became available early in July 1955 and were referred to the ITA where, on the whole, they made a favourable impression. Provision was made by both companies for morning programmes, afternoon programmes, which on weekdays were to consist only of a children's hour from 5 to 6 p.m. but on Saturday and Sunday afternoons films and advertising magazines, and, for the evenings, the main programmes running from 7 to 11 p.m., following the 'toddlers' truce' between 6 and 7 p.m. Three sessions, therefore, separated by intervals – morning, afternoon and evening. The weekday morning programmes were from 10.45 a.m. to 12.30 p.m., and designed for housewives, beginning with a daily serial and including news at 12 noon. The morning transmission on Saturday was to run from 9.30 to 10.30 a.m. as a magazine for the whole family, and plainly derived from the very successful morning magazines which the American networks had developed.

Fraser's comment was that 'they do not in serious content compare at all unfavourably with the BBC television programmes'. He went on:

> I think myself that the restriction of hours so often defended as a brake on programme degradation, works in fact in just the opposite direction. When hours are so restricted, the companies will be disposed to consume every minute in the search for the greatest possible audiences and the greatest possible revenues. They will feel that they cannot afford minority audiences for any part of time that has been made so scarce. And it is worth remembering, on a separate point, that our system does not ban only the tasteless audience-hunting sponsor. It bans, equally, the enlightened sponsor, to whom some of the most striking American programmes are due.[1]

After 22 September there was a month or so of honeymoon before any real hint of critical dissatisfaction made itself known. The comments referred to in Chapter 23 are perhaps to be seen as the end of the beginning. A month later the atmosphere had become distinctly cooler. On 23 November the press reported that the programmes of A-R were to be made more popular and that many of the more serious and cultural items were to be shortened and moved to late evening. The most publicised of the planned changes was the move of the Hallé Orchestra from its position at 8.30–9.30 p.m. every fortnight to 10 p.m. for half an hour. The same reports heralded the arrival of the American 'adult' cowboy series *Gunsmoke*. These perfectly understandable changes were explained by Roland Gillett as a revision of the schedules and a re-timing of items with minority appeal.

If Gillett had stopped there it might have received acceptance from the watchful and jealous eye of the newspapers, but two days later the *News Chronicle* published a leading article headed 'TV on the Retreat'. It said:

> Above the portals of Associated-Rediffusion should be inscribed the motto 'We give the public what it wants'. It was in those memorable words that the company's director of programmes, Mr Roland Gillett, explained the decision to shift the Hallé Orchestra's programmes from 8.30 p.m. (a peak viewing time) to later in the evening. By the same criterion, presumably, it has been suggested that two intelligent discussion programmes may henceforth appear less frequently. Is it wrong, then, to give the public what it wants? Not at all – so long as 'the public' is not automatically equated with 'the majority'; so long as the whole emphasis is not placed on glossy, undemanding entertainment . . . The same proposition surely applies to television. The Act required the Independent Television Authority to satisfy itself that 'the programmes maintain a proper balance in their subject matter'. Until now that obligation has been met. But if this new trend continues, their critics' worst fears will be justified . . . It is not so much the size of its audiences that Asssociated-Rediffusion should be worrying about; it is the quality and ingenuity of its programmes in all departments.

This was not an intemperate comment, although Gillett felt that his words had been twisted by this and other newspapers. But, as Fraser told him in a kindly letter:

> A television company must have a policy of its own and that policy must be something more than 'giving the public what it wants' unless we are prepared to say that we no more respond to the social significance of television than to the social significance of toffee.[2]

25

CRISIS AT ITN

Closely connected with the problem of balance in the programme patterns was the question of the place of ITN in the daily output, its character and its status.

The newest contractor, ABC Television, had not been involved in the discussions leading to the formation of ITN earlier in 1955 (Chapter 12). But the Authority had indicated that they would be expected to join the news company, initially accepting all the obligations of membership, financial and otherwise. In October this company was in touch with ITN with a view to determining the basis on which this would be arranged.

On 1 November, a letter was written to Fraser over the signature of Sir Philip Warter, but in style it betrayed signs of the hand of Dr Eric Fletcher, the Deputy Chairman, and it was with him that Fraser had further correspondence. The letter said that the company were 'appalled at the heavy, indeed reckless capital expenditure which is contemplated . . . There is, in our view, no justification whatever for this grotesquely extravagant capital expenditure on equipment. Moreover the weekly running costs are of an unwarrantably high order – quite out of relation to the results achieved.'[1] These results were 'disappointing in the extreme', and served to confirm ABC's view that the present organisation of the News Company require drastic overhaul. Meanwhile they were disinclined to participate in ITN, and believed they could prepare their own news items at much smaller cost and with much greater efficiency.

Evidently this onslaught took Fraser's breath away. His first reply – also on 1 November – emphasised that the company were completely committed, by virtue of their assurances to the Authority, to join ITN. He then went on to say he was 'somewhat taken aback' at the strength of the criticism of the news programmes. His second reply, two days later, further underlined the incompatibility of ABC's declaration with what had transpired at their interview with the Authority on 18 August.

At that interview they had been given a note prepared by ITN of the prospective financial obligations of joining it. At that date it had been agreed by the foundation members (which included Kemsley–Winnick, ABC's predecessors) that the pre-operational expenses should be capitalised and shared between them – a sum estimated at between £30,000 and £40,000. Capital equipment would be to the value of approximately £230,000 to which had to be added £30,000 to £40,000 working capital to cover spares and initial operating expenses which would be amortised and recovered from revenue over a period. The total of, say, £300,000 would be equally subscribed in the form of £60,000 issued and fully paid ordinary shares and £240,000 unsecured loan stock, if no bank overdraft was available. On this basis the sum required from ABC was £75,000. Total operational expenditure had been estimated at £387,000 per annum (i.e. of just over £1000 a day). ABC's estimated share of this was £77,400 per annum covering the provision of two news bulletins a day, each of 8½ minutes' duration, the second of which would be followed by a 5 minutes newsreel, if required.

'You agreed to join the news company' wrote Fraser, 'on the basis described in the note of 18 August, reserving your right to raise from within, and through your representation on the Board, any aspects of the policy with which you were not happy.' Three weeks later he was again pleading for a better understanding on Fletcher's part of the value of the news and news-interviews presented by ITN. The response was that ABC's worries related very largely to the use of film, 'and to the fear that a management is being built up with views out of harmony with those of the programme companies who have to bear the cost'.

At the same time, however, Howard Thomas was writing to the management of ITN in decidedly hectoring terms, saying that if ABC joined the News Company they would seek to reduce drastically ITN's weekly expenditure. In their view the news service of ITN should be reduced in length. More selective use of film would considerably reduce the expense. There was a wide gap between the actual news programme requirements of the Contractors and the intentions of the News Company.

ABC were hollering on the touchlines rather than taking part in the game. On the Board of ITN there were certainly great differences of opinion. There had been no criticism of the oral presentation of the news but the filmed illustrative material was much criticised on the grounds that it was badly presented and very expensive to produce. This material accounted for some three-quarters of the total expenditure, both current and capital. There was no agreement on the extent to which it ought to be reduced, but all were agreed that its quality needed improving. There were also differences between the Board and its officers about the length and timing of the bulletins. The officers had resented the decision of the companies to shorten the early 7 o'clock bulletin from fifteen to seven minutes, and to put back the time of the later 10 o'clock bulletin to 10.45 p.m. By early December there was already talk of a possible resignation of Aidan Crawley as Editor-in-Chief. Some Members of the Authority were inclined to share the view that the filmed content was 'amateurish'; but it was noteworthy that Lord Layton (who knew more about news than any other Member) stated that:

> he was sure that the illustration of the news would survive and that it was the most difficult thing that the companies had so far had to do. Illustrated news was new to television in this country but it was the coming form of news; he very much hoped that ITV would not revert to the former style of the BBC's news bulletins after only nine weeks' experience.[2]

It is refreshing to read words about ITN at this time which did not subsequently have to be eaten.

From then on the Authority attempted to exercise in this affair its own considerable latent power and this became its first intervention of any magnitude in programme matters. At its meeting on 20 December the Members agreed three propositions which, supplemented by a few adroit embellishments of his own devising, enabled Fraser to take a positive line in the discussions which were proceeding. These propositions were first, that the news company ought to be solely responsible for the national news, only regional news being undertaken by individual programme companies; secondly that the Authority regarded adequate news as part of a balanced programme and interpreted 'adequate' as a minimum of twenty minutes a day; and thirdly that the Authority believed that television news must involve visual presentation, including some use of film.[3] On the evening of that same day Members of the Authority visited ITN, and on the following day Clark wrote to Crawley:

> This is to say two things. First, how much impressed all the Members of the Authority were by what they saw in your department last night and, secondly, to say how glad and relieved I am to learn that, for the time being, your resignation is withdrawn. The news that it had been tendered was a very great shock to the Authority. They are entirely behind the

News Company and I do hope you will not take such a step again without having given me the opportunity of putting your difficulties to them.

That day, 21 December, there was a special meeting of the Board of ITN at which Fraser read out a letter concerning the requirements of the ITA for the presentation of news by the contractors.

Crawley then made a statement giving his reasons for wishing to resign his position as Editor-in-Chief. Fraser and Crawley having withdrawn, the Directors considered Crawley's statement. On his return Brownrigg, the Chairman, stated that the Board intended to review their policy for ITN in view of the ITA's letter and in view of the forthcoming openings of the Midland and Northern stations. They thought it wrong for their Editor-in-Chief to resign before such a policy review was concluded. If, when the policy had been hammered out, the Editor-in-Chief felt he could not accept it, then it would be for him to decide whether to resign or not. Crawley accepted this statement.

It was all to no avail. The Board and the staff of ITN were poles apart. At the next meeting on 5 January 1956, times and lengths of the bulletins were agreed which were just within the terms of the ITA's requirements of a minimum of twenty minutes a day. It was agreed that the newsreel should be discontinued but that the bulletins should be fully illustrated by film. It was then resolved that ITN should be basically staffed to handle news programmes only and that 'near news programmes' should be the responsibility of the contractors; that the management should prepare estimates based on the new schedules and designed to cover news programmes only; and that a sub-committee should be formed to examine the management's proposals. On 13 January a special meeting met to consider Crawley's letter of resignation. He wrote:

It is clear that the Board has no intention whatever of meeting my views, and that our attitudes are too far apart to make it possible for me to continue . . . The Board . . . are determined not only to limit the scope of the News Company's operations to the narrowest conception of news, but to reduce the cost of such news to the barest minimum. Not content with asking the management of the News Company to say what is the absolute minimum on which the new schedule of programmes can be purchased, the Board has appointed a committee of outsiders to examine the management's figures with a view to making further reductions. All this has been done at a time when not only the operations of the individual contractors are being expanded but when, as you know, the BBC is embarking on a vast programme of capital expenditure to extend its television news organization in every region in the country.[4]

This time there was no persuading Crawley to withdraw, but he agreed to serve for another six months 'to facilitate the establishment of the Company and to enable the Board to find a successor'. His deputy, Richard Goold-Adams, also resigned and the morale of ITN sank to its lowest ever. These resignations were then announced to a waiting press which had already scented the most sensational story since ITV had begun transmissions.

It must have been primarily because of ITN's morale, and to prevent the unit's further disintegration, that Clark agreed to be interviewed in that evening's bulletin. It was Robin Day's first important interview, and the fact that he looks back on it as a turning point in his own career is apparent from his chapter 'Personal Milestone' in his book *Day by Day*.[5]

Regrettably, no transcript of this interview survives, for it was a milestone not only for Day but for ITN and the ITA itself. His own account, written within a few years of the event, conveys convincingly the full flavour of the occasion. He wrote:

> It was a crucial moment for me and for the staff of ITN. My colleagues . . . would be watching anxiously . . . Was the news company, for which they had such high hopes, on the brink of extinction? Would a lot of them be sacked? Were they to be denied the chance of building up ITN for effective competition with the BBC News? . . . What, I think, gave the interview its interest was that the chairman of an organisation was being publicly cross-examined about his duties by one of the employees. Though this was unusual, if not unique, I had no option but to put questions as in any other news interview. Was Aidan Crawley right to resign? Did he share doubts which had been expressed as to whether companies whose main business was to run light entertainment were the right people to provide news? What was his answer to press criticism of the ITA for being 'weak-kneed' in controlling ITV? The interview continued on these lines for several minutes and overran the bulletin time.

Though Sir Kenneth Clark avoided giving direct answers to some of these questions, the interview drew from him several important declarations of ITA policy. He defended the amount of entertainment on ITV: 'You must capture an audience first of all. When you are established and secure you can gradually build up to a higher level.' But the Authority, he said, had not approved of cuts in the news nor its placing at a later time. 'The Authority believes that a full and responsible news service of at least twenty minutes a day is essential.' From the start, Sir Kenneth declared, the Authority's policy had been that news should be one of the principal items. 'We intend to uphold that.' These answers, obtained from the chairman of the ITA, did something to raise the morale of the ITN staff and to allay their fears for the future.[6]

Contemporary press reports corroborate this account. In the *News Chronicle*, James Thomas (who never mentioned Robin Day by name but referred to the news staff in the plural) added his own gloss when he said that they drew from Clark the first admission that the ITA was allowing programmes to be overloaded with popular variety so as to build an audience and keep advertisers. This was, especially for the *News Chronicle*, a better and quite fair way of expressing Clark's wish to capture an audience in order to become 'established and secure'.

It was characteristic of Clark that he did not stop to consider whether his appearance was compatible with the requirement that the Authority and companies should exclude from their service any expression of their views relating to current public policy. Over subsequent years the problem of interpreting this clause (3(2) of the 1954 Act) gave rise to incessant difficulty. For ITV the reasoning by which BBC chiefs managed to evade an exactly comparable requirement was not found acceptable. The Day–Clark interview was unique in as much as Clark resorted to no kind of circumlocution to escape clause 3(2): if he did not forget it, then he chose deliberately to ignore it. The new Broadcasting Act of 1980 has removed the difficulty, by specifically exempting broadcasting from the scope of 'current public policy'.

An important factor in this crisis, and it is one which Crawley and his colleagues do not seem to have been given a chance to appreciate, was that ITV was by this time in a grave financial predicament. At its meeting on 17 March the Authority had agreed that, while the possibility of itself having to assume complete responsibility for the news could not be ruled out,[7] alternative ways of strengthening its control of ITN should be discussed with the companies and that, in the meantime, a further approach to the PMG should be made, urging him to make provision in the Broadcasting Vote for 1956/7 for the whole, or a substantial part, of the £750,000 Grant in Aid under Section 11 of the Television Act.

In view of these developments it might have been thought that Dr Fletcher, whose company had so far avoided honouring its pledge to join

ITN and which was not yet transmitting programmes, would have relapsed into silence. On the contrary, he wrote on 16 January saying, 'I am sure you will appreciate that in the light of these events, we must ask to be released from any kind of obligation to join the News Company as at present constituted.'

On 21 January Fraser replied:

I can do no other (and I hope in all conscience you can do no other) than regard as an unalterable governing factor your promise to join the News Company under its present constitution, a promise explicitly required from you and explicitly given in the knowledge of what the capital contribution and the annual operational cost would be. There has been, since then, no change in the constitution of the Company, in its capital structure, or in its running expenses, though I understand that the management is in process of suggesting to the Board some possible reductions in the latter.

It is strange but true that in the discussions at meetings of the Board, Fraser seemed to Crawley and his team to be taking the same attitude as their company critics. Writing to the author in February 1980 – some twenty-four years later – Crawley recalls that in ITN at that time Fraser was regarded as enemy number one. Looking back and knowing more, he is sure this was unjust. Crawley continues:

The proposal was frequently made in conversation by members of the board that $8\frac{1}{2}$ minutes of news twice a day was the wrong format and that the news should be so designed that it could be inserted two or three minutes at a time at intervals through the day. This would give contractors more flexibility in scheduling programmes and allow the viewer to absorb the news painlessly in snippets. I don't think that a formal proposal to this effect was ever made but I certainly got the impression that Bob would entertain the idea. News in that form would not have interested any worthwhile newscaster and would have put an end to ITN as we then conceived it.

Crawley recalls that at one stage it was proposed to cut the budget to £200,000, and that there was a long discussion during which he tried to explain that such an amount would wreck the whole conception of the news company. He had the impression that Fraser sided with the programme companies. It was at the end of this discussion that Crawley said that if they were determined to go ahead with their proposals they would have to get another editor. He felt he had lost confidence in the Board and they in him.

How Crawley and his colleagues received their impression of Fraser's attitude defies precise explanation, and scrutiny of the minutes of the relevant meetings of the Board affords no clue to the mystery. It was a sad misunderstanding. For Crawley could surely not have put better himself what Fraser had written to Fletcher on 24 November 1955:

I have always felt that television must accept, and happily, a great responsibility in the field of public affairs, and particularly the responsibility of giving people each day a lively account of the significant events of the world in which they live. It should, in brief, give the news. More than this, it should present the news in such a way that it possesses what my Chairman once called 'democratic value'. That is to say, the news should not consist of a featureless recitation, but be told or shown to the viewers in such a way as to be enlightening. If that is to happen, not only must the news programmes rest upon these principles, but they must be allowed whatever length and position in the programmes are necessary to let them do this democratic job. They must not be cut to headline length and they must not be relegated . . . I think the News Company has gone quite a long way towards meeting these requirements . . . There is of course room for improvement, but what has so far been done – or so we all think at Princes Gate – is one of the very best things that independent television has done.

ABC Television became a member of the News Company on 1 March. Their behaviour towards ITN perhaps reflected the circumstances of their entry into ITV. What in due course proved to be, as in other cases, a highly lucrative concession had not so much been awarded to, as thrust upon them. Like the other founder companies they were haunted by the spectre of heavy and possibly unbearable losses during the first half of 1956. In this adolescent phase of their life, they were heavily chaperoned by Dr Fletcher, who could hardly have foreseen such a close business involvement in ITV when, as a Labour politician, he was campaigning actively against its introduction. When the company embarked on their allotted programme task they proved both enthusiastic and resourceful. That was only to be expected with a broadcaster as experienced and dedicated as Howard Thomas at the helm.

With the announcement on 7 March that on the principle of rotation Tom Brownrigg would shortly hand over the chair to Norman Collins the first anxious phase in ITN's life can be said to have ended. The ITN Board had found a strong replacement for Crawley. He was Geoffrey (now Sir Geoffrey) Cox, Assistant Editor of the *News Chronicle*, who was not only a leading Fleet Street journalist, but had had (with BBC current affairs) a good deal of experience before the cameras – an advantage he shared with Crawley. Only two months earlier he had presented the BBC's coverage of the Party Conferences, and had conducted the Budget night interviews with the Chancellor and the Leader of the Opposition. He had in fact been urged by Crawley to become one of ITN's opening team of newscasters; and, even earlier, Norman Collins had canvassed his claims to have the Editorship right from the outset.

If the Authority's effort at self-assertion was not spectacularly successful, it could at least feel that it had shielded ITN from a real risk of child suffocation. Brownrigg's own metaphor came, as might be expected, from the Navy not the nursery. He wrote to Fraser on 12 March: 'I think we are nearly through the pilotage waters and the open sea is in sight on the starboard bow.'

26

FINANCIAL AFFAIRS

Some of the policy issues which blew up for the ITA and the companies in
1955 to 1957 proved to be chronic and intractable. Others were acute but
short-lived and were resolved – or within reach of resolution – by the end of
1956. First and foremost, although the economy and finances of ITV were a
perennial issue, the nightmare of prospective financial collapse which began
late in 1955 had by the end of 1956 faded away, never to return. At that time
defeat stared ITV in the face: for the service as a whole, it might be regarded
as their own 1940 and for a few individuals it was their finest hour. In a rare
burst of eloquence one of these few, John Spencer Wills, addressing the
annual meeting of Broadcast Relay Service Ltd – one of A-R's parent
companies – on 27 July 1956, said:

> Never in all the thirty-five years I have been in the business have I come
> across a case in which the task of the entrepreneur has been made more
> difficult. A limited security of tenure from the Conservative Government,
> a threat of extinction from the Labour Opposition, an excessively high
> annual payment to the ITA, an obligation to put on 'minority' program-
> mes of small advertising value, a host of restrictions imposed by Statute
> and by licence, threats of additional competition from BBC – all these
> must daunt the wildest optimist. I remain an optimist.

Seven years later he and his fellow entrepreneurs were to face a sterner
Statute and public control on a scale beyond anything they could have
imagined when they entered television.

Meanwhile this crisis permeated the lives of all who worked in ITV. For the
sales directors and their staff there was the daily grind of looking for business
and the anxious scrutiny of forward bookings for signs of some turn of the
tide. For programme and administrative staff there were aspirations
frustrated by the drying-up of funds and, worse, the ever-present threat of

redundancy: there were minor palace revolutions when men in key positions one day were out on their necks the next. The near-hysteria of the sinking ship was never far away. For the entrepreneurs there were tests of judgement as well as of nerve. In April Cecil Harmsworth King judged the moment right to move in, whilst in July his cousin Esmond, Lord Rothermere, decided to move out – just when the lights were changing to green, as his representative in A-R, Frank Coven, vainly protested. For the Authority there was the problem of observing the requirements of the Television Act for a proper balance in the programmes, focussing itself in a desperate struggle to secure some or all of the £750,000 grant for which provision had been made in the Act. In August Clark placed his resignation in the hands of the PMG, Dr Hill, but before the month was out he was persuaded to withdraw it. Finally, whilst the eyes of the nation were fastened on Suez, came the upturn in revenue and the dawn of the era to be marked by the never-to-be-forgotten phrase of Roy Thomson (later Lord Thomson of Fleet) 'just like having a licence to print your own money'.

All this and much else occupied little more than a single year. The various strands of a complex story must now be traced. We continue in this chapter to recount the history of the financial relations between the ITA and the companies in their early years. In Chapter 27 we shall describe the ITA's attempt to secure the promised slice of the licence revenue and in Chapter 28 we shall look at some of the problems that confronted the tycoons, as inevitably they came to be called. These three chapters, taken together, attempt to convey an impression of the stresses and strains which arise when a new and ambitious enterprise runs into the red, faces the possibility of collapse and then by an astonishing change of fortune meets with success beyond the dreams of 'the wildest optimist'.

The recital of difficulties by Wills, the optimist, included, it will have been noted, 'an excessively high annual payment to the ITA'. Such payments by the companies, or 'rentals' as they were usually called, were required by Section 2(2) of the Act. We have seen in Chapter 13 how the first contracts were negotiated.

The guiding factor in determining what rentals should be paid by the companies was provided by the definition of the ITA's financial duties in Section 10 of the Act. This laid down that the ITA must secure an income at least sufficient to meet all its running costs, to provide for depreciation on its capital assets, to establish a Reserve Fund of an unspecified amount, and to finance the whole of its necessary capital expenditure. As the ITA was liable for income and profits tax, in the same way as a commercial organisation, it had to secure roughly £2 of income for every £1 which it planned to place to

Reserve Fund or use for capital expenditure. So it had to formulate a provisional programme of construction. This programme envisaged the opening of three stations in each of the years 1955, 1956 and 1957. Budgets were drawn up in 1954 to cover foreseen operations until April 1959, and they comprised estimates of captial expenditure on the nine stations then envisaged, estimates of operating costs and the rentals payable to the Post Office for the vision and sound circuits needed to connect the various transmitters one to another, annual cash budgets and annual income and expenditure accounts.

The proposed charges to the companies were the estimated figures necessary to recover all operating expenditure and interest payments on advances made by the Government, build up a Reserve Fund, beginning with £50,000 in the year ended 31 March 1957, and £100,000 thereafter; meet repayments of the initial advances by the Government as they fell due, and set aside a fund to provide for future capital expenditure by amounts of £150,000, £250,000 and £350,000 in the years ended 31 March 1957, 1958 and 1959 respectively; provide for all taxation, and leave a credit balance on income and expenditure account by 31 March 1959, although it was envisaged that a debit balance would arise in some of the earlier years.

In determining the charges to be attached to various stations, the Authority, having decided what total sum was necessary to meet the commitments of the preceding paragraph, allocated it among the companies in proportion to their population coverage. This allocation by population was adopted on the grounds that the more people a station served, the more attractive it would be to advertisers, and so the greater the rental it could bear. American experience indicated the likelihood of heavy losses by the companies in the first year, smaller losses in the second, 'break even' in the third, and thereafter profitability. So provision was made in the first contracts for slightly reduced payments in the first two-and-a-half years of operation, followed by an increase of 8 per cent, and for a further increase a year later of up to 20 per cent at the ITA's discretion. Provision was also made for the rentals to be varied in accordance with changes in the Index of Retail Prices, whenever the cumulative variation reached 5 per cent or more.[1]

However, the precise means by which the rentals were calculated had not been made known to the companies when the contracts were negotiated. By the end of March 1956 the ITA could expect to receive some £423,500 in rental income but this sum was likely to be more than quadrupled a year later, by which time transmissions would have been running for eighteen months in London, just over a year in the Midlands, just under a year in

Lancashire and about six months in Yorkshire. The net advertising income of the companies in the six months to March 1956 turned out to be about £2,750,000 so that the rental payments to the ITA amounted to around 15 per cent of what the two London companies were earning, but, of course, a much smaller percentage of what they were spending overall.

At a meeting on 10 April 1956, arranged at the request of all four companies, the ITA was informed that the three at present operating were all in greater financial difficulty than expected, and in giving their backers an account of their position, would be helped if they knew more of the financial policy and development programme of the ITA. It was suggested that meetings should take place between representatives of the companies and the ITA at which each should disclose their financial situation. The ITA replied that it would be glad to enter into such meetings and welcomed the opportunity to take stock of the financial position of Independent Television in the light of experience. It felt, however, that the experience and evidence necessary for any long-term review could not become available until September or October, when the financial position would be radically different owing to first, the reductions in their expenditure which the companies were seeking to achieve; secondly, the operation by October of the full network in the main areas of population; and thirdly, the substantial increase of advertising income which might be expected to arise after the summer. The existing financial position of the companies was not a safe guide for the future.

The ITA suggested that, in due course, two representatives of the Authority should meet with two similar representatives of the four companies, bringing the whole financial position under review, and disclosing any information necessary, in the opinion of either side, to enable each properly to comprehend the broad financial position of the other.

Recognising that the financial difficulties of the companies might be at their greatest during the next few months, and that any review along these lines could not be completed until the autumn at the earliest, the Authority offered to see what it could do in the way of effecting an immediate, temporary reduction in the current rentals drawing more heavily on the Exchequer loan, so that more of its capital investment would be met from borrowing. The consequent shortfall in its income would subsequently have to be fully made up, including the additional costs of the heavier borrowing.[2]

At its meeting on 1 May, the ITA approved certain suggestions that had been made to Sir Edwin Herbert,[3] who was acting on behalf of the companies. These were that, for the six months from April 1956 until

September 1956 there should be a reduction of all rentals by 40 per cent; during the six months from October 1956 until March 1957, the rentals would be paid in full as provided in the contracts; and that the total rentals payable during the twelve months from April 1957 until March 1958 (or if the companies preferred, during the six months from October 1957 to March 1958) should be increased by an amount equivalent to the reductions, plus interest thereon at $5\frac{1}{2}$ per cent.

At this stage the views of the ITA and the companies began to diverge. The financial review dragged on into 1957, when the circumstances which had given rise to it were altogether changed. It proved completely abortive, and it finally petered out in July of that year, having achieved nothing save to highlight the wide disparity in outlook on financial matters between the public authority and its private enterprise contractors. To that extent it was educative for both parties, but it was rather less than edifying.

In the first place the Authority wanted it established that proposals relating to a temporary reduction in rentals were completely separate from any relating to what it saw as a long-term review. The companies found the distinction difficult to accept.

At the heart of the difficulty lay the dislike of some of the entrepreneurs for working under a public authority which was not just a licensing body but one which possessed wide powers of supervision (however gently it chose to wield them) and which moreover, in financial matters, was subject to government in certain important respects. How different in essentials, the companies began to ask themselves, was this ITA from a BBC dependent on a Government grant-in-aid out of monies derived from a licence fee determined by the Exchequer? In the circumstances of Spring, 1956, the main issue for the company bosses was to discover and, so far as possible, to control what the ITA was doing with the money it was extracting from their firms. They suspected that the Authority might be taking too much in rentals and that in the end the Exchequer might prove to be an important beneficiary. And they could not readily bring themselves to accept that the ITA's role was rather more than to provide them with certain services at their expense.

The ITA on the other hand was aware of its responsibility under the Act to develop and extend ITV as a public service based upon a novel system of private enterprise under public control. To fulfil its task it needed to have considerable knowledge of the financial affairs of the companies which were under contract to it, and, although it was under no obligation to do so, it was ready to trade information about its own finances for information about theirs. Parliament had given it control over the means by which programmes and advertisements could reach the viewers; but it was much more than a vehicle by which the products made by programme companies were conveyed to the consumer. It was responsible to Parliament and public for the character of those products. In the last resort, ITV belonged to the ITA, not company shareholders; and if ITV could not become viable or deliver products which, as custodians of the public interest, Members of the Authority could guarantee, they could not send to know for whom the bell tolled: it tolled for them.

So great was the importance the companies attached to their concept of the unitary character of the long-term financial review that all but one of them (ABC) eventually refused the ITA's offer of a temporary deferment of part of their rentals. They did so with courtesy and only after it became clear that the ITA were determined to separate this matter from the review. Despite the tensions, there was little or no personal rancour between the parties. The two-tiered structure of ITV demanded mutual forbearance, and it required a discipline when issues of importance were at stake which was not easily acquired but, once achieved, it gave certain advantages over the spectacular pyramid of the BBC.

Three firms of chartered accountants were involved in the review. For the companies there were Binder, Hamlyn and Co. (represented by Mr Lawson), and Peat, Marwick, Mitchell and Co. (represented by Mr Leach). Their link with the four companies was Sir Edwin Herbert. For the ITA there were Cooper Bros and Co. (represented by Mr, later Sir Henry, Benson), working with the ITA's Head of Finance (first Mr George Campbell and later Mr Leonard Waight). By 2 October, it was being reported to the Authority that the discussions had so far disclosed little information of real value.[4] Later in that same month, on 26 October, great displeasure was being expressed at a meeting of the Television Programme Contractors Association at what appeared to be delaying tactics adopted by the ITA and it was resolved that a strong letter of protest should be sent to Fraser.[5]

It was against this background that on 6 November – by which time the tide of ITV financial affairs had perceptibly turned – Benson informed the Authority that the information to be provided on its behalf was now complete, but before he handed it over he would welcome guidance on whether the companies' view about the purpose of the financial review was to be accepted and whether the companies were to be given the Authority's information even in the event of their being unwilling to make correspondingly full disclosures. It was decided that, provided the companies undertook to furnish the information requested by its accountants, the review should proceed on the understanding that the ITA was under no

obligation to release the programme companies from any of their contractual obligations and that its own figures would be confined to the
companies' accountants and not disclosed elsewhere.[6]

By the following March it emerged that the companies' accountants were
suggesting that the rentals fixed in the contracts should be reduced by about
20 per cent not just in 1956 but in each year throughout the contractual
period. They were, of course, well aware that the lower rentals would
cripple the ITA's finances so severely that it would be impossible for it to
carry out its programme of development; and so they went on to suggest that
the companies should lend ITA some of the money they would no longer be
paying in rentals. In so far as the ITA had not repaid these loans by 1964, and
if its life was not extended beyond that date, they would take over its assets in
full settlement of its indebtedness to them unless its assets exceeded the
amount of the outstanding loan, when they would be satisfied with the
return of the unpaid portion of the loan.

It seemed to the Authority that a plan so fanciful was an alarming
demonstration of the credibility gap between the companies and itself.
Quite apart from the general question of the independence of the Authority,
it would find itself in a position in which it was ignoring the Act, since the
Act required it to provide capital expenditure from revenue. It was a
revealing feature of the companies' proposals that they provided for a review
each year at which the Authority would be required to produce its draft
trading results for examination. The Authority would no longer be master in
its own house.

Herbert indicated that the financial review had become confined to a
question of whether there were any means by which the Authority's taxation
could be reduced, so that such saving could be passed on to the contractors.
The view was held by at least some contractors that a method had been
found of making arrangements which would enable rentals to be reduced, at
the same time leaving the ITA no worse off, and that, therefore, the only
sufferer would be the Inland Revenue.

What the companies appeared to be suggesting was, in short, that they
should have their rentals reduced by some £4 million up to the end of March
1964, of which they would pay about £1,750,000 in tax, and that they lend
the ITA one half of this £4 million over the period to March 1964, the ITA
paying interest on such loans and beginning to repay loans in 1960/1
onwards. By March 1964, it would have repaid about £1,250,000 and still
owe about £750,000.

So far as the ITA and its advisers could see, the result of accepting the
companies' plan would be that:

1 the ITA would at all times have the contractors as substantial creditors;
2 the contractors' negotiating position at the end of the period (when they would be large creditors) would be very strong;
3 there could not fail to be differences of view between the Authority and the contractors as to how much of the loans should be repaid from time to time, and how much should be kept available by the Authority for capital expenditure, expansion, research and development;
4 these conditions were contrary to the express intention of Section 10 of the Act which was mandatory in wording, the Authority's independence would be impaired and there would be criticism of the Authority in Parliament as its published accounts would show that it was in the hands of the contractors to a considerable extent.

One of the contractors' main anxieties was that, under Section 13 of the Act, the PMG would at some future date require the Authority to pay to the Exchequer the surpluses shown in its accounts – surpluses which had been provided out of their pockets.

The Authority decided that it could not agree to the companies' scheme and that no useful purpose would be served by continuing the joint financial discussions. Letters to this effect were sent to the chairmen of the four companies and to Edwin Herbert.[7] This was, beyond doubt, a crucial stage in the affairs of Independent Television. The issue at stake was nothing less than the one of 'Who rules?'. ITV had survived as a result of calculated risks on the part of a few entrepreneurs. Were they not now entitled to reap for themselves and their shareholders a full reward from their risk bearing? As a matter of political expediency the advocates of commercial television in Parliament had had to concede the establishment of a public authority which not only determined who should receive the franchises and had certain regulatory functions, not unlike those exercised by the Federal Communications Commission in America, but which owned and operated the transmitting stations through which programmes and advertisements reached the domestic television screens. Contracts had been painfully negotiated. All this was true. But in the final analysis who were the principals and who were the agents in this hybrid system? Was this private enterprise or was it not? Whose money was this authority spending? Were not those who paid the piper entitled to call the tune? No such crudely expressed questions were openly posed, but they were present just below the surface. For the next six years they were to remain without a conclusive answer.

Consequently, the long meeting which now took place at Princes Gate on

Monday 3 June 1957, the record of which ran to nearly five pages of typescript, was one of quite exceptional importance. The Chairman, the Deputy Chairman, two other Members and the Director General of the Authority were the nucleus of one side; and the four company chairmen plus Herbert were the nucleus of the other. In attendance were accountants and solicitors. It was a full scale inquest into the whole course of events which had led to the ITA and the companies finding themselves seriously at cross purposes. Herbert's contributions, in which he was speaking for the companies collectively, proved extremely revealing.

He felt that, to remove misunderstanding, it was necessary to go back to the time when negotiations were taking place about the programme contracts. During them the companies had constantly pressed for full information about the basis on which the Authority was assessing the companies' rentals, but this had been refused. He thought that the covering letters to the contracts had recognised the right of the programme companies to ask for full information about the basis of the rentals and this is what had been asked for in March 1956 when the companies had requested the joint financial review. Although at that time the companies were finding it necessary to ask their backers for further money, and for that purpose considered that they should have full information about the basis of the Authority's charges, their serious financial position was merely the occasion for exercising their right to have full information on the. Authority's finances. In the companies' view the accountants' discussions were designed to cover two points which were not really separable one from the other: the first was the immediate relief which could be given to the companies, and the second was a long-term comprehensive review of the Authority's financial policy.

The later stations which the Authority would erect would not only be financed initially out of existing programme companies' rentals but would also be largely depreciated and amortised out of them. Furthermore, in view of the incidence of tax on the Authority, for every £100 spent by it the programme companies were having to provide a much larger sum out of their own pockets, probably a minimum of £180. The companies could not know whether this was right since they had no information on which to reach any conclusion.

The difficulty had arisen in the discussions because each side had a different conception from the other of its terms of reference. The companies felt that they had a clear right to examine the whole financial basis of Independent Television.

The proposals which the Authority had rejected had never been intended as a formal submission from the programme companies but was merely seen as a 'working paper' put forward by the companies' accountants for discussion with the Authority's accountants. It had not been approved formally by the companies although it had been shown to them so that they might give a general assent to it as a basis for discussion. But the Authority had apparently regarded it as a final and definitive document. Herbert hoped that the Authority would accept that there was still an urgent problem to be considered in the review and would agree that the accountants might go on with their discussions with the aim of producing an agreed joint report, or, failing that, separate reports to their principals. He went on to say that the companies were of the view that the Authority might be 'over-insuring' its financial position.

Herbert said that the companies would not have agreed to enter into their contracts unless they had been accompanied by a covering letter which contained the following assurance by the Authority:

> I confirm that it has at no time been any part of the financial policy of the Authority to plan for, or to try to build up, a significant surplus balance over and above such expenditure as the Authority felt proper in carrying out its duty under the Act . . . and that, if for some reason it proved that in fact a signficant surplus was accumulating which the Authority could not, in its view, reasonably use in the provision of a wider or better television service, the Authority would be willing to enter into discussion with the Programme Contractors, during the course of their Contracts, but the final decision whether the fees should be varied must rest with it.[8]

In reply, Clark said that he willingly accepted all the implications of this paragraph which he had signed on behalf of the Authority and gave an assurance that in the view of the Authority a significant surplus within the meaning of the paragraph was not accumulating and was not likely to do so for some time. If, in fact, a significant surplus did accumulate then the Authority would act in strict accordance with the assurance given in the letter, which clearly left the final decision with the Authority. The Authority could not accept any obligation to prove to the companies that a surplus was not accumulating or to defend the manner in which it was conducting its business or to allow the companies' accountants to pronounce on whether or not the Authority was over-insuring or whether or not its programme of stations was or was not reasonable. He added that he would ask his financial advisers if there was any possibility of usefully continuing discussions on the specific amount of taxation on the system as a whole. On this inconclusive note the meeting ended.

On 21 June Clark wrote to Herbert saying how valuable the 3 June meeting had been in clearing away 'some real misunderstanding'. Two subjects of the review were now out of the way: the financial plight of the companies in 1956 and the possibility of reducing the burden of income tax. He went on:

> As I understand it, however, the companies would now like a third subject to be examined – whether the Authority's income is too high in relation to its declared policy of accumulating no significant surplus which it does not need for television. Indeed, I understood you to say that in your mind, this had, from the beginning, been the real subject of our talks, the early financial troubles of the companies and the question of taxation being no more, as you said, than occasions for raising this broader subject with us.
>
> We have given the most earnest consideration to your suggestion that the talks should still continue, but this time I am afraid we do not feel able to agree. In our view the question whether the Authority is accumulating surplus funds it does not need for television could not in any case be profitably considered in only the second year of the rentals. As I said at our meeting, no such surplus is at present appearing, nor can we see any prospect that we shall have such an excess. But I am glad to confirm that the assurance given in my letter to each of the four first programme companies on this subject remains the Authority's policy.[9]

Herbert's reply was non-committal, and this was effectively the end of an episode in the financial affairs of Independent Television. The next episode came two years later when the ITA came under harassing crossfire, not from its contractors but from the Public Accounts Committee of the House of Commons, and not on the grounds that it was taking too much money from the companies but on the grounds that it was not taking anything like enough. That story belongs to Part IV.

27

£750,000: THE GIFT HORSE
THAT BOLTED

The story of 'the grant that never was' is both an intriguing relic of the early history of Independent Television and an illuminating commentary on its law and practices. 'Independent of what?' critics of the system (including Sir Ian Jacob of the BBC) used to ask. The aborting of Section 11 of the Television Act certainly provided one answer to this question. As has been seen in Part I varying descriptions were given in Parliament of the circumstances in which this income could be made available. Traditional government circumlocution when questions about the 'hypothecation' of revenue were raised could not conceal that the source of the money was the licence fee. This had recently been increased from £2 to £3, from which it was considered possible to provide this annual sum to the Authority whilst still leaving the BBC with an adequate and steadily rising income. In winding up the debate in the House of Lords on 14 July De La Warr made what came to be regarded as the definitive statement of the Government's intentions:

> Perhaps in the first year or two they (the programme contractors) will be building up slowly and some of what we should consider the most important programmes may be difficult for them to provide and pay for out of advertisements. It will then be possible for the ITA to say to the programme companies: 'We recognise that you cannot pay for these programmes out of your revenue and we, as the ITA, will make ourselves responsible for their provision' . . . I conclude by saying this. *Whether the whole of this sum of money is spent or not, or whether in the beginning all of it is spent and in later years, perhaps, not all of it will be needed, I regard the provision of the money as vital and essential.*[1] [author's italics]

At the Authority's request a provision of £375,000 was made in the Post Office estimates to cover any payments authorised under this section of the Act during the financial year of 1955/6. But, of course, provision in the estimates was not of itself an authority to spend. For that the approval of the Treasury was necessary.

Since the Act itself said nothing at all about the use to which the money could properly be put the Authority somewhat ingenuously speculated about the possibility of using it for a variety of purposes other than the making of programmes, for which, as it seemed in 1955, the companies would not have sufficient resources of their own. Research into future technical developments such as the opening up of Band IV and the introduction of colour, seemed an obvious choice, as also was a campaign of information designed to extend and improve reception of the Band III programmes by the public. An information campaign about the new programmes, involving press advertising, was also well favoured. But the Authority's Secretary, Wolstencroft, was nearest the mark when he referred to the possibility of one or other of the companies collapsing and the Authority having to fill a programme gap at short notice. For Section 2(2) of the Act envisaged two circumstances in which the Authority might itself provide programmes: (a) to secure a proper balance in the subject matter of the programmes by the provision of items which could not, or could not as suitably, be provided by the contractors; and (b) in the event of 'any temporary lack of suitable persons able and willing to become or continue as programme contractors on suitable terms'.

By the time the lawyers had put Section 2(2)(a) under their microscope in relation to other sections of the Act, including Section 11, it appeared that there were quite a lot of things which the Authority could *not* legally do as regards programme provision. It could not, they said, put on programmes using its own staff; pay the programme contractors for putting on programmes; pay specialist organisations to produce films and then give them to programme contractors free of cost for inclusion in their schedules; or pay a specialist organisation to produce a film and use the technical resources of a programme contractor for projecting it. All it could do, apparently, was to hire a specialist organisation (other than a programme contractor) to produce a programme and deliver it ready for transmission, or arrange for it to be produced by a subsidiary of one or more of the companies and put out through their machinery, the legal requirements of the Act being circumvented by the device of creating a separate production company which would itself not be a programme contractor. At one time it had been taken for granted in the Post Office that the new authority would have its own resources – additional to those of the companies – for making programmes. Detailed plans and costings for ITA studio facilities were worked out and estimates made of the staff that would be required. But their political masters trimmed their sails to an ever-changing wind with the utmost infirmity of purpose.

Thus far therefore – by the summer of 1955 – the Authority had discovered that it was not going to be easy to find a way of spending its promised slice of the licence fee. Later on it was to discover that there was even more of a problem in actually getting its hands on the money or any part of it. For the time being the only sensible course was to wait and see how the programme companies would be able to manage. How to get hold of its money and how to find a means of spending it were problems which would only arise when it was known what programme productions the money would be needed for. It seems to have occurred to nobody at that time to question whether this was a gift horse which should be looked very warily in the mouth. Least of all to Clark.

Clark yielded to no one in his belief that a separate television service additional to that of the BBC was desirable and necessary. But he doubted the wisdom of relying wholly on the fruits of private enterprise to provide it. He clearly attached the greatest importance to the Authority having a source of programme finance separate from that of the companies.

The struggle to obtain this money dominated life at Princes Gate for the Authority and its staff throughout 1956. But if the Authority occupied the centre of the stage, the roles played by the top brass of the companies was not negligible and proved in the end to be decisive. If there was a villain of the piece, it was Her Majesty's Government, represented (this time with no personal reservations) by Dr Hill. The legendary dead hand of the Treasury could be felt unmistakeably in the background. It was largely a public performance, with the Press providing a lively running commentary; but some scenes were enacted in private, notably the one in which the Chairman of the Authority resigned. A decorous veil was drawn over the proceedings in the Authority's annual reports. It might even be better regarded as a cover-up. The furthest the official record ever went to disclose the ITA's deep sense of frustration was in the report for 1955/6 which said: 'As regards this subject, therefore, the year ended on a disappointing note. The Authority felt its ability to discharge one of its leading statutory duties had been impaired in that a source of income on which it had counted had thus far been denied it.'[2]

At a meeting on 15 November 1955, the Authority was told that the Post Office now needed to know what sum was to be provided in their Vote for 1956/7 and also to have a forecast of requirements for the following financial years. They had stressed that the Treasury would expect estimates and forecasts to be based on a reasonable assumption of actual requirements.

After some discussion, and noting the impossibility of giving at that stage chapter and verse of projects for which Treasury money might be needed, the Authority decided to ask for the full £750,000 as a contingency fund for emergencies.[3]

The Post Office flatly refused to act, explaining that it would be improper to ask Parliament to vote money until it was established that the money would be required and some information could be given of the cost of the projects on which the money would be spent. If this could not be done, then the only recourse would be to seek a Supplementary Estimate at a later date. This made the Authority a bit uneasy. 'Some of us', wrote Clark to the PMG on 22 December 'have had personal experience of the obstacles which may arise when a Supplementary Estimate is proposed.' Replying on 11 January 1956, Dr Hill said 'I do want . . . to dispel your fears about a Supplementary Estimate. Any case you may put forward later in the year would be considered on its merits, and I can give you an assurance that I would not be prejudiced in any way by reason of its being a supplementary.'[4]

In the meantime, the BBC happened to have issued its annual handbook for 1956 saying on page 22 'A Grant of £375,000 has been made by the Treasury to the Independent Television Authority for 1955/6'. Much huffed, Fraser wrote brusquely to Jacob on 25 November denying that the Authority had received a penny for 1955/6 or would do so. There is perhaps an implication here that Fraser himself did not greatly care for receiving public money for private enterprise television. 'We are always trying to track down and stone to death the story that the ITA has received, does receive, or is in process of receiving a grant from the Treasury.' A corrigendum slip was asked for, and it was duly provided without quibble on 3 January. The point was hammered, almost bludgeoned, home by a press notice issued by the ITA on the same day.

It is widely believed that the ITA receives automatically a grant of £750,000 each year from public funds. This is not the case. The Television Act permits the Postmaster-General, with the consent of the Treasury, to make payments to the Authority within this limit for approved purposes. No such payments have so far been made, and none are at present in view.

Be that as it may, it had by this time begun to dawn on the ITA that, at the level of Treasury officials, if not above, the Government were deliberate in wishing to evade the implications of what various Ministers had at certain times said in Parliament during the passage of the Bill. The autumn budget of October 1955 had introduced an era of financial retrenchment designed to effect substantial reductions in public and consumer expenditure. Assistance to commercial television from public funds, even though they derived from the licence fee, would hardly be timely in political terms. It was decided that Clark should pursue the PMG further, confronting him with the undertakings that earlier Ministers had given and itemising the make-up of an envisaged expenditure of £750,000 in the following terms:

Religious services and programmes	£ 50,000
News and related programmes	£ 350,000
Educational programmes	£ 200,000
Minority programmes	£ 150,000

In a long letter on 20 January, he also said ' . . . I told Earl De La Warr that I could not have accepted his invitation to be Chairman had I not been assured that sufficient money would be available for the Authority to fulfill its responsibilities in the matter of balance'.[5] On 31 January the whole Authority trooped off to the House of Commons to lobby the PMG and Assistant PMG with senior Post Office officials in attendance.

The Chairman had armed himself with an advance copy of a letter written next day by John Spencer Wills, requesting that the cost of 'balancing' programmes, or at least a high proportion of it, should be borne by the Authority and saying that over £500,000 of his company's advertising had been cancelled during the first three months of operation, because the schedule had contained news and programmes of a religious, artistic and educational nature which were of very limited public appeal and were 'uneconomical'.

Clark told Dr Hill that he saw in what had happened confirmation of the views of many who had deeply considered the implications of the provision for grants during debates on the Bill. The success of the whole enterprise depended on the companies building up an audience as fast as possible to achieve financial stability, if not prosperity, after which they could themselves afford to maintain a proper balance and cater adequately for minorities. Meanwhile, the ITA should be in a position to contribute towards the general well-being of the enterprise by using monies made available under Section 11. He had been assured by the Chairmen of both London companies that when financial security had been achieved, their aim would be to improve their prestige by including cultural programmes. But in the meantime, the two companies were losing money at the rate of £2½ to £3 million a year and were securing on average only about three minutes of advertising an hour.

After reviewing what he called the 'technical' aspects of grant provision the PMG counter-attacked, fastening particularly on the proposal that the ITA rather than the companies should finance the news. He suggested that the Authority might be underestimating the force of public reaction which could follow the grant of public funds for an ITA news service. It could well be argued that a good news service, in one form or another, should be one of the first costs in a programme contractor's budget, even for a basic schedule in the 'build-up' period. By the time he had finished Dr Hill had killed stone dead the idea that had been current in ITA since the earliest days that the news service could be financed by the ITA separately from the main stream of programmes; and he had skilfully removed one of the cornerstones of the case the Authority was making. For the rest he could afford to adopt a more conciliatory attitude. With regard to religious, educational and minority programmes generally, concrete proposals were essential to any provision in the Estimates and nothing would be lost if the Authority took time to develop the case for further discussion. On this note the engagement was broken off: but it was clear that before long the battle would be resumed.

The more the ITA considered the PMG's demand for 'concrete proposals' the less it liked it. From a study of the debates on the Bill it seemed clear that Parliament wished there to be made available, as part of the new arrangements made in 1954 for the distribution of the annual yield of the licence fees between the Exchequer, the Post Office, the BBC and the ITA, a sum of money which was not to exceed £750,000 a year to enable the Authority to see that balanced programme schedules were provided by the contractors if circumstances aross in which advertising income alone was insufficient. Such circumstances had come about. At that very moment the Exchequer was holding the full £750,000 deducted from the yield of the licence fees over and above the amount required to defray the Post Office's collecting expenses and the £2 million at which it had been announced in 1954 the Exchequer's own share of the licence fees would be stabilised. So what was all the fuss about? Agreed that, in the light of the debates, the Authority would have no title to the money unless it were used for the improvement of the programmes, then under Section 2 (1) of the Act it had the direct and uncircumscribed power 'to do all such things as are in its (or 'their' as the Act preferred to say) opinion necessary or conducive to the proper discharge of its (their) function as described in subsection (1) of Section 1 of this Act' (i.e. the provision of television programmes of high quality additional to those of the BBC). So, if the Authority were given the money or some of it, what was to prevent it, at its discretion, applying it to a reduction in the rental payments made by the companies, according to the extent to which individually they complied with the ITA's requirements for a proper balance? It was for the Authority to require the companies to increase the share of serious programmes of various kinds and arrange for the appropriate abatements. Was it for the PMG to involve himself in detailed programme proposals? Had not Maxwell-Fyfe said in the House on 4 May 1954 'The Government are not going to insist that because the Authority gets that money it should act under the control and supervision of the Postmaster-General'? Presenting the PMG with 'concrete proposals' as a precondition of any grant would be tantamount to handing over to the Government the power of deciding what, in certain areas of programming, should or should not be broadcast.

Fired by these reflections, the Authority renewed the offensive in a letter dated 29 February. It must have taken Hill and his cohorts by surprise. They withdrew to defensive positions, and made preparations for a war of attrition. On 8 March Hill sent Clark a non-committal reply saying that the matter was being considered, but would take some time. The move he had decided to make soon became clear; he would seek the instructions of the high command in a memorandum to the Home Affairs Committee of the Cabinet.[6] It thus became inevitable that in an increasingly difficult financial situation delay would be encountered in reaching a settlement, and the outcome was unpredictable. At the national level, the set-back in the economy which had been registered by Butler's autumn budget of 1955 remained a continuing problem, and financial restraint was the order of the day.

It is a reasonable assumption that by this time Dr Hill, even though he thought that a great fuss was being made about mere 'chicken-feed', was ready for a negotiated peace: but a simple gentleman's agreement between him and Clark – two reasonable men – was not practical politics. His officials, however dutiful, had the Treasury to contend with. He himself had to go to a Cabinet, of which he was not a member, and which had much else on its mind. On his side, Clark had the companies on his tail, headed by the redoubtable Spencer Wills. Before long wires had begun to cross. Early in April Stuart McClean and Edwin Herbert were calling to see Hill on behalf of A-R, but not without the knowledge of the ITA. By the end of May, Fraser was sufficiently hard pressed to be writing direct to a high official in the Treasury, a move which would have greatly displeased Sir Ben Barnett of the Post Office had he known of it.

But this is to anticipate. The first thing to be done was to ensure so far as possible that the PMG made the kind of case to the Home Affairs Committee that best suited the Authority and the companies, and on 22 March a complete draft of a suitable memorandum was dispatched to the Post Office. It was thought better that an appraisal of the problem should appear to come from within the Post Office rather than in the form of a letter from the Authority which Ministers might well discount as special pleading. It took the form of a report by the PMG on the operation of Independent Television over its first six months. The comings and goings between Post Office and Authority staff over subsequent weeks leave little doubt that the document which eventually reached Ministers was different from the one drafted at Princes Gate, but there is no reason to believe that the main drift of it was materially changed. It was in two parts: the first was in the nature of a general report and the second dealt with the question of grants-in-aid to the ITA under the terms of Section 11 of the Act.[7]

Up to a point Part 1 was a success story. There had been, as we saw in Chapter 23, a remarkably rapid rise in the number of homes equipped to receive ITV, and audience measurement figures continued to show a marked preference in those homes for ITV as against BBC programmes.

That was the good news. The bad news could hardly have been worse. The advertisers were holding back. Projected to annual rates, the current losses of the first two companies (A-R and ATV) were:

Expenditure	Income	Loss
£8,500,000	£5,500,000	£3,000,000

As far as could be estimated at that stage A-R would lose about £4 million in its first year and ATV about £1,500,000. As it happened, and as will be seen in Chapter 28, there was additional financial help ready at hand for both these companies; and, as it happened too that year, the advertising recession which had set in after Christmas 1955 reversed itself with dramatic suddenness. But meanwhile, from the standpoint of the ITA, this situation had two bad consequences: first it created a state of uncertainty in the minds of potential contractors for future stations, particularly those planned for Scotland and Wales, and secondly it impelled the companies to concentrate all their efforts on obtaining the highest possible audience ratings by the presentation of programmes of proven popularity at the expense of those with only a minority appeal. In the ITA's considered opinion this second consequence was nullifying its ability to maintain a proper balance in the programmes by procuring from the companies elements such as good music, good theatre, discussions, reviews of current affairs, etc.

Expressed in statistical terms which, it was thought, would impress Ministers more than an account of the trends in programme output about

168 IN AND OUT OF THE RED

which most of them were likely to know almost nothing, the retreat from balance was indeed startling (Table 27.1). Saturdays and Sundays were ignored for the simple reason that programmes capable of being described as 'balancing' barely existed. *International Theatre* (90 minutes) was included as a balancing programme, although not all the plays genuinely qualified. In October the series was fortnightly: in March it was weekly in London and the Midlands. This accounted for the relatively good figures for Mondays in March.

TABLE 27.1   *Balancing programmes – time allocated on weekdays (in minutes)*

	October 1955	March 1956 (London)	March 1956 (Midlands)
Monday	67	120	90
Tuesday	67	15	15
Wednesday	52	15	–
Thursday	60	30	30
Friday	60	30	–
Total (5 days)	306	210	135

The effect of carrying these balancing programmes on the advertising revenue of the companies could be assessed in a variety of ways. The example chosen by the Authority was that of the Hallé Orchestra concerts on alternate Mondays during October and November 1955 between 8.30 and 9.30 p.m. The audience measurement was a rating of 10, i.e. 10 per cent of the homes in the London area able to receive ITV. Advertisements during this hour would on average have cost advertisers £27 8s 6d per thousand homes. On the Mondays when the Hallé did not perform the programme at the same hour (*Your Kind of Music*) was viewed in 27 per cent of the homes. The cost to advertisers during this hour was on average £9 3s 6d per thousand homes, that is approximately a third of the cost when the Hallé was playing. Had the alternative programme to the Hallé been one of great popularity, the comparison would have been much more striking. On Monday 27 February 1956 excerpts from *Hamlet* were presented from 8 to 9.30 p.m. Sixteen per cent of the so-called Band III homes were tuned to *Hamlet* initially, but this audience fell to 8 per cent in the first quarter of an hour and never subsequently rose above 15 per cent. This presentation led to the concurrent BBC *What's My Line?* achieving the distinction of being the first BBC programme since October reaching number one in the 'Top Ten' list regularly issued by the Nielsen Television Index.

All this and a lot more was packed into the draft that was put in the hands of the Post Office officials on 22 March. Sporadically over the next month they were on the telephone with supplementary questions, the main drift of which soon became clear. The Governmen: were wanting to know whether the Authority could not itself provide out of its own income the money which it was seeking in the form of an Exchequer grant. This income came exclusively from the rentals which the companies had contracted to pay to it. The argument was that, if the Authority could abate these rentals by an equivalent sum, this would enable the companies to afford to provide the balancing programmes which the Authority considered necessary for a proper observance of the Act and the Government would then be spared having to make any grant. In fact, as seen in the previous chapter, the companies were themselves beginning to seek such an abatement, not in order to provide balancing programmes, but in order to reduce their losses. The answer finally given on 26 April to the Government's enquiry was that the Authority could contemplate nothing beyond an emergency reduction in the rentals of an order of one-third until September 1956, the re-establishment of the present rentals from October until March, and the full recovery of the sums abated in the financial year 1957/8. That amounted to some £300,000. Even this concession was contrary to the advice of Cooper Brothers, its auditors and independent financial advisers. It was imperative for the Authority to retain the means to construct transmitting stations sufficient to secure coverage of at least 80 per cent of the population by 1960, if only in order to provide the economic conditions in which Independent Television could thrive.

The matter must have been on the agenda of the Home Affairs Committee of the Cabinet early in May, which is not to say that the item was taken or fully considered then. Clark reported to the Authority on 1 May that he had again discussed it with the Minister and also with the Home Secretary, Gwilym Lloyd-George. But on 30 May he was writing yet again to Hill and in decidedly reproachful terms. 'I have forborn from worrying you about the £750,000, although it is six weeks since you said that the question was just about to be considered.' He said that when Members of the Authority were appointed it was impressed upon them that their chief responsibility would be for the quality and balance of the programmes and that there would be this money at their disposal to assist them in their task. He went on:

The appointment of the Chairman of the Arts Council as Chairman of the ITA clearly implied the Government's intention to maintain standards and balance. The present programmes are often extremely embarrassing but, as you know, I have defended them, because I have always assumed that means of improving them would be forthcoming.[8]

Not even an acknowledgement was received, a fact which Clark did not conceal from the Conservative Broadcasting and Communications Committee which he met on 27 June.

In the meantime *The Times* had published on 23 June a report correctly explaining the niceties of the issue. It was linked, however, with the publication of the autumn schedule of A-R, the company which, it will be recalled, had made approaches direct to Dr Hill. It quoted 'someone in everyday touch with trends in commercial television' as having said that theirs was not only a good schedule from the advertising point of view but also 'an astute schedule from the political point of view'. From this *The Times* correspondent drew the conclusion, accurately enough, that if the grant was forthcoming 'there will be no outraged cries from the programme companies about the Authority's interfering with their sovereignty as contractors'.

With the inevitability of gradualness the issue moved towards its climax. The Minutes of the ITA for 3 July record that:

> The Chairman had seen the PMG and the Financial Secretary of the Treasury and had gathered that there was virtually no hope of the Authority being granted any part of the £750,000 during the financial year. He, the Chairman, was therefore going to see the Lord Privy Seal to inform him of the Authority's serious disquiet that the means for implementing its statutory duties were being withheld.[9]

The Financial Secretary of the Treasury was Henry Brooke and the Lord Privy Seal was now R. A. Butler. So, by this date, four Ministers had been approached, two of them (Butler and Lloyd-George) senior members of Anthony Eden's Cabinet.

Two weeks later Clark reported that Butler had agreed to recommend to his colleagues in the Cabinet that a Supplementary Estimate should be immediately presented to Parliament for a token payment from the Grant-in-Aid for religious and educational programmes. In addition to the token payment, the Government would be prepared to give a written acceptance of the Authority's right in principle to the grant when the country's financial position improved. The Authority decided that the Government's offer should be accepted.[10]

The idea of a 'token' payment seems to have evolved out of the meeting with Hill and Brooke and had been developed by Clark in subsequent discussion and correspondence with Hill. He felt that it would be a foot in the door and that the principle of a subvention from the product of the licence fee would have been established. In the meantime the PMG on 11 July answered a Parliamentary question by baldly stating that he had received a request for a grant and that it was being considered. In the course of supplementaries the following astonishing exchange took place:

Mr Herbert Morrison: Can the Rt. Hon Gentleman say whether this indicates that there is a deficit commercially on ITA workings and that that is the reason for the request for the money, or is it wanted merely for fun or for pocket money?
Dr Hill: The application which has been received in no way relates or refers to the general financial position of the programme companies. The case is not put on any such basis.[11]

That says more about politics than it does about broadcasting. So far as Independent Television was concerned, seeking to confirm the principle rather than insisting on the substance of the grant altered the whole basis of the argument to an extent which was not fully realised until the final stages of the battle had been reached.

In the event Butler failed to deliver even the promised sample let alone the goods. A letter from the PMG of 31 July arrived in time for the ITA meeting on that day, and it said that the conclusion the Government had felt bound to reach was that, because of the general economic situation, no grant could be made under Section 11 in the current financial year. The decision was publicly announced in a written Parliamentary answer on the following day, and simultaneously the Authority published its reaction. It said:

The setting aside of a maximum sum of £750,000 each year from the rapidly increasing yield of the licence fees for the support of such programmes was an integral part of the arrangements approved by Parliament and embodied in the Television Act in 1954, and has always been regarded by the Authority as crucial to the proper discharge of its duties in this field.

So completely did it seem to be accepted that the money would be available if the Authority judged it necessary, that the Treasury began deducting this additional £750,000 from the licence fees in the financial year 1955/6, and the deduction is continuing this year. The Treasury has now received, during the last sixteen months, a million pounds under this arrangement. Requests for this grant were made in November 1955 and repeated during the following eight months . . . The Authority is conscious, and its view is shared by the programme companies, that the present programmes, although extremely popular, do not contain a sufficient number of programmes of information and discussion or of plays and performances of lasting value. For this the explanation is the very simple one that such programmes, whether transmitted by the Authority or by the BBC, do not attract relatively large audiences, despite their national value. The possibility that this situation would arise was clearly foreseen during the debates on the Television Bill, and it was precisely in order to make such programmes possible that the £750,000 provision was included in Section 11 of the Act . . . The Authority appreciated that the Government might reasonably take the view that the payment of the full sum should be deferred while the country's present financial difficulties continue, and so made it clear that it would for the present rest content with the payment of only a small part of the sum so that at least a start could be made in the provision of balancing programmes, and in token of the acceptance of the principle that independent television, if it is to grow to its proper stature, should not be dependent on advertising revenue alone. Even this modest proposal has been rejected.

If only the matter had rested there the Authority would have notched up an honourable defeat. It had striven to do its duty to maintain a proper balance in very difficult circumstances but had been cheated by a Government which broke its word. It had quite a sympathetic press. The *Observer* wrote on 5 August:

> The Government's decision implies either that it knows better than the Authority whether commercial TV programmes are up to the standard required by the Act, or that if they are not, the country cannot now afford to improve them.

The harsh rebuff was very dispiriting and seemed likely to delay the attainment by ITV of a reasonable balance, or synthesis, between the popular and the serious, the satisfaction of both majority and minority tastes – express it how one will. The procurement of licence money would have been a short-cut to this objective but it was unlikely to be a permanent solution. There was a longer, more reliable route which Fraser and a few others both in ITA and the companies were prepared to travel. For his part, Fraser, as will be seen, set out upon his journey in September 1956.

Parliament had gone into an uneasy recess and members of the Government were snatching some holidays. Dr Hill took his family to Sandwich Bay during the second half of August. On 21 August he received a letter from Clark tendering his resignation as Chairman of the ITA. This letter had been three weeks in gestation, Clark being at pains to consult with fellow Members scattered about the country. Copies of it, with brief covering letters, were sent to the Lord Chancellor, Lord Kilmuir, the Lord Privy Seal, R. A. Butler, and De La Warr, now no longer in the Government. (The Editor of *The Times*, Sir William Haley, who had been closely consulted by Clark, received one on a personal basis.)

Inevitably, since he was writing with a view to publication, Clark's letter traversed the old familiar ground: the statements made in Parliament in 1954 by De La Warr and Maxwell-Fyfe (now Lord Kilmuir), the assurances he received before accepting his appointment, the letters he had written to Hill and the talks they had had. He recalled the painstaking efforts of Fraser and the staff to deal with Post Office enquiries and objections over five patient months. The national economic situation had not figured as a factor in these exchanges, he observed.

> The first time it was put forward as a determining factor was in a meeting I had with you and the Financial Secretary of the Treasury on 27 June. I knew that this would weigh heavily with the Authority, and therefore told you that I would ask them to accept, instead of £750,000, a token payment which would have no budgetary significance, but would maintain the principle, provided that it was accompanied by some sort of assurance that a grant more in accordance with the original intentions of Parliament would be favourably considered when the financial situation improved. Your letter of the 31 July refuses to make any payment whatsoever and, what is worse, contains no such assurances.
>
> I believe that any unprejudiced person, reviewing these events, will feel that a fundamental difference has taken place in the Government's attitude towards the Independent Television Authority.[12]

The fact that the letter had now been sent was disclosed to Members at a meeting of the Authority that same day – 21 August. Dilys Powell said that she too would resign immediately. Other Members decided to issue a statement expressing their full accord with their Chairman, but explaining that they did not have the same compelling personal reasons for resigning.

Efforts to persuade the Government to change its mind were to continue.[13]

For Dr Hill the whole thing was a confounded nuisance and little more. He had sensed all along that the financial position of the companies would change for the better, and sooner rather than later. As it seemed to him, it was all a storm in a teacup; and, writing his own memoirs some eight years later, he could not bring himself to give the matter more than a page. But there he was on his family holiday at Sandwich Bay with Butler asking on the telephone what was to be done. Fortunately, he was due back in London within a few days and would, he hoped, be able to sort something out. 'I was very glad,' wrote Butler to Clark on 22 August, 'to learn from Charles Hill that you have agreed to defer its publication until you have had a talk with him on his return to London next week. I shall be in touch with him as soon as he is back, and shall, of course, do anything I can to help to straighten this thing out.'

By Monday, 27 August, the ITA staff had a draft Press Notice ready, covering a copy of the Chairman's resignation letter and inviting the press to come to Princes Gate at 12 noon the following day when Clark would be ready to answer questions. It was never issued and the press never came. That same afternoon Clark, on invitation, called upon Dr Hill who had doubtless spent some of his first morning back from the seaside in consultation with more senior colleagues. Returning from the interview Clark wrote at once to Hill, at the latter's request, to tell him formally what assurances would lead him to reconsider his decision to resign.

> In the first place, I feel we must know that the Authority has the full support and sympathy of the Government in discharging its responsibilities under the Television Act for maintaining high quality and proper balance.
>
> Secondly, that it still supports the principle enunciated by the Government spokesmen that there will be times when quality and balance cannot be achieved by the programme companies out of advertising revenue alone and that, under these circumstances, it will be proper for the Authority to see that they are maintained by grants that can be made under Section 11 of the Act.
>
> Thirdly, we should, I think, have some confirmation of the point made by Sir David Maxwell-Fyfe and Lord Selkirk that the Authority is the judge of when this money is needed . . . Finally, I come to the question of the Estimates for the coming year. This, really, is the essential point. I must be sure that the Government will not resist the inclusion of an adequate sum of money in the Estimates for the year 1957/8. Were they to

do so, we should be exactly where we are and I should have to go through this whole painful business all over again.

Hill replied with remarkably little delay on 29 August:

> The Government recognises . . . that there may well be times when the quality and balance of the programmes cannot be achieved . . . out of advertising revenue alone . . . It is agreed that it would be appropriate for the Authority to use grants made available under Section 11 of the Act for the purpose of balancing programmes.
>
> The Government reaffirms the statements made by its spokesman to the effect that responsibility for judging the quality and balance of programmes rests with the Independent Television Authority.[14]

He went on particularly to reaffirm the statement that had been made by Maxwell-Fyfe on 4 May 1954 and to explain that the Government would shortly be preparing the Estimates for 1957/8 and that it was desirable that any application the Authority wished to make for 1957/8 for a grant under Section 11 should be submitted by 1 October. While stressing that the Government could not be expected to give an undertaking about a particular Estimate before it had considered the Estimates in general as well as those relating to particular services. But in reaching its decision on this matter the Government would take fully into account the points which Clark had made with such emphasis and the Authority would be informed as soon as a decision was reached whether there was to be in the Estimates for 1957/8 provision for a payment under Section 11 of the Act.

Clark received this letter with the utmost relief. True, there was no money on the table, nor even a post-dated cheque. But, for the moment, the procuring and the spending of the promised grant took second place to the issue of confidence – the question whether or not the Government could be made to keep its word.

Talking to the author in May 1979 Hill was not disposed to attach much importance to the question whether Clark stayed or went. The problem, as he recalled, was 'David Kilmuir's conscience'. When he was Home Secretary in 1954, Kilmuir (then Maxwell-Fyfe) had made a commitment in the House of Commons. As Lord Chancellor in 1956 he could not bring himself to be a party to dishonouring that commitment, however inconvenient it had turned out to be. Kilmuir's conscience won the day. The matter was settled; it only remained to make provision for the token payment in 1957/8 which, back on 1 August, the Authority had publicly expressed its readiness to accept in 1956/7. This was a formality over which the civil servants felt able to take their time. By their standards they did not take long; but it was long enough to involve Clark in a humiliation which was as painful as it was unnecessary.

On 12 September Clark wrote to Dr Hill to convey the Authority's 'very great satisfaction' with the assurances it had received. He went on to urge that the decision about what to provide in the 1957/8 Estimates should be taken not later than the end of October. By then the winter schedules, effective from 1 January, would be in an advanced state of preparation and the Authority was anxious that its first attempt to achieve a better balance should be made in the winter months. 'As I told you, we would be prepared to help those sustaining programmes out of our own resources for one quarter, but we could not do it for longer than this. Our support of the first quarter's programmes would be dependent on whether or not an adequate sum of money was going to be in the Estimates.' Hill replied on 27 September saying that he could not guarantee the date by which the decision would be given 'but I will do my best to let you have it as soon as I can'. This masterpiece of bureaucratic verbiage reflects perhaps something of Hill's feeling of boredom.[15]

Clark asked the Chairmen of the programme companies to come and see him on 28 September. 'I should like to let you all know how things stand, and also have some preliminary discussion as to how the money should be used in the event of our getting it.' They had not been told of the events of the past month, although they could be expected to have read the Authority's statement on 1 August.

The formal application required by the Post Office went off on 4 October. It said that the programmes necessary for a balanced output were religious, political and 'discussions of international and national problems' to which should be added scientific, documentary, educational and cultural programmes. The programme companies had in some degree succeeded on their own account in making a worthwhile contribution under these heads. But this contribution was, said the letter, insufficient in quantity and not wholly adequate in quality, and the Authority's immediate concern was that its weight and range should be significantly and speedily increased. Such a development could not be secured from the companies' current financial resources.

The grant was needed both to sustain and improve current programmes and to introduce about four more each week within the stated categories. The provision required for 1957/8 totalled £515,000. In conclusion Clark said: 'Perhaps I should add that I have had preliminary discussions with the Chairmen of the four programme companies now operating and am assured of their co-operation in achieving the Authority's intentions'.[16] This request fell short of seeking the maximum grant but went well beyond the naming of any token sums, such as on 1 August the Authority had declared it would have been ready to accept in the current financial year of 1956/7. There had indeed been an exchange of information with the companies which seemed to show that the full cost, direct and indirect, including all overheads, of the five current balancing programmes (excluding news) as well as the four or five additional programmes the Authority would like to introduce would be some £700,000 over a year. It was thought unwise for the Authority to provide the whole of this sum, leaving the companies to spend nothing.

It took Dr Hill until 27 November – nearly eight weeks – to convey the Government's decision which was that provision would be made in the Broadcasting Estimate for 1957/8 for the payment of £100,000 as a 'purely temporary device . . . for the purpose of procuring the inclusion in the programmes of items which in its opinion are necessary for improving the balance of the subject matter of the programmes'. The day was Tuesday and Clark was abroad in India, but he was expected back early the following week. On Wednesday the position was made public by arranged question and answer in Parliament. On Thursday the four programme companies collectively issued a statement declaring that the proposal was unrealistic and that they [sic] did not wish to avail themselves of the offer. Informed of it by Adorian of A-R shortly before its impending release, Fraser made clear that the Authority would be greatly displeased.

After the lapse of twenty-five years the companies' statement can still only be described as both arrogant and artless, and it caused great distress at Princes Gate. These four Chairmen had, of course, laboured during 1956 under almost ceaseless financial strain, and Wills in particular had staked a fortune on his belief that all would come well within the foreseeable future. By November he knew, as did the others, that the tide had indeed turned: his relief and his pride can be understood even if this first demonstration of them was maladroit.

The press observed these proceedings with a pretty cynical and jaundiced eye. Nobody was awarded good marks; neither the companies nor the Authority nor the Government. Given that, in common with the rest of the press, they were unaware of what had happened back in August (for this was a story which never leaked), the *Observer* made fair comment in their issue of 2 December:

Last spring, the Independent Television Authority informed the Postmaster-General that Commercial Television programmes were so 'unbalanced' – that is so lacking serious and informational content – that the Television Act of 1954 was not being complied with. The Authority asked the Government for the £750,000 which may annually be spent to maintain 'balance' . The Postmaster-General, on grounds of economy, refused. Now the Government has suddenly announced that next year the sum of £100,000 will be available for 'balancing'. Has the Government suddenly but belatedly come to the conclusion that the case of the ITA is two-fifteenths better than it seemed in July, or, alternatively, that the country's economic situation is going to be two-fifteenths better next year than this? The Government's eccentricity has already received a prompt comment in the action of the four companies that put on programmes: they have refused to have anything to do with the paltry sum. But that should not be the end of the matter: MPs should press the Government to explain the reason for this extraordinary decision.

Actually Members of Parliament did nothing of the kind. Like Dr Hill himself they were not all that interested, and following Suez, they certainly had other things on their minds.

The Authority did not immediately see that the money provided for in the Estimates could not now become available. But it had been irreparably tainted. Dr Hill's diagnosis had been maddeningly right; there was nothing wrong with the patient which could not be cured by a dose of nasty medicine administered by the ITA.

So the youngster was to survive and thrive and be properly brought up without assistance from the State. It was the concept of grants from public funds which died. The obsequies were all over before Christmas. On 30 November, the day after the companies' statement, Littler of ATV wrote to Fraser saying that, since they had agreed to associate themselves with the application for a grant, his Board has 'come to the conclusion that it would be unwise to accept Treasury money in respect of an operation which can be made self-financing' and they had found that two of the other programme companies (about the third he did not really know) shared their views. They were intending to seek the earliest opportunity of telling the Authority so after Clark had returned. So the PMG's statement, of which they had had no prior notice, had been a disturbing shock.

Clark's first act after his return from India was to write on 5 December to Dr Hill expressing his astonishment at the statement put out by the programme companies.

I must tell you, firstly, that for a year they (the companies) have been urging me most strongly to ask the Government to provide some money under Section 11 and have frequently charged me with slackness and inefficiency in not getting a grant sooner; and secondly that, before finally applying to you for the grant, I saw all the chairmen of the companies and explained to them precisely what I was doing. They all agreed enthusiastically, and we even went so far as to consider the ways in which such money, should it be forthcoming, should be used.

I need not describe my feelings about the programme companies' volte-face. It remains to be seen what we can now do with them.[17]

To see what he could do with them, as Clark put it, was the occasion for a meeting on 14 December – Bernstein, Littler, Warter and Wills on the one side, Clark and Fraser on the other. Clark did not mince his words. Small as the sum might seem to the companies, the Government's agreement to it was a remarkable gesture of confidence in the Authority and established an important point of principle. The companies' purported rejection of the grant had come as an unpleasant shock, had neutralised his efforts and made them appear foolish. In any case the grant would be made to the Authority and it was not for the companies to claim to reject it. Wills replied that he had sincerely expected Clark to share the companies' view that £100,000 was so small as to be insulting. His Board wished him to ask whether any indication had ever been given that less than the full £750,000 would be granted. Clark said that the PMG had mentioned the possibility of a token grant and he, Clark, had taken the view that this would be better than nothing at all. Wills went on that he had been instructed to make a strong protest that the companies had not been consulted about the acceptance of a lesser sum than £750,000: his company had never wanted to incur the odium of accepting public assistance for less than £750,000. Clark rejected the protest; he had been in no way bound to consult with the companies about the size of the grant. Warter and Bernstein both also dwelt on the smallness of the grant as the determining factor, but Littler repeated that his Board was on principle against any grant, even the full one.

Clark stressed his view that the most important thing was the precedent for payment of a grant in future years. Meanwhile, however small the grant might be, there would always be programmes for which its use could be justified. The chances of receiving any further grant had been prejudiced, perhaps irretrievably. He could accept the logic of ATV's argument of principle, but could not see the validity of the argument of the other three.

There was a meeting of the Board of A-R on 18 December 1956, when Wills reported fully on the row with the ITA. The Board unanimously decided to convey to the ITA their regret that the public announcement made by the four contractors had proved unwelcome to Clark, and their surprise that Clark should, without prior consultation with, or even subsequent notification to, the four companies, have varied his approach to the PMG from that agreed as recently as September 1956. Action was duly taken by Groocock, the Company Secretary.

Meeting that same day the Authority took note of 'the greatly improved financial position of the programme companies'. It agreed that as a first step it would formulate an opinion on what was necessary for balance, as a basis of discussion with the companies; if they felt that the Authority's demands were too extragavant it would then be open for them to ask for a grant from the £100,000.[18]

Littler wrote again to Clark on 20 December saying how distressed he would be that any action to which he was party could have caused Clark any embarrassment. 'It is so unfortunate that the Postmaster-General should have made his statememement before the Chairmen of companies involved could seek another interview with you to make known their change of attitude in the matter.' He went on to say, as regards balance, that 'in the new schedules which will be operating in the Spring, I do not think you will have any cause for disappointment'. To which letter Clark, after Christmas, gratefully replied, adding that 'if balanced programmes of high quality can be achieved without the expenditure of public money, it will be the best justification of those who sponsored the Television Act and we shall all be delighted'. Clark might also justifiably have said that it was equally unfortunate that the PMG had not made his statement a couple of months earlier, in which case there would have been no talk from the companies' side of the odium of public assistance or of being insulted by the smallness of the grant.

The Secretary of the Authority (Anthony Pragnell) replied to Groocock:

The Authority cannot accept that its Chairman was under some obligation to consult the four programme contractors or even inform them about a private exchange of views with the Postmaster-General. The question of its right to grants under Section 11 was well known to be one on which the Authority had very decided views. The further question whether, in the light of the national economic position and other factors, the Authority would regard a much smaller sum than £750,000 as a sufficient recognition of its claims was one which called for a reply on the

Authority's own behalf, irrespective of any opinions which the programme contractors might have.[19]

The new companies which had been appointed to serve parts of Scotland
and Wales were not yet ready to provide a service, and can hardly therefore
be said to have *locus standi* in this dispute. However, the ingenious Mark
Chapman-Walker, whose role in establishing Independent Television has
been described in Part I and who was now Managing Director of Television,
Wales and the West (TWW Ltd), wrote in January to Fraser:

> I mentioned to you that my Board was not in agreement with the other
> contractors about the refusal of the £100,000 offer of the ITA. Since then I
> have had a Welsh Board Meeting and it was generally felt that some part
> of this money should be allocated to our station to help with the provision
> of Welsh language broadcasts. It seems to me that this type of broadcast is
> the exact form of programme for which the money was intended, and
> therefore this is to formally let you know that when we are in a position to
> do so we shall apply for a sum to be agreed, at the same time being of the
> opinion that the amount proposed is totally inadequate for the services of
> Independent Television as a whole.[20]

On 5 February the Authority decided to consider this request later in the
light of circumstances. When it did so in August it gave TWW a dusty answer
(Chapter 29). In any case within a month of TWW going on the air in
January 1958, the Supplementary Estimates of the Post Office recorded the
earlier provision for a grant of £100,000 to ITA as a 'saving'. That was, in the
correct Parliamentary form, the official burial of the prospective grant.

Consulted by the author in July 1979, Spencer Wills (whose memory of
these events, as of others in 1956, was exceptionally clear) was surprised to
hear of the statement issued by the four companies on 29 November. He did
not himself recall anything having been said on behalf of his company until
the meeting with Clark on 14 December and it seems probable that he did
not personally authorise it.

This long-forgotten affair of the £750,000 may seem of small importance
now, but it has a constitutional significance which surely merits the
attention it has received in the first three parts of this volume. We have noted
how ambivalent about it were Ministers and Parliament in 1954, and we
have described the lengths to which the first Chairman of the Authority was
prepared to go to establish that Independent Television should be financed
not solely out of advertising income but, to some extent, out of income from

the licence fees. We have seen how government at the departmental level sought to make payments from the 'fund' dependent upon their own valuation of the programme plans. Furthermore we have seen how the companies, when *in extremis*, were keen to get the money, but how, for differing reasons, they spurned it once their own income was secure.

The difficulties for Independent Television in its relations with government have been increased by the fact that it can easily speak, and often has done, with different voices. The ITA and the companies, collectively and individually, have sometimes been at cross purposes. This hapless episode was an early example. It would be some time yet before the shrewder company bosses learnt that progress could best be made by resolving so far as possible their differences among themselves and then approaching government, when that was necessary, collectively rather than severally; and never without the foreknowledge, if not always the agreement, of the Authority.

Charles Hill was a man of action, but he also had a sixth sense for discerning when masterly inactivity should be the order of the day. Instinctively rather than rationally, he recognised Section 11 as a horse which would not run, and his tactics were brilliantly successful. We shall encounter in Chapter 30 another instance of this sixth sense. His abrupt dismissal from the Macmillan government in 1962 was to prove in due course to be of great value to British broadcasting.

28

MEN AND MONEY

(i) THE 'MAJOR GAMBLE' OF JOHN SPENCER WILLS

If in the closing stages of the ITA's struggle to secure its promised slice of the licence fee the behaviour of John Spencer Wills appeared arrogant both to the Authority and some detached observers, it can at least be said in his defence that he had a great deal to be arrogant about.

In January, 1946, at the age of 41 Wills had become Managing Director of the British Electric Traction Company, of which Harold (Harley) Drayton became Chairman in June of that year. Immediately, these two men were engaged in a fight with the Labour Government to avoid nationalisation. It was the risk that confronted their bus, electricity and gas interests which led them and their fellow directors to diversify into other areas. One of these was the acquisition in 1947 of a substantial interest in Broadcast Relay Service Ltd which had been founded in the twenties to offer subscribers a better reception of their wireless programmes than was possible by means of aerials of their own. Wills took over the Chairmanship and Managing Directorship, and so well did he develop the company that by 1954 they had over half a million subscribers to their wired sound service in more than 120 towns and cities and were also providing wired television services in some of these same places. Overseas in many Commonwealth countries their development had been even more remarkable. By this time the relay company had become generally known as Rediffusion, and in the ten years of their association with BET their group assets had increased from £4 million in 1947 to £25 million in 1956.[1]

Initially Rediffusion regarded the prospective arrival of commercial television with some aversion and their Board unanimously approved on 9 January 1953 a resolution that it would not be in their interests for commercial television to be introduced. At that time they were thinking more in terms of wired relay than of set rental and they did not rate the business prospects in the field of television very highly. But later, Wills persuaded the Board that, as commercial television was bound to come, they ought to be involved in it. In doing so, he was strongly influenced by the imaginative and ingenious Paul Adorian, who had become Deputy Managing Director. Interviewed in connection with ITV's twenty-fifth anniversary Adorian claimed that 'between January 1949 and June 1954 I wrote fifteen papers assessing the various aspects of a television operation'.[2] These considerations coincided with similar thinking in Associated Newspapers on the part of Stuart McClean and Frank Coven. Wills was acquainted with McClean and so it turned out that over lunch on 21 April 1954 Lord Rothermere as Chairman of Associated Newspapers, McClean as Managing Director and Wills as Chairman of Rediffusion reached an understanding whereby if either company decided to go in for commercial television, it would only do so in partnership with the other company.

The opening words of the resultant application to the ITA for a London contract on 8 September were:

> Broadcast Relay Service Ltd (associated with the British Electric Traction Company Ltd) and Associated Newspapers Ltd are in a position jointly to form and operate a 'Programme Contractor Company'. It has not yet been decided under what name the company should operate but for the purpose of convenience this partnership is referred to throughout this application as the 'Television Company'.

Possibly the most significant words in this paragraph were those in parenthesis. Rediffusion's very rapid development and the difficulty of getting permission from the Capital Issues Committee to raise more money had left them short of capital, and so they decided to invite BET to share equally with them their 50 per cent participation in the Television Company. Directors and senior executives were also invited to put up money on the same terms as the three companies: some did and some did not.

The legendary Harley Drayton was a financier from the world of investment trusts and investment banking, and head of what was known as 'the Drayton Group', with its nerve centre at 117 Old Broad Street. He liked nothing better than being legendary, and he probably did not greatly mind the highly inaccurate assertion made later by Clive Jenkins: 'Associated-Rediffusion Ltd *is* Mr Harold C. Drayton. To understand the structure and the interlockings in the commercial television programme contracts, this is a central fact which must be seized and never relinquished.'[3] Drayton was

certainly important to ITV, as we shall see, but the leadership of this
television company belonged to Wills, and it was upon his shoulders that fell
the main burden of sustaining Independent Television during its year of
agony – 1956. The importance of Drayton in this context was his association
with Wills: too many commentators have put the names the other way
round.

By November 1954 'Programme Contractor Company' had become
Associated-Rediffusion Ltd with Arthur W. Groocock as its Secretary, and
Captain Tom Brownrigg RN as its General Manager. One half of the shares
in the new company was taken by Associated Newspapers and a quarter
each by BET and Rediffusion. Wills was the Chairman and Stuart McClean
the Deputy Chairman. The preparations already described in Chapter 20
were wildly expensive and, as BET's official history puts it: 'Money poured
out faster than it came in. The total losses for the period up to July 1956 were
a fearful £2.7 million, and in the following April the company's total
unsecured advances amounted to the huge sum of £4.75 million'. (In 1981
terms these figures would be at least five times greater.) Professor Mingay's
restrained history[4] of the events that occurred in August 1956 (just at the
time when Clark was preparing his letter of resignation to the PMG) barely
conceals the tension of those days:

> At this point, with Associated-Rediffusion in very deep financial water
> and the future at best obscure, there occurred a crisis of confidence. Could
> the company weather the storm? Could it eventually make profits, and
> profits large enough to recover the frightening losses and repay the very
> heavy borrowings which had been incurred? Mr Wills, at any rate, had
> no doubt that what he had originally conceived a 'reasonable
> speculation' still remained reasonable. Associated Newspapers, however,
> had taken fright. There transpired the famous lunch and dinner in August
> 1956 when a most remarkable transaction took place.

An account of this transaction by Wills himself was published in the April
1961 issue of 'Fusion', the A-R house magazine. The lunch was with Mr Neill
Cooper-Key, a director of Associated Newspapers. Cooper-Key asked Wills
what he thought of the prospects of A-R in view of its enormous losses. Wills
replied that he thought the company would start to earn profits as from next
January, and would not lose much more in the meantime.

> He asked, if I was so optimistic, would I care to buy Associated
> Newspapers' holding? I replied that I would certainly be prepared to

recommend my Boards to do so, at a price. He asked 'What price?' and I replied 'Probably at 25 per cent discount'. He suggested that this would not be very generous but I replied that as we had lost 75 per cent of our money, it would really be a very high price. Nothing more was said about this subject and I thought little more about it.

On the next occasion Lord Rothermere was also present:

> When the ladies had left us after dinner, Lord Rothermere said, without any preamble, 'Are you still willing to buy us out?' I replied that I hadn't thought any more about it but, when he pressed me, I said I would be prepared to recommend my Boards to do so at 25 per cent discount. He at once said, 'Would you be prepared to sell us your shares?' This was completely unexpected. Nevertheless I replied, 'Yes, at a price!' 'At what price?' he asked. My reply was 'At 25 per cent premium – I think that would be a fair "jobbers" turn!' 'But you would be willing to buy ours at 25 per cent discount.' 'Yes.' 'Done,' said Lord Rothermere.

With Drayton's agreement the transaction was completed. Professor Mingay's BET history records:

> Thus, confessing to one sleepless night, Mr Wills completed a deal which involved the cash payment of £1.65 million for the purchase of 200,000 shares and £2 million of unsecured loans and loan stock – and this at a time when, under the restrictive eye of the Capital Issues Committee, the chances of raising new capital were, to say the least, slim.

As recently as 6 July, Rothermere had said at the Annual General Meeting of Associated Newspapers that set growth and the results already attained by advertisers 'encourage us to view the future with confidence'.

Wills told Rothermere that the easiest and quickest way to put through the deal would be for him to act on behalf of the British Electric Traction Co. Ltd, leaving the division of shares between BET and Rediffusion and individual shareholders to a later date. However, he would only agree to buy four-fifths of it, because he thought it politically inexpedient to let Associated Newspapers out of television altogether. His account went on:

> As soon as the terms of the Agreement had been settled between Lord Rothermere and myself and committed to writing (all of which took over a fortnight), I telephoned to Mr Drayton . . . and told him about the

deal. He asked me if I would mind going over to see him in Suffolk and taking Mr Adorian with me, so that he could satisfy himself that he would be justified in supporting it. This was arranged, and Mr Adorian and I stayed the night at Plumton Hall where we discussed the pros and cons of the bargain and the likely division of shares between BET and Rediffusion and the individual shareholders. Mr Drayton agreed to join me in my recommendations to the Board and he and I accordingly signed three copies of the Agreement, which I had taken with me. After my return to Sussex I took them to Lord Rothermere and procured his signature.

This deal was approved and ratified by both the Rediffusion and BET boards at their September meetings . . .

The Rediffusion board subsequently decided not to take up its full entitlement, and so it turned out that BET became the majority shareholder in A-R. By early 1958 Associated Newspapers had secured an opportunity to become shareholders in a new company, Southern Television, but the ITA's approval was conditional upon their divesting themselves of their remaining 10 per cent holding in Associated-Rediffusion. These were bought by Rediffusion Ltd at, as Wills described it, a 'generous premium of 400 per cent'. Wills remarked in April 1961 that the result of his major gamble was that the annual profits of A-R were by then double the combined annual profits of the BET and Rediffusion Ltd at the time the project started.

In evidence to the Pilkington Committee in December 1960, A-R described themselves as a private company formed on 18 November 1954 having its share capital held as to 50 per cent by the BET company, a public company with upwards of 35,000 shareholders, as to 37 per cent by Rediffusion Ltd, a public company with upwards of 10,000 shareholders; and as to 12 per cent by private individuals.

At a meeting of the shareholders of Rediffusion Ltd on 29 July 1959, Wills, as Chairman, said:

You may have wondered why you do not own more than 37 per cent of an undertaking which bears the name of your company. The reason is simple: right up to the end of 1956 the enterprise remained so highly speculative, and needed such large sums poured into it, that your board just did not feel justified in risking any more of your money . . . When, in 1956, the losses of Associated-Rediffusion had amounted to £2,600,000 and Associated Newspapers decided they had had enough (later the losses reached £3,250,000) your board thought it prudent, in view of our then strained financial position, to ask British Electric Traction to take up more than their share. Now that Associated-Rediffusion has had such an outstanding commercial success it may be difficult to realise how worried and depressed we all were for so long a period. I, perhaps, more than most, have every reason to remember.

In the light of all this what needs to be said of the claim in 1961 by Clive Jenkins that Associated-Rediffusion *is* Mr Harold C. Drayton? The short answer is that it does not make sense, and has no relation to the reality of the distribution of power in ITV. In those days the men who ran A-R were John Spencer Wills, who gave a disproportionately large amount of his time to their affairs, Paul Adorian who became Managing Director in 1956, supported by their indefatigable General Manager, Brownrigg, and the Secretary, Arthur Groocock.

Drayton died on 7 April 1966 at the age of sixty-four – 'a commanding figure in the City' as *The Times* obituary expressed it. As the years had passed between 1945 and 1966 the range of his financial, commercial and industrial interests had become more and more extensive.

Although he was never in the public eye, the *Financial Times* obituary was wrong in describing him as 'the magnate who was self-effacing'. He was very much an extrovert, and as those rare few who knew him well, such as Lord Barnetson and Wills, would probably concede, he was not above claiming personal credit for achievements which were by no means exclusively his own. The account given of an interview with him in Anthony Sampson's *Anatomy of Britain Today*, which implied that he himself masterminded the deal with Rothermere, provides a good example: the name of Wills did not get a mention.[5] Drayton cultivated his own legend.

Drayton's interest in television was something of a self-indulgence, as was his interest in newspapers. However, as regards the latter, he genuinely saw himself as a newspaper proprietor in the tradition of Northcliffe, Beaverbrook and Camrose, and it would certainly have occurred to him to wonder why he never received similar 'recognition'. United Newspapers were a greatly cherished enterprise. Of course, he became very dependent upon 'Bill' Barnetson (the late Lord Barnetson) who joined the Board in 1958 and came south from Edinburgh to become joint Managing Director in 1962. Comparing Barnetson's role *vis-à-vis* Drayton in newspapers and Wills' role as regards television, the distinction to note is that Wills was from the outset Chairman of A–R whereas Barnetson only became Chairman of United Newspapers after Drayton's death.

It will be recalled that Wills effectively struck his bargain with Lord Rothermere entirely on his own, telling Drayton about it afterwards and securing his indispensable support. Barnetson's great achievement in securing the United Newspapers merger (by acquisition) with Yorkshire Post Newspapers came in 1969, three years after Drayton had died. In his careful and skilfully written account of Wills' 'coup of the century' in 1956 Peter Black does justice to Wills' achievement; but at one point he says 'Drayton's confidence was unshakeable'.[6] If by that he was referring to Drayton's confidence *in Wills*, then doubtless he was right. But in ITV circles in 1956 there was one man, and only one man, who was unreservedly prepared to back his hunch with all the financial reserves he could get his hands on. That man was John Spencer Wills. Black writes: 'It is doubtful whether the companies of 1956 really were, as the ITA afterwards told the Pilkington Committee, "on the brink of complete collapse". It is unimaginable that Harley Drayton and British Electric Traction would have allowed this to happen.' But to those involved it was quite imaginable. It did not happen principally because Wills was BET, Rediffusion Ltd and A-R all at the same time. If he was not arrogant, then at any rate he was proud and very, very determined.

To recognise that Wills and his associates were ambitious for power is not to endorse the facile theories of Clive Jenkins and other searchers for blues under the bed. Challenged about the alleged pervasive interest in ITV of the Eagle Star Insurance Company (of which Drayton was a director) Ivone Kirkpatrick, Clark's successor as Chairman of the ITA, said to Jenkins in 1960 'We have no attitude to cross-directorship and are interested only in controlling interests. . . . This question of cross-directorships is not one of principle but of quantitative judgement. You can't raise thirteen effective companies without cross-directorships.'[7]

(ii) THE PERFECT TIMING OF CECIL KING

We saw in Chapter 11 how the *Daily Mirror*, campaigning against the participation of Associated Newspapers and the Kemsley Press in Independent Television, set about rocking the fragile little boat in November 1954, but how Cecil King later declared his continuing interest in commercial television and his decision to move in 'after the second bankruptcy'.

In 1951 King – nephew of Lord Northcliffe – had managed to become Chairman of the *Daily Mirror*. The story of his move into television began with a meeting of some gravity which took place at Princes Gate on 25 January 1956 between Sir Mark Turner and Mr J. A. L. Drummond from, respectively, Robert Benson, Lonsdale and Co. and S. G. Warburg and Co., acting on behalf of ATV, and Sir Ronald Matthews and Sir Henry Hinchliffe, representing the ITA. It was explained that the television company were in 'temporary financial difficulties' because they had had to start operating for only two days a week on the London station but had had to make the capital outlay and carry all the overheads made necessary by the fact that they would eventually be operating on a seven days a week basis. The gap between their start in London at weekends and their start in the Midlands on weekdays had been widened by the time wasted over the abortive plan to use existing BBC masts to accommodate ITV Band III aerials. The Authority representatives were reminded that the company had no private shareholders willing to put up extra finance and, although certain measures could be taken, it was going to be extremely difficult to raise in time all the extra £500,000 (additional to their existing £1 million) of capital necessary to finance their operations in the Midlands, which were due to begin in the middle of February. They could perhaps get by if the Authority were able to defer for about six months some £200,000 of rental. All the difficulties in the way of the Authority doing this at a time when it was financing itself out of a Government loan were rehearsed and the meeting broke up inconclusively. Subsequently, it was understood that the company were not going to press their request.

When the company next approached the Authority they did so, not in order to say that Benson, Lonsdales and Warburgs had solved their problem, but to say that the problem could be solved provided the Authority was prepared to agree to a certain course of action. Littler and 'Jamie' Drummond called on Clark and Fraser on 4 April. It was now clear that the company were grossly under-capitalised; they were losing money at the rate of just under £1 million a year. Unless fresh capital could be found they would be forced into liquidation. It had not been easy for the company to find anyone willing to put a large sum of money into a concern which had been losing so heavily, but nevertheless an offer had come from the *Daily Mirror*. When the Authority next met on 10 April they agreed with alacrity that ATV might accept the offer provided only that the *Mirror*'s holding of ordinary shares did not exceed 25 per cent of the total and that they did not have more than three directors on the Board.

Cecil King's story as recounted in his letter to Norman Collins on 1 April 1979 is as follows:

I wanted to join a group that had expertise on the electronic side and, above all, in light entertainment to which we could provide a knowledge of the outside world. I told my people we would come in after the second bankruptcy, as I foresaw a large expenditure before any possible return. But one day I had lunch with Donald McClean, then Managing Director of the *Daily Mail* and a sort of cousin. From him I got the impression that there would be no bankruptcies and that I had better move fast if I did not want to be left out in the cold. At that time it seemed the most promising group was ATV as it included Pye and Prince Littler. We had been in touch at various points – including a young woman from California whose name I forget . . . Actually I was very lucky as you did not really need our money. The tide had already turned. Don McClean then went out with cancer of the throat and Esmond sold out . . . We and Rediffusion were lucky.

I do not recollect any opposition to the *Mirror* becoming involved. I was in favour of commercial television from the start as the only way of putting some life into BBC television.[8]

Donald was the name by which Stuart McClean was known to his friends, but for rather obvious reasons it had fallen out of use. The young woman from California was Suzanne Warner, a friend of Littler's and a shareholder in ITPC. Esmond was, of course, Lord Rothermere, whose dealings with Wills have already been described. There was indeed no opposition to the *Mirror* joining ATV: not from any quarter.

But the story was fully reported in the national press on 21 April. ATV's announcement had spoken of a new capital issue of £750,000 which would help to double their capital: this new issue, together with other money to be raised, would increase the company's capital from £1,020,000 to £2,020,000, subject to the approval of the Capital Issues Committee; and it would be used for the 'general development of the company'. Cecil King's statement said that the entry of the *Mirror* into the television field should create no surprise. 'The possibilities of commercial television are vast, and it would be quite ridiculous for modern expanding newspapers to ignore the fact.' He went on to praise the 'progressive course' already followed by Associated Newspapers in taking a 50 per cent interest in the running of A-R and to condemn as 'prejudiced and unreal' the attitude of the *Express* in attacking commercial television.

The deal went through on 29 May. To the existing 75,000 ordinary shares and 657,000 'A' ordinary shares were added a further 75,000 ordinary shares and 670,000 'A' ordinary shares all for cash at par. Half of the new shares were offered to the existing shareholders in proportion to their holdings; the other half were bought at par by the *Daily Mirror* Group. Ellis

Birk, accountant and business adviser of the *Mirror* Group, and Hugh Cudlipp, editor of the *Daily Mirror*, joined the Board of ATV. Subsequently Patrick Gibson also became a member of the Board, representing the Westminster Press Provincial Newspapers Group and the *Birmingham Post and Mail*, both being already substantial shareholders in the company.

In the end, by 1960 when the Pilkington Committee began its work, the *Daily Mirror* and *Sunday Pictorial* each held 13 per cent of ATV's shares; Littler as nominee of Moss Empires 27 per cent; Pye 11 per cent; Westminster Press 7 per cent; *Birmingham Post* 5 per cent and AEI 5 per cent.

A year or so after these events, in August 1957, *The Times* published an article entitled 'Moving Out of the Red' which elicited a letter from Val Parnell who had become Managing Director of ATV in their darkest days of January 1956. This letter highlighted the situation of the company when Cecil King decided to come in from the cold:

> He (your Special Correspondent) said we had the luck to start with London weekends commanding an audience the early advertiser would be bound to covet. Here your Special Correspondent is entirely wrong. The luck would have been with us if we had the five London week days, which we would have much preferred to our seven days a week operation of London weekends and Midland week days, for this, as you will appreciate, entailed expense of two complete operations, one mounted in London and one mounted in Birmingham. Furthermore, early television advertisers are interested mainly in week days, and Saturday was in the beginning considered by them to be a very unsuitable day because it preceded a non-shopping day. It was only because my company provided programmes that consistently secured the top ratings that we were able eventually, after nearly a year, to convince the advertisers that it was worth while advertising with us on Saturdays.

King himself says that, in the event, ATV did not need his money. It is true that revenue mounted so fast that the company could have managed without the *Mirror* money. Nevertheless it was timely reinforcement and the contribution of the *Mirror* to the company went well beyond mere financial backing.

The mystery remains, and it belongs more to the history of Associated Newspapers than of Independent Television. How could it have been that, in face of the example set by cousin Cecil, despite the praise publicly lavished on him by that cousin for taking a 50 per cent share in the plum of the four franchises and despite the protests of the well-informed Frank

Coven, Rothermere thought it prudent to divest himself of four-fifths of his holding as late as August of that year? Peter Black loyally does his best when he says: 'All that can be said is that on the information available of the projections made Wills's assessment was careful, reasoned and right, and Rothermere's was careful, reasoned and wrong.'[9] Well, yes, perhaps so. But if King regards himself as lucky, how much more so was Rothermere who, after making what still appears to be a serious misjudgement, was given the chance to take a major holding in Southern Television at a time when those first hazardous franchises had, together with those awarded in 1957 and 1958, become concerns of plenteous profitability.

(iii) HOW 'MR SIDNEY' RODE THE STORM

The personality of Lord Bernstein, now in his eighties, has somehow eluded everyone who has so far tried to write about it. The character of his brother Cecil, whose name is as indissolubly linked with ITV as Sidney's, is less complex and less elusive, but even he – whose contribution to the development of ITV has most certainly been greatly underrated – presents the other problem of understanding the closely knit relationships within the Bernstein family. It baffles outsiders to determine what, within the Granada complex, has derived from Sidney and what from Cecil. And then it is also necessary to take account of those very few outsiders who have been admitted to the inner counsels of the company, such as Victor Peers, Joe Warton and Denis Forman. Together, under Sidney's leadership, they created Granadaland – Granada From the North.

As well as being (what no employee in Granada was ever allowed to forget) a life-long admirer of Barnum, Sidney counted among his greatest friends Lord Radcliffe – Cyril Radcliffe, former Director General of the Ministry of Information, a Lord of Appeal and the most extreme of all the opponents of commercial television. It is in one respect a sad deprivation that Radcliffe never had the opportunity of exercising in relation to Bernstein that remarkable insight he possessed into the characters of people who are at one and the same time almost flamboyant and extremely reserved. He displayed just this insight in his privately circulated memoir of Brendan Bracken, the wartime Minister of Information. It is a loss which we can, however, gratefully accept; for Bracken died young in 1958 at the age of 57, whereas, happily, Bernstein has continued to enliven the worlds of broadcasting, the cinema, publishing, television rental and (astonishingly) motorway catering right through the 1970s.

These three – Radcliffe, Bracken and Bernstein – shared in common a profound admiration for the BBC, which in differing ways determined their approach to Independent Television. A fourth name should be linked with this trio – that of Sir William Haley – who was Director General of the BBC from 1944–52 before he became Editor of *The Times*. Radcliffe and Haley eventually forgave Bernstein for throwing in his lot with ITV; Bracken's position was different because his political convictions demanded his tacit support for ITV – tacit because he could not bring himself to join with the young men of the Conservative One Nation Group in action hurtful to the BBC. Not all readers will perhaps recognise these four men as having been close wartime associates or be able to appreciate how deep was the influence of those years on their attitudes to the media and in particular to broadcasting. So it came about that Granada's opening programmes on 3 May 1956 included a tribute to the BBC.

Granada Theatres (subsequently Granada Group Ltd) was a family business and strongly wished to remain one. The Authority was no less keen to preserve the character of the company, and its contract with Granada Television contained a special provision requiring that its consent was needed for any transaction that would have the result that a specified list of persons, mostly members of the families of Mr Sidney and Mr Cecil, would cease to hold at least 51 per cent of the voting shares of Granada Theatres. Here, therefore, was a highly reputable family concern founded on the cinema, which had now diversified into television. Any threat to the Granada Group's control would be anathema to the Bernsteins and also to the Authority.

As has been seen in Chapter 14, Bernstein had been upset by the breakdown of the plan for sharing the BBC's television mast and the consequence that programme transmissions began in Lancashire on 3 May and in Yorkshire on 3 November. It is indisputable that these dates would in any circumstances have been less than ideal, to say the least, for a company starting a new television service designed to pay its way and eventually become profitable. How much worse were they when the country was experiencing a sharp recession and advertisers were holding back from the London and Midlands transmissions to such an extent as to place the first two companies on the air in financial difficulties which were already widely known and were generating much alarm and despondency.

As early as 5 September 1955 – before ITV began – and before the plans for sharing the BBC mast at Holme Moss high on the Pennines, broke down – Bernstein had said in a letter to Fraser 'we have begun to doubt that starting during the summer months would be economical or advisable'[10] and correspondence on this and related subjects between the two continued right up to Christmas. By 4 January 1956 Bernstein was asking for an opportunity to address the Authority personally at one of its meetings and later made clear that the points he wished to discuss referred to the double payment for outside broadcasts reception equipment (there now being two masts rather than one); the cost and problems involved in operating a station for a population of 5 millions (i.e. west of the Pennines only in the first instance) as against the 12 to 13 covered by his whole contract area, and the cost of commencing a station in the summer instead of the autumn.

Eventually, but not until 18 April, Bernstein got his meeting with the Authority. When, on returning from a visit to America, Clark had received a note from Fraser explaining all the issues that had arisen with Granada he noted 'This really demands a meeting with Mr B'. Then on 19 April, he added in red ink 'And what a meeting!' Perhaps as much because he had been kept waiting so long as of his persuasive eloquence, Bernstein left the meeting with the ITA's agreement that he would be required to pay for outside broadcasting equipment at only one transmitter, the cost of the second set of equipment, about £15,000, being borne by the ITA itself.

Quite apart from the other ineluctable reasons for abandoning it, the one-transmitter plan would not have provided a Band III coverage in the northern area of more than 10 millions, whereas with two stations a coverage of a good 12 millions could be, and was, secured. The fact that Band III channels did not have as good a reach as the BBC's Band I channels was known to all four companies before the contracts were signed. If Granada had to wait six months without a Yorkshire income, so also did ABC. Their position was not really special: all four companies would have benefited if it had been possible to open all four stations simultaneously.

By the middle of June Granada were in real financial trouble and Bernstein's sense of grievance against the Authority which had led to the meeting on 18 April was, if anything, intensified. In a letter of 18 June he represented that all his oft-expressed forebodings had been realised. Advertising revenue had been seriously affected by opening in the summer; advertisers' budgets had been spent or allocated earlier in the year to contractors already on the air; and many advertisers were holding up orders until the additional potential of the Yorkshire area was available. ABC Television, the weekend contractor, had been able to start operating in the Midlands in February, and by offering both areas to advertisers had secured a great number of contracts which would otherwise have been at least shared with Granada. Since 3 May the other three contractors had cut their advertising rates, and given free bonus showings.

It certainly seemed to the Authority from the information it was able to gather that Granada's advertising revenue was very much lower in relation to coverage than that of the other companies; and on 19 June it decided to offer to absolve Granada from all liability for rental for six months on the understanding that the unpaid rental would be repaid later and subject to the agreement of the other companies.[11] However, on 3 July Clark reported that he had been informed that Granada did not wish the other companies to be approached about this offer.

From that time on Granada's financial problems receded from the Authority's agenda and were never to return. At a later date Bernstein was to reproach Fraser for having said something which might imply that at this time Granada were on the verge of bankruptcy. It was, of course, true that Barclays Bank had always stood stolidly behind Granada Theatres and were hardly likely to fail them now. Perhaps it is enough to rest on Bernstein's own words to the Authority on 18 June: 'Our losses are staggering but not as a result of any extravagance on capital expenditure, or operational costs'.

If the agreement which was shortly to be made between Bernstein and Wills had become public knowledge it is possible that the cry of 'collusion' would have reverberated around Westminster and the city. Precisely who, in addition to the two principal parties to the agreement, the Secretaries of the two companies, Joe Warton (Granada) and Arthur Groocock (A-R), and their legal advisers were aware of it remains obscure, although it can be taken for granted that the Boards of the two companies were informed, and it is inconceivable that Clark and Fraser at the ITA did not know enough to lead them to ask some very searching questions had they judged it prudent to do so. In the event the first public acknowledgement that this agreement had been made came in Bernstein's speech to the Granada Group shareholders in January 1959, and the first general account of the transaction was written by Peter Black in *The Mirror in the Corner*, published in 1972.

Bernstein spoke of 'a working arrangement with another programme contractor for the exchange of programmes and networking. It was made in 1956 when we went on the air and protected our television subsidiary from heavy losses. We think the agreement was in the best interests of the company and of Independent Television.' It was signed by Wills, Groocock and Warton on 26 July. The actual text did not come into the hands of the ITA until 1 April 1959 in response to a request from Sir Ivone Kirkpatrick, the Chairman, addressed to the two company chairmen on 24 March.

The agreement was brief but none the less expressed with the utmost precision. It established the following arrangements:

1 Complete networking between London and the North.
2 Production by Granada of 15 per cent of the joint needs.
3 Supply by A-R of the balance of 85 per cent of the joint needs, either by production, purchase from other contractors, or supply of films.
4 Granada could network its 15 per cent live production to other contractors, in which case the revenue was credited against the costs of such programmes.
5 Arrangement terminable on 29 July 1960 by nine months' notice, otherwise continued to 29 July 1964.
6 A-R paid to Granada, for programmes received, the total costs of producing those programmes. Although A-R could require Granada to reduce their costs, and might take them to arbitration, the arbitrator would not consider the costs too high if they were no higher than A-R costs.
7 Up to February 1958 Granada paid to A-R the following percentages of net revenue received from advertising in the North:

   90 per cent of the first £1 million,
   87 per cent of the next £3 million,
   85 per cent on all above £4 million.

The net revenue of Granada was deemed to be 45 per cent of the combined net revenue received by A-R and Granada from advertising in the London and Northern areas; against payment so due was offset the payment due from A-R to Granada for production costs ((6) above) and this gave a 'net amount payable to A-R', the rest of the net revenue (i.e. 10 per cent, 12 per cent, and 15 per cent) being 'retainable by Granada'.
8 As from 1 March 1958, following amendments to the original agreement, the 'net amount payable to A-R' and the 'amount retainable by Granada' in the previous year became a basic figure. If the sum of those two amounts in the year commencing 1 March 1958 exceeded the figure for the year ended 28 February, A-R received the 1957/8 amount plus one half of the excess, with the proviso that if the total amount exceeded £4 millions, the A-R payment was reduced by one tenth of that excess. In brief, A-R got the 1957/8 amount plus 50 per cent of any extra up to £4 millions and 40 per cent of any extra above that figure.

Kirkpatrick's letters to Wills and Bernstein had spoken of the 'somewhat critical tone of some of the comments in recent months', for the city pages of the press had indeed contained a good deal of cautious comment, the bluntest of which came from 'Lex' of the *Financial Times* on 24 December 1958.

The smallness of the trading profit of the Granada Group whose
subsidiary, Granada TV Network, is the weekday Lancashire and
Yorkshire programme contractor for commercial television, is something
of a puzzle. Associated-Rediffusion reported a trading profit of £5.1
million for the year to April 30 last, and Associated Television an
operating profit of over £4 million for the same year. Granada now
reports a trading profit for the year to September 27, that is, a period
ending five months later, of only £1.1 million. So far as can be seen,
Granada's advertising revenue ought not to have been greatly different
from that of Associated-Rediffusion and ATV. Granada has, of course, also
cinema interests. Shareholders will naturally want to know why Granada
has not done as well as other programme contractors. For some time, City
rumour had had it that a profit sharing arrangement was entered into
when commercial television was passing through its bleakest phase. This
could explain the apparent relatively low level of profits. It would be
useful to have something official on the point, whether the rumour is true
or not.

A close study of the agreement in relation to the circumstances of the time
leaves it difficult to dispute the conclusions reached by Peter Black:

> Faced with the possibility of running out of money, and of having to part
> with family control as the price of getting more, at a time when the money
> was flowing out in thousands of pounds a day, an agreement that, as he
> had said, protected their television subsidiary from heavy losses was
> obviously in Granada's interests. It was a shrewd stroke that put the
> company on a fortune to nothing . . . Among some of those in Granada
> who knew of it, the agreement caused anguish. But Bernstein may have
> reasoned that either ITV would collapse or it would become open-cast
> goldmining. If it collapsed at least his deal with the Granada theatre
> chain would not go down with it.
> Meanwhile the arrangement left him free to create a company style.
> Nor were the terms onerous except by reference to the way things turned
> out. Nobody had forseen how huge the profits would become. With
> Granada's later earnings on such a scale Lord Bernstein may well look
> back and reflect that a man with two legs does not fret because he has not
> three.[12]

Another advantage to Granada which Black does not expressly mention
was the guarantee of exposure in the London area for the bulk of their

programme output. Both ATV and ABC came to see the importance of this factor too, but in this respect (as in some others) Bernstein was quicker on the ball.

Yet it is possible to question whether Bernstein might not have foreseen by July 1956 that the bonanza was already on the horizon. Was he not perhaps almost as guilty of misjudgement as was Rothermere one month later? Opinions differ as to exactly when signs of the turnround began to show themselves. Casting his mind back to that year, when he was sales director of ABC Television, George Cooper (later Managing Director of Thames Television) informed the author in August 1979:

I would say that the key month if one can be selected was probably May 1956, and then it began to be apparent that we were moving into a healthy situation for the autumn of that year, and although we may not have had all the bookings on the charts, discussions and meetings with agents and advertisers indicated that television was becoming a prime medium on the autumn schedules.

It is fair to say that Cooper would be the first to admit that he could be mistaken in setting the date so early and that others perhaps equally well placed to know would place the date some months later. There could perhaps have been in those days a communications weakness between the sales directors and their top managements; or, more likely, the former shrank from committing themselves to hasty judgements on which the whole future of their businesses depended.

So far as the Authority was concerned it might have asked for a copy of the Wills–Bernstein agreement much nearer to July 1956 than March 1959 when there was little more than a year to go before its expiry. Section 5 (2) of the Act had, as has been seen, made it the duty of the Authority to do all it could to secure that there was adequate competition to supply programmes between a number of contractors independent of each other both as to finance and control, and to this end it had devised the 'competitive optional network'. Neither Wills nor Bernstein were men who would with deliberation have acted in breach of the Act or of the contracts which were based on it. They had legal advisers of the highest competence and integrity from whom they accepted the advice that the agreement did not make Granada less than 'independent as to finance'. Preoccupied as they certainly were by the problems of ensuring survival until better days arrived, Clark and Fraser accepted this view without insisting, as they were empowered to do, on independent scrutiny by the Authority and its lawyers. They had regarded the arrangement as a commercial one between two companies and not of a kind that impaired their independence one from another.

Granada's own contractual obligation to the Authority was fulfilled if it produced (as indeed it did) 15 per cent of the programmes transmitted in its service area, and that was the quantity of programmes which, subject to the terms described above, A-R undertook to accept at a price that would meet the cost of production. In effect, Granada looked to A-R to guarantee the money which they had to spend to fulfil this minimum requirement which the Authority had laid down. Scrutinising the agreement in 1959 the Authority's own legal advisers questioned whether it left Granada 'independent as to finance'. If the price to be paid by Granada had been determined not by reference to their actual production costs but by prescribing a fixed sum equivalent to their foreseeable production costs the question would not have arisen. This legal issue was never argued out because in the totally changed financial situation of all the companies the guarantee had lost its original relevance. 'For all practical purposes' wrote Fraser in an internal memorandum dated 10 August 1959 'the guarantee is a dead letter.'[13]

Because of the huge advertising revenues which Granada, in common with the other companies, earned between 1957 and 1960, Granada paid A-R a very high insurance premium. According to Peter Black, the total sum taken by A-R within the four years was £8,044,238.[14] But the Northern company could well afford it. Bernstein achieved all his own objectives; and, moreover, Granada's reputation as a provider of enterprising and lively television grew apace. It is beyond dispute that Independent Television drew benefit from the deal and the programme dividends have been substantial ever since.

29

SCOTLAND, WALES AND THE SOUTH

(i) ROY THOMSON'S LICENCE

In 1956 I wrote to Roy Thomson, Chairman of Scotsman Publications Ltd, the letter he was most eagerly awaiting and which was destined to start him on a new life at the age of sixty-two and to transform, not so much the face of British broadcasting, as of the British press. For, as a direct consequence of the huge financial success of Scottish Television in the late fifties, he was able to acquire the entire chain of Lord Kemsley's newspapers and so lay the foundations of the Thomson press empire, and all the other enterprises of the Thomson Organisation which came about during the sixties.

My letter of 24 May described arrangements the ITA was making for a press conference in Glasgow about its plans for Scotland on Wednesday 30 May 'or on such other day as we may have to choose in the light of your negotiations with the Independent Television News Company'.[1] It enclosed a draft press statement stating that the Authority had decided to accept, subject to contract, the application of Scottish Television Ltd to supply all the programmes from the Authority's station in Central Scotland. It did not contain any formal offer of the contract: that did not reach him for another five days. Indeed it might not have reached him at all had he not recognised the implied message of my letter, which was to say that the time had come for him to end his protracted haggle with ITN over the fee he would pay for the national news service. Otherwise, it would be necessary either to call off the conference or to hold it in order to say that no appointment had been made and might well not be made for some time to come.

On the day of its receipt, 25 May, he wrote to Adorian, who had been acting for ITN in this matter:

We now accept that you will not allow us $33\frac{1}{3}$ per cent discount for the first three years but that you have confirmed a discount for that period of 25 per cent per year. I also confirm that I told you in view of these circumstances we will demand and expect to receive a news service for the Scottish station as satisfactory to us for our requirements in every respect as your newscasts are satisfactory to the other contractors for their requirements.

Just for good measure he added: 'We enter this whole arrangement with a deep sense of grievance and with considerable resentment.'[2]

Actually, of course, Thomson was walking on air. But it was not so apparent then as it is now that his intense eagerness to get into British commercial television had become an obsession which was almost irresistible. He was one of the few who then believed that commercial television in Britain could and would succeed financially, for to him it was axiomatic that what could succeed in North America could succeed in Britain too. Yet, as ever, he was looking for bargain basement prices and he would allow nobody to suppose that he would pay the price which was on the label in the window. Besides, he knew how much the early extension of ITV into Central Scotland, with a population within the prospective service area of nearer four millions than three, meant both to the Authority and to the financially hard-pressed contractors in England.

Of all the many open secrets that have existed in twenty-six years of ITV none could have been more open than the fact that Thomson would get the Scottish contract provided he could swallow its terms. This had been widely predicted ever since January. However, every propriety was observed. The Authority interviewed two other applicants as well as Thomson and his associates: it is sometimes forgotten that there were any at all. And I told him that he would have to arrive at the conference 'unheralded' and make sure that *The Scotsman* did not scoop the story – an exhortation which, according to Russell Braddon, he found most difficult to obey.[3] But he succeeded.

Thomson had arrived in Edinburgh to live as the new owner of *The Scotsman* in January 1954. The son of a barber in Toronto, he had made his way in Canada first as a salesman of spare car parts, radio sets, washing machines and refrigerators and then running radio stations on a shoe-string in small mining towns. He bought a newspaper and by 1953 he owned thirty of them, some as far south as Florida. His first contact with *The Scotsman* had been Colin McKinnon, an executive and minority shareholder, whom he had met at an Empire Press Union conference in 1950; but it was not until 1952 that he heard that a majority holding in the paper was up for sale. As soon as he could extricate himself from his none-too-promising political involvements he went over to Edinburgh and the deal was done with James

Whitton, *The Scotsman*'s financial adviser. The Royal Bank of Canada helped him find the cash; he had a remarkable talent for engaging the assistance of bankers at crucial periods of his career. He was the first of his family to return to live in Scotland since his great-great-grandfather, Archibald, left it for Canada in 1773. He was a widower, his wife having died in 1952, leaving two daughters and a son, Kenneth, the present Lord Thomson of Fleet.

There can be no doubt that, without Thomson, the Authority would have lacked a Scottish contractor until well into 1958 at the earliest. The whole development of the ITV network would have slowed up.

In July 1954, even before the Authority came into existence, Thomson informed the PMG of his intention to apply for the programming of the Scottish station, together with a group of associates ('important people').[4] Subsequently, both before and after advertising the contract, the Authority received from Thomson several applications of varying degrees of formality. By no means all the 'important people' he had in mind when he approached the PMG in 1954 relished the idea of putting their names, still less their money, into an enterprise which, against the background of the formidable losses being incurred by the four main companies in England, seemed destined to sink without even floating.

James Coltart came over from managing Beaverbrook's *Evening News* in Glasgow to join Thomson as Managing Director of Scotsman Publications early in 1955. Acquiring Coltart, a typical Beaverbrook retainer, rather in the mould of E. J. Robertson, was one of Roy's greatest masterstrokes. These two men had much in common. Both were self-made and largely self-educated. Both were brilliant with figures. Together they forged an alliance which led on to Scottish Television and the Thomson Organisation and never ever looked like breaking up.[5] It was fortunate for Thomson, at any rate in a financial sense, that their efforts to secure broad and influential support in Scotland met with so little success. By the time that STV began transmissions at the end of August 1957, advertising revenue was beginning to pour into Independent Television and the Scottish company was profit-making from the outset. Roy Thomson hit a jackpot compared with which previous ventures in press, radio and television in Canada were puny. These days, however, still lay ahead.

In the beginning Thomson was thinking in terms of a 60 per cent holding by Scotsman Publications and 40 per cent shared amongst a variety of Scottish persons and interests. He ended up with an 80 per cent holding, and the single other major holding was 10 per cent by Howard and Wyndham, the only Scottish theatre company of any substance which owned two theatres in Edinburgh and three in Glasgow. One of these, the Theatre Royal, Glasgow, was acquired by Scottish Television for conversion into television studios. Most of the 'important people' brushed Thomson off or displayed initial interest only subsequently to turn cold. Disbelief in the prospects for ITV during the winter, spring and early summer was not the only reason why he was denied support; his brash, thrusting manner offended a large part of the Scottish Establishment; and, furthermore, there were influential people in the city who considered him a small-timer. These included Harley Drayton and Brendan Bracken. For example, Sir Alexander King, the greatly respected and wealthy owner of some Scottish cinemas, who would have made an excellent partner in this enterprise, held aloof doubtless on the advice of Bracken to whom he was devoted and whom he believed to be infallible. Drayton may have been motivated by his ownership, through Provincial Newspapers, of the *Edinburgh Evening News*, which under the skilful leadership of Bill Barnetson was the rival of Thomson's *Evening Dispatch* and had an established readership amongst thinking people in Edinburgh and Leith.

Virtually the only entrée Thomson had to the Scottish élite in those days was Sir Edward (Teddy) Stevenson, Purse-bearer to the Lord High Commissioners to the General Assembly of the Church of Scotland. He made great play with Stevenson's name and lent him the money to buy a few shares. Sadly, however, his friend died shortly after Scottish Television began to provide a service. Otherwise, only Lord Balfour of Inchrye and his brother-in-law John Profumo broke ranks and acquired personal holdings. To these should be added the name of Iain Stewart who became a director of STV and was described by the Authority's Member for Scotland (Dr. Tom Honeyman) as an 'up and coming industrialist'. In 1980 Sir Iain Stewart (as he now is) was still a director of this company amongst a host of others, and as forecast, an eminent captain of industry.

Actually the Authority, by its own standards at this time, undoubtedly erred in allowing the Howard and Wyndham holding without requiring that company to divest itself of their holding in ITPC. They received one tenth of all classes of shares in STV – rather more if one adds in the personal holding of their nominee on the Board of the Company, Charles McQueen, the Edinburgh stockbroker. They were already holding one tenth of the shares of ITPC, which held nearly one third of the capital of ATV. Added to this Prince Littler, Chairman of ATV, was also Chairman of Howard and Wyndham. It was to be through ATV that Scottish Television secured their supply of network programmes at one of the best bargain prices Thomson ever negotiated. There was no deception here on anybody's part; nor is there the slightest evidence that this cross holding limited the independence of Scottish Television. It was just not the kind of situation which the Authority in general thought desirable, and Fraser was exceedingly mortified when he realised what had escaped his vigilance. But there could be no doubt that Thomson's control of Scottish Television was absolute.

In those days of 1955–7 dealing at the ITA with Roy and Jim, as they liked to be known, was always stimulating, sometimes tough going, but never downright disagreeable. Determining the rental for the Scottish station presented the Authority with a new problem. With the first four stations, the rentals accepted by the companies did not reflect the varying capital and other costs of the different stations, or their links, but only the ratio of coverage achieved by stations with the technical characteristics specified in the contracts. Rentals worked out on this basis came to some £62,000 per million of population covered. For Central Scotland, however, the Authority was fixing a rental for one station at one time, not four stations simultaneously. In seeking £300,000 a year from STV in relation to a predicted coverage of 3.7 millions, account was being taken, amongst other things, of Roy's known propensity for doing deals; there was going to be some bargaining.

He had known that this was the figure in mind for some months before the Authority even called for applications, but it was not until the formal interview on 28 February 1956 that he disclosed that his own objective was to pay £150,000 or as near to it as he could get. It was plain to the Authority that, on the basis of £62,000 per million, a correct rental was of the order of £225,000 – less than the sum it had first asked but substantially more than Roy was offering. It was one thing to inveigle him towards this 'true' figure ahead of the formal interviews and quite another to do so afterwards, when he was fully aware that he was the only effective 'runner'. (The *Daily Herald* ran a story on the very day of the interview headlined '"Scottish ITV prize in the bag" says Thomson'.) Moreover, his indiscretions were such that it rapidly became known to the existing companies that the Authority was lowering its financial sights, seemingly at their expense. As Fraser said to the companies on 13 April, by means of a letter to Sir Edwin Herbert, the £62,000 ratio was 'the one basis which it seems to us no one could feel to be preferential . . . If the application of this formula over Scotland had brought us down to a figure which involved a subsidy, we would of course have had to think again'. To the Authority he said: 'Our consultations with the parent programme companies about the Scottish rental . . . have made it only too clear that the slightest vestige of preference or discrimination . . . will meet with fierce objection.'[6] And to Dr Honeyman he wrote ' . . . the one thing we now know and have to remember all the time is that, whatever Roy Thomson's merits may be, they do not include discretion'.[7] Necessarily, all the original enquirers about the Scottish contract had to be informed of the revised rental terms, and this resulted in one additional applicant having to be interviewed.

The issue with the Board of ITN, which nearly wrecked the long-delayed announcement of the offer of a contract to Scottish Television, was not exclusively a consequence of Roy's inability to resist a haggle. With rather more justification than Dr Eric Fletcher and ABC, he was not enamoured of taking his national and international news from the metropolis. If, as he recognised, the Authority could compel him to do so as part of his contract and had no intention of compromising on this score, that was all the more reason why he should be uncompliant about financial terms, over which, at that time, the Authority had no power to dictate.

Russell Braddon says 'There are a thousand anecdotes to hand of Thomson's thrift, to put it euphemistically; and he himself confirms them all. "The driving force of my life" he recites, "was poverty." But adds cheerfully: "I *like* to save money" . . . '. Again: ' . . . even the cynical must accept him as a singularly unaffected, unostentatious, unmalevolent and honest man'. Braddon quotes the silver-voiced Canadian broadcaster, Leonard Brockington, as saying that Thomson's honesty blows through the stale air of all his deals like a gust of innocence.[8] ITV can truly say 'Amen' to that.

Thomson and Coltart moved confidently forward through the winter, spring and summer of 1956/7 towards the opening night on 31 August 1957. They showed rare skill both in business negotiation and in public relations, and they always seemed unerringly to get their priorities right. Most, but not all, of their activities were extensively publicised in the Scottish press including, of course, but on the whole with studied moderation, *The Scotsman* and the *Edinburgh Evening Dispatch*.

Amongst Thomson's least conspicuous deals was the one he made in July 1956 with ATV. His North American experience had taught him the value of 'affiliating' to a larger company which would guarantee him his supply of programmes from the network. He dealt with ATV rather than another of the existing four companies perhaps because of the Howard and Wyndham link or, more probably, because they just seemed kindred spirits. The arrangement gave access to all ATV's programmes and also all they had acquired from other companies. The ITA took no exception so long as the contract was not an exclusive one, which would have denied Thomson the right to acquire programmes direct from one of the others. 'We would not' wrote

Fraser, ' . . . wish him to be a pure affiliate, in the American television sense, of ATV. We would on the whole prefer him not to enter into a block commitment to take programmes, but this we could not prevent, for he could plainly circumvent by buying the same programmes individually.'[9] Circumstances were already edging the ITA away from its early ideal of complete free trade within a competitive optional network.

It is almost unnecessary to add that the financial terms on which Thomson secured his programme supply were highly favourable. Although the precedent of 'affiliation' was to be followed by subsequent new regional companies, none of them ever secured terms anywhere comparable to Thomson's bargain. His courage in assuming a commitment in days when precious few believed it to be aught but a passport to penury was to be amply rewarded.

The ATV connection led him in January 1957, through C. O. Stanley, to make a contract with Pye Ltd for the supply of all television equipment for studios, together with a complete outside broadcast unit. Delivery of the studio equipment was set for the early summer, but the outside broadcast unit was to be delivered in February.[10] This unit was put to work almost at once as the centre-piece in a series of twenty-one exhibitions in the principal towns and burghs within the reception area. These exhibitions were supplemented by a twenty-four page television guide providing a 'colourful picture of the programmes'.

Early in January Rai Purdy flew in from Vancouver to become executive producer for STV. For seven years previously he had been a producer for CBS in New York. But there was to be no mass importation of staff from across the Atlantic, nor yet any raids upon the personnel resources of the BBC. 'I want to get Scots and train them, rather than import outside help,' said Purdy. Furthermore, 'we expect to carry the best programmes from London, as well as some of the top American shows with, in addition, drama, comedy and variety, developed with the pick of Scottish talent'.[11] Shortly after, Anthony Jelly came up from ATV to become Sales Director, announcing that 30-second spots could be bought for as little as £35 and as high as £210.

The influential Church and Nation Committee of the Church of Scotland was none too happy about all this. A report in May said that ITV in Scotland could 'bring Sundays with an even more worldly weekday tone than at present . . . Other dangers of ITV which must be guarded against are the encouragement of a buying spree and the dilution of Scottish culture by programmes initiated in the South.'[12] Yet, if Purdy's claims were to be believed, there was to be a minimum of ten hours a week of local productions to start with, and an emphasis on news, including a thirty-minute programme of 'controversial discussion' about things of current Scottish interest and a Sunday night religious programme from Glasgow churches of all denominations.[13] On 16 May, Thomson said in one of his many speeches: 'there is every reason to expect that television will have a greater impact in Scotland than in America where, last year, in houses with television sets more total time was spent watching television than in any other single activity except sleep'.

It may well have been the flair which Thomson and Coltart had for publicity which led them to show so much consideration and forbearance towards the ITA when shortly before the opening day its transmitter at Black Hill turned out to be a maverick one. In order to radiate the maximum possible allowable powers in directions which would ensure the best overall population coverage a new 'inside the mast' type of aerial had been decided upon. It failed to live up to expectations, and as soon as a test signal was put out radio dealers were thrown into confusion by finding that the shape of the radiation pattern was different from what they had been led to expect; and – even more disconcerting – some of the power, particularly that directed towards the Ayrshire coast, was radiated in the horizontal plane instead of in the vertical plane appropriate to the station. Hopes that a generally acceptable signal would reach Dundee were far from fully realised, but fortunately the Glasgow and Edinburgh areas received pictures which were substantially unaffected by the trouble. Despite valiant and by no means unsuccessful attempts to effect major modifications and improvements during the few weeks before the opening, the service had to begin in the knowledge that a replacement aerial would need to be developed and manufactured by Marconis and placed in position probably during the summer of 1959. Initially at any rate, this technical hitch inflicted on STV a loss of coverage, in terms of population, of around 10 per cent and some loss of advertising and goodwill.

But Thomson turned it all to his advantage. 'Triumph at Black Hill' ran the headline in the special opening day supplement of *The Scotsman* which, for that occasion, its pawky editor, Alastair Dunnett, allowed to be more lyrical than was customary. Tom Robson, the Engineer-in-Charge, would say only this: 'A maximum effort has been made and is continuing'. Now Director of Engineering at the IBA, Robson recalls a visit from Roy Thomson at 8 a.m. seeking a first-hand report on the proceedings. Later, on 25 October, Fraser wrote to Thomson: 'I really must tell you how greatly we all, and particularly the writer of this letter, appreciate the way in which you have borne with us in our common troubles'.[14] Thomson sought no compensation for his financial loss.

On 20 May, the ITA had announced the appointment of a Scottish committee to advise concerning the general conduct of ITV in Scotland, and also the appointment of an executive officer, Noel Stevenson. Dr Honeyman, the Member for Scotland, badly wanted this committee and he became its chairman. Its seven members ranged from Frank Donachy, past-president of the Scottish TUC, to Barbara Napier, general adviser to women students, Glasgow. 'It is no part of their function,' Clark said at a press conference 'to interfere directly with the programmes of Scottish Television Ltd.' The appointment of this committee was, amongst other things, intended to underline that Central Scotland, in which STV operated, was not the limit of the ITA's territorial sway. Other areas in the Highlands and on the Borders would be covered in due course, and this by no means necessarily involved any extension of STV's contract. Some counter to Thomson's openly expressed ambitions to extend his licence was especially necessary at that time, and I was reported as saying on behalf of ITA that there was a population not far short of three-quarters of a million in North-east Scotland and I would be surprised if they did not find that there were independent groups interested in trying to secure the contract.

Noel Stevenson was a man of many parts – lecturer in social anthropology in the University of Glasgow, and a prominent local BBC broadcaster: many years of his life had been spent in Burma and during the war he had become first commandant of the Burma Levies, with the rank of lieutenant-colonel. I tried to tell him that the post available was too minor for a man of his background, but he was determined to get into ITV on the ground floor. In the early sixties he was to become, at Coltart's invitation, Managing Director of STV.

The first phase in the life of ITV ended on 31 August 1957. The atmosphere throughout the day was euphoric. As his memoirs record,[15] Clark steeled himself for his final arduous duties as Chairman of the ITA until, when midnight came, his term of office ceased; and, literally within minutes, he reached an understanding with Val Parnell and Lew Grade which started a new career as a brilliant television presenter of the arts, which earned him world-wide renown.[16]

According to *The Scotsman* (2 September) more than one million viewers watched the opening show *This is Scotland*, 'a spectacle sumptuously mounted and manned by one of the most brilliant collection of Scots artists ever to amalgamate their talents in a single production'. Clark made several speeches that day, all charming and elegant, but none were quite in tune with the atmosphere of the occasion in which the dignitaries of Scottish public life joined zestfully with show-biz personalities from the South in affable celebration.

Despite his setbacks, Clark enjoyed his sojourn among the purveyors of 'people's television'. It pleased him to be serving the patrons in the public bar, and possibly doing something to cultivate their interest in more refined kinds of refreshment. It was truly ironical that his exit should have coincided with the entrance of the man who, in bursts of outrageous self-mockery, not only said that having a television franchise was just like having a licence to print money but went on to say later that there must be something wrong with a country in which he could make money so easily. In Howard Thomas's vivid phrase, 'Roy Thomson came in with the harvest'.[17]

(ii) LORD DERBY'S CONSORTIUM

The first ITV 'consortium' was established in the autumn of 1956 to serve South Wales and the West of England; and it brought into being a new style of contractor which seemed to derive from the nature of the contract area itself. It was a hybrid area determined in part by what was considered the necessary population coverage to sustain a viable independent company and in part by the ineluctable fact that no transmitter located near the Bristol Channel and, as technical factors dictated, near the Wenvoe transmitter of the BBC, could throw a signal to the north and west of the estuary without also reaching the south and east.

The consortium was the result of a merger between several groups, all of which had set out independently to apply for this contract but had found difficulty in securing sufficient financial backing. The man who, after some initial jockeying for position, emerged as head of it was the eighteenth Earl of Derby, the thirty-eight year old John Stanley of Knowsley Hall, Lancashire. The fact that this aristocrat had formed an association with the leading show-biz and theatrical impresario, Jack Hylton, might at first sight seem incongruous. The explanation is simple. It had fallen, naturally enough, to Lord Derby as Lord Lieutenant of Lancashire to receive and entertain The Queen in the North-West during her tour of the country after the Coronation. After taking advice, he had invited Jack Hylton to arrange the light relief and his choice proved to be a successful one.[18] Together with Sir William Carr, owner and Chairman of the *News of the World*, and a wide range of others, they applied for and secured the ITA contract for an area covering South Wales and territory to the east and south of the Bristol Channel with an expected population coverage of 3.28 million. It will be recalled that Lord Derby had been appointed Chairman of the Popular Television Association in 1953/4: the family seat of the Derbys is, of course, near Liverpool, the city in which Lord Woolton had spent much of his working life, and from a suburb of which he took his title. Mark Chapman-Walker who, on Lord Woolton's behalf had helped to form this Association, had now become Managing Director of the *News of the World*. Thus the basis of a working relationship between the two major participants in the consortium existed ready-made.

The fact that Derby and Chapman-Walker had been so closely associated with the campaign for commercial television was inevitably grist to the mill of the conspiracy theorists. Eventually remarks made by Lord Ogmore in the House of Lords on 9 July 1963 drove Derby into issuing a statement the next day in his own defence:

I would like to make it quite clear . . . that when I first joined the Popular Television Association campaigning for an independent television service I had no intention of going into commercial television myself.

Indeed at the time commercial TV was being discussed I expressed to Lord Woolton my interest in becoming a vice-chairman of the authority which would have to be set up to administer the scheme. It was some time after commercial TV had been agreed upon and started that I was approached by Mr Jack Hylton to join him in forming a television contracting company.

By then independent television was already on the air, and this presented me with an opportunity of justifying the view I had held publicly and privately for some years before.[19]

The application arrived at the ITA in the form of a memorandum from a firm of solicitors named Goodman, Derrick and Co., headed – so its notepaper informed the ITA – by a Mr Arnold Goodman, MA, LLB (Cantab) LLM (Lond), who is now Lord Goodman of the City of Westminster and Master of University College, Oxford. Jack Hylton was but one of a list of well-known people who were clients of Goodman, Derrick and Co.[20]

Between them, Lord Derby and Jack Hylton owned some 25 per cent of the company which was to become known as Independent Television for South Wales and the West of England – TWW Ltd for short. Hylton was at the height of a career that spanned the entire range of entertainment, and he was currently packaging light entertainment and comedy shows for A-R. The *News of the World* was to own 20½ per cent of the shares and an associated company, Berrows Newspapers of Worcester, 4 per cent. Sir William Carr had close connections with South Wales, where his paper had a very high readership density: in fact, of the estimated population of the whole area, 58 per cent read the paper. Although the Board was to include a number of distinguished Welshmen, little of the share capital came from either South Wales or the West of England. The Imperial Tobacco Company of Bristol was, however, to hold a 6 per cent interest, having been recruited by Sir Alexander Maxwell, Chairman of the Bristol Tourist and Holidays Board, and an associate of Hylton's. Like Scotland before it, Wales was reluctant to furnish risk capital for an enterprise which in England had been sustaining such heavy losses. The film industry joined in with a small holding by Launder and Gilliat Productions, as also did RCA, Great Britain.

If capital from Wales was in short supply, there was no reluctance on the part of prominent people to join the Board. There was the immensely distinguished Huw T. Edwards, who had been appointed by the Labour Government as Chairman of the National Council for Wales, the precursor of the Welsh Office; Sir Ifan ab Owen Edwards, Founder-President of the Welsh League of Youth and holder of many other offices; Percy Jones, High Sheriff of Monmouthshire; D. V. P. Lewis, the future Lord Brecon, soon to become the first Minister of State for Wales; Sir Grismond Philipps, Lord Lieutenant of Carmarthenshire and Chairman of the Historic Buildings Council for Wales; and Captain Harry Llewellyn, Captain of the British Show Jumping Team at the 1952 Olympic Games. The man designated to become Chairman under the Presidency of Lord Derby was Viscount Cilcennin, formerly J. P. L. Thomas from Llandilo, First Lord of the Admiralty from 1951–6.

Roy Thomson would have given his eye-teeth for a comparable team. Add to these Herbert Agar, the anglophile former assistant to the American Ambassador, Alfred Francis, Administrator-General of the Old Vic Theatre, Sir Alexander Maxwell, the somewhat solitary Board member from Bristol, and there was created a group against which the existing companies, which all applied (and amongst which A-R were the most pressing in their claims), could not hope to prevail before an Authority enthused by the concept of regional television.

A month or so after the group was offered the contract on 24 October, the Authority gave its approval for the Liverpool Post and Echo Ltd to acquire a holding of just over 14 per cent. This newspaper had been interested in Independent Television from the outset but had failed to apply in time for one of the original contracts, and, as has been noted already, a subsequent attempt to join up with either Granada or ABC came to nothing. Like the *News of the World*, the *Post* described themselves as independent in politics; but their antecedents were Liberal. The two papers were represented on the Board of TWW by Sir William Carr and Mr A. G. Jeans (Assistant Managing Director of the *Liverpool Post*).

Let it be said, because it has sometimes been implied otherwise, that the blue-blooded Earl of Derby did not intend to be merely a decorative leader, nor did he ever become one; if he and others like the Marquis Townshend of Raynham and the late Earl of Antrim were to occasion Sampson's phrase 'a large bonanza for the local aristocracy',[21] it should not be thought that ITV's aristocrats were mere passengers on the bandwagon. The alliance between Derby and Hylton was forged out of mutual respect and regard. And, once the initial problems of the merger had been surmounted (the sort of work which Goodman has always relished), the consortium displayed a remarkable degree of cohesion. When in 1960, Lord Cilcennin died suddenly, Lord Derby was persuaded to resume the Chairmanship temporarily, but, in the event, continued to hold it until the company failed to secure a renewal of its contract in 1967/8.

If the ITA had a penchant for groups containing blue blood, it certainly had an aversion for any non-British elements, particularly American ones. Lord Derby's group, as originally composed, included the National Broadcasting Company of America as a small but significant shareholder. Whether or not Section 5(1) of the Television Act, which placed certain disqualifications on foreign holdings in a television company, constituted an insuperable bar, the Authority thought this proposal 'undesirable' and politely asked Lord Derby to drop it. With equal politeness, he acquiesced. Fraser was at pains to ensure that NBC did not take offence. In a letter dated 31 October he said: 'The Authority would be very grieved if, in any way whatever, or in any quarter, this initiative was construed as a reflection upon NBC, for whose general standing in the field of private enterprise television we have nothing but respect and admiration.'[22]

Nevertheless, this was not the end of TWW's American connection. As Chapman-Walker (who took over the Managing Directorship on secondment from his newspaper) saw it, American experience could be of great value to a new regional station. The company therefore decided, and the Authority saw no reason to object, to enter into a service agreement with NBC for the provision of 'pick up and transmission engineering techniques, programme planning and presentation, research, sales, advertising and promotion and operational management in order to assist TWW in the planning, organisation, construction and operation of its business as a television programme contractor'. Under this agreement, NBC provided the company with the services of a senior representative from New York, Bob Myers, who stayed for two years. He provided 'invaluable technical and administrative advice'.[23] The purpose-built studios, constructed around a farmhouse at Pontcanna, Cardiff, were one memorial to this sensible and successful relationship.

As Thomson had found, a newly appointed regional company had to secure, on the best terms it could, access to the available supply of programmes from the four central companies. For the new regional companies, long-term programme planning required that there should be deals which procured a guaranteed, continuous supply in bulk from which each company could draw and to which it could add its own local originations and acquisitions, the minimum amount of which was pre-determined by the Authority. Whilst no company could simply 'ride the network', the actual quantity of programmes they could make for themselves was limited by their resources in income and manpower and was not expected to be more than 15 per cent of regular transmissions and often substantially less. Scottish Television, as has been seen, 'affiliated' them-selves to ATV, which undertook to supply them the full range of network programmes produced by the central four companies. This established a procedural precedent which later companies followed. It was a British variant of the system already fully operative in the United States.

For TWW the most natural source of this programme supply was one or other of the London companies, which were situated at the centre of the Post Office links which carried the vision and sound signals from one part of the country to another. It was good business for both A-R and ATV to endeavour to secure TWW's affiliation. The former, frustrated in their aspirations to add South Wales and the West to their London franchise, made the initial running: but, whereas in the case of STV and ATV the deal had been done for a fixed sum, A-R proposed an annual payment which would be a percentage of TWW's gross income – an arrangement in some ways comparable to the one which Wills had made with Bernstein earlier in the year. Ingeniously, however, A-R incorporated in their offer a guarantee of profit. In effect they said, 'We will take x of your gross income, but if your annual profits fall under y in any year, we will make them up to that figure.' In consequence, TWW would make certain of a minimum profit, y, and would therefore be safeguarded to that extent against the possibility that x may have been fixed so high that their profit otherwise would be less than y and perhaps less than nothing. As A-R saw it, their offer increased their chances of securing an affiliation and also of getting TWW to agree to a higher x than it would accept without the guarantee.

Acceptance of the proposed guarantee by TWW, especially if it was accompanied by the express or even tacit assent of the ITA, would have had far-reaching consequences. The giving of such guarantees by large companies to smaller ones could have become a means by which a large company could extend its sway over the entire system. Moreover, the accepting company would no longer be 'independent as to finance', as the Act required. At their negotiating level TWW were initially tempted by the prospect of guaranteed profit, but their Management Committee baulked at the idea and the Authority in turn made it clear to Wills that in its view such an agreement would be in breach of the Act, and, if made, would have forced it to withhold the contract from TWW until such time as it could be amended to preclude any such development. Clark and Fraser were dismayed by this revelation of what seemed to them A-R's imperialistic ambitions, and Lord Derby hastened to assure them that his company 'have every intention of carrying out the pledges we gave when we applied for the licence, and have no intention of selling ourselves to any other company'.[24]

It cannot be said that the temporary Managing Director, Chapman-Walker, (he was later to be succeeded by Alfred Francis) had an easy run up to the opening transmissions. Attempts to negotiate a satisfactory affiliation with either A-R or ATV having run into heavy weather the eventual outcome was a deal with Granada whose claims to be TWW's 'parent' were in no way freakish, bearing in mind that they were already providing a service which reached extensively into North Wales. Although the agreement with Granada was skilfully formulated by Goodman to secure conformity with the ITA's requirements and was not in practice different from the arrangements previously made between STV and ATV, a somewhat boastful announcement of it was made on 24 May 1957, not by TWW, but by Granada; and it was made in terms which suggested far too great a dependence by TWW on Granada's advertising organisation. 'It is not suitable', wrote Fraser severely 'that one programme company should be ensuring the effectiveness of advertising in the programmes of another company.'[25] However, Chapman-Walker managed to persuade Fraser that Granada was to be no more than an agency through which for certain limited purposes TWW's separate and autonomous sales organisation worked, and that, in fact, he himself had made the arrangement public, though less formally, a month earlier. 'I have been anxious and at pains all along not only to ensure in fact, but also to publicly proclaim, that TWW have done nothing to abdicate their full independence.'[26] Nevertheless Fraser's intervention was timely.

The worst of the obstacles which had to be surmounted in TWW's preparatory phase were of a technical character. The selection of the best possible site for a transmitting station near the Bristol Channel began as early as July 1955. About ten different locations in areas such as the Mendips, the Quantocks and in various parts of South Wales itself were considered in detail but all in turn were rejected, mainly because they gave less population coverage for South Wales than that predicted from a site on the coastal ridge between Cardiff and Cowbridge. This was St. Hilary Down. Having proceeded thus far and having obtained approval in principle from all the authorities concerned, the ITA heard early in December 1956 that the Minister for Housing and Local Government had asked the Glamorgan County Council to suspend planning permission for it to build its station at St. Hilary. Objections had been made by the principal airline companies operating from Rhoose Airport, near Cardiff, that the erection of the 750 foot mast would endanger air navigation. These objections were heard at a public enquiry held at Cardiff on 7 March 1957. Fortunately, the Minister's formal decision, made public on 21 March 1957, did not uphold the objections and granted permission for building at St. Hilary subject to certain conditions. This unexpected delay of nearly four months in securing planning permission held back progress, but even so it was hoped that sufficient time might be regained to enable the first programmes to be transmitted before Christmas. So well did Marconis work that by 6 August Fraser was able to commit the Authority to an opening on 14 December, 'subject only to the usual "escape clause" in the event of serious unforseeable trouble, either on your side or on ours'.[27] This date was by agreement subsequently amended to 17 December.

Serious unforeseeable trouble was, alas, precisely what arose; for the St. Hilary aerial was basically similar to the maverick one which caused such confusion in Scotland prior to the opening day of STV. It was judged best by the ITA and most reluctantly accepted by the company, that the opening should be postponed until after Christmas, and it was on 14 January 1958 that TWW eventually opened their service.

One consequence of the delay meant that the star-studded showpiece programme with which they had planned to grace their opening night under the title *The Stars Rise in the West* had to be pre-filmed. Introduced and linked by Jack Train it included Stanley Baker, Donald Houston, Harry Secombe, Petula Clark, Sir Ralph Richardson and, of course, Shirley Bassey, but according to some observers it had lost some of the impact that the live show was hoped to have. Actual opening was at 4.45 p.m. 'We're brimful of happiness to be on the air!' cried the announcer, Bruce Lewis. The ceremonial was brief and to the point with speeches of welcome from Lord Derby and Sir Ifan ab Owen Edwards and Alfred Francis. The networked Granada programme *Youth Wants to Know* was also shown, and to honour the occasion featured Lady Megan Lloyd George, Raymond Gower, MP for Barry, and schoolchildren from North Wales. The early ITN news was appropriately read by Llanelly born Huw Thomas, who opened with a Welsh greeting. There were estimated to be some 84,000 sets (45 per cent of those with a choice) tuned to the new station at opening time. By 7.15 the 'Stars' rose on an audience of 115,000 homes. And the top rating of the evening – on both channels – was reached with the quiz *£1000 Word* which followed, bringing in the Bristol element with Bert Tann, manager of Bristol Rovers FC, as a prize winning participant. In all over 90 per cent of all two-channel sets were tuned to TWW at some time during the evening.

The new company's success was very obviously never in doubt; and this was amply born out in the weeks that followed. By April a survey published by the *News of the World* revealed that out of 310,000 homes equipped to view ITV as well as BBC only 8000 were not regular TWW viewers. During the first three months 'running in' period the Authority had allowed the company to fall short of their contractual obligations to provide 15 per cent of locally originated programmes. In the following quarter local productions were therefore increased, including a number of series in the Welsh language. The latter, together with series from Granada, made up the 200 minutes of Welsh to which the company had already committed themselves. It was at this early stage that the two series *Amser Te* (*Tea Time*) and *Gwlad y Gan* (*Land of Song*) started their long and successful runs, the latter finding a regular place on the network during the Sunday 'closed period'.

The company's application for a contract had not in so many words proffered programmes in Welsh; nor for that matter did the Authority's initial prospectus state that they would be a requirement; and nor, to go back a stage further, did Parliament in the Television Act go beyond providing that the programmes from any station should 'contain a suitable proportion of matter calculated to appeal specially to the tastes and outlook of the persons served by the station'. However, the need to provide Welsh programmes had been stressed in the Parliamentary debates of 1954. The first mention of the language in the ITA's own records appears to have been an enquiry at a meeting on 6 November 1956 from the Member for Wales, Jenkin Alban Davies, whether the company would accept a contractual provision that, so far as was economically possible, they should provide a certain amount of broadcasting in the Welsh language.[28] At the next meeting on 20 November it was reported that this had been agreed with the company.

Alban Davies' move coincided with the visit of a deputation to the PMG on behalf of the New Wales Union (Undeb Cymru Fydd). Early in 1957 a joint committee was formed representing the Union, the Welsh League of Youth, the National Eisteddfod Council and the Honourable Society of Cymmrodorian, and this committee got into communication with the BBC, ITA and TWW urging the presentation of programmes in the Welsh language. At a meeting of the Council of the Union at Borth in Cardiganshire, arrangements were made for a conference at Llangefni during National Eisteddfod week to discuss the importance of the Welsh language in everyday life in the home and at school and in literature. In those days outside pressures on the broadcasters, both in Wales and elsewhere, were incredibly sedate compared with those of recent years.

It was not until 30 July 1957 that, in response to a strong representation from Alban Davies, the Authority decided to inform the company that there should in its view be at least one hour a week of Welsh language programmes, and that no more than half an hour of these should be mixed Welsh and English programmes. In the meantime, the PMG had agreed that Welsh language programmes should be included in a strictly limited category which would be 'off the ration' so far as permitted transmission hours were concerned. This meant that such programmes would not have to be counted as coming within the Government's prescribed limits of 50 hours a week and 8 hours a day and could be shown during the 'closed period' between 6.15 p.m. and 7.30 p.m. on Sundays, without the Central Religious Advisory Committee having any necessary right to object. In the meantime too, Chapman-Walker had put in his plea for some portion of the Government's proffered grant of £100,000 to be allocated to help in financing such programmes (see Chapter 27).

The question came to a head at the Authority's meeting in Glasgow, of all places, on 31 August, of all days. (It was the opening day of STV and Clark's last day as Chairman.) Given that the company were being in no way uncooperative, or dismissive of their obligations towards Welsh national culture, the Members' attitude might almost be described as pernickety. The last recorded remarks of Clark as Chairman of the ITA were to point out first that if the programmes were attractive to non-Welsh viewers TWW (and Granada too if they undertook them) would in effect be getting additional time not available to other companies, and secondly that, if financial assistance were given to TWW, it would be difficult to refuse it to Granada (which had not in fact sought it). Others remarked that all TWW's Welsh language programmes would 'earn' advertising time, whether inside or outside normal hours, and it was eventually concluded that no grant should be made to TWW or Granada for Welsh language programmes and that TWW would be expected to place one half of the minimum supply of one hour a week within normal programme time. It was also agreed that for a programme to qualify as being in the Welsh language it must be Welsh in performance and exclusively Welsh in language. But it was concluded that programmes of Welsh song could be treated as being 'in the Welsh language'.[29]

Over the next few years TWW's record of service to Independent Television, to Wales and also to their area was all that could have been asked of them. They were one of ITV's golden boys: not only immensely profitable but lively and adventurous in their programmes and eager to expand, first by constructing modern studios in Bristol to meet their West of England responsibilities, and also, had they been allowed, to pioneer a truly Welsh service in west and south-west Wales and co-operate actively and positively with any new contractor for south-west England.

The ITA paid an official visit to TWW at Cardiff on 28 November 1960. Before meeting the company it held one of its regular meetings in the Park Hotel, the agenda for which included a report on the company by its own Welsh officer, Lyn Evans. Kirkpatrick thought the report 'most encouraging'.

Evans recalled that in January 1959 the number of homes able to view ITV had increased to 445,000 and in November 1960 it was 673,000. That represented a population of $2\frac{1}{4}$ millions, slightly more than half of whom were on the Welsh side of the Bristol Channel. The weekly total of local origination amounted to an average of $8-8\frac{1}{2}$ hours of 'live' origination, and $1\frac{1}{4}-1\frac{1}{2}$ hours of acquired film, which brought the percentage to approximately 15. Of the 'live' origination, just under three hours were in the Welsh language. During the year the company had shown 'conspicuous inventiveness and originality in new programming in both English and Welsh'. He listed some of these programmes and their average 'rating': if they did not perhaps quite bear out Evans' lyrical description, they were both varied and worthy and they drew very substantial audiences.

Regular news bulletins were transmitted on five weekday nights following the 5.55 ITN bulletin. A 15-minute sports programme proved so popular that it was extended to half an hour and was now transmitted regularly on Thursday evenings at 6.15. Among occasional programmes were two special reports on the Royal visit to Wales and daily reports on the National

Eisteddfod of Wales. That month a special half hour programme had been devoted to the Ebbw Vale by-election. On Sunday, 20 November, at 8 p.m. a 45-minute special programme, *First Night*, had been broadcast from the company's new Bristol studios.

These studios, built at a cost of £250,000, had been officially opened in October. Up to then transmissions were limited to news bulletins from a small studio opened a year previously. From now on many more programmes would be mounted and transmitted from Bristol, and among those already planned were a quiz panel game, *Claim to Fame*, and a West Country edition weekly of *Here Today*. A number of improvements and extensions to the Pontcanna studios had been carried out during the year.

Evans went on to say that more than 750,000 of Wales' population of 2.6 millions were Welsh speakers, and a significant proportion lived in South-West Wales. From the beginning this language minority had been closely watched by the company's Welsh Board, and Welsh language broadcasts were started early in 1957. During the year the company continued to produce 5-minute news bulletins and a 35-minute feature on four days of the week and to relay Granada's Monday feature *Dewch i Mewn*. Independent Television thus provided for Welsh speakers a weekly average of over 200 minutes of programmes in their own language – albeit at a low viewing period of the day, namely from 4.10 to 4.50 p.m. In addition, there was *Gwlad y Gan (Land of Song)* at 6.15 every fourth Sunday, which could be seen throughout the ITV network.

The company had been taking all the schools programmes produced by A–R and Granada, and proposed to transmit the new ATV series in the New Year. In September 1960 two conferences, at Bristol and at Cardiff, had been arranged to inform local authorities and educationalists of the facilities available. They were proposing to appoint an education officer to liaise with schools. Network religious programmes were taken and local epilogues transmitted on Sundays and Wednesdays. During Holy Week The Revd. Gordon Lang had delivered a series of epilogues which were well received by churchgoers and Sunday School workers. On 7 August a *Hymn of Praise* Festival recorded at a Llanelly chapel was transmitted. Popular Welsh hymns were sung by a 1000-strong congregation which included the Morriston Orpheus Choir. The company hoped to arrange similar programmes in the New Year. Religious topics were discussed from time to time in *Challenge* and in the Welsh language series.

The dual character of TWW's service area did, as will be seen, create problems of inter-company friction. But it also led very naturally to developments which were to be important pointers to the way in which ITV's continuing pursuit of the decentralised regional interest could be realised. In the words of the *Bristol Evening World* TWW made television history when a special edition of their local news magazine *TWW Reports* provided linked news output from both Bristol and Cardiff with numerous switchovers from item to item between Ludovic Kennedy as presenter in the Bristol studio and Maureen Staffer in Cardiff. 'Last night's programme,' added the newspaper, 'made it quite clear that the West Country is going to get its fair crack of the whip.'

But this was only a first step towards the creation of a full-scale all purpose studio centre in Bristol. With the completion of this centre, TWW became the first ITV company to be operating from two focal points within the same contract area, situated indeed in two different countries. The sophisticated master control arrangements handling the output from the two centres were well ahead of their time and became a legitimate source of pride within the company, and especially to their Chief Engineer Dr Walter Kemp, another of those brilliant engineering graduates from Norman Collins' High Definition Films.

Thus equipped the company were, in the remaining years of the contract, to go from strength to strength. Financially they prospered most handsomely. Profits before tax in 1961 were £1,277,648, and shareholders' dividends of the order of 100 per cent. Yet as their Managing Director, former Old Vic administrator Alfred Francis, put it: 'We like to think of ourselves as a TV company that makes profits, not as a profit-making company that does television.'

(iii) THE SOUTHERN INHERITANCE

The contract for which applications were sought in May 1956 was described by the ITA as covering a service area consisting of a rough half circle of which the base ran from a point west of Weymouth around the Isle of Wight to Newhaven and of which the topmost point lay near Newbury. The population of the 'primary' and 'secondary' areas[30] of the transmitting station at Chillerton Down, Isle of Wight, was expected to be around 2.3 millions, and some 270,000 people amongst those would already be able to receive good signals from the London transmitter at Croydon, a figure which would rise to 750,000 when the initial temporary transmitter there was replaced by a permanent, more powerful one.

A group formed by the Rank Organisation, Rothermere's Associated Newspapers and the Amalgamated Press (the Camrose–Daily Telegraph group), was among nine new applicants for the contract, and it was clearly the most powerful of them, in terms both of finance and media resources. Indeed in business and media terms it would be hard to imagine a more high-powered combination. Perhaps five out of the nine could be classified as local groups and the other four, including, of course, Rank/Associated Newspapers/Amalgamated Press could be described as national. For the first time the Authority had to ask itself what kind of programme company it wanted in an English regional area.

This question had not really had to be faced in the case of Scotland and Wales/West of England, if only because STV and TWW were respectively the sole credible applicants for their concessions, and in neither case had it been clear that lucrative contracts were on offer. Nobody could dispute that Thomson worked from a Scottish base or that Derby was amply supported by Welshmen of distinction. The situation was now transformed: already profits on a soaring scale were being made by the first four companies and STV had been in profit from their first day on the air. The facts in the case of Southern England were that one or two of the 'local' groups could probably do the job, whereas there was at least one competent 'national' group in additon to Rank/AN/AP.

Instinctively, Fraser's preference was for local identity, much as it had developed in radio and television for smaller stations in America, Canada and Australia. The analogy of local newspapers producing local material for local use and fed from the centre by the Press Association and Reuter was the one which sprang most readily to his mind. Clark, on the other hand, thought primarily about the balance of power. As he saw it, the Authority's influence over the programme companies was likely to be increased by the addition of a further powerful company; a number of powerful companies would more readily retain their independence one from another and would then be individually more amenable to suggestions from the Authority. Clark's view was endorsed by the Authority and the contract was consequently offered to the group under the Chairmanship of John Davis, Managing Director of the Rank Organisation, with Stuart McClean, Managing Director of Associated Newspapers, as Deputy Chairman. While Lord Rank played no direct part in the enterprise, Lord Rothermere was forced into personal involvement at one critical stage. It was said that John Davis held ninety-six other directorships, perhaps more; but this made no difference, and from 1957 through to 1976 he was a vigorously active chairman of the company.

It was Frank Coven, the man who had warned Associated Newspapers a year previously that they were pulling out of A–R just as the lights were turning green, who prompted Stuart McClean now to bring them into an alliance with the Rank Organisation in a bid for the south of England contract. Only McClean, however, could have brought it about. He had foresight as well as dynamism, tireless energy and an ability to inspire enthusiasm amongst his colleagues. Although, rightly enough, he is remembered mainly for his services to Fleet Street, there can be no doubt that, had he lived beyond the age of fifty, he would have been a tower of strength in the collective affairs of ITV.

Clark's expectations were not entirely well founded. However, the danger that had arisen earlier in the year that TWW would come under the domination of A–R made a deep impression on him, and he was determined that there should be a company in Southern England strong enough to preserve its independence. When other new contracts became available, Clark had departed and genuine local roots became an increasingly significant factor in securing the Authority's favour.

The new company, with capital subscribed in equal proportions by the three groups, was registered as Southern Television, with C. D. Wilson, an executive of Associated Newspapers, as its general manager. The company would have preferred 'South of England' or 'Southern England' to be incorporated in their title, but the Authority was averse to regional titles because they were generally too wide and imprecise. 'Southern Television' was in fact its own suggestion, given that the company was reluctant to have some made-up title such as 'Wessex Television'. Wilson's own bright idea had been 'English Channel Television'. The company assented to the ITA's suggestion without enthusiasm. Arnold Goodman (who had bobbed up again as a legal adviser) thought that it was rather the worst of both worlds.[31]

Southern Television (although not yet under this name) were offered the contract on 10 July subject to one important proviso. This was that Associated Newspapers should dispose of their remaining 10 per cent interest in A–R. Section 5(2) of the Act (independence as to finance and control) clearly precluded their having a foothold in both camps. Stuart McClean promptly gave an undertaking to this effect, but asked that nothing should be said or done to inflict on his company a forced sale of this now valuable interest. It was indicated that the disposal would be necessary before Southern Television went on the air, that the Authority could not guarantee to keep the proviso secret and that, pending the disposal, Associated Newspapers should not exercise their voting rights either in A–R or in the new company. The announcement of the acceptance of the application which was made on 22 July merely added in general terms that the Authority had received satisfactory assurances from the group in relation to the requirements of Section 5(2).

Implementing this undertaking was perhaps the most difficult of the problems which beset the preparatory phase of Southern Television. Sadly, by the time it was resolved, McClean was mortally ill, and he eventually died in June 1960.

A letter from him arrived at the ITA on 17 February 1958 saying that he had been negotiating actively over the disposal of the A–R holding since July 1957 but he had come up against difficulties he had not anticipated: however he was pressing on in the hope that a solution could be found which was satisfactory to everyone. 'I cannot help wondering,' wrote Fraser internally, 'whether it (the letter) does not go some way to confirm the rumours now in circulation that Associated Newspapers may be having second thoughts about their investment in Southern Television and be asking themselves whether it might not pay them better to retain their shares in A–R.'[32] On 19 March McClean met Kirkpatrick and Fraser (his illness had prevented any earlier meeting) and told them that the controlling shareholder in A–R (i.e. BET–Rediffusion) was offering 35/- for shares which were generally admitted to be worth £30 and would refuse to allow them to offer their shares to any one else. The owners of 90 per cent of the shares in A-R were willing buyers and under these circumstances the company's Articles of Association precluded a sale to any outside party. In view of this 'derisory price' McClean appeared to take it for granted that his company had the option of pulling out of Southern, although the agreement of the previous July was explicitly to the effect that they would divest themselves of their shares in A–R.

Actually this was not the outcome which, over the preceding months, McClean had been seeking. He had been exploring indefatigably devious ways and means of coming to an agreement which would effectively keep the 10 per cent holding in A–R without interfering with the Southern contract. Maybe it was a long shot, and doomed to failure from the start, but he was an ingenious man and he knew that Wills and others in A–R had no wish to part altogether with the Associated Newspaper connection. Wills and McClean had a natural rapport with one another: and they shared an equal zest for a business gamble. Persons working close to McClean at the time doubt whether he seriously entertained the idea of pulling out of Southern, but confirm that he did envisage the possibility of discovering a means of staying in A–R – some method which would not be incompatible with the assurance given to the Authority back in July 1957.[33]

On the instructions of a full meeting of the Authority Associated Newspapers were bluntly and officially informed on 2 April that a failure on their part to divest would automatically result in the lapse of the offer of a contract to Southern Television.

McClean was now very ill. There followed a meeting on 10 April between Lord Rothermere and Mr R. A. Redhead on the one hand and Sir Ronald Matthews and myself (deputising respectively for Kirkpatrick and Fraser, who were away) on the other. Lord Rothermere stated that his company were honourably bound to their colleagues in Southern not to take any steps which would jeopardise their contractual position, but Redhead nevertheless suggested that if the Authority could agree to their being released from their obligation to dispose of their holdings in A-R, they might temporarily hold their one-third interest in Southern for allocation at par elsewhere and that it was not necessary for the ITA to consider afresh the allocation of the Southern contract. My reply was that the Authority in granting valuable programme contracts had so far proceeded with a high degree of informality and privacy. This was not so in other countries where the granting of licences to broadcasting companies was in many cases carried out by means of public enquiry. It was therefore incumbent on the Authority to see that it gave no grounds for criticism that it did not act with scrupulous fairness to all applicants. That was the reason why the Authority was not able to give any assurance that, if the group to which the Southern contract had originally been granted ceased to exist in its original form, the Southern contract would be reoffered to a reconstituted Southern Television. However, Sir Ronald said he would arrange for Lord Rothermere to state his case to the full Authority; and this he did on 22 April.[34]

There was much goodwill but no lenity on the ITA's part. Kirkpatrick wrote to Lord Rothermere next day:

The discussion showed that the Members of the Authority were unanimous in believing that if Associated Newspapers left Southern Television it would be the duty of the Authority to reopen the allocation of the southern contract with no certainty that, as a result of such reconsideration, the contract would be offered to a reconstituted Southern Television. In these circumstances and in the light of the statement you made in regard to your sense of obligation to your partners in Southern Television, the Authority, whilst sympathising with you in your predicament, felt that it had no alternative but to ask Associated Newspapers to take steps forthwith to fulfil their undertaking and to divest themselves of their interest in Associated-Rediffusion. You were good enough to say in your letter of 15 April to me and again at the meeting that you would do this if it was the Authority's wish.

Rothermere duly replied, adding that 'the price we have been forced to accept under your decision is one which bears no relationship to the current market value'.[35]

Need the Authority have treated Lord Rothermere with such severity? There could be no doubt that his company's holding in Southern could have been taken up either by their two existing partners or by a responsible new participant. The 'know-how' possessed by Associated Newspapers which had seemed a significant factor in the application a year previously had already to a large extent been utilised by Southern. A competent staff had been appointed and the directors from Rank and Amalgamated Press had learnt the ropes. The ravages of cancer meant that the dynamism of Stuart McClean – an asset to any organisation – was virtually certain to be lost. The Authority had agreed to a significant change in the composition of A–R to bring Southern into being. Would it have been so wrong now to allow Southern to be changed in order, after all, to leave A–R unaltered?

However, the outlook and attitude of the Authority had been steadily changing since the heady days of 1954/5. Bitter experience had taught it scrupulous vigilance, and, as contract succeeded contract, so the provisions for 'control of control' became increasingly meticulous. There had been the collapse of Kemsley–Winnick and the procurement of ABC as a substitute, the conversion of ABDC into ATV, the move of the Mirror group into ATV, the withdrawal of four-fifths of Associated Newspapers from A–R, and Howard and Wyndham's foothold both in Scottish Television and – indirectly – in ATV. A–R and Granada had done a deal of which the Authority had at the time no official cognisance. Something akin to a take-over of TWW by A–R had been mooted earlier in the year. The financial stresses which had brought about these various developments had now quite disappeared and had been replaced by nagging anxieties about exorbitant profits. Several more contracts – valuable concessions – were in the offing. Small wonder that the Authority now placed a high premium on probity and rectitude in the exercise of its supervisory role.

Whilst Associated Newspapers were thus preoccupied with their painful dilemma, John Davis and his chief executive, David Wilson, were pushing ahead with their plans for providing a television service for the area which had been allotted to them. They too became rapidly aware that the so-called 'toothless watchdog' was a force to be reckoned with. Clark had departed on 31 August and the first of the interregnums to which the ITA came to be accustomed was in operation. Kirkpatrick did not succeed Clark until 7 November and the Acting Chairman for two months or so was Ronald Matthews. He was diligent, but his other activities precluded regular attendance at Princes Gate. Confident of his support – more so than of Clark's – Fraser was pressing ahead on all fronts. He took a determined line regarding Wilson's plan to establish Southern's main administrative and production base for the deep south, not in Southampton or Portsmouth, but in London. This was not as heretical an idea in those days as it would have been regarded later; and, as has been seen, the company had been offered their contract despite (indeed almost because of) their lack of any significant regional characteristics. One of their arguments (for Wilson had the support of his board) was that the Southern area was not naturally a homogeneous one and had, other than London, no focal point to which people looked or travelled. Nearly all the main lines of communication ran to and from London. But Fraser was not to be persuaded. Brushing aside the Authority's deliberate choice of a contractor for the South whose power-base was elsewhere he wrote:

> When the Authority decides to find and appoint a new and independent company for any region, its main reason lies in its desire to initiate a local operation in which *local* talent and *local* interests should lead to the production of *local* programmes . . . If this were not the Authority's policy, it would usually be much simpler to let one of the existing network companies supply the programmes, dispensing completely with any local studio or local staff . . . the Southern region has a real and massive centre in the Portsmouth–Southampton–Isle of Wight triangle, where the population must exceed 600,000 . . .[36]

Fraser did not stop at that. Four days later he wrote at length again to Davis setting out in some detail the categories of programmes which he would like to see presented in order (to quote the Act) 'to appeal specially to the tastes and outlook of persons served by the station'. This plan involved local production of rather more than six hours a week or about 11 per cent of fifty-six hours a week. Davis replied on 21 October, unreservedly accepting Fraser's views about location of studios and far from resenting Fraser's range of programme ideas, the company welcomed them saying that they had been thinking along similar lines. Southern were no different from other regional companies: they recognised in Fraser an overlord who knew about, and cared about, programmes more than about anything else.

In March 1958 the Authority was asked by John Davis if the Rank
Organisation's holding in Southern Television (£250,000 out of a total
capital of £750,000) could be held beneficially as to 60 per cent by the
Rank Organisation and as to 40 per cent by Gaumont–British. The Rank
Organisation would remain as registered holders of the shares and
debentures in Southern Television and would retain the full voting rights,
Gaumont–British's beneficial interest being secured by a Deed of Trust.

An abrupt rejection of this proposal by the Authority took Davis by
surprise and was something of an embarassment within the Rank
Organisation. In truth it was only the timing of the request which really
bothered the ITA. Had the proposal been explained, as it ought to have been,
at the time of the application, it would almost certainly have been
acceptable. There had been an oversight. Apart from its dislike for
approving any changes in the structure of a programme contractor from
what had so recently been described in the contract application, the
Authority could not feel too happy about the American Twentieth Century
Fox having, through the Metropolis and Bradford Trust, an indirect share,
amounting to about 19 per cent of the equity in Gaumont. This would under
the proposal entitle them to between 2 and 3 per cent of the earnings of
Southern, although not, of course, to any voting interest in the company. It
was pretty small beer, and probably of less significance to commercial
television conspiracy theorists than the fact that, through Midland Bank
(Threadneedle Street) Nominees Ltd, the Eagle Star Insurance Company,
of which Harley Drayton as well as Davis was a director, owned about one
seventh of the voting shares in Rank. Doubtless a knowledge of this latter
fact would have been grist to the mill of the author of *Power Behind the Screen*.[37]

With characteristic good sense Davis accepted Fraser's advice not to press
the matter further at that time, even though it involved some inconvenience
and embarassment within Rank. His patience was rewarded a year or so
later when the ITA accepted without demur a revised plan designed to secure
precisely the same result.

The final episode in the saga of Southern's financial structure began in
November 1958 when it was announced in the press that sale of the share
capital of Amalgamated Press was to be negotiated with Daily Mirror
Newspapers Ltd, in which for the future Sunday Pictorial Ltd would have
an increased interest. If the sale went through a situation would arise where
the *Daily Mirror*, having a 25 per cent interest in ATV, would also have a
33 per cent interest in Southern. Such a situation would be anathema to the
ITA, but it was doubtful whether it had powers in the contracts to prevent it.
Happily for the ITA, Cecil King was ready to agree to sell the shares in

Southern if they came into the *Mirror*'s possession. The Articles of Association required a departing shareholder to offer his shares *at his price* to the other shareholders; only if they failed to accept could he sell elsewhere.

King fixed a price of £45 a share which took account of Southern's enhanced earning power from having had the Dover area added to their franchise with effect from January 1960.[38] All the same Davis believed that £30 was a more realistic price, as also did his partner, Redhead, of Associated Newspapers. But King was buoyantly unwilling to negotiate a compromise. The outcome was that Rank and Associated Newspapers increased their respective holdings to 37½ per cent and not to 50 per cent, as, without demur from the ITA, they might ordinarily have done. King then found a willing buyer for the remaining 25 per cent in D. C. Thomson and Co., proprietors of the *Dundee Courier* and other journals, who consequently, and with ITA approval, replaced Amalgamated Press as the third member of the Southern triumvirate. There the financial structure stabilised and remained intact right through the sixties and seventies, until on 28 December 1980 the IBA decided not to renew the company's contract. Ever since Roy Thomson was required to dispose of his majority holding in STV in 1967, no company in ITV save Southern was predominantly controlled by newspaper interests.

The correspondence that passed between King and Davis was typical of the cheerful insouciance of the early ITV tycoons. It was punctuated by one agreeable but unproductive lunch *à deux*; but it was the only one, for Davis refused a repeat performance unless it involved real negotiations which King had not the slightest intention of conducting. He politely reminded King that he had 'a few other jobs to do'.

With the first transmissions from the Chillerton Down transmitter over 80 per cent of the United Kingdom population came within range of an alternative television service. It was, as the *Financial Times* put it, 'an auspicious time to open . . . ITV has just entered its years of prosperity . . . [Southern Television's] capital could well be recouped within 18 months to 2 years'. The prophecy was amply fulfilled. By the end of their second year, profits had topped £1 million and in 1962 dividend payments on the £100,000 capital totalled £650,000.

But it was no passive ride on a rising wave. Both Davis and Wilson were men who would, in whatever circumstances, always insist on paddling their own canoe. From the start their programme contribution showed those qualities of business-like, independent initiative which the Authority doubtless expected from the company's antecedents. Certainly there reigned during the weeks before opening night an atmosphere of expectant optimism among the 200 young staff – reputedly with the lowest (thirty years) average age in the industry. In the new two-studio centre created out of Southampton's former Plaza cinema there prevailed, said *TV Times*, 'an air as keen and bracing as that of the many famous seaside resorts . . . within the boundaries of the region'.

Opening night itself on 30 August 1958 was undramatic. Promptly at 5.30 p.m. were heard the strains of Richard Addinsell's specially composed station identification music, 'Southern Rhapsody', and programme controller Roy Rich was seen exchanging pleasantries with Brighton resident Alan Melville on the boat deck of Cunard liner *Caronia*, at Southampton. No solemn speeches: just a few words of welcome to ITV's new viewers. After the 5.40 p.m. ITN bulletin and a 'filmed drama' with Eric Portman about the reunion of a wartime aircrew, *Coming Shortly* at 7 p.m. offered preview glimpses of forthcoming episodes from popular imports like *Dragnet*, *I Love Lucy*, *Gun Law* as well as from *Robin Hood*. At 8 o'clock came the evening's main offering, an hour-long nationally networked variety show – also titled *Southern Rhapsody* – presented by Alan Melville. It started with a film montage showing aspects of the region: stately homes, industry, Glyndebourne, the beaches, the ships and went on to feature popular performers like Line Renaud, Gracie Fields, Frankie Vaughan, Anne Shelton and Charlie Drake. It included also a return visit to the *Caronia* where Southern region residents J. B. Priestley, Tommy Farr, Uffa Fox and Gilbert Harding were interviewed at the dinner table and Lionel and Joyce Blair did a lively dance sequence round the swimming pool.

From the beginning there were to be at least six regular home-produced programmes a week. On weekdays at 1.25 p.m. and 6.25 p.m. were local news bulletins. On Mondays, Tuesdays and Wednesdays appeared *Flotsam's Follies* – lunchtime variety introduced B. C. Hilliam ('Flotsam'). Saturday afternoons saw *Southern Heritage*, conducted tours for teenagers of places of historical interest in the region; and in the early evening episodes of the drama serial *Mary Britten M.D*, a networked programme starring Brenda Bruce (Mrs Roy Rich) which, though by no means of indifferent quality, had to cease production after $4\frac{1}{2}$ months when the Big Four lost interest. On Sunday afternoons journalist Cyril Ray presented *Southern Affairs* a weekly news magazine, subtitled 'a programme from the south for the South'. On Tuesdays at 6.30 p.m. A. G. Street introduced *Farm in the South* followed at 7 p.m. by *Sportsclub*, presided over by Berkeley Smith.

The influence of Berkeley Smith, who had been Peter Dimmock's right hand man at the BBC, was apparent in the substantial commitment to one form or other of outside broadcasts. He had recruited a highly professional outside broadcast unit and was destined to play an increasing role in the company's programme policy. Even before air date, the network had agreed to take his unit's coverage of eighteen events; and in the years ahead he would maintain such regular access to the national audience, for which his crowning achievement was doubtless the two-hour long coverage of the enthronement of Archbishop Ramsay at Canterbury in June 1961. Southern's outside broadcasts in their first three weeks included for example Farnborough Air Show, Brighton Races, Salisbury Cathedral floodlighting, sailing on the Hamble and Hampshire county cricket, a game to which they consistently gave more exposure than any other ITV company.

This bias towards the real 'live event' – a mixture of sport and 'you are there' programmes – coloured most of the company's programming during their first contract period. Out of an average of nine hours a week of home production more than five and a half were given to local current affairs, regional news, instructional and other factual material, and in all this the authenticity of on-the-spot reporting had prominence. In an area which the company's own contract application had described as 'heterogeneous' without 'any individual local characteristics throughout' it made good regional programming sense to take cameras out and about in order to portray as many varied interests and activities of the region as possible. *Probe*, a series of thirty-nine visits to towns in the South in which local inhabitants were able to question Town Hall officials attracted, in the familiar pattern of investigative journalism, its fair share of indignant protest from local mayors and councillors. But at least viewers throughout the area were made to feel that others outside were interested and concerned about their local doings and affairs. When the South Eastern extension to their franchise area came about in January 1960 the Mayor of Dover expressed his delight that this would put Dover 'on the map!'[39] Small wonder that the company's Monday to Friday news magazine *Day by Day* which replaced the earlier once a week *Southern Affairs* in April 1961 earned for itself an enviably high reputation in a programme genre which ITV was to make peculiarly its own.

There were, naturally, ventures into other programme fields, not all of them successful. Persistent attempts were made to collect an audience for lunchtime light entertainment, sometimes exploiting local talent; and continued in various guises until their final abandonment in April 1961. More ambitious was the arrangement with the Old Vic for transmission of one production of a modern play every eight weeks for two years. Like the ill-fated *Mary Britten* drama series, this project came up against the rigidities of the networking system and was terminated after five network showings at unfavourable times. Another venturesome enterprise which, for quite other reasons, terminated prematurely was the late night satirical revue *Melvillainy* presented by Alan Melville. It ran for twenty-four editions from January to July 1960 and was probably the first television programme of this type, in some respects a forerunner of the BBC's *That Was the Week That Was*. It was withdrawn because the company felt it conflicted with their obligation, under Section 3(1) (a) of the 1954 Act, to avoid 'offensive representation of, or reference to, a living person'.

Southern soon reached the conclusion that the proper policy for regional ITV companies with networking ambitions should be one of increasing specialisation. For themselves they saw greatest scope for possible future development in the fields of information and education and in programmes for children. They had already given practical expression to their interest in the educational possibilities of the medium in a co-operative experiment with the Hampshire County Education Authority, for three of whose schools near Southampton a complete closed circuit TV installation had been provided.

In their original 1957 contract application the company had proclaimed an intention to make themselves 'a significant factor in independent commercial programming'. By the end of 1961 they were well on the way to succeeding. It would have been surprising had they been less than successful. They were the last of the really big-business contractors to be appointed and, without incurring the slightest risks, they trod the primrose path to fortune.

30

TWO OBSTACLES REMOVED

(i) THE FALL OF THE FOURTEEN DAY RULE

On 23 February 1955 in the House of Commons the Prime Minister answered a question concerning the operation of the Fourteen Day Rule (or Fortnight Rule as it was sometimes called). This 'rule' had come into being in 1944 as an informal understanding between the BBC and the Government and it precluded the broadcasting of talks, discussions or debates on any issues being discussed in Parliament, or for two weeks before such a parliamentary debate was due to take place. It was invented by the BBC as a convenient means of avoiding pressure from Ministers wishing to broadcast on matters of current legislation at a time when plans for post-war reconstruction and the approach of the first General Election since 1935 were beginning to place a strain on the wartime coalition. In the 1950s, the BBC were coming bitterly to regret the arrangement; but, having once landed themselves with it, they were finding it, despite strong support from the Beveridge Committee, decidedly difficult to liquidate, especially when the Prime Minister was Sir Winston Churchill:

> *Mr Grimond*: Will not the Prime Minister reconsider the matter? Could it not be left to the good sense of the BBC to exercise discretion?
> *The Prime Minister*: No, Sir. I will never reconsider it. It would be shocking to have debates in this House forestalled time after time by expressions of opinion by persons who had not the status or responsibility of Members of Parliament . . . I am quite sure that the bringing of exciting debates in these vast, new robot organisations of television and BBC broadcasting, to take place before a debate in this House, might have very deleterious effects upon our general interests, and that hon. Members should be considering the interests of the House of Commons, to whom we all owe a lot.[1]

Fraser was quick to notice the existence of this 'queer rule'. He did not lack understanding of the view which Churchill took, dogmatically as it was expressed, but in a letter of 26 February to Clark he was saying:

> People say that the rule is ridiculous and ask why it should not be applied to the newspapers. But the newspapers speak with the many different voices of democracy. If there were only one newspaper in the whole land it seems to me very possible that members of Parliament might wish to place the same rule upon the press. But when we have in prospect alternative programmes and the public begins to look at these different programmes just as it buys different newspapers, the position surely begins to change.[2]

But the Authority had no inclination to be rushed into a controversy which was just beginning to build up, and decided to shelve the matter for the time being. On 2 March Gammans stated in the House that it was intended that the arrangements with the BBC would also be applied to the ITA. Meanwhile the BBC were making no progress in relieving themselves of their ten-year-old commitment and decided to challenge the Government to issue a formal directive if they wished the rule to persist. If they thought the Government would shrink from doing so, they were mistaken, and on 27 July they received a directive from the PMG, who was now Dr Charles Hill. So also did the ITA, in accordance with the terms of Section 9(2) of the Television Act.

Charles Hill wrote that he hereby required:

(a) that the Authority shall not, on any issue, arrange discussions or *ex parte* statements which are to be broadcast during a period of a fortnight before the issue is debated in either House or while it is being debated:

(b) that when legislation is introduced in Parliament on any subject, the Authority shall not, on such subject, arrange broadcasts by any Member of Parliament which are to be made during the period between the introduction of the legislation and the time when it either receives the Royal Assent or is previously withdrawn or dropped.[3]

He had the support of the Labour leadership, but not of the Liberals. Most Labour members followed their leaders but it was on the record that, during the Committee stage debates on the Television Bill, Anthony

Wedgwood Benn had expressed his strong personal disagreement with his own Party Front Bench's support for the rule.[4]

The companies received the news of this Government direction with dignified concern. The newspapers and periodicals were full of it. Not a single voice was raised in support of the prohibition and many were fierce in their condemnation: but initially the BBC, the ITA and the companies preserved their reticence, saving for one letter in *The Times* from the Editor-in-Chief of ITN, Aidan Crawley. To the Authority on 15 August came a letter from the Television Contractors Association registering their unanimous view that 'at some time in the future they will wish to contest what appears to them to be an arbitrary check on their freedom and independence and one which surely conflicts with our national traditions'.[5] Against this background the Authority decided on 16 August that the Chairman should attempt in conjunction with the BBC to discuss the matter with the PMG.

The latter was not to be drawn (nor for that matter was the Chairman of the BBC), and he declared emphatically that there was absolutely nothing he could do until the matter had been debated in the House. A meeting in September with Government and Opposition representatives was equally unforthcoming. The Prime Minister stated at question time in the House on 8 November 'This was an arrangement originally voluntarily arrived at. I think it is a reasonable arrangement in the interests of Parliament and everybody concerned, and I see no present cause to vary it.'[6]

'Originally voluntarily arrived at' described accurately enough the position so far as the BBC were concerned. There had been no prior consultation with the ITA before the PMG's directions were issued and published. The Authority and the companies had never freely consented to the arrangement; on the contrary they had always been most strongly opposed to it.

For once, Independent Television could sail before a wind of public opinion which was making itself felt even within the precincts of the Palace of Westminster. In a leaflet widely circulated by the National Council for Civil Liberties shortly after Churchill's statement on 8 November they said:

> Censorship as blatant as this may seem quite incredible but this is not just nonsense invented overnight by a bureaucracy which has not woken up to the fact that we are living in the twentieth century. The letter from the Postmaster General [Dr Hill] merely makes an official ruling on a matter which had previously been the subject of a 'gentleman's agreement' [i.e. between the BBC and a previous administration] . . . All measures that are taken to restrict Freedom of Speech, Freedom of the Press and

Freedom of the Air are measures which are designed to keep public opinion less informed, particularly at crucial moments, and thus to make it less effective.

That was one way of looking at it. A memorandum by the PMG, possibly intended for his Ministerial colleagues, shows that he was, at that time, stating the position quite differently. He pointed out that the BBC not only sought the rule in the first place, but while operating it justified it. In their memorandum to the Beveridge Committee they described the object of the rule as 'to ensure that the BBC at no time becomes an alternative simultaneous debating forum to Parliament'. In their 1954/5 Annual Report, they stated that 'the object of the rule has been to give effect to the principle that broadcasting should not be allowed to encroach on the position of Parliament as the supreme forum for the discussion of public issues'.

The memorandum went on to point out that the rule had worked successfully and without noticeable oppression. Could it be said to have prevented free speech on the air? The conversion of the rule into a formal prescription was sought not by the parties but by the BBC. There were important differences between the press on the one hand and the BBC and ITV on the other. An article in the press or a statement at a meeting was open to immediate challenge or rebuttal. The press was so varied in outlook and policy that anyone with a point of view worth expressing could ventilate it in that medium. In controversy, there was a 'free for all'. The citizen could write to the press with a reasonable prospect of having his letter published in one or other newspaper. On the air, on the other hand, the number of people who could express views on a given subject was very small and these people were selected by the broadcasting authority. The air was not available to anyone to say his piece. Was it unreasonable to ask that, when Parliament was to discuss an issue within the following fortnight, the BBC should avoid the topic? If this was done, Government and Opposition speakers could deploy their facts and arguments and public debate could follow on them. If it was not done, there was a danger that broadcasters, representative and unrepresentative, accurate and inaccurate, informed and uninformed, selected by a Director of Talks because of their broadcasting technique and photogenic qualities, may form public opinion and prejudge the issue to a vast audience before Parliament had had an opportunity to get to grips with it. What freedoms were diminished as a result of the fortnight rule? It was not the freedom of the press, for they were not subject to, and would not be subject to, any such limitations. It was not the freedom of the public, because they had no say in the selection of the speakers or opportunity to answer them.

What was at stake said Hill, was the position of Parliament, to quote the BBC's own words, 'as the supreme forum for the discussion of public issues'. Parliament should be the principal forum for the discussion and debate of public affairs – not the only forum but the principal forum. If it were true that broadcasting, because of its very nature, could easily supplant Parliament as the principal forum for the discussion and debate of public affairs, should we stand aside and let it happen? This was the crux of the matter. The maintenance of the prestige of Parliament was an essential ingredient of freedom. If it was necessary to impose limited and sharply defined restrictions on broadcasting in order to sustain the prestige of Parliament and to protect the public, then it should be done. For a few broadcasters to be in a position in scripted and unscripted discussions to prejudge issues immediately before Parliament was proposing to consider them would mean granting freedom of speech for the few at the expense of the many, and at the expense of Parliament.

The Government had already decided that the matter would have to be debated in Parliament itself and expressed the hope that 'it may be possible' to arrange one in the week beginning 28 November. This lack of precision gave ITV a chance to make a tactical manoeuvre and the subject was chosen for discussion in an edition of ATV's political programme appropriately called *Free Speech* on 20 November. The ITA raised no objection to ATV's choice, arguing that as it had not been announced that the debate would take place within fourteen days, it had no right to prohibit discussion of the rule on television and that, had it done so, it would have exceeded the duties placed on it by the PMG's direction. On 25 November Clark wrote officially to Hill saying that the Authority felt quite unable to agree that so powerful a limitation on the right of free speech and free discussion was justified.

In the House of Commons on 30 November, the PMG proposed the appointment of a Select Committee to consider whether any changes were desirable in the method of giving effect to the principle of limiting the anticipation of debates by broadcasting. He indicated that the BBC were just as intent as were the Party leaders on some limitation:

The BBC agreed that there should be a limitation – indeed it had devised one. It had worked to an agreed limitation. It was still prepared to operate a limitation provided that it was within its own discretion. What was unacceptable (i.e. to the Party leaders) was that the Corporation, and the Corporation alone, shall have full responsibility for working that limitation and for modifying it . . . It was the BBC which, having failed to persuade the party leaders that the Corporation should decide and operate the rule, insisted on a direction.[7]

In what was otherwise a fair and balanced speech, recognising the existence of different points of view, Hill failed to state that, for its part, the ITA was opposed (as were the companies) to any such limitation, whether by direction or by agreement.

The motion was supported by the leader of the Opposition, Mr Attlee, speaking for himself (for there was to be a free vote). 'The odd thing is,' he said, 'that despite all the cries now that this is a terrible infringement and a hardship, nobody noticed it for about seven years. As long as the practice was not reduced to writing it worked perfectly well, as so many of our conventions do.'[8] Throughout his speech, which was brief, Attlee spoke about the wireless and never mentioned television at all, let alone Independent Television. Actually he was also wrong. It was incorrect to imply that, prior to that direction, the practice had not been reduced to writing. What had been bothering the BBC was precisely that fact – that in 1948 it had been incorporated in an unpublished *aide-mémoire* primarily designed to settle the basis on which they would transmit Ministerial broadcasts. The BBC had allowed themselves to be hoisted with their own petard; for by introducing safeguards in the *aide-mémoire* against Ministerial broadcasts of a controversial character, they had removed the danger from which they had originally sought to defend themselves by inventing the Fourteen Day Rule. The *aide-mémoire* was not published until the Report of the Beveridge Committee came out in January 1951.[9] The Report itself was explicit. 'We do not see why the British democracy should not be allowed to have microphone debate of a political issue at the time when debate is most topical and interesting, that is to say when the issue is actually before Parliament.'

Since 1953 the BBC had struggled in vain to persuade the Party leaders to release them from their commitment. From August 1954 onwards there was a further reason why something should be done. Referring to a meeting with the Parties, Asa Briggs has described the argument put by the BBC Chairman, Sir Alexander Cadogan, and says: 'The imminent advent of commercial television, Cadogan went on, made it essential to have a definite Government statement one way or the other'.[10] This was the origin of Dr Hill's specific regulation in 1955.

The ITA was not brought into the BBC's discussions with the Parties and their reluctant spokesman, the PMG. That Dr Hill was now reluctant was no secret. 'Of course, it is quite well known,' said Harry Crookshank, the Lord Privy Seal, in winding up the debate, 'that this difference of opinion, if that is the right word to use, started long before he took his present office. It was also quite well known that, as Postmaster-General, he would not have been taking action of this kind on his own initiative.'[11] Years later Hill wrote: 'Freedom of expression has its dangers like any other freedom and my hunch was that it would be wiser to take the risks than yield to any amount of logical and reasonable argument for its limitation.'[12]

An amendment designed to give the proposed Select Committee a free hand to make its recommendations untramelled by any commitment to the principle of limitation on the anticipation of debates was rejected by 271 votes to 126 and the PMG's original motion was then carried without a division.

One striking characteristic of this rather desultory debate was the evidence it contained of the distrust, even resentment, with which broadcasting continued to be regarded by the political parties. For some members, of course, the arrival of ITV on the scene had only served to deepen this distrust. Patrick Gordon-Walker, faithful henchman of Herbert Morrison, said that there was no knowing what would happen if the rule were abandoned. 'This is going to be settled by the people who broadcast, and among these is commercial television. This alters the situation. If it were only the BBC I could understand some argument for a gentleman's agreement, but with commercial television we are, by definition, not dealing with gentlemen.'[13] To which Robert Boothby, a professional broadcaster like Hill himself, replied: 'I am fascinated to hear . . . that the view still lingers among honourable gentlemen opposite that one cannot engage in trade and remain a gentleman.'[14] Like Jane Austen's Netherfield ladies, socialist Gordon-Walker (a former fellow and tutor of Christchurch College, Oxford) had difficulty in believing that men who lived by trade could be well bred and agreeable.

Boothby himself had, of course, been one of the stars of *In the News* which, together with *Press Conference* was the BBC's regular provision on television for politically interested viewers. Its regular team, which included Bevanite Michael Foot as well as Boothby had their appearances rationed in the interests of political balance, and the programme suffered constraint also under the provisions of the *aide-mémoire*. Early in 1955 virtually the whole outfit transferred their allegiance to Norman Collins, reappearing in September of that year as *Free Speech* when ITV took to the air. Small wonder that the only utterances expressed with passionate conviction during the debate came from Boothby. He deplored the rule and added:

I think broadcasting and television have one specific advantage over the Press in that on any controversial issue both sides of the case are presented. I would say – and I beg honourable members on both sides of the House to consider this – that during the last few years millions of people in this country have heard the other side for the first time.[15]

When the Select Committee got under way in February 1956, the distinction in broadcasting between the position of MPs and of other citizens was further pursued in BBC memoranda and in oral evidence by Jacob. 'It only seems to me that if there is any substance in any of this at all, then that is one of the places where it resides; namely that we shall not provide, on important matters, an alternative for a Member of Parliament to come and make his speech on the BBC, when the debate is, in fact, taking place in the House'.[16] Giving evidence for the ITA, Fraser demurred to this attitude of the BBC's. 'I am afraid I take a very different view. I would even go further and say that I cannot think of anyone who, on the face of it, could more appropriately take part in such discussions.'[17]

Try as both authorities did to keep in step it proved impossible to conceal from an intelligent Committee, brilliantly chaired by Sir Lionel Heald, QC, fundamental differences of approach. Both bodies were willing to concede that with subjects of high national importance about which new and crucial information was expected to be disclosed in a debate known to be taking place within a week, it would be prudent to avoid prior discussion on television or radio. Beyond this what mainly preoccupied the BBC was their desire to recover for the Governors the full freedom to exercise their own discretion which they had surrendered when subscribing to the *aide-mémoire*. What mainly concerned the ITA was the difficulty of finding and operating any intermediate position between full freedom for the companies to proceed as they wished, so long as they were not in breach of the Act or their contracts, and the continuance of a formal prescription.

There were clear differences in style between the evidence presented by the old body and the new. Rightly or wrongly, the Committee acquired the impression first that the BBC were being deliberately perverse in their interpretation of the directive so as to make it seem nonsensical and secondly that the BBC were determined to exclude MPs from any political programmes even remotely affected by it. The ITA on the other hand appeared as a body dutifully doing its best to comply with the rule but handicapped by its own lack of direct control over the relevant programmes. Clark made it quite clear that, if relieved of the prescription, ITA would still be prepared to exercise restraint on the discussion of subjects on which, prior to debate in

Parliament, the public was insufficiently informed; and he was quite optimistic about the Authority's ability to secure such restraint from the producing companies. He was also as positive as had been Fraser that there was no need to draw a distinction between broadcasters who were MPs and those who were not.

The Committee's report was finalised on 17 May, less than a month after hearing its last two witnesses, Cadogan of the BBC and Clark. It occupied just over two pages, and doubtless its Chairman had much to do with its lucidity as well as its brevity. It recommended that any restrictions should be reduced to the smallest extent that was practicable. It said that the only justification which could be claimed for any policy of limitation was the necessity of upholding the primacy of Parliament in the affairs of the nation; and that in view of the advent of competition in television it was doubtful whether even this provided anything more than a temporary justification for a special rule not applicable to other organs of publicity. It thought the development of radio and television and the broadcast discussion of public affairs which had followed it had done much to encourage intelligent interest in the work of Parliament.

On the question whether the limitation, as well as its administration, could be left to the organisations concerned, the Committee noted that the BBC appeared to desire this, but the Independent Television Authority expressed a clear preference – if there has to be any limitation – for a definite rule of guidance to be laid down by Parliament. It had no doubt that the view of the ITA was the sounder of the two and recommended that the Government should take the responsibility of laying down and *enforcing* any restriction which Parliament might deem necessary. Further, it recommended that in future any limitation upon anticipation should apply only from the time of the announcement of business, and that the limitation should not begin to operate until seven days before the business in question was to be taken.

As regards the rule which applied the prohibition to all legislation pending in the current session, the Committee thought it unnecessary and undesirable, and recommended that no rule other than that already proposed should apply to any legislation, and that, in the case of a Bill that has passed its Second Reading, no restriction should apply at all.

The Committee was clear that MPs should be treated in exactly the same way as other persons in the administration of any restriction upon broadcasting and it could see no justification for confining the restriction to Members, as the BBC had suggested.

Although the proposed restriction should be embodied in a prescription issued by the PMG, the Committee was strongly of the opinion that some flexibility should be allowed for in its application and therefore recommended that it should be so drafted as to allow for relaxation at the discretion of the PMG in individual instances.

Finally, it was recommended that the House should appoint, at any rate for an experimental period, a small committee or panel of Members, who would be available to advise the PMG in connection with any application for relaxation.

Whilst the Committee were in the final stages of drafting their report they had received a joint personal memorandum from Clark and Fraser[18] which proved to be very closely in line with the conclusions that were being reached. As regards the apparent difference in attitude between the BBC and the ITA to which paragraphs 5 and 6 alluded, the two ITA men said:

> We see an insuperable objection in principle to any substitute rule imposed by the broadcasting organisations themselves: namely that the prohibition of public discussion in a free country is so grave a matter that it could be justified on no authority less than Parliament itself.

The BBC felt that the Committee had misunderstood their attitude, saying that what they had suggested was that if there had to be some limitation the extent of it should be defined by Parliament, but the Governors should be trusted to interpret and apply it. They also represented that it was wrong to infer that they believed in restricting MPs more than others. They did, however, express great dislike of the proposal to allow the PMG discretionary powers. The Authority gave the Report a warmer welcome, but it shared the BBC's misgivings that the new rules proposed by the Committee might be meant to apply to the House of Lords, and that the word 'issues' might be replaced by 'subjects' in any new prescription. Hitherto, the broadcasters had on occasions been able to escape the full severity of the restrictions by arguing that some topics were not 'issues'.

The Government showed marked reluctance to take action. However, Dr Hill – by now a convinced abolitionist – felt that time was on his side and he was not too sorry that the great issue of Suez raised acute problems in relation to the direction that was continuing to operate. Writing to the Post Office early in November Fraser said:

> The truth of the matter is surely that when the country is confronted with an issue of great magnitude the broadcasting organisations are under a moral obligation to contribute towards a public understanding of it, and

that in fact this contribution can be made without conflicting in the slightest degree with the primacy of Parliament as the great forum of the nation.[19]

It was apropos of this situation that Hill reminded the readers of *Both Sides of the Hill* that there were more ways than one of killing a cat.[20] Conversations took place between the usual channels and it became a question of how the party leaders could back down without too much loss of face. Both Chairmen of both broadcasting bodies were asked to undertake – and they did – that they would continue to act in a way which did not derogate from the primacy of Parliament as the forum for debating the affairs of the nation and would intend to act within the spirit of the Resolution approved by the House of Commons on 30 November 1955. The Authority, after consultation, coupled the companies with its assurance. The PMG revoked on 18 December the notice he had issued on 27 July 1955 and the Prime Minister announced on the same day the decision to suspend the rule for an experimental period of six months. On 8 July 1957, a new PMG, Ernest Marples, notified the two Chairmen of the decision that 'the present arrangements and understandings should continue for an indefinite period'.

The politicians never subsequently showed any wish to disinter the rule. The quid pro quo assurances have never been withdrawn; but with the passage of time they have ceased to be meaningful. It was a famous victory for freedom of speech in which Independent Television played an honourable part. By themselves the BBC might have had far greater trouble in exorcising a ghost from a former regime. More recently Lord Hill has told the author that repeal would have been more difficult had it not been for Suez. He himself, whilst remaining PMG for the time being, had been given the task of co-ordinating Government information and so he attended all Cabinet meetings relating to Suez. He was thus able to choose the right moment for getting the agreement of the Party leaders. He acted with skill and determination, which were all the more necessary in view of the fact that senior officials at the Post Office were recommending maintenance of the rule.[21]

(ii) THE END OF THE 'TODDLERS' TRUCE'

There were those who were disposed to see it as the end of civilisation as they knew it. Dr Hill was not one of these: and when asked to reflect on the developments of broadcasting that occurred during his short sojourn at the Post Office, it is the opening of the closed period on television between 6 p.m. and 7 p.m. on weekdays that springs most readily to his mind. The Sunday closed period – sometimes irreverently called the 'God-slot' – was quite a different matter. That was to remain closed to general broadcasting for another twenty years.

Hill inherited a responsibility for prescribing television hours which he would have preferred not to possess. If the Television Bill had remained in its original form and not been amended in the Lords all he would have had to do was prescribe maximum and minimum hours. The phrase 'as to the hours of the day in which such broadcasts are or are not to be given' which appeared in Clause 9(3) was proposed by Lord Jowitt at the Report Stage on 20 July 1954 and grudgingly accepted by De La Warr, who recalled that in Committee Lord Simon of Wythenshawe (a former Chairman of the BBC) had actually proposed an amendment to the effect that ITA's hours should always be the same as those of the BBC.[22] In the Commons, David Gammans, moving 'that this House doth agree with the Lords in the said Amendment', said 'it does not mean that the hours broadcast by the BBC will be the same for the new Authority'.[23] Philip Bell (Bolton East) said, 'I hope that this power will not be used to protect the BBC.'[24]

For nearly the next twenty years Philip Bell's hope was to be largely unfulfilled, and the work of the BBC's well-organised lobby at this late stage of the Bill was to be amply rewarded. Even in Charles Hill's time as PMG, the practice developed in the Post Office of refusing to act in liberalising control of hours unless both broadcasting services could first reach agreement between themselves. His action over the toddlers' truce was a rare exception.

When the initial deal was done over television hours (Chapter 15) this evening break was already established practice in the BBC service, and the ITV negotiators were counselled by the Post Office not to question it; to do so would be to rock the boat.[25] It was the Authority's opinion that the 'social justification', i.e. giving parents an opportunity to get the children to bed, of which some play had been made in the House of Lords, was an afterthought. It appeared more likely that it really owed its origin to the lack of any positive desire on the part of the BBC to stay continuously on the air once the day's television had begun.

By the summer of 1956, this closed hour had become for the companies – now in dire financial straits – a very serious handicap, and the only surprise for the Authority was that they left it until early July to agree joint, formal representations seeking its abolition. When their letter arrived Fraser described it as 'a dear little mouse'. From their point of view, the case was overwhelming and their failure to present it sooner despite constant pressure by the ITA is a commentary on the rudimentary nature of their arrangements for concerted action in matters of common concern. The Authority's own data showed that the approximate percentage of television sets in use consistently conformed to the following pattern:

	Summer	Winter
3–4 p.m.	18	24
4–5 p.m.	24	42
5–6 p.m.	44	57
6–7 p.m.	–	–
7–8 p.m.	53	67
8–9 p.m.	68	83
9–10 p.m.	69	82
10–11 p.m.	49	56

From these figures it looked certain that the percentage of receivers that would be in use if the evening break were abolished would be not less than 50–60 per cent. It was estimated that the total financial benefit accruing to the whole system from the abolition of the break (without any increase in the overall maximum hours of programme transmission) could in 1957 be of the order of £2½ million. These and other data were assembled by the ITA and on 3 August Clark wrote officially to the PMG requesting the removal of the ban on television between 6 and 7 p.m. on Mondays to Saturdays. The agreement of the BBC to seeking this concession had been sought but refused.

So far as Hill was concerned, Clark was pushing at an open door, but he had his administrative problems. Later he wrote:

This restriction seemed to me to be absurd, and I said so. It was the responsibility of parents, not the State, to put their children to bed at the right time. Many people get home from work between 5 and 6 p.m. and it was unreasonable to deny them the opportunity of watching television between 6 and 7 p.m. . . . I invited the BBC and the ITA to agree to its abolition.

The BBC would not agree. It would not even agree to a compromise suggestion that, as a first step, the break should be reduced to half an hour. A few days later, the Governors of the BBC passed a resolution strongly in favour of the maintenance of the whole hour of silence. I abolished it altogether.[26]

Actually it was not until 31 October that Hill could inform Clark confidentially that the Government had now accepted the principle that within a maximum of fifty hours weekly, and not more than eight hours on any one day, each authority should be permitted to broadcast in the hours it deemed appropriate with such local and daily variations as it thought wise. This was to be subject to the maintenance of a Sunday evening break and the ban on television broadcasting before 2 p.m. on Sunday. It was another month before formal revision of the rules and a public announcement became possible. Part of that month was occupied in resolving the difference between BBC and ITV as to when the change should take effect: the former wanted 1 April 1957, the latter 29 December 1956. Hill split the difference, and decided on 16 February 1957.

On 23 January 1957, the House of Lords had a debate on broadcasting – its first since the Television Act was passed in July 1954 – which gave an opportunity for reviewing the Government's decision. To say that the debate lacked distinction is the least unkind comment that is possible. Lord Simon of Wythenshawe asked what enquiries the Government had made before making its decision:

> Did they consult the National Union of Teachers? Did they consult the Mothers' Union? I know that they consulted the BBC and that the BBC objected strongly, saying that it would cost them £500,000 a year . . . surely it is almost unthinkable that for no adequate reason this extra burden should be imposed on the BBC – the only reason being, presumably, to increase the profits of Independent Television.[27]

To which the Government spokesman, Lord Munster, could only reply that the BBC did not have to make the change if they did not want to.[28]

The press coverage of this development was generally cynical. Some newspapers carried 'vox-pop' interviews reflecting a wide spectrum of opinion amongst the general public. School homework was brought into the issue, and there was no shortage of teachers and education administrators who could be found to deplore the development. There was talk of getting up protest petitions; for it could hardly be disputed that the change was going to make things difficult for a child in a home where there was only one room in which the whole family could live. Nevertheless, on balance, the press gave a mild welcome to a new freedom. 'TV to be freed' said the *Manchester Guardian* headline. 'The Way is Clear for High-Tea TV' said the *Daily Mail*.

But, of course, as ever, the press continued to imply that it was all achieved by the pressure exerted on Government by the Machiavellian companies. Commentators would have found it hard to accept the truth, that all running was made by the ITA and that, in any event, the PMG had made up his own mind that the rule was 'absurd'. That was not the sort of story their editors wanted them to write.

The question that remains is whether ITV – and the BBC too – put the concession to any good use; whether it made for an improvement in the programme services. One answer is clear. It greatly extended the opportunities for regional television.

31

PROGRAMME DEVELOPMENTS

(i) STOP-GO

As the financial problems of the London companies became more acute so did the 'retreat' which the *News Chronicle* had detected at the end of November 1955 become more evident. In January 1956 the Authority was shocked to find that ATV had published their first programme schedule for the Midlands at the same time as it was delivered to its own headquarters at Princes Gate, and its Chairman promptly informed Prince Littler that this was not the way to run a railway.

Incidents of this kind were not uncommon in the early years of ITV. The failure of the ITA to secure any public knowledge or understanding of its role and of the two-tier system over which by statute it presided was matched by a comparable failure within the companies at any level below their top managements to appreciate the implications of conducting private enterprise television under public control. Nor was there any spontaneous readiness on the part of the company chiefs to inform and educate their staffs about the responsibilities of the ITA under the Television Act or to regard it themselves as having any close involvement in the programme output.

The ATV schedule, for the Midlands, was made up predominantly of variety, drama or dramatic series. Presentations from real life or discussions of serious subject were conspicuously lacking. Nevertheless, ATV's success in London with *Free Speech* and *About Religion*, two outstanding programmes of their kind, showed what could be done when the company gave their mind to it. And there were other programmes of the kind available from A-R on a network basis.

The first few weekends from ABC Television revealed somewhat nobler intentions, although the standards of competence in presentation were dismally low. Their saving grace was a real and quite successful attempt to supply features of local interest on the two days of the week when they might have been forgiven for offering fare which had a safe, conventional and universal appeal. Before long, however, ATV started to embark on the same course, and, with five days at their disposal, soon began to make the stronger impact.

The ITA was destined for some years to be seen by supposedly informed observers either as a 'sleeping watchdog' or as a timid, censorious brake on enterprise and initiative. It was not uncommon to find the same observer saying both things at different times. The bulk of the audience was indifferent to such matters, and appreciated the new freedom to choose between the services by the flick of a switch. Yet the measurement figures revealed right from the outset a disconcerting tendency to settle down with one channel or the other, choosing whichever seemed in general to provide the kind of entertainment that was most liked rather than to select individual programmes irrespective of the service which provided them. Consequently, for an ITV struggling for survival as a viable business enterprise 'capturing the audience' was the first priority: securing what the Act called a proper balance in the programmes was not of immediate importance and any reference by the controlling authority to such an objective was deemed unrealistic. As has been seen, the Authority itself saw no alternative to endorsing this attitude in its public utterances as Clark himself had done on ITN in January (Chapter 25).

All this having been said it was significant that a Gallup opinion poll conducted in the middle of March showed a marked preference for the ITV programmes over those of the BBC, and a striking similarity between the degree of preference in London and in the Midlands. The figures were as follows:

	London	Birmingham
Prefer ITV	60	58
Prefer BBC	16	16
No choice	19	20
Don't know	5	7

So there was nearly a 4 : 1 preference for the ITV programmes among those who had a feeling one way or the other. If those who felt no particular preference were distributed equally between the two, the degree of preference was about 3 : 1. The rapidity with which the preference had been established in the Midlands astonished even the two companies which provided the programmes.

Meanwhile, Northern England, Granadaland as it soon came to be called, was awaiting the arrival of the new service which was due to begin on

3 May in the area west of the Pennines. The newspapers there began to treat the approaching day as big news. For example, the *Bolton Evening News* on 27 April under the banner headline 'You're Going to Like the New TV', carried a long report from an anonymous north countryman now living in the south, which was calculated to make its readers' mouths water. It attempted a comparison between the BBC they knew and the ITV which they were about to meet.

This absentee from the north seemed not to appreciate that Granada Television were in no mood to have their programme service regarded as a carbon copy of the ones provided further south. Tom Driberg had told readers of the *New Statesman* on 18 February that Granada's whole approach to television was strikingly different from that of the London contractors: 'more philosophic, more methodical, and also more reserved in the imparting of information and the soliciting of trade . . . Mr Bernstein was obstinately reticent on the nature and content of the programmes'. Bernstein certainly had a knack of using his own instinctive reticence to advantage. 'The fact remains' said the *Manchester Evening News* on 9 March 'that by his silence Mr Bernstein has attracted as much attention as has ABC Television, the other Manchester company, which has announced its programmes in full.'

Bernstein promised no immediate successes, either in programme or in financial terms. Referring in April to developments in the South, he said that not only had money been lost but people had also lost their jobs. 'We cannot start too big or else we crash . . . The only way is to start small and build up.'[1] It was true enough that around the beginning of May the auguries from the South could hardly have been worse. Losses mounting daily; programme budgets being pruned; schedules being 'adjusted'; and staff departing either from frustration and disillusionment or because their services were no longer required.

On 27 January that youthful, engaging, plausible impresario of international television production and distribution, Harry Alan Towers, abruptly left the boards of ATV and ITPC. Towers had done ATV no small service, for he had put them on the London screen on time. Val Parnell became chief executive of ATV and, frostily, the announcement said: 'The boards of the two companies acknowledge Mr Towers' efforts in connection with the start of commercial television'. Towers had, amongst other things, produced *The Scarlet Pimpernel* series and it was clever of the *Daily Mail* to name him 'Pimpernel Man'. His counterpart in A-R, Roland Gillett – the man who two months previously had dared to speak of giving the public what it wants – departed by a coincidence on the selfsame day. John

McMillan, who had been with A-R six weeks took over as programme controller – after having been appointed business manager earlier in the day! Cecil Lewis, who had been Gillett's deputy, departed on 28 May. Some creative people, such as Desmond Davis, head of drama for ATV, seem to have moved out more because they lacked the opportunities they had expected than because they did not relish the heat of the kitchen.

Granada's arrival on the Northern scene was a deliberately muted one, and yet it attracted more critical attention than ABC's at the weekends – perhaps because most of the critics were already familiar from their Midlands transmissions with ABC's style of popular entertainment. Five days after their opening night Bernstein summed up Granada's performance as 'singularly free from praise and abuse'.

The development that by itself justifies speaking of 'progress' in 1956/7 was the formation of the central network and the consequent opening up of new sources of programme supply. In September 1955 the programmes had come from two companies based in London; in May 1956 the sources comprised four companies operating from London, Birmingham and Manchester. And, moreover, each of the four were as distinguishable in character one from another as ITV as a whole was distinguishable from the BBC.

An immediate consequence of this completion of the first phase of the ITA's development plan (saving for the delayed extension to Yorkshire of the Granada/ABC service in the North) was a recognition by A-R that they were very substantially over-equipped and over-manned. Spencer Wills and his management saw more quickly than did ATV that networking arrangements were essential to the economy of the system as well as to the quality of the programme service overall, and there was a period during the summer of 1956 when arrangements between those two companies completely broke down. A-R braced themselves to secure the unions' agreement to the redundancy of between 200 and 300 employees. This was achieved on 21 August after successful negotiations with the ACTT, the ABS, NATKE and the ETU. By the standards of the day, the compensation paid by A-R was munificent. At this juncture, the Wills–Bernstein agreement had already been signed (Chapter 28 (iii)), and ATV had been brought to see that no company could be an island unto itself. A-R was able to announce that from 14 September onwards their share of the London transmissions would be reduced by twelve hours a week – no less than 35 per cent. The makeshift studio at the Granville Theatre, Walham Green, was to be closed, one outside broadcast unit was to be put in moth balls, three telecine projection channels were to be frozen and two interview studios at Television House were to be dispensed with.

At the annual general meeting of A-R on 18 November, Wills speaking of networking, said:

> These arrangements are, in my view, essential to the success of the contractors who now cover the main areas of the country. Comprehensive networking arrangements are now in force and we are grateful to the other contractors concerned for their co-operation. So far as new and undeveloped areas are concerned, it is my belief that no new programme company can in itself have any possible economic justification; it could only avoid insolvency by taking practically all its programmes on network from the existing contractors.

The last sentence struck an ominous note. The pure ITA doctrine of the 'competitive optional network' seemed quite unrealistic to Wills. He had succeeded against all odds, and might be forgiven for feeling that he held the whole of Independent Television in his hand. But he was no tyrant. He was genuinely concerned with the public good as he saw it:

> We do accept that we have a duty, in serving our viewers to cater for a reasonable minority as well as for the majority. No one in his senses would, however, expect us to put on a programme wanted only by a small minority at an hour at which the large majority expect to be served. My opinion is that a surfeit of any type of programme brings its own cure. A proper balance is essential to our continued existence.

Wills also said that what constitutes 'balance' was a matter of opinion. In the judgement of the Authority there had in this respect been a year of recession which was endurable only so long as heavy financial losses were being incurred and the Government was refusing to implement its pledge to make a financial grant. The facts spoke for themselves. In October 1955, there had been about sixteen regular programmes outside the field of entertainment. By summer and autumn 1956 there were barely half a dozen, as Table 31.1 shows.

Presenting this data to the companies early in September at the Standing Consultative Committee, Fraser stressed that the Authority could not ignore its statutory obligations, although it was unwilling to make demands on the companies which were unreasonable in relation to the state of their finances. He acknowledged that the news from ITN was both high in quality and sufficient in quantity: that *This Week*, due to be fully networked that autumn, was an excellent weekly news magazine; and that *About Religion*

TABLE 31.1 *Programmes outside the field of entertainment*

ITA October 1955	ITA (London) Summer 1956	ITA(London) Autumn 1956
Public affairs Free Speech Wide World (F) Assignment Unknown (F) Foreign Press Club	This Week	Free Speech This Week
Social questions Points of View (F)		We Think (20) I Remember (15)
Science Scientist Replies (F) Peaceful Atom (F)		
Religion Epilogues (D) Billy Graham (M)	Epilogues (D) About Religion	Epilogues (D) About Religion
Documentary British Heritage (F) Out of Town (F) Personal Call (F) Orson Welles (F)	Look in on London (15)	
The arts Hallé (F 60) Debut (15) Sunday Afternoon (45)	Music Sets the Scene (F 45)	
Approximate running time 4 hours 50 mins	2 hours	2 hours 30 mins

NOTE: This table excludes the news, children's programmes and any other relevant afternoon programmes except on Saturdays and Sundays. All programmes belong to a series, mostly weekly. Where they were daily, fortnightly or monthly, this is indicated by (D), (F), (M). Where programmes ran for less or more than 30 minutes this is indicated by the figures, in numbers of minutes, after the title.

was a creditable weekly religious series. But he thought that there was need for a good, regular general discussion programme of adequate length; documentaries which were windows both on Britain and the world; a 'person to person' series such as Ed Murrow had pioneered in America; and a regular programme in which viewers could be presented with good plays, old and new, good music (for the Hallé concerts seemed to be petering out), opera and ballet. In other words, something like America's famous *Omnibus*. 'In the light of experience so far, it seems to the Authority that little is gained by way of balance in having a lot of small programmes tucked away in odd corners. It prefers to look for a limited number of programmes of outstanding character which will make their mark and become respected.'[2]

Six months later, in March 1957, Fraser had a very different story to tell the Authority. In the general field of public affairs, science and religion, ITV now had in addition to the fifteen national news bulletins, ten regional bulletins, and five two-minute bulletins, eleven weekly programmes most of which were networked. They were:

1. *Free Speech* (topical political discussion between well-known commentators)
2. *About Religion*
3. *Outlook* (scientific programme)
4. *This Week* (topical news magazine)
5. *Roving Report* (a feature programme from ITN highlighting other countries and people in the news)
6. *What the Papers Say* (London and the North) (review of events of the week as reflected in the press)
7. *Members Mail* (showing how MPs dealt with constituency problems)
8. *Under Fire* (North) (an audience in the North questioning a panel of experts in London)
9. *Paper Talk* (Midlands) (interviews on topical subjects)
10. *Youth Wants to Know* (prominent experts questioned by a group of young people)
11. *Round Peg* (vocational guidance)

In addition, there were the daily *Epilogues* in London and the Midlands. Numbers 3, 5, 10 and 11 were all to be found in the period 6–7 p.m. which, as we have seen, had been opened to television a month earlier by Dr Hill against the wishes of the BBC.

In the field covered by these eleven programmes, the BBC only had three regular weekly programmes, together with its new 'topical programme for all the family' called *Tonight*, which was difficult to classify. They had good science and current affairs programmes on an irregular basis. These usually came to three or so a week. They also had a regular ten minute Sunday religious programme for children, but still had an epilogue only on Sundays. In music, with their usual hour and a half of good music on Sundays, and in classical drama (though no longer in modern plays) the BBC retained their higher standards, and had a clear field in their practical programmes for women during the afternoon. ITV no longer had a women's programme at all, as the successful network programme *Lunch Box* at 12.45 exhausted the permitted 50 hours. The BBC also retained their lead in documentaries on subjects other than current affairs; but these did not amount to more than a programme or so each week, and ITV now had, after much trial and error, a successful weekly Person-to-Person type of programme in their new Bernard Braden series.

Retrenchment, recession and rationalisation, the three imperatives of 1956, involved everyone and everything connected with the making of programmes. On the trade union side collective attempts to contain the flow of redundancy by ABS, ACTT, NATKE and ETU were severely tested as the dovelike ABS fell foul of their more hawkish brethren. ABS would not join in the goslow which followed A-R's redundancy announcement in May: they thought it more seemly to concentrate in gentlemanly fashion on securing the best possible compensation terms. The guerrilla war between ACTT and ABS which had broken out a year earlier lasted a further year. It ended in August 1957 when the companies (but not the ITA) finally gave the ABS three months' formal notice of termination of their agreements with them. Even though their membership in the companies was numerically smaller than that of ABS, the experience of ACTT in the film industry proved to be more effectual in television than experience as a staff association of the BBC monopoly. The first national agreement between ACTT and the ITV companies was signed on 14 August 1957, a date which proved to be one of great significance in the ITV calendar.

(ii) POLITICAL BROADCASTING

ITV were not yet transmitting programmes at the time of the General Election in the summer of 1955. On BBC Television there were three formal election broadcasts by the Conservative party, three by Labour and one by the Liberals. Except for these official broadcasts, the BBC followed their established practice of ruthlessly excluding from their programmes everything that could conceivably be held to influence opinion on election issues. Save for references in the news and for the official broadcasts, radio and television avoided the election campaign like the plague.

But, quite apart from election broadcasting, during the spring and summer of 1955 the Authority and the companies had to sort out their attitude to the arrangements made between the Corporation, the Government and the Opposition for the annual series of party political broadcasts in the year 1 April 1955 to 31 March 1956. These were announced by the BBC as two television broadcasts each for Conservative and Labour with an additional option of taking two further television broadcasts each in lieu of sound broadcasts. The Liberal party were allowed to take their allocation of one broadcast either on sound or television or on both simultaneously. It had become the custom for the BBC, which had been transmitting party political broadcasts ever since 1933 (except during the war years), to settle the number and allotments of these broadcasts at informal meetings with leaders of the two main political parties.

To the discomfiture of the Authority and the satisfaction of the BBC, these broadcasts were described in Section 2(5) and Section 3(2) of the Television Act as 'the British Broadcasting Corporation's party political broadcasts'. It was permissible for the Authority to include in its programmes relays of the whole (but not some only) of a series of such BBC broadcasts, and these (and the sound radio broadcasts) could be transmitted by the Authority in sound only as well. But the Act did not *require* the Authority to do these things – only that, if it did do them, *all* of a series must be taken.[3]

There were other prevailing arrangements between the BBC and the parties to which the Act did not refer. In the first place there were broadcasts by the Chancellor of the Exchequer following the presentation of his Budget and provision for a reply by the Shadow Chancellor on the following day: in effect these constituted a small, separate series of party political broadcasts additional to the main annual series described above. Secondly there were the Election broadcasts which were also, in effect, a special series of party political broadcasts. Thirdly there were the Ministerial broadcasts, arranged under an *aide-mémoire* dating from 1947, which were assumed to be no more than factual statements, explanations of policies approved by Parliament, appeals for public co-operation in national policies such as fuel economy etc, or broadcasts on State occasions. If the Opposition thought that any such broadcasts were in the event controversial they could seek to persuade the BBC to allocate time for a reply. So far these 'Ministerials' had been only on radio but were repeated by the television service in sound only at the close of the television transmissions for the day.

It took the companies and the Authority effort and time to overcome an instinctive reluctance to offer a positive response to Government overtures, made through the PMG, inviting them to come aboard the party broadcast bandwagon. But, by the end of July 1955, the PMG had been told in oral discussions that ITV would be disposed to do so on three main conditions: first that there should be a television series separate from the one on radio, secondly that they should not be publicly described as 'BBC party political broadcasts' and thirdly they should have a say, together with the BBC, in the number and timing of these broadcasts. The principle which the companies sought to establish was one of 'absolute parity' with the BBC, which, if fully observed, would involve them in some arrangement for producing a proportion of the broadcasts in their own studios.

'Absolute parity' with a BBC, already some thirty years old and recognised as 'the main instrument of broadcasting in the United Kingdom', was an objective not easily reached by a new born ITV which had yet to transmit a single programme. Moreover, issues of principle regarding broadcasting were, as ITV representatives soon found, apt to become somewhat blurred when it came to discussion with political parties. Nevertheless in this first year the three main conditions on which ITV were ready to transmit party broadcasts secured general acceptance. But the legal requirements of the Act could not be brushed aside. Since an annual series was already under way for 1955/6, ITV could not participate right from the outset of its transmissions, but needed to wait for a new series to begin on 1 April 1956. Government legal opinion was that a 'relay' from the BBC implied simultaneous transmission; and because times could not be found which were acceptable to the single programme company concerned (A-R), the BBC and the parties, a separate budget series arranged in October 1955 was left to be transmitted by BBC Television alone.

Shortly before Christmas 1955, the Government Chief Whip, Edward Heath, was enquiring of the ITA and the BBC whether they had been able to make any progress on matters relating to party political broadcasts which they had undertaken to discuss with each other. The truth was that the two broadcasting authorities had been occupied with other things. The reminder was a timely one.

Early in 1956, Harman Grisewood, then Chief Assistant to the BBC's Director General, and I began informal conversations which continued intermittently throughout the year. Our working assumptions at the outset were threefold: first that ITA would join the party broadcast 'club' for the year April 1956 to March 1957, secondly that it would not be practical politics to ask the parties to accept fewer or shorter television broadcasts than previously, and thirdly that it would be an advantage to both bodies to find transmission times between 7 and 7.30 p.m., so that the broadcasts were out of the way before the evening competitive struggle began. This meant that Conservative and Labour would have four programmes each, of which two would be fifteen minutes and two thirty minutes, and the Liberals one of fifteen minutes. My only reservation was that it would suit ITV better if the thirty minute ones were reduced to twenty-five minutes. I learnt from Grisewood that it had been BBC practice to ask for six weeks' notice of an impending broadcast, but that the parties were apt to brush this requirement aside when it did not suit them. The companies were much bothered by this, as it seemed to them, cavalier attitude of the parties and were disposed to make a strict adherence to the six weeks' notice a condition of their agreeing to show the programmes. There was nothing in the Act or the contracts which enabled the Authority to insist on the party broadcasts being taken.

The stage was set for a meeting of that rather indeterminate Committee on Party Political Broadcasting, traditionally convened by the office of the Government Chief Whip and composed of representatives 'For the Government', 'For the Opposition', and 'For the Liberal Party', together with representatives 'For the BBC' and also now 'For the ITA'. The senior Government Party representative, usually the Leader of the House, took the chair. Whilst the Prime Minister never attended, the Leader of the Opposition almost invariably did. The date was to be 6 March.

In those days meetings of this committee seemed to be carefully stage-managed; in addition to a galaxy of stars there tended to be on stage a positive horde of extras supplied by the well-known party agencies. On this particular occasion, the Small Ministerial Conference Room at the House of Commons accommodated no less than twenty people of whom five came from broadcasting, two from the BBC, two from ITA, and one from the companies. There were three Ministers and three members of the Opposition. On this occasion the Liberal Party was unrepresented. It was then normal for the PMG to be one of the Ministers (the others being the Leader of the House and the Government Chief Whip), although in later years the PMG came to be conspicuous only by his absence, perhaps because these were essentially meetings between the parties rather than part of the machinery of Government. But four voices – no more – found their way into the record, namely those of the two Leaders (Butler and Gaitskell) and the two Directors General (Jacob and Fraser).

In politics, party leaders are in the nature of things more often to be seen in disagreement than in agreement. These occasions tended to be seized upon as an opportunity for a display of unity against a common foe – or victim – the broadcasting bodies. Over the years, the atmosphere at these meetings – rarely predictable – varied between one of positive *bonhomie* to one of disdainful *froideur*, with many intermediate gradations. Occasionally one of the leaders – usually of the Opposition of the day, for the Government one did, after all, have to function within the constraints of the chair –

would embark on a course of downright vituperation. As for the broadcasting chiefs, the knowledge that respectful meekness was what was expected of
them sometimes led them towards displays of proud but impolitic obstinacy.

On 6 March 1956, *froideur* was the order of the day, an atmosphere with
which Jacob was more familiar than Fraser. By the end, while Jacob was
certainly cross and peppery, Fraser was nothing less than hurt and
indignant. His political antennae were highly developed, but he was by
nature sensitive and he could never bring himself to relish these affrays even
though they held for him a certain compelling fascination.

What stuck particularly in the gullets of the politicians was the proposal
(a new one for them) to transmit these television broadcasts between 7 and
7.30 p.m. The facts and figures of television viewing in no way convinced
them: for this was not 'peak-time' as they understood the term. They were
being asked to accept the position that the public's attachment to their
recreational programmes was so great that it admitted of no disruption even
to allow matters of 'immense public importance' to be brought to their
notice. The leaders were willing to meet the convenience of the broadcasters
but not to that extent: 7.30 p.m. would be acceptable, for by then an
audience would have assembled following the toddlers' truce between 6 and
7 p.m. Wittling thirty minutes down to twenty-five was just as undesirable,
and really the fifteen-minute broadcasts at any rate ought to go into the
middle of the evening. Fraser spoke no more than the truth when he said
that, had they known such times were in contemplation, the companies
would have asked to be excused transmitting the broadcasts at all: for they
had no obligation either to the Authority or the parties beyond what their
public service impulses or their notions of expediency suggested. In their
parlous financial situation the possibility of the BBC carrying these
programmes alone had its short-term attractions: the sound of the switches
turning away from these programmes of importance to ITV programmes
more in tune with what most viewers were wanting would have been sweet
music in their ears.

If the broadcasters themselves had already learned the lessons which
audience measurements were later to teach, this early confrontation with
the parties could have been avoided. They could have dangled the carrot of
simultaneous transmissions at the high peak-time of, say, 9 p.m. in return for
an agreement to limit the length of all the broadcasts to fifteen minutes. The
public would with patient resignation have kept their sets switched on to
await the succeeding programmes on the respective services. A very high
rating for such transmissions could be guaranteed: techniques for the
measurement of appreciation were not at that time highly developed, and

the parties would not have heeded evidence of this kind. Much has been said over the years about the low motive of the ratings and its influence on the broadcasters: those early pioneers of access broadcasting, the political parties, were not immune from it.

There was one subject that came up on 6 March on which Government and Opposition were at variance. This was the question whether Ministerial broadcasts under the *aide-mémoire* should in future be transmitted on television. It had come up before and the division was clear-cut. The Government claimed the right to ask the BBC for television facilities as occasion required: the Opposition challenged it, saying that party advantage would always accrue to Ministers making use of such facilities. Gaitskell stressed that his opposition did not extend to Ministerial appearances on occasions of national emergency of a special kind (his example was flooding), but he thought that in such circumstances an Opposition spokesman should be invited to make a similar appearance. No agreement was reached, but the BBC, asked for a view, considered the question to be simply at what point in the growth of the television audience that medium should be used for Ministerial broadcasts. There were 21 millions who had access to radio, 15 millions to television. The average evening audience for television was over $5\frac{1}{2}$ millions; the average audience for radio was just under 5 millions. An attempt by Gaitskell to get a working party set up to consider the position of ITV in relation to broadcasts under the terms of the *aide-mémoire* was rather skilfully sidestepped by Fraser and Jacob. And Butler moved in swiftly to give an assurance that the Government would be ready to consult with the Opposition on the matter.

A question was asked whether ITV intended to follow the BBC's practice in regard to local news broadcast reports at the time of local, by- and general elections. Jacob explained that at these times the BBC confined their broadcasting to reports of the machinery and facts of the election and party manifestos; they did not report electioneering speeches. They had found, he said, that it was only by so confining their reports they had been able to achieve impartiality. Fraser said that ITV would be most reluctant so to confine themselves; and he thought it most important that they should give full news reports, including reports of speeches. Eyebrows were raised all round the table, for here was a unilateral declaration of independence and it could not pass without comment. Gaitskell averred that the ITA would run great risks and would have to be watched. Once again, Butler blocked a potentially acrimonius debate by requesting Fraser to 'keep in touch' with both the Opposition and the BBC.

The three men from ITV left this meeting with much food for thought. The shape of things to come could be fairly clearly discerned. Writing personally to Gaitskell the very next day (for the two men were old friends) Fraser said:

> There is nothing wrong with the segment of time between 7.05 and 7.30, I assure you. The audiences are very big and do not grow much between 7.30 and 8. Really, you should jump at the offer, made in a very friendly, responsible and thoughtful way. Yet this was what you called 'frosty'. I do really think it a bit hard.[4]

As for the companies, they had, not without difficulty and disagreement among themselves, agreed to take the party broadcasts on condition that they took place between 7.05 p.m. and 7.30 p.m., or after 10 p.m., when they put on their own serious programmes. They regarded this as a generous and responsible offer, for the broadcasts were most unwelcome to the viewing public. In the BBC transmissions since ITV programmes began they had failed to attract more than about one-tenth of the audience in those homes equipped to make a choice. Companies were unwilling to face either the financial losses or the hostility of viewers that would arise from the transmission of the party broadcasts in peak hours, and they thought that the broadcasts, even between 7.05 p.m. and 7.30 p.m., would depress viewing levels. Their offer had not been met at all graciously, but rather with grumbles and suggestions that they were lacking in public spirit. They would prefer not to take the party broadcasts at all if they were not available within the time offered.

Reporting the companies' attitude to the Authority, Fraser said:

> If the Parties do not accept our offer, then I would propose to say that this is for us a matter of regret and that we would wish to consult with the Parties to see whether we could not make our contribution to their need to make their policies known through television in some different way that would fit in better with our own system, and I would suggest that discussions are continued with the Party leaders on this basis.[5]

In saying this Fraser was well aware of the collective views, not yet fully articulated, of the people who exercised effective power in the ITV companies. What followed was a series of discussions with the party leaders which were, and remain, unique in the annals of party broadcasting. A serious attempt was made by ITV and the main parties to find a new and better way of providing access to television for party propaganda. Regrettably, it failed. For the next quarter of a century no comparable effort was ever made; and the fundamental basis of party broadcasting as inherited from radio remained unchanged. It has to be stated that this was an effort in which the BBC played virtually no part.

Two more 'meetings on broadcasting' were held that month in Butler's room at the House of Commons, following the inconclusive result of the one on 6 March. They were attended by the two leaders (Butler and Gaitskell), the two Chief Whips (Heath and Bowden) and the two Directors General – six instead of twenty, plus one other at the second meeting only – James Griffiths, Deputy Leader of the Opposition. Fraser took the plunge if only to test the temperature of the water, which turned out to be less freezing than might have been expected. Perhaps the reproachful letter to Gaitskell had generated more warmth. He said that he had been considering whether there was any alternative to the ITA's taking the proposed party political broadcasting series, which was not attractive to them, whilst at the same time keeping within the requirements of the Television Act, and yet satisfying the legitimate desire of the parties to use television to expound their policies to the public. His tentative ideas were, first, a 'round-table' type of television programme, similar to the BBC's *In the News* and the ITA's *Free Speech*, but with the differences that the parties should have the right to choose the participants, who would be declared to be speaking for their parties, and that junior Ministers might participate (he recognised that senior Ministers might have difficulty in reconciling such appearances with their obligations to Parliament); and secondly, programmes in which a person (generally a senior Minister or a senior member of the Opposition front bench) might be interviewed by a number of journalists in a way similar to that in the BBC's *Press Conference* programme, but with the differences that the parties should have the right to choose the person to be interviewed, and that the journalists should be Parliamentary Lobby correspondents, thus assuring responsible questioning and opportunity for the person interviewed to develop his themes satisfactorily.

The meeting was adjourned after little discussion for the parties to consider the matter and for Fraser to have discussions with the companies. So far, so good.

At the second meeting Fraser was able to report that the companies were agreeable to arrangements such as he had proposed. Butler said he had sought the views of the PMG as to the compatibility of the proposals with the Television Act, and it was considered that the first proposal would be admissible on the assumption that there was a proper balance, but that the second proposal presented difficulty. Everything would depend on whether the programme was 'balanced' politically; if the interviewers behaved in a certain way it could be, but the chances were that it would fail to be so, and in this event it would be held to be contrary to Section 3(1) (g) of the Act. He also pointed out that in the debate on the relevant Section of the Television Bill when it was in Committee it had not been contemplated that there should be any other form of party political broadcast than the traditional one.

Gaitskell's reaction was that the plan ceased to be very attractive if proposal (2) was ruled out, unless proposal (1) was extended to senior Ministers and senior members of the Opposition. He also considered that if in future such proposals were adopted, it might be more suitable if both the BBC and ITV participated in them and combined them with a reduced number of the traditional party political broadcasts which both the BBC and ITV might also continue to take. This compromise proposal could well have transformed party broadcasting, had it ever been followed up by BBC and ITV, acting together.

Both Leaders recognised the desirability of getting away from the stereotyped political broadcast. However, the general opinion of the meeting was that there was too little time to work out satisfactorily any arrangements on the lines of Fraser's proposals, or a combination or a variation of them before the new party political broadcasting year, starting on 1 April, got under way. Yet it was apparent that the barometer had moved significantly away from *froideur* in the direction of *bonhomie* and the parties registered this by accepting, after all, that television broadcasts in the year 1956/7 should normally take place at 7.05 p.m. and that the longer ones should be of twenty-five rather than of thirty minutes' duration. Moreover, it was agreed that the proposals for an alternative form of broadcast to meet the political wishes of the parties should be examined in the course of the next year.

This subject out of the way for the time being, there were, even in broadcasting, a few other things to occupy the attention of the political leaders before the year was out, to say nothing of Crichel Down, Hungary and Suez. The last of these crises precipitated a crisis also in British broadcasting by reason of the attempts by the Prime Minister to impose unacceptable restraints upon the BBC. The story has been related by Asa Briggs who remarks that: 'the most serious threat to the BBC as an institution . . . came from the Government of Sir Anthony Eden, not from the competitor'.[6] It suffices here to record that according to the measurements available to ITV, on Saturday and Sunday 3 and 4 November at 10 p.m. 76 and 77 per cent respectively of all homes in areas served by both BBC and ITV were switched to Ministerial broadcasts by Eden and Gaitskell.

The audience split 54 per cent ITV, 46 per cent BBC in the case of Eden and 71 per cent ITV, 19 per cent BBC in the case of Gaitskell.[7]

During that autumn the ITA and the companies discussed both within and outside the Standing Consultative Committee what plan should be put to the parties for party broadcasts in 1957/8. All were agreed that they wished to break away from the traditional broadcasts established by the BBC and that the initiative taken by Fraser at the meetings in March should be followed up. The BBC were informed of this attitude but, as Grisewood put it in a letter to me on 30 October, they were 'not inclined to favour a change of the sort you indicate'.[8] He did, however, add that if a separate ITV series of broadcasts were to emerge on the lines proposed on 29 March, the Corporation would want to reconsider the existing system of party political broadcasts. There is no record that either of us referred to Gaitskell's compromise proposal in the discussions we had following our exchange of letters.

It took some time to reach agreement within ITV on the plan to be put before the parties, but the proposal eventually forwarded to Heath and Bowden on 3 December was clear and concise and consisted of six propositions:

1. That the best alternative to the present party political broadcasts would take the form of an interview programme between newspaper editors (or possibly lobby correspondents) and senior party spokesmen nominated by the parties.
2. That the programmes should be telecast on a weekday at 10 p.m. – the day of the week to be decided later; and that they should be scheduled to run for a minimum of twenty-five minutes.
3. That there should be annually, nine such programmes – one a month between September and May.
4. That the programmes should either be produced in the studio of one of the programme companies or possibly, if it could be arranged, somewhere in the Palace of Westminster.
5. That the programmes should be an ITV production, entirely separate from anything the BBC might choose to do.
6. That the companies should agree on the appointment of a single producer to be responsible to the companies for the programmes.

In the event the parties expressed a wish to have a first discussion of this proposal with representatives of the ITA alone, who were on this occasion (Fraser being away), Clark and myself. The date was 5 February 1957 and the next day I sent a full report to the four companies.[9] The leaders expressed appreciation of the constructive nature of the proposal but said they had come to the conclusion that it could not be made compatible with the terms of the Television Act. It would, they thought, involve a series of programmes which were not in any real sense party political broadcasts; the only essential difference between them and ordinary programmes would be that the parties themselves would put up speakers, turn and turn about. The question at once arose whether the press conference formula guaranteed due impartiality under the terms of the Act. Whilst they could see that in certain circumstances balance might be achieved under the formula we had proposed, they could also visualise circumstances in which it would not be achieved, and they did not feel that they could co-operate in a project which ran the risk of contravening the Act.

They went on to say that they attached importance to the BBC and the ITA being treated in the same manner in regard to party broadcasting and they thought that they would be in great difficulty with the BBC if they swallowed our proposal whilst continuing to expect the BBC to carry a conventional party series. These considerations had turned their minds back to the existing arrangement whereby both the BBC and ITV were transmitting the party broadcasts, and it was their definite and agreed wish that this arrangement should continue during the period from April 1957 to March 1958.

We put to them the principal arguments which had convinced us that the parties would get a better deal if they were to co-operate with us in a series which was separate from that presented by the BBC. We also pointed out that the public ought to be considered and that the Act required us to provide programmes *additional* to those of the BBC. We were bound to concede that the press conference formula had possible flaws from the point of view of strict conformity with the Act, but we argued that this was a direct consequence of the maladroit wording of the Act which narrowly defined party political broadcasts as a series emanating from the BBC. Why, we asked, could not the parties agree to let us undertake our own distinctive service of party broadcasts? And if, to make this possible, it was desirable to amend the Act by deleting the reference to the BBC why could not this be done quite quickly and non-contentiously? Their response to this argument was a virtual acceptance of our criticism of the way in which the Act was worded but a most non-committal attitude to the idea of taking steps to put it right.

They assured us that they were as much interested in getting the broadcasts into a form which attracted a good audience as were the companies, and that they were very ready to listen to any advice we had to give to this end. They went on to ask whether it would be helpful (if this could be squared with the Act) to arrange that a share of the series was originated by Independent Television instead of the whole series originating from the BBC (the Gaitskell compromise). We replied that this would indeed be a step forward, assuming a situation in which the programme companies had agreed to renew the arrangements for a joint BBC/ITV presentation of party political broadcasts. But we emphasised that the programme companies were free agents in deciding whether or not to take the party broadcasts and that we were quite without authority to commit them in any way to do so in 1957/8. The meeting ended with their saying that they would think the matter over again and asking us to do the same. Although they took their stand on the impossibility of squaring our proposal with the terms of the Act, they did not conceal their scepticism concerning our claim that they would get a better audience by substituting our proposal for the arrangement which was currently operating. They had no illusions about how a BBC series would fare if it had to compete against one of ITV's normal programmes. We were, in fact, back to square one.

The ITA's position was a delicate one, for the companies were far from pleased by the reluctance of the leaders to meet them direct. On 20 February Clark wrote to Butler and the other leaders involved (Gaitskell, Bowden and Heath) in the following terms:

> I must tell you that they [the companies] are at present still much opposed to the continuance of an arrangement whereby they relay a series identical with that of the BBC and at an identical time. The strength of their resistance is greater than I had expected.
>
> In the circumstances I think it would be a prudent step if you and Mr Gaitskell could manage to arrange a further meeting at which the programme companies can be represented. You will remember that at our talk on 5 February I said that such a meeting might be necessary . . . They recognise the limitations which the Television Act imposes but they remain anxious to find a way of presenting what would in effect be a separate party series, although, of course, this could not be in the traditional form. They believe that a formula can be found which would reconcile the requirements of the Act with the needs of the parties, and they still think that the proposal which they have put forward could by various means, such as careful pre-scripting, sufficiently conform with the Act and at the same time provide the parties with an effective new platform for presenting political argument on television.[10]

Another month passed before the companies were given their opportunity to meet the party leaders. The lapse of time was of critical importance, for, by 20 March, when the meeting was held, a new party broadcasting year was less than two weeks away and the routine annual meeting, with the BBC and the party officials present, was already due. The chances of a real breakthrough had receded and ITV would be confronted by the need to make a decision whether or not to take the conventional series jointly with the BBC for another year.

A full memorandum sent to the parties well ahead of the meeting stressed the unpopularity of the conventional series. Over the past year the average rating on ITV had been 35 and on BBC 20 and the effect of placing the transmissions at 7 p.m. had been to lower the average rating of all subsequent programmes on the same evening by eight points. On the other hand, political programmes on ITV, such as *Members' Mail*, *Under Fire*, *Change at Downing Street*, *This Week* and *People Are Talking* had obtained an average rating of 51 and had not damaged the ratings of subsequent programmes. The principal advantages of the companies' proposal were that the public would always have an alternative programme available which was one of the objects of the Television Act; and more people would see political programmes since twice the number would be transmitted and since the ITV programmes would be so produced and 'slotted' as to ensure a rating of at least 50. The companies would undertake to allocate a fifteen-minute slot on the third Tuesday of each month (October–July) for programmes on subjects chosen by the parties, the same split between the parties to be made as was agreed for the BBC's broadcasts; and the programmes would be scripted so as to ensure a sufficient impartiality to meet the requirements of the Act, i.e. by arranging a suitable mixture of critical questions and answers by spokesmen whom the parties had nominated.

For the companies and the ITA to have collectively produced an agreed programme plan was a remarkable achievement at that time. Even the parties were impressed, but they were not persuaded. They could not bring themselves to abandon the prospect of simultaneous coverage on BBC and ITV, affording the viewers no chance of escape save by actually switching off their sets – a simple action which set-owners were in the main notoriously reluctant to take. But in discussion they rested their objection first on the legal doubt and secondly on the fact that the proposed programmes were not party political broadcasts as they understood them, since they were merely being given the right to nominate someone to be questioned by a panel. With surprising submissiveness, in view of all that had gone before, the companies agreed to toe the line and to accept renewal for 1957/8 of the broadcasts in their existing form. Reservations expressed about length, about timing and about frequency were of relatively minor consequence. The course was set for the next quarter of a century: not even the arrival of BBC 2 in the sixties was to change it, even though for a while the Conservatives and the Liberals ventured in the seventies to experiment with non-simultaneity. Another experiment in non-simultaneity was begun in 1980 and it remains to be seen whether the arrival of the Four Channel and other developments in the eighties will provide a further impetus for change.

It is easy to deride the institution of simultaneous party political broadcasting, but over the years it has performed one considerable democratic service, namely a means of ensuring that some at least of the party faithful are exposed to the viewpoints of the other side. Looking back on this episode, one is left with the feeling that, if ITV had taken better advantage of the seeming readiness of the leaders to consider a mixture of old BBC-type and new ITV-type party broadcasts (the Gaitskell compromise) the course of television in this respect might have been changed for the better. The mere fact that ITV-type broadcasts would look very much like ordinary programmes was not an insuperable bar.

Ironically, some days after the meeting, viewing figures were issued by the Nielsen organisation for a Conservative party broadcast on 14 March by Henry Brooke (Minister for Housing and Local Government), entitled *House to Let*. Among three million homes able to view both BBC and ITV, 1,316,000 watched the programme on ITV and 245,000 on BBC. 'Sensational' was the word used by Fraser in reporting this to Heath. However, the Conservatives had been procuring other research from Nielsens and were more concerned by the fact that, in general, party broadcasts collected audiences 12 to 13 per cent below the average for the time segment (26 per cent if ITV alone was examined) and they concluded that the right course was to maintain simultaneity and progressively seek to raise their standards of production. Such resolutions were frequently made by the party organisations over subsequent years, but successful and convincing party broadcasts have continued to be the exception rather than the rule.

(iii) INDEPENDENT TELEVISION FOR SCHOOLS [11]

Symbolising recovery in 1957 and demonstrating unequivocally the public service intentions of 'commercial' television was the entry of A-R into formal educational broadcasting. This gave every sign at the time of being no less startling – not to say traumatic – for the established order in this specialised field than had been the breaking of the monopoly itself. As with that earlier event, how it was regarded depended largely on personal outlook. It could be seen as a brash and clumsy intrusion by the hucksters into the sacred groves of Academe – and there were many, not least in the BBC-financed School Broadcasting Council, who did so regard it. Alternatively, it could be seen as a public spirited venture by pioneering private enterprise perceiving a public need and, in order to serve it, brushing to one side the doubts and hesitations of entrenched bureaucracies.

On 18 December 1957 John Spencer Wills made his Chairman's address to the annual general meeting of A-R, and in it was included one innocent-seeming sentence: 'We are now proposing a series of schools broadcasts sometime next year, as we think the medium of television has great and useful potentialities in this direction'. As a clear statement of purpose and public commitment surely a not unworthy response to the reminders that had recently been given that the programmes of Independent Television were expected to maintain a proper balance in their subject matter? One might have thought so. Some clearly didn't. All the passions of the earlier television debate seemed to have been re-awakened.

The day after Wills' announcement, national dailies carried front page headlines. 'The ITV project emerged as a surprise, especially to the BBC', said the *News Chronicle*. 'A bolt from the blue' said *The Times*. Leading spokesmen of national educational organisations were quoted as saying 'first we have heard of it', 'scatterbrained' and complaining that they had not had any hint of A-R's intentions communicated to them – 'Trying to butt in with a pirate programme' quoted the *News Chronicle*.

The wonder lasted well over nine days and spread to regional newspapers all over the country. 'Education authorities and school staffs must be rigorous about this' said the *Manchester Evening Chronicle* of 28 December, 'the advertising world has long had eager eyes on the mass of children in schools.' The *Wolverhampton Express and Star* pontificated: 'It might be worthwhile returning to elementary instruction in reading and writing rather than taking a backward step to the picture language of primitive man.' Whereas the *East Anglian Daily Times* thought on 29 December that 'competition could provide a welcome opportunity for wider and more varied experiments', The *Daily Telegraph* had difficulty in making up its mind. On 31 December it said 'ITV has rushed into schools broadcasting to remove the reproach that its programmes lacked serious balance' whereas on 2 January the same paper commented 'The object is clearly to catch future audiences and carry advertising into the classroom . . . We do not expect from commercial television any spontaneous compliance with the nation's standards of taste'.

A rare note of moderation was sounded by the editor of the NUT's own weekly *The Schoolmaster* on 4 January:

> It would be a pity if the suddenness with which the Company has chosen to announce its plans should prejudice teachers . . . against these broadcasts before they have been given a fair trial. Undue distrust . . . simply because the methods of the commercial company are not those of the Schools Broadcasting Council would be ill-advised.

These measured words contrasted markedly with the *New Statesman*'s statement that 'the hostility of the educational interests . . . seems to be the result of a very recent decision taken in the slaphappy haphazard way typical of ITV'.

As early as the first meeting of the Authority's Children's Advisory Committee in November 1955 the possibility of educational programming, whether of a formal or informal kind, had been mooted. It was an item of discussion at more than one subsequent meeting. At its fifth meeting on 6 December 1956 Brownrigg attended and in broad outline described plans for weekday afternoon programmes for children, of which one half hour per day would be intended for schools. The latter, he suggested, would be primarily for children of fifteen and over; and the five half hours would be devoted to science, art, domestic science, history and geography, civics and/ or modern languages.

There was one important point of difference with the programme company that remained to be resolved after the 6 December meeting. The CAC, on which teachers and education authorities were represented, had always insisted to the ITA that any programmes intended for classroom use must be the subject of previous consultation as to their purpose, level and content with qualified representatives of the education system; in other words they expected a pattern of consultation similar to that established over the previous twenty to thirty years for school radio by the BBC through its School Broadcasting Council. A-R's intention had been to seek such advice from a small panel drawn in the first place from three educational institutions in the London area. The company felt that it would be unnecessarily cumbersome to establish anything resembling the complex hierarchy of the SBC committees for what was after all at that stage no more than an eight-week experimental project. But, after further discussion with the ITA and representatives of the CAC, they set up in the course of the first weeks of 1957 both an Educational Advisory Council (to advise the company in educational matters generally) and a Schools Broadcasts Committee (to advise on the programmes intended for classroom use), both under the Chairmanship of Sir John Wolfenden,[12] and on which education authorities and teachers' professional organisations were adequately represented.

In the meantime, however, feelings between the CAC and the company became strained because under the impact of the unexpectedly strong press interest roused by the original statement more was being leaked, by company staff among others, about details of programme intentions that were still at that stage very provisional and that were still awaiting ITA approval. The pressure became so great that A-R felt obliged to hold a press conference on 28 December at which the newly appointed Head of Schools Broadcasting, Boris Ford, spoke of plans to broadcast a daily half hour from Monday to Friday in May and June 1957 for eight weeks. If the experiment was successful, he said, then a regular schools service would be established for the school year beginning in September 1957 and running throughout all three school terms. 'We shall think up the kind of programmes we would like to do,' he was reported as saying, 'and then consult chief education officers, headmasters, individual teachers and, where appropriate, the National Union of Teachers.'

That statement together with the mistaken impression probably created by the press conference that the project had already been approved by the ITA, to say nothing of a company advisory committee that was still in course of formation, caused some resentment. But it was of brief duration. Good sense and the desire to see sincere good intentions translated into early action prevailed. By the 8 February meeting of the CAC, Sir Ronald Gould – General Secretary of the NUT as well as a member of the committee – was able to say that any impression that the arguments that had taken place meant that the committee was trying to wreck the projects should be dispelled: the company advisory committee should be appointed quickly so that broadcasts could begin as intended in the early summer.

In giving qualified approval in principle to the undertaking, the members of the CAC had recognised that their concern, as laid down in the 1954 Act, should be with the *principles to be followed* and not with programme detail. That, they saw, would be better left to the producers and the company's own advisers. They did, however, insist as a matter of policy, with the ready agreement of the company management, that, whatever the nature or content of the programmes, they should carry no advertising.

a-r's Educational Advisory Council held its first meeting on 19 February 1957. The Minutes of that meeting record regret that insufficient time had been given for full consideration of plans that had already been formulated. But not wishing to handicap Ford in carrying out an important experiment, the Council decided to recommend that the programme plans should be issued to schools with a foreword explaining their experimental nature and that the Council and Schools Committee would be considering further programme plans on the basis of the outcome of the experiment.

Following that Council meeting, the company's Schools Committee met to consider preliminary plans for 1957/8. Thus, despite the sound and fury that greeted the first announcement of a-r's intentions, it can be said that when itv broadcasts finally took the air in May, they did so with the blessing of representatives of the educational establishment. It remains nevertheless difficult to suppress the suspicion that, given the wide-flung network of long-established contacts linked with the School Broadcasting Council, some at least of the rancorous clamour that marked the first weeks of over-reaction to Wills' December statement had been inspired by resentment that the upstart commercial newcomers were about to steal a march on the bbc.

The bbc had conducted their own first schools tv experiment on *closed circuit* with six schools in Middlesex as long ago as 1952. Since then they had been carefully studying the effects of that experiment and deliberating with the School Broadcasting Council how soon and how much might be risked in 'open air' transmissions. It was not until November 1955 that they had finally made known their intentions to make a start on a limited scale, with two programmes a week, and that not until the autumn of 1957. One result of a-r's initiative – not untypical of the impact of itv in other spheres – could be seen in the bbc's change of plans. When the bbc started their schools tv service that autumn the output had been increased from the original two to four programmes a week.

But it would be wrong to make too much of the idea of rivalry or hostility between the two organisations in the field of education. It has had little lasting importance for programme people. It soon became apparent that whatever the situation at managerial or advisory body levels or with the general evening output, there could be no defensible case for a 'ratings war' in the provision of programmes for schools. As indeed was recommended by the cac, a pattern of consultation and liaison both formal and informal was soon established at staff level. Over the years it was developed and has been maintained in good shape ever since.

Moreover, it would be too facile to dismiss with the wisdom of hindsight the doubts and hesitations of the early fifties as mere bumbledom or bureaucratic pusillanimity. Risks, uncertainties, there undoubtedly were. If ITV's earliest schools broadcasts, shown in the London and Midlands regions only, reached hardly more than 100 scools in their first experimental summer term and a few hundred in their first complete school year, the BBC too, in spite of their entrenched position in educational radio and with the schools of the whole United Kingdom as potential audience, could scarcely achieve more than one thousand. As late as 1957 important sections of the educational world harboured strong doubts about the medium itself. Lord James (at that time High Master of Manchester Grammar School and at all times a master of the calculated indiscretion) was not untypical when he remarked that television would enter his school 'over my dead body'.

It is true that there was already a considerable weight of prestigious educational theory in favour of 'visual aids'. Yet in practice, educational films had made no startling progress in spite of official encouragement and support. Too many school projectors remained in store cupboards gathering dust and rust. School broadcasts on radio on the other hand had been outstandingly successful over close on thirty years. But to the academic mind it was clear that radio, relying as it must on carefully chosen words and therefore on a response to rational process, was a very different thing from this new broadcast medium exploiting the immediate emotional appeal of the moving picture, and only too likely to become – if reports from other lands were accurate – a serious threat to literacy and the use of 'good books'. Moreover, television for schools was appearing in Britain precisely at the moment when many feared that with the introduction of a commercial system the British broadcasting services were likely to be increasingly 'Americanised'.

Too much of the news about ETV in the States suggested use of the television receiver as a substitute teacher, as a means of coping with teacher shortage. 'In America, it would appear,' wrote a secondary Headmaster in *The Schoolmaster*, 'experiments have been conducted in which the class teacher took no part whatever in the teaching, all this being done by the TV teacher.' British teachers were suspicious of a device that could perhaps appear temptingly convenient to hard pressed authorities at a time when post-war school population 'bulges' were making their impact and when the teacher supply situation was far from being what it is today. 'There will be tut-tutting and head shaking when we start using TV in schools in Scotland,' said Scotland's Chief Inspector of Schools at a conference in Edinburgh in August 1957. But he did then go on to say: 'TV cannot replace the teacher, but it can make a contribution to education'.

In general, neither government nor local education authorities seemed over-confident that television could make a worthwhile contribution to education, let alone ease the difficulties. It was a time of financial strain and, true to tradition, education was bearing the brunt. The Ministry of Education made it known that in their view schools television was no more than a dubious experiment; and during the first three experimental years they said they would limit the number of receivers for which a grant (of 50 per cent) would be made to one per 100,000 of school population. This meant that in London, for example, grants would be forthcoming for about twenty sets. In actual fact the governmental restraint was removed well before the three years were up. (The introduction of 'block grants' to local authorities had deprived it of much force.)

Given such circumstances and the generally critical, suspicious or at best dubious attitudes of educationists towards television as such, and towards ITV especially, it is understandable that the CAC (with several members representing major educational interests) should have reacted in such stern schoolmasterly fashion to A-R's well-intentioned initiatives. However, as already noted, the company were fully prepared to recognise that without the ready co-operation of the teaching profession the children in the schools would not see the programmes: and to do whatever they could to reassure doubters about the sincerity of their intentions. Since the educational value of the service they were planning would clearly benefit from a regular supply of firsthand information on the effectiveness of the broadcasts in the classroom, they offered to supply a set to any school willing to report back on the usefulness of the programmes viewed by their classes. Even this offer was greeted with suspicion in some quarters and interpreted as a sly device for wooing the younger generation to become viewers of television advertising. The unequivocal public statement by the Authority that no advertising would be allowed during the period set aside for schools programmes, nor for two minutes before and one minute after, was conveniently ignored.

Clark himself wrote in *TV Times* for the week in which the experimental transmissions began: 'This is an imperfect world and some who pride themselves on not being deceived have questioned the intention behind these proposals'. But for him they appeared as

a remarkable act of faith in the future. It represents a disinterested desire on the part of the directors and in particular of the Managing Director, Mr Paul Adorian, to use the great franchise with which they have been entrusted in a responsible and farsighted manner. . . . The publication of the programmes should allay the misgivings of the doubters.

He was right. In the last resort the only reassurance worth having would be found, if anywhere, in the programmes themselves.

When on the afternoon of Monday 13 May 1957 there started the first regular schools television service to be seen in the British Commonwealth, there were eighty schools registered with a-r as intending viewers. The programmes were also simultaneously shown by atv in the Midlands. One estimate puts the number of schools that eventually used the series at 125.

The service in that first term consisted of five programmes shown in the afternoons at the rate of one a day, Monday to Friday, during eight weeks. On Mondays was *Looking and Seeing*, which flung down the gauntlet on behalf of 'visual education', demonstrating how we can learn to 'use our eyes'. Tuesdays had *The Ballad Story*, aiming to relate the 'pop ballads' with which children would be familiar to the poetry read in the classroom. The series on Wednesdays, *On Leaving School* tried, as its title suggests, to give helpful information on finding a job and on the worrying problems to be faced at the beginnings of responsible adult life. The Thursday series exploited the fact that 1957 was International Geophysical Year: *A Year of Observation* offered up-to-date statements by leading scientists on the influence of the sun on 'planet earth', on earthquakes, ocean movements, the atmosphere, space rockets. Finally, Friday's programmes, *People Among Us*, made a contribution to history, geography and social studies by having immigrants tell about their countries of origin and how they came to be in Britain.

Already this first group of programmes (perhaps even more so than those shown in the following 1957/8 school year) illustrated, in their chosen subject matter, in the problems encountered by their producers and in the reactions of schools, several of the salient features and concerns of school television ever since. For example, when one looks at the total output over the past twenty-five years it is striking to note how it has tended to reflect both in content and in approach the current preoccupations of the educational world in any given year. These first five series were all addressed to pupils aged fourteen and over, more particularly in the Secondary Modern School. At that time, in the aftermath of the Spens and Norwood Reports, children were being divided, like Gaul, into three parts, in the so-called 'tripartite system'. The largest part, to be served by the Secondary Modern School, was thought to be made up of children of a predominantly non-bookish, practical cast of mind with little or no inclination towards abstract thought. How to devise a satisfactory curriculum and teaching methods for such pupils, and above all how to create 'parity of esteem' for their schools, was certainly a matter of concern in the 1950s.

The first efforts in 1957 were not all equally successful. Some teachers found it difficult to fit series such as *Looking and Seeing* or *People Among Us* into their curricula. The former seemed to be part science, part art; the latter part geography, part history, part civics. Others, however, welcomed the bridges created across artificial subject divisions. Criticism was much more marked of *Year of Observation*. Some of the eminent scientists did not communicate successfully; there was too much 'lecturing'; and too much background knowledge was assumed. On the other hand, it was agreed that valuable material was brought into the classroom which an average teacher would seldom, if ever, have been able to provide himself.

It is not clear from available reports how far *The Ballad Story* succeeded in its aim of showing that poets can be both entertaining and relevant. Complaints that the series was not sufficiently visual were balanced by praise for the encouragement given to young viewers to write their own ballads: which many did. Because it was so clearly close to the natural preoccupations of fourteen-year-olds, *On Leaving School* came in for more general praise. Singled out for approval was the use of dramatisation to illustrate the problems facing school leavers. This was the only series of the five against which there was virtually no complaint against 'overloading': too much new material to be assimilated in the limited time. This latter criticism is still heard.

However, already, by the end of May 1957, Adorian was able to state publicly that, in his view and that of his Board, the experiment was proving successful and that they therefore intended to make arrangements to put the service on a more permanent basis. Plans were already far advanced for the provision of daily programmes during the new school year 1957/8. It was also announced at that time that Scottish Television were preparing to appoint their own educational advisory committee as a preliminary to joining ATV in the relaying of A-R's productions.

With the lessons learned and the confidence gained in that first term, the programmes of the school year that followed showed an increased range in subject matter and target audiences. It had been observed that schools were having difficulties in adjusting class timetables to transmission times. To help ease that problem it was decided to repeat each day's programmes later in the same afternoon; and to provide four rather than five programmes a week so that the programme with the widest age-range (*The Farming Year*) could be seen on two days a week, with a repeat on each occasion. The ten new series shown during the year revealed yet more of what has since come to be recognised as salient educational characteristics of schools television;

not to mention one or two of the more awkward policy problems that cause irritation and vexed misunderstandings from time to time.

All the series were still for the Secondary level, but whereas the art series *Shape in Your Hands* (modelling, carving, pottery), *From Cover to Cover* (books) and *Invitation to the Dance* (ballet and folk dancing) were aimed at 11–13 year olds, *Music in the Making* (including the Hallé Orchestra), *Producing Macbeth* (ending with a performance of the play starring Donald Wolfit) and *Judge for Yourselves* (critical approach to the media) were all planned for the 12–16 age group; *World of Figures* (maths), *More Power* (atomic power) and *Easier Living* (science in the home) for 14–16; and the filmed programme *The Farming Year* for the whole school audience from 11 years upwards.

Much satisfaction was conveyed, more especially by schools with specialist maths teachers, at the use of visual techniques to illuminate mathematical concepts in *World of Figures*. Classes were apparently stimulated by *Shape in Your Hands* to clay modelling on their own. *The Farming Year*, filmed on location during the course of the term in which it was broadcast, was an early and striking example of the use of the medium to broaden children's horizons beyond the classroom walls. Not unexpectedly it was found more interesting by town children than their country cousins. The girls loved the animals: the boys enjoyed the machinery and the craft processes. The series was thought by a number of teachers to be so useful as a substitute for school 'visits' (without the trouble and expense) that it was repeated in a shortened version at their request in 1959/60.

There can be few clearer demonstrations of the power of television to give an added, live dimension to classroom studies than the presentation of television studio productions of drama, especially of Shakespearian and other classical drama. Very many schools are still without easy access to the live professional theatre; and even where there are theatres within reach the chances of their giving performances of such plays are not great. For some children seeing the *Producing Macbeth* series was their first experience of Shakespeare in performance. 'They were gripped and listened and watched intently,' said one report. Over the past twenty years, such programmes, calling on the services of the best available performers of the professional stage and the most skilful and experienced TV drama producers, have been a regular continuing feature of ITV's school broadcasts.

With the series *Judge for Yourselves*, shown in the Autumn Term 1957, ITV school broadcasting encountered for the first time and in its very first year of existence that perennial problems of broadcasting policy, the preservation of due impartiality in all programmes dealing with current public policy or matters of political or industrial controversy. The ITA drew the attention of A-R's management to the possibility that a programme series intending to encourage and exemplify a critical (possibly cynical) attitude towards the role played by the press, television, films and advertising in influencing the public mind, might run the risk of offending against this provision of the Act.

After reading the scripts, the management considered it necessary to make certain changes. In a controlled classroom situation contentious political material could be handled by a competent teacher with complete propriety without any justified charge of introducing political propaganda into teaching. But it was a different matter when the material in question, although intended primarily for classroom use, was also being broadcast on a public television service bringing the programme to a potentially very much larger, undifferentiated audience. There the law governing public broadcasting was bound to apply.

A-R's recently appointed educational advisers found this difficult to accept. Believing themselves appointed as trustees on behalf of the educational world, with powers to accept or reject any programme included for broadcasting to schools, they took particular exception to the company's action in changing the content of a programme without previously consulting with them.

The arguments that followed, sometimes conducted in public, sometimes in private, were long and bitter. It took all the famous diplomacy of Sir John Wolfenden and – since it involved a question of principle as well as one of programme content – intervention by the CAC before it could be brought to a satisfactory solution in March 1958. The outcome was both a reaffirmation of the committee's role as 'sponsor' for the programmes *vis-à-vis* the school authorities and a mutually agreed reformulation of the procedures for internal company editorial 'regulation' of programmes, in which the respective roles of Authority, company and committee were more clearly defined. But by the end of the affair, the company found itself without a permanent titular Head of Schools Broadcasting for more than a year – indeed until early in 1959, when Miss Enid Love came over from the BBC to take charge.

As if (or perhaps in order to) proclaim their independence of A–R, Granada did not take the first school programmes on the network, and for all of two years these were absent from the ITV transmissions in the North. ATV on the other hand took the A-R programmes in the Midlands from the start. Scottish Television did not join in until the summer term of 1958. Scots are ever ready to emphasise the differences between their educational system and that south of the border. Ideally STV would have liked to produce school programmes of their own, but through a combination of Roy Thomson and native canniness, they decided to hasten slowly and profit from experience in the south. In the school year 1958/9, they began making programmes for inclusion in certain of A-R's series.

However, when in 1960 ATV also decided to become producers of schools programmes (Sixth Form French and Junior Mathematics) it became evident that some joint planning for a nationally networked service would be desirable. An educational sub-committee of the existing inter-company Network Planning Committee was established and by late 1960 all companies were appointing education officers. By early 1961, it was agreed that from September, for the school year 1961/2, there would be a nationally networked balanced five hours a week of schools programmes provided jointly by A-R, ATV and Granada. From that time on consultations at staff level in order to avoid wasteful duplication became possible with the BBC's Schools TV Department, both organisations having agreed that competition for audiences was out of place in education. The next stages in the education story were to come in the wake of the Pilkington Report of 1962, the White Papers and consequent legislation – with the advent of adult education programmes from ABC and ATV and the creation of a central educational advisory structure by the ITA. They will be described in Volume II.

(iv) RELIGIOUS TELEVISION

In the beginning there was, as Chapter 16(ii) related, the Central Religious Advisory Committee and the small Advisory Panel, the three members of which were described in the Annual Report for 1955/6 as 'consultants'. CRAC's first step, and one which at that time seemed quite revolutionary, was to support a proposal from ITV that religious programmes should be shown during the Sunday evening 'closed period' which at that time was prescribed for 6.15 p.m. to 7.30 p.m. It is paradoxical that this period, intended to prevent members of the Church of England from having any incentive to absent themselves from evensong, became the main outlet for the very programmes which might have seemed most calculated to offer the faithful a valid excuse for not taking part in the corporate worship of their church. The paradox was defended in a statement issued on 2 January 1956 by the ITA with the agreement of the Chairman of CRAC[13] and the BBC, saying that CRAC had had in mind:

the fact that already from various quarters the churches have been strongly criticised for not being more quick to take advantage of the opportunity offered by television to reach those large numbers of people who are not connected with the life and worship of the churches. The committee thought they ought to recognise the immense missionary opportunity which religious television presents and to seek by every possible means to ensure that the quality of religious programmes is such as to be an effective Christian witness to television viewers.

Shortly after this statement, on the initiative of Norman Collins and Harry Alan Towers, *About Religion*, the first regular weekly religious television programme to be presented in Britain, began its life which was to last for just over ten years. At 7 p.m. on Sunday 8 January ATV presented a discussion between Prebendary Douglas Owen and Father John Groser of Stepney on 'aspects of religion in relation to everyday life, and especially to the colour question'. This was a challenging start, for in those days the public at large were virtually unaware of even the existence of a colour problem in Britain. It lasted twenty-five minutes and there were no advertisements either at the beginning or at the end. The producer was Bill Allenby who was later to divide his creative time mainly between the coverage of church services and of racing. From the first day, however, A-R had been providing nightly epilogues – short messages of religious significance immediately before close-down – an innovation which became a tradition in most ITV areas, but never on the five weekdays in the area covered by Granada. From time to time the ITA was asked to press Granada into line with the general practice: it considered doing so more than once, but never did.

In those days some importance was attached to 'denominational balance', although never in terms comparable to those governing party broadcasts. The rule of thumb guideline was 7 Church of England, 4 Free Church and 2 Roman Catholic. Later on, when ITV reached Scotland, Wales and Northern Ireland, appropriate variations were determined for those territories. Denominations outside the British Council of Churches were not in the early days admitted to the club. At a meeting of the panel in February 1956 it was reported that the Seventh Day Adventists, the Pentecostal Group and the Christian Scientists were asking for 'time' between 7 and 7.30 p.m. on Sundays, and it was agreed not to accede to these requests. A few months later an approach from the Salt Lake Mormon Tabernacle Choir met the same fate. But Dr Marsh did not want the door to be permanently closed on religious minorities and Canon Heaton pointed out that in sound broadcasting the BBC had provided time for the Unitarians. Moreover, in epilogues presented by ATV, no objection was raised to the appearance of Billy Graham. In one way or another secular or at any rate pantheistic tendencies crept into epilogues and never ceased to infiltrate as opportunity offered. In fact they proved far more formidable than Moral Rearmament as diversions from the pursuit of 'mainstream' Christianity. On Sunday 5 February, for instance, ATV's epilogue had consisted of a reading of Keats' sonnet 'Bright star, would I were steadfast as thou art'.

In the autumn of 1956, CRAC formally agreed that three religious minorities, the Jews, the Society of Friends and the Salvation Army should be allowed access to television. Only the last of these showed any enthusiasm for taking advantage of the opportunity.

Modest as the programmes were in terms of cost and in production values, the opening up of television by ITV for regular religious programmes at a good viewing time, and the knowledge that there were other vacant times on Sundays, for example between 6.15 p.m. and 7 p.m. and possibly in the morning, attracted widespread attention in religious circles. In March there was an approach from the Rank Organisation which was willing to finance the presentation of non-denominational services from a 'television church' – St. Paul's Church, Portman Square. The panel was attracted by the concept but dubious about the possible use of it for 'evangelical propaganda'. Delicate issues relating to sponsorship were involved and neither the panel nor the ITA (nor the London companies) were inclined to rush a decision. Another factor involved was the question whether or not the Authority would secure some or all of that slice of the licence revenue (see Chapter 27) which might conceivably enable it to finance the undertaking. The project never materialised any more than did a similar plan for equipping the church of St. George's-Tron, Glasgow.

ATV's *About Religion* steadily consolidated its position. In the spring of 1956 Michael Redington took over its production and was to work in this capacity for the next five years. He was supported by two particularly tireless advisers, The Revd Simon Phipps (now Bishop of Lincoln) and The Revd Michael Hollings. Writing in 1963 Redington said: 'Everyone who has been connected with *About Religion* has always brought to it enthusiasm and found in it enjoyment'. From May 1956 onwards the programme was also transmitted by ABC in the Midlands and the North, but later in the year ABC began to provide in those areas comparable programmes of their own, a few of which were in turn relayed in London. Originally it was envisaged that ABC's contributions would be embodied in certain editions of *About Religion*. This arrangement soon broke down, however, and ABC went ahead with their own series under the title *Living your Life*. By March 1957, the average audience for the programmes in these three areas was approximately 300,000 homes containing an audience of some 750,000 people.

Enthusiastic company producers and advisers were soon expressing to the panel decided feelings of frustration at the limitations of their budgets. In the absence of any vigorous competition from BBC television, there was little incentive for the managements to become more generous: the programmes earned no revenue from advertising and there was a readymade audience available in homes where newly-acquired television sets were more often switched on than off.

However, new development was at hand, stemming in large part from the restless energy of Howard Thomas. An idea for a 'Sunday School of the Air', designed for a teenage audience and to be shown between 6.15 and 7 p.m., was first discussed by the panel in October 1957, but by January 1958 it had been overtaken by a plan for a series set in a typical youth club and to be called *Facing Tomorrow*. A dry run of such a programme was shown on 3 February, by which time Penry Jones and Ben Churchill had been engaged to work on it. The former hailed from the Iona Community and had run a youth club in Glasgow.[14]

After discussion it was decided that a further dry run was needed and that there should be a change of title. For some reason a suggestion of mine that it should be called *The Sunday Break* (a term often used to describe the 'closed period') caught on, and it was under this title that a remarkable and quite revolutionary new religious programme began its life. The first edition was transmitted on Sunday 16 March, 1958.[15]

In the context of religious television, and of *The Sunday Break* in particular, a Gallup Poll of 1957 about 'Religion' had made interesting reading. Of the 16–30 year olds, 32 per cent believed in a personal God, 36 per cent in some sort of spirit and only 5 per cent didn't think there was any kind of supernatural spirit. Of the 32 per cent, 64 per cent believed Christ was the Son of God, 10 per cent that He was just a man and 8 per cent that it was just a story. 45 per cent believed in life after death and only 17 per cent believed that when you were dead you were done for. When it came to churchgoing 26 per cent claimed to go once a month or more, 38 per cent never, 15 per cent at Christmas and family occasions. The biggest part of these stopped going between the ages of ten and fifteen. As Penry Jones expressed it: 'This might be summed up as "Christianity Yes, the Church No – except for young children".'

The Sunday Break made an immediate impact. It was noticed. Moreover, as the company's mail bag established, it attracted and held the attention of many among those it was designed to serve; that is to say young people mainly between the ages of sixteen and twenty-five. The programme time was apportioned between jazz music, dancing, discussions and competitions in such a way as to introduce the religious interpretation of life in a context which affirmed as good in themselves the activities which many young people enjoyed. It also appealed to many more youngsters of school age than had been expected, such as the one who wrote to Ben Churchill 'Please could you tell me when you are dead do you become old or young or do you stay the way you deaded?' Later developments in religious television will be discussed in Part v.

(v) SUCCESS ON A SHOESTRING: ITN

Despite the unhappy story told in Chapter 25, the field in which ITV was to achieve its greatest distinction in its first two years or so was that of news.

1956 had begun badly for ITN with the resignation of its first Editor, Aidan Crawley, and his deputy. It suffered an even more spectacular blow in April, when Christopher Chataway, who seemed to embody not only the new concept of newscasting, but the character of the new service, followed Crawley across to BBC current affairs. Yet by the end of the year ITN was widely acclaimed as having not only out-matched the BBC in liveliness of presentation, but also in the quality and content of the news service it supplied. In particular ITN had come with flying colours through the two big news stories of the autumn of 1956, Suez and Hungary. The Suez crisis, with its involvement of Britain in a new (if brief) war, remains perhaps the story which has most deeply affected the feelings of the British people since 1945. It was a tough test for a new service in the television era.

'Of the two television news services ITN have so far convincingly out-pointed their BBC rivals', wrote *Truth* in January 1957. 'ITN with deft flashbacks and live interviews with bystanders, established their usual lead over the BBC's News Department', was the *Observer*'s comment on coverage, early in 1957, of another big story, the replacement of Anthony Eden as Prime Minister by Harold Macmillan. 'You can tell there is a good newspaperman behind ITN. News treatment, in fact, is almost the only aspect of ITV worth watching. Geoffrey Cox's team beat the BBC on the big story', was *The Sunday Times*' comment on the same event.

The new Editor had a clear idea of what he wanted to do when he took over in the spring of 1956. He believed that in the press a gap existed between the popular papers and the quality papers, which could be filled by a news organisation which, whilst retaining the human approach and the simplicity of language of the popular papers, provided a larger ration of more significant news, whether it be political or foreign or economic, than was the habit of the popular papers of the day. It was a recipe for a *Daily Mirror*, with an added dash of *The Times* and the *Manchester Guardian*. This approach happened to fit the needs and the potentialities of British television at that time. BBC News resembled in style and news value the quality papers such as *The Times* and the *Daily Telegraph*. Television viewers were ready for a news service which spoke to them in the terms of the newspapers they read and which gave them, in good measure, reports of sport, of crime and of human interest which those papers provided. At the same time the techniques of television, with its ability to depict, illustrate and personalise the news, could help greatly by adding the further ingredient of making significant news more interesting, more comprehensible and more acceptable.

Cox found in the ITN team, small though it was, a group of men and women well fitted to achieve this aim. The survivors of the early storms were united by a passionate common interest in developing to the full this new form of journalism. Their deep satisfaction in their work outweighed all the fears and alarms about whether the commercial system would survive. An able replacement for Chataway was found in a young writer, Ludovic Kennedy, whose 'fine voice, dark good looks and warmth of manner were to have a strong appeal to viewers'.[16] Kennedy and Day were to prove an admirably balanced pair of newscasters, providing a strong central pillar around which ITN could be developed from its early role as a fresh and entertaining programme of news into a major daily news service, able to hold its own, not merely in the way it gave the news, but on the extent and quality of that news.

Day's interview with Clark (Chapter 25) had shown that a hard, probing interview could be successful if it was designed to elicit information rather than to stage a scene. This technique was developed until the forthright, probing interview became an ITN hallmark. John Hartley, who had come to ITN from *The Times*, George Ffitch, and young Reginald Bosanquet proved themselves particularly adept at it. Arthur Clifford as News Editor fought stubbornly to get those in power to be interviewed on these terms, which were markedly different ones from those prevailing in the past. In the days of the monopoly, public leaders, if they agreed to be interviewed at all, had wanted to appear on their own conditions and not on those of the broadcasters.

Clifford's gifts for spotting not only quirky human interest stories, but for expressing major, important news in human terms, were given full rein.

Two examples must suffice. When the Home Secretary ruled that a Hungarian refugee family could stay in Britain, the ITN cameras were with them when they learnt the news, and were able to reveal their relief and joy. When the Army reservists were called up for Suez, ITN not only showed them being kitted out and drawing their weapons, but found time to film the marriage of one man only two hours before he had to report. This sense that news was in the end about people and was best expressed through people, was to be the basic ingredient in the ITN formula. From the first, too, ITN had had in Lynn Reid Banks (soon to win fame as the author of *The L-Shaped Room*) and in Barbara Mandell a regular feminine presence in the bulletins. Both of them covered not only art and fashion, but did their stint of harder news stories as well.

Above all, the bulletins were filled with pictures. Having very few reporters, ITN sent out its cameramen to cover news on film. Many of them were the cream of the cinema newsreel camera crews and they responded to this challenge with technical skill and a news sense of their own. Sport, too, was filmed on a regular, rather than an intermittent, basis, and techniques devised to allow coverage in compact form of long-running events like Test Matches and Wimbledon. Foreign film was, for reasons of cost, mostly limited at first to a daily package of half a dozen stories provided by CBS of New York from their fairly extensive world coverage. But home stories were covered with vigour and speed.

In the summer of 1956, a big new step forward was taken when, in covering a strike at the Austin works at Longbridge, the natural sound of a scuffle at the plant gates was recorded by the ITN crew at the same time as the scenes were filmed. This brought an added authenticity as well as vividness, and set in train the practice now virtually universal, under which action scenes are shot with sound as well as picture. A quip added by the newsreader to round off the bulletins became a further and popular element in the programmes.

This pattern, hammered out by the new Editor and his small band of colleagues, was soon to be put to a severe test. In mid-summer Nasser seized the Suez Canal. For three months the country turned night after night to television as well as radio, to know if we were, once again, to be drawn into a war. Late in October the Hungarian people made their short-lived and abortive bid for freedom, stirring fears of an even more lethal conflict. In November came the brief but dramatic onslaught of French and British forces on Port Said.

Had not ITN risen to this occasion, the damage to its standing and that of the new Independent Television network could have been very great. There was a risk that ITN could have been seen merely as a personalised and cheerful programme, good viewing in normal times, but no substitute in a crisis for the tried and tested BBC. In practice ITN dominated the television coverage of those grave months in late summer and autumn, and dominated it by high professional standards. They had not only the first but the only British film coverage from Budapest, and they followed this by having the first film of the landings at Port Said, providing the pictorial evidence on which turned much argument about the damage done by allied bombing.

From the gallery of the House of Commons, Day demonstrated a further skill, to add to his ability as an interviewer and newscaster. Speaking often only from notes he gave night after night vivid word pictures of the battles between Eden and the Opposition.

One chance factor helped ITN to make the most of this material. At that time the late bulletin, beginning at 10.45 p.m., was the last scheduled programme of the night. This enabled it to be extended when the news ran big. No crippling penalties were then exacted by unions if the service extended beyond its normal close-down time and the doctrine of the 'unforeseen overrun' enabled the ITA to square the practice with the prevailing limitations on broadcasting hours. During the peak of the Hungarian and Suez crises ITN bulletins ran at times for twenty, twenty-five and even on one occasion for twenty-eight minutes – an unheard of scale of news for those times.

All this brought ITN not only a good press, but a big viewership. Moreover, the crisis months established links between the news company and its audience which were reflected in a flood of letters praising not only the efficiency of the coverage but the warmth and humanity with which the newscasters presented it. Nor were the events of the autumn of 1956 a flash in the pan: on the contrary they forged ITN into an instrument which was to prove well fitted for the next stage of television news, as film coverage expanded throughout the world. Competition came from the BBC late in 1956 when they moved towards the ITN approach by naming their newsreaders and by forming a small cadre of readers specialising in television, headed by Robert Dougall and Richard Baker.

ITN's success was all the more remarkable because it was achieved throughout 1956 and 1957 with a tiny staff and on a tight budget. Its total editorial staff including its newscasters was never more than twenty-three, charged with the preparation of at least two, and often three news programmes a day, seven days a week. Although Cox, when he took over the post of Editor and Chief Executive, was able to resist most of the drastic staff reductions which were proposed by the Board Committee whose appointment had finally clinched Crawley's resignation, three senior staff had to go and the total expenditure of the company was kept down to just under £1000 a day. Out of this sum had to be financed not merely the coverage of the news, but the operation of ITN's own studio, its own equipment, its own premises, its own management. For the news company was not just a programme-making department but a small television station in its own right, responsible for all a station's costs, except gathering advertising revenue. Its achievement in 1956 and 1957 was possible only because the staff, swept up in their enthusiasm for this medium, and stimulated by success, were prepared to work long hours, and to put their hands to any task which came their way. The unions turned a blind eye to practices which later would have brought the network to a halt. Not only did sub-editors and script writers double up as reporters on their days off, but there were even occasions when a cameraman acted as questioner for a film interview. This pattern could not, of course, be maintained, if only because even the most ardent people in the end tire. In due course the news company had to lengthen its stride and began to expand its staff and its facilities; yet its early achievement is all the more remarkable because of the short commons upon which it was done.

This success on a shoestring was, however, to bring in time one bad by-product. The programme companies, seeing that good results had been achieved at a very low cost, were reluctant to accept the fact that much more money would in due course have to be spent on news. The tendency of managements and accountants to measure the pleas of the programme makers in percentage terms weighs unfairly against those who have, in the first instance, cut their costs back to the bone. For these then seem to be demanding the biggest proportionate increases. Such calculations became all the more important as television news, from 1957 onwards, began to turn its cameras more and more on overseas events, with a corresponding leap up in costs.

In June 1957 ITN won for the first time a reputation abroad as well as at home when it secured a scoop of international proportions by interviewing Nasser in Cairo. It was Nasser's first contact with Britain since Suez. It secured headlines in papers throughout the world and a column of space in *Time* magazine, which described Nasser as 'sending an amiable grimace into several million British living rooms'.

In that year two fresh newscasters joined the news company. One was Huw Thomas, the other Ian Trethowan, who had been a colleague of Cox on the *News Chronicle*, and who embarked at ITN on the broadcasting career which was to carry him to the post of Director-General of the BBC.

When, in February 1957, the Toddlers' Truce ended (Chapter 30) ITN was asked to fill half an hour at 6 p.m. once a week. It developed *Roving Report* as a vehicle for covering foreign news in depth on film and on the spot. This programme was to run for seven years, before making way for other in-depth programmes, such as *ITN Reports*. In that time it was to bring in many scoops, of which the Nasser interview was merely the first, and to range far and wide, greatly helped by the fact that the unions permitted it to work with a two-man camera team, instead of the cumbersome and costly crewing forced upon the current affairs units of the programme companies. Among other achievements it greatly improved, by good script writing, the quality of travelogues, then regarded as a lowly form of film making.

Roving Report became the first of a number of news feature programmes undertaken by ITN for one or another of the companies, but chiefly for A-R who were to make full use of the news company's resources. The next venture was, however, for the weekend companies, ATV and ABC. It was a series of interviews under the title, *Tell the People*, conducted by Robin Day. They included the first extensive interview on British television by a single interviewer with a Prime Minister, Harold Macmillan. Although the programmes went out at the unfashionable hour of 6 p.m. on Sundays, they attracted great publicity, providing as they did, excellent copy for the news-hungry Monday morning papers. The Macmillan interview, in which the PM was asked bluntly if he intended to dismiss his Foreign Secretary, hit the biggest headlines of all. Another series, done for ATV in the summer of 1958, under the title of *Look Ahead* was based on the ingenious idea of looking forward to the news of next week, rather than reporting on the news of the week just past.

Such series, though of great value to ITN at the time, particularly in offering outlets to its ambitious and talented staff, tended to be short lived. As each programme company's current affairs staff found their feet, they wanted the scarce air time for themselves. Only A-R, with the sure prestige outlet of *This Week* for their own staff, tended to come back to ITN for supplementary programmes. *Dateline*, a programme which pioneered the idea of a nightly examination in depth of the day's news was launched in the first instance for A-R in 1960, and spread in time to a number of companies as a supplement to the main evening bulletins. Eventually in 1967 it was merged in *News at Ten*.

For the news bulletins, the basic formula established in 1956, modified only by a wide extension of filming abroad, was to prove remarkably durable throughout the period leading up to the Pilkington Inquiry. Although the placing of the bulletins was changed first to the grotesquely late hour of 11 p.m., then to 10 p.m. and again to 9.25 p.m. and finally in 1962 to 9 p.m., and although the BBC competition mounted in force, the same fundamental principles prevailed at ITN – those of aggressive news coverage, of uncompromising interviewing and of newscasting which was both human and yet authoritative. They provided a durably attractive format which not only held the audience but made ITN the one part of Independent Television to win unreserved approval from the Pilkington Committee.

Part IV

THE NEW MONOPOLY

Commercial television has undeniably done many stimulating things in its first six years. But it has become a monopoly – a collective monopoly, perhaps, but a monopoly just the same . . .

> (Hobart Paper 15. TV: From Monopoly to Competition. Published by the Institute of Economic Affairs 1962, p. 67)

The Authority first let it be known three years ago that profit levels were developing which it could not defend. Such profits can be secured for one reason only: monopoly.

> (ITA Memorandum to the Pilkington Committee (October 1960) paper no. 68 Report of the Committee on Broadcasting, vol. i., app. E)

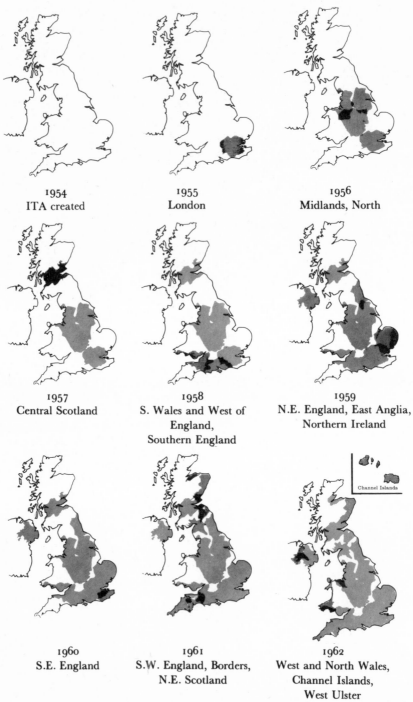

1954 ITA created	1955 London	1956 Midlands, North
1957 Central Scotland	1958 S. Wales and West of England, Southern England	1959 N.E. England, East Anglia, Northern Ireland
1960 S.E. England	1961 S.W. England, Borders, N.E. Scotland	1962 West and North Wales, Channel Islands, West Ulster

The spread of Independent Television is progressively traced in these nine maps. The Television Act was passed in July 1954 and the Authority first met in August. The service began from Croydon on 22 September 1955. The service areas shown in the final map include about 94–5 per cent of the population.

SOURCE ITA Annual Report 1961/2.

32

UNACCEPTABLE PROFITABILITY

Between 1958 and 1962 Independent Television spread across the United Kingdom in the manner illustrated by the maps on the facing page and described in the extract from the ITA Annual Report for 1961/2 which is reproduced in Appendix 1. By the end of 1961 six companies additional to the seven already described had been appointed, and two more were to be added in 1962. How each of these appointments came to be made, and what befell those who received them, will be described in Volume II. This rapid growth created problems, not just for each company as it arrived on the scene but for the system as a whole, and not least its supervising authority. Growing pains, however, were only to be expected: what was certainly not foreseen was the rapid and indeed fabulous expansion in the advertising revenues accruing to all the companies appointed on the mainland of Britain between 1954 and 1959. Fortunes were made, but, as regards the system itself, it seemed as if having too much money imposed stresses as great as, if not greater than, having too little.

On 10 March 1959 Fraser suffered a long and gruelling inquisition by the Public Accounts Committee of the House of Commons. When he had appeared before the Committee two years earlier, it had shown little interest in the finances of the programme companies and in fact questioning about them had been stopped by the Chairman of the Committee on the ground that they were not its concern. However, on this occasion, practically all of the questions were about the huge profits being made by the programme companies and the relationship between the Authority's financial policy and those profits. It was apparent that several members of the Committee felt that the Authority had not been doing all that it should to moderate the profits and that it should, in fixing the rentals, have provided for a regular surplus for the Exchequer.

It was also suggested that the Authority should be putting its programme contracts out to competitive tender. Fraser pointed out that there was no suggestion in the Act that in appointing programme companies the ITA should pay regard to anything other than their ability to provide a satisfactory programme service and that it had had to plan for a predetermined income and not one that depended on the chance of what applicant groups were prepared to pay at any given time. He argued that Sections 10 and 14 of the Television Act defined very clearly the financial duties which the ITA was expected to discharge. It had to ensure for itself an income at least sufficient to meet all sums properly chargeable to revenue account and to make provisions for necessary capital expenditure. Section 13 provided that any excess revenue could, if the PMG with the approval of the Treasury so directed, be paid into the Exchequer. The payments made to the Authority by the companies under the contracts between them were of an order that fully complied with the ample discharge of all these responsibilities.

The PAC were told that the income necessary to achieve these purposes involved the Authority in securing from the companies annual payments about three times greater than the actual cost of the engineering and administrative services it provided. The Act did not require the Authority to provide itself with an income out of which sums in addition to income tax should be paid to the Exchequer, though it would have been possible for Parliament to add such an obligation to those defined in Section 10 had such been its wish. If the Authority, having established rentals amply large enough to fulfil its duty as defined in the Act, had then made a further increase designed only to make inroads into the companies' profits, it would not only be exceeding the clearly defined duties laid upon it by Section 10, but would be assuming responsibilities of a fiscal character proper only to Parliament and to the Ministerial responsibilities of the Chancellor. In fact, the profit levels of Independent Television were not the result of under-charging by the Authority, whose income was three times greater than the actual cost of its services, but of the inability of the Authority to introduce directly competitive services on the number of channels available to it.

It was no part of Fraser's duty to disclose to the PAC the discussions which had taken place within the Authority and between it and the companies which had been offered contracts back in March 1955. These have been described in Chapter 13. It then made, as we noted, a crucial decision. In selecting programme companies, it was to pay sole regard to those qualifications that bear upon the relative ability of applicant groups to provide the best possible television programmes, subject always to the assurance that a group which it had in mind to select would be financially secure. The Act had instructed the Authority to provide television services of high quality, and contained many directions about the standards to be observed. It would be difficult, if not impossible, to reconcile this duty with the selection of programme companies by competitive tender, and the Authority would be obliged to reserve the right not to accept the highest bid.

Yet neither in this interrogation, nor in a second one on 5 May and not in a memorandum which was presented between the two occasions, did either Fraser or Sir Gordon Radley, Director General of the Post Office, succeed in convincing the Committee that the financial affairs of the ITA had been properly conducted. It became necessary to send the contracts to the Committee for inspection and also, of course, Clark's letter to the first three contractors declaring that it was no part of the ITA's financial policy to try to build up a significant surplus balance over and above such expenditure as it felt proper in carrying out its duty under the Act – the very letter which in June 1957 these companies had asked Clark to reaffirm (Chapter 26). When it reported on 9 July 1959 the Committee declared it to be unfortunate that the opportunity had not been taken for more frequent review of rentals; that therefore future contracts should take full account of capacity to pay; and that the rentals in these contracts should be arrived at by competitive tender. Furthermore, following some questions which had been asked but not pressed about the nature of the arrangement between A-R and Granada, the Committee stressed that the Authority should pay particular regard to the requirement in Section 5 of the Act that contractors should be independent of each other.[1]

Constitutionally, a public authority has a right of reply to such a stricture. The ITA's comments were sent to the Post Office for onward transmission to the Treasury and subsequently embodied in a Treasury Minute to the Committee which was eventually published on 15 December. By that date there had been a General Election and a new Parliament had appointed a new Public Accounts Committee.

The comments were put together with infinite care and reaffirmed the Authority's view that if it went beyond the explicit requirements of the Act it would be assuming responsibilities of a fiscal character proper only to Parliament. It noted that the Committee recognised that the Act did not *in terms* require it to earn excess revenue for payment into the Exchequer. In its own early discussions the Authority not only had the assistance of its legal and financial advisers but also consulted the PMG. It was his opinion that the Act did not charge the Authority to make profits beyond the surplus necessary to meet all capital expenditure and create its statutory Reserve Fund. Both De La Warr and Clark had been asked to confirm this, as there was no clear record of it either in the Post Office or the ITA. Both did so.

The Authority had become a very prosperous public corporation. Its income was three times greater than its revenue expenditure. It had no public debt, and met all its capital expenditure from income. At the end of its ten-year life, it would hold, on present calculations debt-free physical assets of £5 million at first cost, on which depreciation of £2¾ million would have been provided; would have accumulated in addition in the Reserve Fund, or in other reserve income, some £4 million; and would have paid £7 million in taxation. This income, and these reserves and assets, amply fulfilled the whole of the statutory requirements placed on it by the Act. Its rentals were far greater than its costs and had been planned from the start to be so. As the Authority's charge for the services it rendered already exceeded the commercial cost of them by 200 per cent, the profit levels of Independent Television could not be said to be the result of undercharging by the Authority for the services provided.

It was true that the Authority's contracts ran until 1964 without a break. In view of the financial and political uncertainties then unresolved, the earlier ones could not have been negotiated for a shorter term. Even so, earlier contracts did provide for increases during their term, and these had been made effective. They now amounted to 45 per cent over the initial rentals. In the result, the Authority would have received by 1964 some £5½ million more than would have been yielded by the maintenance of the initial scale of rentals in those contracts. The charges in later contracts, which were for increasingly shorter terms, were from the beginning at a level some 50 per cent higher pro rata than the initial rentals in the earlier contracts.

Since the Committee's interrogation, the Authority had once more considered at length the Committee's view that its three remaining contracts should be offered to the highest bidder, subject only to the condition that he should be of standing and technically and financially competent to provide the service. The effect of compliance with this recommendation would make length of purse the governing factor in selection, for the great majority of applicant groups would pass the general test of standing and technical and financial competence. Its own considered opinion was that the introduction of selection by competitive tender would be radically inconsistent with the discharge of its duties and functions under the Act. The very foremost of these was the selection, from the many qualified applicants, of the companies that appeared to offer most, not in money, but in public responsibility, in talent and ability, in a lively sense of the social gains that would accrue from good television, and in the case of regional companies, in the reality of their local associations with the communities they would be serving.

The position had been reached where the Authority had at most only three more new companies to appoint in order to complete its present television service. These could not expect to be as profitable as the early ones. Existing contracts already covered some 95–6 per cent of the population that would be finally reached by the Authority's transmissions. The three remaining companies would serve only comparatively small numbers of viewers, and would have only about three operational years before the Act – and consequently the contracts – expired in mid 1964. The Authority was therefore going ahead on its established basis, but would, in accordance with the Committee's wishes, provide that these contracts could be reviewed during their course.[2]

Any faint hope that the Public Accounts Committee of the new Parliament would disavow the views of its predecessor was in due course snuffed out. At the end of July 1960 it reported tersely in these terms:

> Your Committee attach great importance to the principle that economic prices arrived at by competition should be obtained for all public concessions. This was the only case known to them where a franchise amounting to a monopoly, in this case highly profitable, is disposed of without financial competition and with no provision for the Exchequer to share in the profits. They therefore asked the Treasury why they said nothing to recognise the principle when they transmitted the reply of the Authority in the Treasury Minute. It was explained that under the Television Act the matters raised are the responsibility of the Authority, and the Treasury did not consider themselves entitled to express any views in a field where they had no jurisdiction at all. But your Committee note that the Treasury . . . gave an assurance that the Government will take into account the Report of the Committee of Public Accounts of Session 1958/9 when it is considering what it should do on the expiry of the Television Act 1964.[3]

And so, as we shall see in Volume II this question of the monopoly profits of ITV companies became the central issue of Parliament's new legislation in 1963. By October 1960 the ITA would be telling the Pilkington Committee that, while most businesses with a similar ratio of turnover to capital employed would be more than content if they could retain as profit before tax about £1 out of every £10 income, the programme companies as a whole were able to retain roughly £6 out of every £10 of income as profit, subject to tax.

The PAC reports made no special public impact at a time when ITV profits had become a continuing story in the newspapers. But they most certainly had a profound effect on the Treasury, the Post Office and the Authority itself. On 20 November, in a personal letter to the Editor of *The Times*, Sir William Haley, Fraser wrote:

> Of course, as we were saying, the real problem, and it is a massive one, is the present level of profits, which are likely to increase, not to fall. For at least two years now, we have been trying to warn Ministers about the reality of this problem, and have never concealed our view that public opinion would come to regard such profit levels as insupportable. Indeed, we first told Ministers what was going to happen long before anyone outside Independent Television could have guessed. The only thing that surprises us is that trouble with Parliament and public opinion is so long delayed.
>
> It remains the simple inescapable truth of this situation that these profit levels can be materially affected in one of only two ways – by the introduction of a directly competitive self-supporting service, which would solve the problem at one stroke, and which has been the Authority's steady policy and proposal since 1954, or else by some form of discriminatory taxation on television programme companies. Certainly they cannot forever remain.[4]

Somewhat earlier, on 20 October, Sir Thomas Padmore, Second Secretary to the Treasury, had said in a letter to Radley at the Post Office 'I still do not find the Authority's arguments in the least bit convincing'.[5] The writing was on the wall.

It was certainly writing that the Treasury was trained to read. Sir Thomas Padmore's men moved into action. The Authority's Annual Report for 1960/1 contained the following passage:

Contribution to the Exchequer
It will be noticed that, for the first time, there appears under this heading an amount of £450,000 payable to the Exchequer under Section 13(2) of the Television Act, 1954. The Authority has been directed by the Postmaster-General to make this payment which represents approximately one half of its available surplus for the year after providing £405,000 under capital expenditure reserve for the increase in the net

book value of fixed assets plus payments on account during 1960/1.

The Authority, through its Chairman, was consulted by the Postmaster-General, as required by Section 13(1) of the Television Act, before this direction was made. It was the firm view of the Authority that, at least until the cost and incidence of its future capital requirements can be estimated, it should be allowed to build up its reserve fund to the maximum extent possible. No such estimate can be made until, following the report of the Committee on Broadcasting, the decisions of the Government are known on such matters as the transition from 405 to 625-line definition, the introduction of further services and the introduction of colour television. The Authority's established policy of being self-supporting, which is based on the requirements of the Act, could well be prejudiced if its annual surpluses are not left intact in the meantime, because clearly the future capital commitments could be formidable.[6]

Nevertheless in 1961/2 the Exchequer claimed £531,311.

There was one more card up the Treasury's sleeve and it proved to be the joker. It was duly played by the Chancellor of the Exchequer (who was, of all people, Selwyn Lloyd) in his Budget speech on 17 April 1961. He proposed the imposition of an excise duty of 10 per cent on advertisements inserted for payment in television programmes broadcast from stations in Great Britain on or after 1 May. The duty was payable by the persons who provided the programmes, i.e. the programme companies. Subsequently, before the Finance Act became law, the rate was lifted to 11 per cent. So far as the Authority was concerned, its first reaction at its meeting next day was to note that the imposition of the duty need not preclude it from putting to the Pilkington Committee its own suggestions for the most equitable method of taxing the companies.

Reactions on the part of advertisers and advertising agents were much less placid. 'Bad as such a tax is, it cannot even be defended on the grounds of reducing the large profits of the television companies, for these will be protected if they are allowed to pass on the tax to industry.'[7] So said ISBA, representing over 500 members responsible for some 70 per cent of all advertising. They had their answer very shortly when on 27 April the Financial Secretary to the Treasury, Edward Boyle, confirmed that 'any suppliers of goods or services on which an indirect tax is imposed is able, so far as supply and demand permit, to pass on the tax'.[8] Later, on 6 July, when the Finance Bill reached its third reading, the Chancellor was to say: 'the conduct of programme companies . . . will be closely watched. It is my view that they should assume a reasonable part of the burden.'[9] And he added that he considered this had been done in a number of cases. It was R. A. Bevan, as President of the IPA who, in a statement made simultaneously with that of ISBA, first pointed out that the effect of the duty was likely to be more severe on the smaller television companies than on the larger. This view was endorsed in a *Financial Times* leader on 20 April which said 'some advertisers may choose to drop the smaller stations from their schedules to the advantage, probably, of the four networking companies'.

As for the companies themselves, 'discrimination' was the word most frequently on their lips. A-R expressed surprise that the burden should have been placed on one advertising medium only. 'We had in mind increasing our charges but in view of this new tax upon the advertisers [*sic*] we shall have to think again'. The reaction of their Sales Departments varied. Some announced that the normal eight weeks cancellation clauses would be waived or eased: others did not. Peter Paine, Sales Director of Tyne Tees Television, serving North East England, was venturesome: he boldly announced that all rates on his current rate card would be reduced by 10 per cent from 1 May to 16 September, subject only to existing bookings during this period being guaranteed non-cancellable. In other words Tyne Tees would for this period carry the burden of the duty. The first of the smaller companies to display anxiety was Grampian Television, serving North East Scotland, which on 5 May sent an emissary to the Post Office and at the same time sought urgent consultations with the ITA. Later they were to secure a temporary abatement of their rental.

The implications of TAD for Independent Television only slowly became clear, but by the end of July the Authority for its part had decided what it wanted to say. It had three audiences to address: first the Pilkington Committee, now one year old; secondly the PMG and his officials; and thirdly the Chancellor of the Exchequer and his Treasury brains trust. It therefore set out its views in a wide-ranging memorandum to the Committee[10] and on 15 August it sent copies of the memorandum to the Post Office because 'it is anxious that its views about the Television Advertising Duty should be made known to the Government'.[11] Summarising its argument in para. 10 of the memorandum it said:

In summary, a television advertising duty contracts the margin of profitable operation, and competitive services would render the problem more acute. From the point of view of the Authority's own plural policy, the duty is objectionable in that it hurts small companies more than large ones and could reduce the number of companies that either single or competitive services can securely sustain. It could also give rise to a situation where the economic survival of a programme company could be maintained only by limitation of expenditure, which would inevitably fall in large part on programmes and result in a reduction of programme standards.

Six months later the ITA became aware that, whatever the Post Office might have done with the memorandum and whatever the Pilkington Committee might be doing, its views were quite unknown to Treasury Ministers who would by then be preparing the next Budget. There was no chance of the tax being removed or reduced, but something would be achieved if an increase could be prevented. So on 31 January 1962, Sir Ivone Kirkpatrick, Clark's successor as ITA Chairman, wrote to Selwyn Lloyd in language best calculated to engage the sympathies of a Chancellor whose personal views about television were just about as close to those of the ITA as could conceivably be hoped for from any member of the Cabinet:

The policy of the Authority has been to disperse power as much as possible, to create as much competition as is practicable on one channel and therefore to establish a large number of television companies in Scotland, Wales, Northern Ireland and the English provinces.

Of the fifteen companies now in existence, four may be described as large, five as medium and six as small. The present tax falls without discrimination on all three classes; and there is reason to believe that the small companies who make relatively meagre profits are the principal sufferers since some advertisers are inclined to economise by cutting their appropriations in the smaller provincial areas. It could well be that our very smallest companies will now make a loss instead of a modest profit because of the incidence of the duty.

If a special tax is to be imposed on television companies, it seems to us that it would be as profitable for the Exchequer and fairer to the small companies to impose a graduated tax on profits. We have given very careful consideration to this problem and my colleagues on the Authority would be grateful if you would receive me so that I may convey their views to you.[12]

Kirkpatrick described the outcome of his subsequent meeting with the Chancellor on 20 February in characteristic language, some trace of which survives in the official minute:

He had found the Chancellor not unsympathetic to the Authority's view. Officials of the Board of Customs and Excise and of the Inland Revenue who had been present at the meeting had, however, sought to claim that, on grounds of fiscal principle, it would be undesirable to graduate an excise duty of this kind by reference to the size of the companies charged with the duty. They had seemed to regard programme companies as being on the same footing as distillers and other purely commercial concerns. He himself had pointed out that there was a precedent for graduated taxation in other fields and he had emphasised that the programme companies operated in a field of activity governed by statute and were subject to control by a public authority.[13]

It is almost needless to say that neither this appeal nor the more passionate pleadings of the Presidents of ISBA and IPA, who had jointly seen the Chancellor on 31 January, impelled him to remove or abate TAD. The general effect of the duty on the fortunes of the smaller companies eventually proved to be somewhat less harsh than was at first feared and, except in the special case of Wales, West and North, was within the Authority's power to contain by judicious and selective abatement of rentals. Nevertheless, as will be seen in Volume II the PMG and Parliament generally did come to realise that, as a means of curbing the stupendous profitability of the major companies, TAD was pathetically ineffective. But as a means of jeopardising the prospects of the smaller and newer companies and of nullifying the ITA's policy of utmost diversity, as well as inflicting an unwarrantable deterrent on industrial and business enterprise, it was quite an efficacious instrument. It died an ignominious death in the Budget of 1964. In Volume II we shall see what took its place – and why. One thing had become abundantly clear. The great television bonanza was intolerable to all except its immediate beneficiaries and their friends in Parliament and elsewhere. Something had got to be done.

33

THE NETWORK CARVE-UP

Towards the end of 1959 – nearly a year before evidence was to be submitted to the Pilkington Committee – the ITA was reminding itself that a 'network' (in the sense of a primary source of programmes of 'national' appeal and standing) was a basic feature of virtually all broadcasting systems, whether sound or television. The reasons for all this centralisation were readily apparent. First of all, virtually every country had its clearly distinguishable 'talent capital' for certain aspects of its entertainment and culture. In this country it was London; in France it was Paris; in the United States it was New York for 'live' entertainment in broadcasting and the theatre, and Hollywood for filmed entertainment destined for showing in the cinema or on television.

The Authority's policy had always been to moderate this metropolitan tendency and that was why it had appointed companies not for the whole network of London, Midlands and the North, but for individual areas. Three companies had between them set up substantial centres of programme production in Birmingham and Manchester. It had to be admitted that there was a 'pull' in programme production towards London, and a good many of the programmes produced by ATV, Granada, and ABC Television were, in fact, produced there. Nevertheless, in the central network there were not only four separate companies but significant non-metropolitan elements. Additionally, there had thus far been appointed six purely regional companies for stations outside the central network and there could be three or four more before the first round of stations was complete.

The second reason for the emergence of television networks was an economic one. Not only was it cheaper and more convenient to produce television programmes where the primary pool of talent existed, but it was just not possible, given the costs of television production, for there to be a number of independent major centres of production each providing all the programmes for the local area. ITV, however profitable it had turned out to be, could not operate economically if each programme company was responsible for all its own output. Nevertheless, on output of some 60 hours a week on each station, 115 hours of new programme material was being produced each week. (This compared with an overall BBC figure of some 70 hours a week for a similar station output.) Without networking, Independent Television would have had to produce 540 hours of programmes each week.

As has been seen in Chapter 10, the Authority, when deciding on the pattern of the system in 1954/5, envisaged the use of the 'network' as an important step in the fulfilment of its duty under Section 5(2) of the Act to secure adequate competition. Apart from this aspect, the network was obviously sensible as a means of enabling Independent Television to compete economically with the BBC and as a way of encouraging powerful and resourceful companies to establish themselves in the provinces in spite of the predominance of London as the centre of the entertainment industry. At a time when nobody could accurately forecast how the system of exchanging the programmes would work, the ITA saw the buying and selling of programmes as being much less stable and systematic than in practice they turned out to be. It thought that there would be many more single transactions between the companies for individual programmes or series of programmes than proved the case. This original idea would have led to a highly competitive arrangement under which each company would, as it were, display its goods for sale to the others who would buy those which they considered the most attractive.

When the first four companies were struggling for survival, there were many good reasons why they should seek to make economical use of their studio facilities and their staff, by arranging between themselves that, over a given period, each should be responsible for producing a certain number of programmes of a particular kind and length. These arrangements were never questioned by anybody, least of all by the Authority itself, since they helped to ensure that the total output of the companies was properly balanced. Indeed when, in 1956, they broke down for a period owing to disagreement on terms, there was considerable public criticism of the fall in overall programme quality which ensued.

The advance planning of the network programmes was done by a committee of the four companies. The newer and smaller companies tended to resent the main programme fare, which in practice they had no option but to use, being planned by a consortium from which they were excluded and on whose decisions they had little or no influence. The 'parent' companies, however, saw the arrangement in quite a different light and, to varying extents, regarded the independence of the committee as fundamental to their own independence. They argued that each individual company had a contract with the Authority to supply a balanced programme of high quality and that it must be for each company to plan its own programme in the light of this commitment. While they were ready to make available the full range of their programmes to the smaller companies for a fee, they accepted no obligation to allow their customers a share in the planning of those programmes. When, in a discussion of the autumn programme schedules on the Standing Consultative Committee, Fraser said that, before giving a final blessing to them, he would want to be assured that the interests of the smaller companies had been taken fully into account, A-R demurred and argued that it would not be strictly correct for the Authority to object to the programme plans of one company on no other ground than that they might adversely affect the operations of another.

The pattern which had emerged was broadly as follows (Monday to Friday):

5.00–5.25 p.m.	Networked children's programme.
5.25–5.55 p.m.	On two days, local children's film.
	On three days, networked children's programme (usually cartoons).
5.55–6.10 p.m.	National and local news.
6.10–6.30 p.m.	Usually networked programme, mostly about current affairs.
6.30–7.00 p.m.	Local filmed programme or advertising magazine.
7.00–7.30 p.m.	Mostly networked light entertainment.
7.30–8.00 p.m.	Fully networked 'quiz' or fiction series.
8.00–8.30 p.m.	Networked programme, usually a 'quiz'.
8.30–9.25 p.m.	On three days, an hour-long networked programme.
	On two days, a half-hour networked programme, followed by a half-hour local film.
9.25–9.35 p.m.	News.
9.35–10.30 p.m.	On three days, an hour-long networked programme.
(or 11.00 p.m.)	On one day a local programme (usually a feature film), or networked balance programme.
	On the remaining day, a networked $1\frac{1}{2}$ hour play.
Remainder of evening	Mixed local and networked programmes.

On Saturday and Sunday, there was a similar alternation of local and networked programmes. 'Local' in this context did not necessarily connote a programme of primarily local or regional appeal but rather a programme, whether locally produced or acquired from elsewhere, which was being presented by a company independently of the network.

From an economic point of view this broad programme pattern seemed sensible enough. The major or most popular items were usually fully networked, but local initiative was relied upon for the remainder of the programmes. Each company had, therefore, some scope for putting into practice its own ideas, both on what made a good television programme schedule and on what the local audience liked. The arrangements for the supply of network programmes from the parent companies had become standardised. The practice was for each smaller company to 'affiliate' to the parent company of its choice and for all financial transactions and programme booking arrangements to be made with that parent company alone. Despite the fact that affiliation was with one company only, all the other parent companies agreed to make their programmes available to the smaller company for the single fee it paid to its parent. The share-out of money between the four parent companies then took place as a separate transaction with which the smaller company was not concerned.

The network programme agreement provided for the supply of the full range of programmes, past, present or future, filmed, taped or live, carried by all the parent companies. The financial arrangements were that the affiliate company paid a fixed charge of so much an hour for programmes supplied (the charge, like the ITA rental, being proportional to population coverage) and a percentage of net advertising revenue (increasing by various steps according to the revenue received). As an example, Southern Television paid £60 an hour for programmes supplied plus the following percentages of net advertising revenue:

> 10 per cent up to £1 million
> 12½ per cent on the next £½ million
> 15 per cent on the next £½ million
> 20 per cent thereafter

New companies, when appointed, were eager to enter into their network programme agreement, so as to guarantee a regular, dependable supply of programmes. The grumbles came later. The first ground of complaint was that the smaller companies had a disincentive to produce programmes over and above their minimum commitment to the ITA since, as the percentage of advertising revenue still had to be paid in full, they lost money by not taking the maximum amount of network programmes. The second compliant was that, whatever programme company they approached as a prospective parent, they were still offered exactly the same terms.

On the first point, the defence of the agreement was that the smaller companies' profits (which some had been making from the beginning) were a direct result of the established popularity of the network programmes and that it was unreasonable for them to expect a rebate if they chose from time to time not to take full advantage of the agreement. (They did not have to pay the *hourly* charge when they opted out of the network.) Furthermore, the loss sustained by occassionally replacing a network programme by a locally produced one was not likely to be significant against the background of profits.

On the second point, the strength of the objection depended to a great extent on whether or not the charges were reasonable. In the ITA's view, it was difficult to say that they were unreasonable. Apart from this question of cost, the very compactness of the four programme companies was a form of safeguard to the smaller companies, in that it ensured that programmes from all the parent companies were available. Yet there seemed to be an agreement among the parent companies which prevented them from undercutting one another in the terms they offered to affiliates.

The outside strictures which by late 1959 were being voiced were understandable. On the other hand, the parent companies genuinely believed that the price they were offering to the affiliates was a fair one and that any reduction would mean that they were subsidising the operations of the smaller companies. Therefore, if the parent companies were to seek to attract affiliates by offering reduced charges, this could, in theory at least, lead to a position where the regional companies were carrying on over-profitable enterprises at the expense of the parents.

The smaller companies also had a sense of grievance over the fact that it was only rarely that they could export any of their own programmes to the network, and they felt that the decision of the parent companies often rested not on an objective assessment of relative programme quality, but on a definite policy of not normally accepting programmes from the smaller companies. It was true enough that the parents wished to spread their overheads by utilising their own resources to the fullest practicable extent. Yet the urge of the regional companies to obtain a nation-wide showing for their programmes was a very natural one: it was a reflection of the fact that with a shortage of channels and restricted hours of broadcasting, there were not sufficient national outlets for all the creative talent in the system. With the high profitability of Independent Television, the smaller companies had generally been able to equip themselves in a manner which created a surplus of regional studio capacity. In other words, there were now regional companies which felt capable not only of meeting their regional obligations but of operating, given the opportunity, on a national scale. There was also some dissatisfaction among the regionals at the quality of some of the network programmes: they felt that, if they could sell programmes to the network (and thereby cover part of their costs), they could improve the general quality of the ITV service as a whole.

It was noticeable, however, that the kinds of programmes which the smaller companies usually sought to have networked fell into categories of which there was already an abundant supply. If a regional company was to succeed in reaching the network, it behoved it to look around for the type of programme which was likely to be of interest to the parent companies because it fell outside the normal run of their own productions.

Of course the Authority's main aim in appointing regional companies had been to provide a television service which served the special tastes and outlook of the local viewers and it had often, when interviewing applicants, sought to discourage them from putting forward grandiose ideas for the networking of their programmes. In the case of southern England, north-east England and East Anglia, the Authority did not itself provide, as part of the contract, return lines to London, but left these to be asked for and paid for by the individual programme companies. The producing of programmes for the network by the smaller companies could, therefore, be regarded as in a sense a diversion of their efforts from their proper job of serving their local area. Unless it would clearly improve the balance and quality of the programmes as a whole, and would not lead to any reduction in regionalism, there seemed little justification for the ITA to give any encouragement to the regional companies to try to break into the network.

As has been seen in Part I, it was generally recognised during the 1954 debates that initially, if only because of the shortage of frequencies, competition to supply programmes would be limited and this point was made more than once by the PMG and other Government spokesmen. It was not suggested that the Authority could do much more than ensure that the programmes of more than one programme company were seen on each of its stations. Competition was, in fact, equated with the idea of there being no local monopoly of programme supply. Thus De La Warr said in the House of Lords on 13 July 1954:

I can quite visualise that the best system – and I mean the best system from the point of view of introducing genuine competition and also for the commercial success of the scheme – is likely to be a system of time-sharing under which the whole network will be allocated between shall we say, two or more contractors, each of whom may have the sole use of it for a number of days in the week. This could be . . . supplemented by smaller local companies in the individual regions. These would provide local regional programmes with what seems to me extremely import-ant . . . regional roots.[1]

If the PMG was prepared to regard that arrangement as representing 'genuine competition', the actual position achieved was more satisfactory in several respects. There were four programme companies in the central network. By means of the 5:2 system, local monopolies at the first three stations had been avoided. Instead of one programme company responsible for the whole network on certain days of the week, there was a system where, on any given day, a viewer could see programmes produced by three, four and sometimes more different companies. Finally, the regional companies had a wider function than was contemplated by De La Warr. They were not responsible merely for certain fixed periods not allocated as part of the concession to the network companies; they had been given responsibility for the whole time on the stations with power, at any rate in theory, to select programmes from a number of network companies as well as to produce as many programmes of their own as they wished.

The movement away from the ITA's original concept of a competitive optional network had its beginnings in 1956 and gathered momentum as the major companies came to learn the advantages of collective programme planning. This movement did not by any means proceed smoothly; it was punctuated by frequent hiccoughs. Each company – with no existing source of accumulated experience on which to draw – made pragmatic judgements in which self-interest, the overall interest of the system and the requirements of the Act and the contracts all played a part. There were disagreements, even conflicts. As the years went by, the means of resolving them changed; they became more sophisticated as the companies began to take the measure of each other. By the beginning of the sixties the 'carve-up' was virtually complete; and the uneasy alliance between the Four was forged by such people as Cecil Bernstein, Lew Grade, John McMillan and Howard Thomas. Within the main alliance, subsidiary ones emerged. Given the lack of formal powers in the hands of the ITA, it was largely by observing the drama from the wings and interjecting the occasional timely prompt that its staff could most effectively exercise on behalf of the Authority a significant degree of influence.

There is on record a copy of a note I wrote to Clark (in Fraser's absence) as early as 23 May 1956, which began:

> I listened to a somewhat rambling account from John McMillan on the telephone yesterday evening of the course of events which have led to the breakdown of the A-R/ATV negotiations about networking . . . the more I think about it the more I feel that the situation is distinctly ominous and I do not think we can properly stand by in complete silence.

Clark wrote letters to Wills and Littler next day and they may have contributed in some degree to the solution which these two found to that particular difficulty. The dispute worried the Authority Members who, at a meeting on 15 June, came to the conclusion that A-R were 'at variance with the Authority's original conception of a "competitive optional network" '.[2] Consulted at the Members' request, Geoffrey Sammons, of Allen & Overy, the ITA's solicitors, advised that it could be argued that the companies would be putting themselves outside their contractual obligations if they introduced a system under which there would be at any given time only one source of programmes (or one programme) available so that there could never be any competition to supply programmes 'between a number of programme contractors'. But he did not recommend that the ITA's approach should be based on this strict legal interpretation. By 17 July, Fraser could report that there had been a marked improvement in the networking position: arrangements between the companies would mean that the network 'would be open again by the middle of September'.[3]

McMillan's information may have been 'rambling' but it was timely. About that time an understanding developed between him, Fraser and myself which proved of importance certainly to the ITA and probably to ITV as a whole. In those far-off, haphazard days, when established relationships between public authority and private enterprise in the programme sector were in process of formation, the presence in a key position within the companies of a man who seemed more than most to be in sympathy with the ITA's aims and objectives was a useful asset to those whose task it was to try to implement the Authority's wishes.

The establishment of the actual networking machinery came about in the following way. In the autumn of 1955, a series of informal discussions took place between A-R and ATV about the exchange of programmes between the two companies once daily transmission began in the Midlands in the following February. They culminated in the convening of a formal meeting at Television House on 3 February 1956. R. T. Harris, Brownrigg's deputy, took the chair and there were three representatives from each company, headed by McMillan for A-R and Grade for ATV. The first recorded Minute referred to Draft Heads of Agreement, intended to be converted into a contract to regulate the networking arrangements between the two companies. This contract was in fact never completed, although networking continued on an *ad hoc* basis until 9 January 1959, when formal agreement of important points was recorded in Minutes.

At a further meeting on 10 February it was agreed to invite Granada to send representatives to future meetings, because the first of the Northern transmitters was due to come into service early in May. Consequently, Robert Heller attended the next meeting on 17 February – and thereafter Granada was always represented. The meeting on 9 March 1956 was the first meeting at which Brownrigg was chairman – an office which he held until 20 January 1961, when he retired in favour of Cecil Bernstein of Granada.

The Minutes of the meeting of 6 April 1956 record a decision to terminate the then existing networking arrangements between A-R and ATV, but 'it was reaffirmed that the mutual aim was for maximum networking of the best possible programmes, and the mutual benefit of all concerned'. For a time thereafter the meetings, which had hitherto taken place weekly, became less frequent and regular, and were not always attended by all three of the companies. This was the period of 'breakdown' which gave rise to the Clark–Wills–Littler correspondence already mentioned.

Early in 1957 the second 'series' of meetings began and continued at fairly regular intervals of about one month until, in October of that year, it was agreed to constitute the Committee on a firmer basis and to appoint an official Secretary. L. T. Thornby, who had acted as such at most of the meetings since early 1956, was appointed the first Secretary of the 'Weekday Network Committee'. The meeting of 6 December 1957 was the first attended by representatives of ABC Television as observers.

On 9 May 1958, the Secretary was instructed to invite representatives of the affiliate companies then operating or about to operate to attend as observers at future meetings. Until then their interests had been looked after by the company to which they were affiliated.[4]

Within the Weekday Network Committee disputes were constant and Lew Grade had ample scope for exercising all those wiles which have made him something of a legend. But there were certain restraints that he could not evade. First and foremost there was the special relationship between A-R and Granada which always tended to place him in a minority position within a consortium consisting, to all intents and purposes, of three. This axis between A-R and Granada was strengthened by the fact that, in general, both companies had a closer identity of view with staff of the ITA, at any rate so far as schedule planning was concerned, than did ATV. Secondly, both Brownrigg and Bernstein were in different ways chairmen of exceptional skill. True, within a 'star-chamber' of three the arts of committeemanship could scarcely be fully deployed but, as time went on, the occasional open sessions, in which all companies could take part, gained greater importance. Grade was not at his best round a committee table, but Bernstein, in particular, had a talent for allowing argument to run on until, with adroit timing, he would intervene, somehow extracting a decision rather like a dentist extracting a tooth.

In relation to the weekends the situation was altogether different. Networking was a matter of what Howard Thomas has described as 'bazaar-type bargaining' between two companies, ATV with the London audience and ABC Television covering the whole of the Midlands and the North.[5] As has been noted Thomas did not join the Network Committee until December 1957. Writing to the author in January 1980 he said:

> When the Midlands transmitter began in February 1956, ABC became responsible for two-thirds of the weekend programmes and ATV one third. This output was planned by Harry Alan Towers and myself. When Towers left suddenly, Lew Grade joined Parnell as Deputy Managing Director and the three of us did the planning.
>
> Eventually Lew and I planned the programmes on a very informal basis, with constant battles over peak times and payments to each other's company. Thus, Sunday night was shared by ATV's London Palladium and ABC's Armchair Theatre. Although ABC reached 66 per cent of the audience (Midlands and North) Lew had the strength of London exposure. How he first refused to transmit such programmes as *The Avengers* in London, and my battle to alternate the Palladium show with our Blackpool Variety Show is told in my book.[6]

In some ways the situation at weekends in the first five years conformed more closely with the early ideal of a competitive network than it ever did on weedays. Thomas writes: 'The weekdays were a single network, but at weekends ATV and ABC had different programmes and their own planning, so the regions took their choice'. In his book[7] he blamed Fraser for failing to give ABC Television more help in securing a London outlet for their drama, particularly the early series of *The Avengers*, and suggested that Fraser was 'too susceptible to the strong-arm tactics of Val Parnell and the beguiling persuasion of Lew Grade'. But the Authority was in those years opposed as a matter of principle to directing one company to transmit particular programmes produced by another. In standing back from such issues, Fraser was implementing an ITA policy which he himself had done much to formulate.

As can be seen in Appendix 1, the ITA was openly critical of the way the network had developed in practice and thought that new arrangements were required to permit the more flexible supply of programmes of which the system had become capable. The nature of those new arrangements became a subject of protracted debate over the next two years amongst the informed and the ill-informed, between the companies themselves and between them and the ITA, between ITV as a whole and the Ministers and officials of the Post Office, and with the Pilkington Committee. Finally, of course, inevitably, in Parliament itself.

Precisely what did the ITA find wrong with the networking arrangements that had come about in 1960/1? This was spelt out in a memorandum dated October 1960 to the Pilkington Committee.[8] First, the Authority's forecast of 'free trade' on a competitive network had not been borne out in practice. The four network companies each produced a more or less fixed amount of programme material for the network and, at any given time, there was usually one programme on offer for network showing. Secondly, a regional company had difficulty in getting its programmes on the network. Thirdly, the parent companies all offered the same standard terms to an affiliate who, because there was no other source of supply, had no choice but to accept them. Fourthly, there was the disincentive in the financial arrangements to regional companies originating programmes in excess of the Authority's minimum requirements and exchanging them between themselves.

The Authority's recommendations for rectifying the defects of the present system were first, that it should have the power to ensure that no programme company withheld its programmes from any other company which wanted to use them and was prepared to pay a fair price for them; and secondly, that it should have the power, in the event of a dispute between companies, to fix the price at which programmes should be made available. It pointed out, however, that these powers would not enable it to oblige a company to take a particular programme from another company or enable it to ensure that companies wishing to purchase network programmes would have a choice of programmes. But it stressed that, given the further powers proposed, it would be able to get rid of the inbuilt disincentive to regional company production. Finally it said that if a higher degree of competition was envisaged than then existed, further channels would have to be made available.

It believed that, given the continued limitation on the frequencies which it could use, it could not have done more to fulfil the objects of the 1954 Television Act. With only one station in each service area, there could be no competition for the viewing audience between simultaneously operating programme companies, nor, as it had turned out, was there as high a degree of competition as was originally expected among the network companies to supply programmes to the regional companies. They had preferred a programme pattern based on regularity, which was not only popular with viewers but also enabled them to deploy their production facilities in an orderly manner over a long period; there were, so to speak, only infrequent changes in the goods displayed for sale by the main producing companies. Furthermore, they had built up such great resources of studios, technical equipment and talent that they were all reluctant to surrender any network time to their own competitors, whether they be network companies or regional companies, since to do so would mean that they would be forced to reduce the economic use of their own productive capacity. It was not an exaggeration to say that there was productive capacity within one service to support two.

Except at weekends a regional company had rarely any choice between a major programme produced by company x and one produced by company y and it could only make up its programmes in succession from items produced by the four network companies, from films acquired from those companies and from programmes originated or acquired by itself. Given the general quality of the network programmes, the pattern of programming which had evolved could not be said to be unsatisfactory considered solely from the point of view of what audiences in any part of the country saw on their screens, and it could be argued that the necessity for regional companies to use their resources almost entirely for local programmes was advantageous for the regional system. But this system could not be said to be as competitive as it should be.

This was not to say, however, that competition was so absent as to make it possible for a network company to go on regularly providing a programme which did not commend itself to other programme companies. For a period, at the start, the programme would normally be the only one available for network distribution at any given time. But the other network companies were not obliged to take it if it fell below an acceptable standard; they had the resources to produce an alternative programme. The alternative programme could then be on offer concurrently, giving the other companies a choice, or it would replace the original one. There was, therefore, however small and slow the resultant turnover of programmes might be, a standing competitive incentive to the network companies to maintain the quality of their programmes. The word used by the ITA was 'quality', but others would consider it more realistic to say 'audience appeal'.

Granada told the Pilkington Committee that each of the three companies jealously protected its place in the sun, but the basic principles of working together had long been agreed. The first of these was that each company would contribute live network programmes approximately in proportion to its population coverage (for weekdays, Granada two-fifths, A-R two-fifths, ATV one-fifth). The second was that the general schedule of programming would be settled jointly, but that each company would have sovereign rights over its own programmes and could transmit them without preliminary vetting or inspection by the others.

It was at about this time that the idea was first floated of the regional companies, collectively, having 'a quota' of network time. It was an idea which was to persist for a long time, partly because it was one which politicians were able readily to grasp and partly because there was a confusion of voices among the regional companies themselves. At least some of the major companies would have settled for some such plan as a simple means of getting the problem off their backs. The shrewd and realistic Cecil Bernstein, for example, saw it as the most effective cure available for a disease which came to be known as 'network itch'. The most perceptive of the regional company executives saw it from the first as a snare and a delusion. One of them told the ITA that he was 'entirely averse from the proposal . . . This might appeal to a regional company thinking only of the network distribution for some of their programmes, but it would cease to appeal as soon as this regional company saw that it would be itself landed with programmes from other regions instead of network programmes.'[9] This view was supported by four others. Commenting on the dilemma seventeen years later Cecil Bernstein said to the author in September 1980:

The truth of the matter is that the four central companies, together perhaps with one additional company in Scotland, Wales and Northern Ireland respectively, could very easily have covered the whole of Britain and provided all the programmes that the ITA wanted for serving local tastes and interests. But we understood why the Authority saw the matter differently and we were fully prepared to work along with the new regional companies so long as they controlled their itch to do major programmes which we were well able to produce ourselves at a higher standard. From a programming point of view the Majors didn't need the Regionals but they needed us more than they needed each other. That's why, when it was suggested by us that a regular network slot should be reserved for regional company productions, they fought shy!

As was seen in Chapter 13, the idea of a network quota for regional companies had its origins right back in the days when the first contracts were being negotiated in 1955. The pitfalls so clearly seen by some of the regional company executives were beyond the comprehension of many members of company boards. The notion that it provided a solution to the problem of the 'stranglehold of the network' lingered on into the sixties. For a time, as will be seen in the next volume, it was taken up again by the ITA itself under the chairmanship of Lord Hill. Variations of it, such as the development of 'little networks' between certain regional companies were tried with differing degrees of success.

Such matters were now about to become issues in the public and political discussions about the future of ITV which began with the publication of the Pilkington Report in June 1962 and continued for over a year until the new Television Act reached the Statute Book on 31 July 1963. Independent Television was to come under intensive scrutiny – warts and all. The broad question was not whether it should survive – that had been decided long since by public acclaim – but whether such deficiencies as had emerged could be remedied by adroit adjustments or whether, as the Pilkington Committee would argue, only a major reconstruction – 'organic change' – would suffice. How Parliament came to decide that adjustments rather than major surgery were preferable, what these were to be and how they were effected will be related in Volume II.

Part V

PEOPLE'S TELEVISION

If you decide to have a system of people's television, then people's television you must expect it to be. It will reflect their likes and dislikes, their tastes and aversions, what they can comprehend and what is beyond them. Every person of common sense knows that people of superior mental constitution are bound to find much of television intellectually beneath them. If such innately fortunate people cannot realise this gently and considerately and with good manners, if in their hearts they despise popular pleasures and interests, then of course they will be angrily dissatisfied with television. But it is not really television with which they are dissatisfied. It is with people.

Sir Rober Fraser: Address to the Manchester
Luncheon Club, 17 May 1960

34

THE FIRST SIX YEARS

(i) 'THE GARDEN OF EDEN': 1955

The Gala Opening on Thursday 22 September 1955 is better remembered as an occasion rather than as a series of programmes: the ceremonious welcome of the new channel in the heart of London, a triumph over many tribulations, the first showing of advertisements on the small screen in this country. Nevertheless, many beginnings were modestly made in those programmes, and certain promises were implied in them. For example, Bill Ward's *Channel Nine* displayed the talents of many variety artistes like Shirley Abicair, Reg Dixon and Leslie Welch who were already well known on BBC TV. But *Channel Nine* also introduced new personalities to the television audience – Hughie Green, Michael Miles and others who were to become identified with ITV. From the very beginning the new channel gave notice that it was going to develop its own characters and also that its approach to the viewing public was to be different from that of the BBC.

Over the first weekend, with the euphoria of that evening only a comforting memory, the two pioneer companies began the long haul of regular broadcasting and the prolonged trials in practice of the ideas they brought to the task. Much later Sir Denis Forman spoke of the 'Garden of Eden' into which came a serpentine intruder in the shape of the Pilkington Committee which put an end to this age of innocence.[1] But, looked at from another angle, the age of innocence lasted a matter of weeks rather than years. By November 1955 ITV planners were already beginning to wonder if they had got it right; they also began to ask themselves questions about the nature of a commercial channel. The real serpent which intruded into this Garden of Eden had a double tongue: unexpectedly high operating costs, and unexpectedly low advertising revenue.

But in so many ways things were going well. Although in these early months ITV was pent within the London area, it was evident by mid-

November 1955 that the new channel, as we saw in Chapter 23, was not only capturing the existing audience but was also creating a new audience for itself among sections of the population the BBC had hardly touched. On the first Friday the day's programme started at 10.45 a.m. with the first ITV serial *Sixpenny Corner*, which was followed by a programme for housewives, *Hands about the House*. There was then a half-hour break with the test card, after which Douglas Warth introduced *Book Case*, discussing her auto-biography with the American actress Yolande Donlan. At 12 noon a news bulletin and a programme trailer occupied ten minutes and were followed by a five-minute entertainment feature and a short programme for under-fives, with close-down at 12.30 p.m. At 5 p.m. children's television started by explaining the plan on which children's programmes were allocated between age groups; the term 'children's TV' was rarely to be used, the titles of individual programmes being left to speak for themselves. The 'toddlers' truce' enforced a close-down from 6 to 7 p.m.; evening programmes began at 7 p.m. and continued until about 11 p.m. No less than thirteen were screened between 7 and 11 p.m., including *Take Your Pick* with Michael Miles, *Dragnet*, and comedian Reg Dixon's *Confidentially*, named after his signature tune. Dixon was a roly-poly performer from the Midlands who had topped the bill on BBC Variety shows as well as in music halls; and *Confidentially* was the first of the ITV shows built around one principal performer, who is both the star of the show and also its anchorman or anchorwoman.

The other two shows, *Dragnet* and *Take Your Pick*, at once entered popular mythology. *Dragnet* was an American police series, one of the first to deal with the routine work of a city police department, with a leading character called Sergeant Joe Friday, played by Jack Webb. Friday's manner of speech became stock material for comedians and impersonators; by some quirk of communications the joke was understood and appreciated even by people outside the range of ITV. This, and other similar instances, were valuable forms of publicity for the new service. *Take Your Pick* was ostensibly a quiz which became an excitable three-sided dialogue with the presenter, Michael Miles, the contestant and the studio audience all taking part. Correct answers to three not very exacting questions allowed the contestant to 'take his or her pick' of the keys to thirteen numbered boxes, each containing a prize voucher ranging in value from expensive top prizes to ludicrous booby prizes. On occasions Michael Miles would offer sums of money to buy back the key: the problem of choosing between cash in hand, the hope of a substantial reward, and the dread of a worthless booby prize – the problem confused by contradictory shouts of advice from the studio audience – almost deserved the epithet 'agonising'. It was regular viewing in thousands of homes and was invariably in the 'Top Twenty' charts; it was also the first TV programme in this country to use the studio audience as part of the show, helping to create and at the same time to emphasise the tensions of the game.

Next day, on Saturday, morning programmes began betimes with *Weekend* at 9.30 a.m.: this was an 'informal magazine programme' presented by Daphne Anderson 'with something for every member of the family'. At 3 p.m. 'pop' music raised its head in *ABC Music Shop*, with Gerry Wilmot; this was a 'rendezvous of popular recording stars from both sides of the Atlantic', with competitions and prizes. It is probably true to say that ITV, with its ear closer to the ground than the BBC, understood the 'pop' sub-culture better than its older rival and was able to make better programmes in that area. The main feature in the afternoon was *My Hero*, an American comedy series with Bob Cummings; it was followed by the home-produced *Home with Joy Shelton*, a twenty-minute feature for housewives. Armand and Michaela Denis, a Belgian husband-and-wife team of naturalists, had already made a name for themselves on BBC; they presented a series of short films about wild life in Africa early on Saturday evenings.

People Are Funny was the Saturday evening comedy show, and the first to become mildly controversial. The object of the show was to submit the people who volunteered to take part in it to ingenious practical jokes. The volunteers were generously rewarded for their various ordeals, and they clearly had no inhibitions about appearing in the programme. But almost from the beginning *People Are Funny* was condemned as cruel, tasteless and pointless, an exploitation of people taking part. In the course of time the ITA thought it wise to intervene, and eventually the programme was quietly dropped – much to the disappointment of the people on its long waiting list of volunteers.

Saturday Showtime, at 8.15 p.m., featured the famous music-hall trio Wilson, Keppel and Betty, along with Harry Secombe ('the Goon with the Golden Voice'), and Norman Vaughan, soon to achieve stardom on ITV. There was a regular play-spot at 9 p.m. on Saturdays; on this occasion it was *Mid Level*, by Berkeley Mather, a thriller set in Hong Kong with a cast including Michael Gough, Betty McDowell, Jack Allen, Rupert Davies, Hilda Fennimore, William Franklyn, and Stratford Johns. Most ITV plays then and later seemed like a theatrical *Who's Who*, because the frequent practice of filming plays rather than screening them live meant that distinguished actors were often able to fit in ITV plays whilst they could not spare the time for BBC drama productions. Saturday evening closed with a mixture of music, interviews, and gossip from the Embassy Club in London's West End. The producer was the immensely popular Jack Jackson, trumpeter, former band leader, and a considerable innovator in presenting pop music on TV and radio.

Sunday's programme also introduced people and shows destined to be closely identified with ITV. They included *Liberace*, another source of endless parody; *Free Speech*, the political discussion programme with Robert Boothby, W. J. Brown, Michael Foot and A. J. P. Taylor, and Kenneth Adam in the chair; *The Adventures of Robin Hood* with Richard Greene; *Sunday Night at the London Palladium* with Tommy Trinder as the first of many well known presenters; and *I Love Lucy* with the indefatigable Lucille Ball, whose comedy shows became a fixture on either ITV or BBC for many years to come.

Sunday Afternoon was a magazine programme which was intelligent, ambitious, highly praised, and over-crowded. The list of people taking part in this first edition justifies all those adjectives: Penny Knowles, Tom Driberg, Dame Edith Sitwell, Ludovic Kennedy, Mervyn Levy, Jill Craigie, Anthony Wedgwood Benn, Chin Yu, and Leslie Welch; all these in a forty-minute programme! Nevertheless it was successful, always favourably reviewed, and much enjoyed by a variety of viewers. It was followed by an innovation, startling at the very least – a cowboy film on Sunday!

Sunday Night at the London Palladium was the ultimate expression of the 'showbiz' element in ITV, relying heavily on the reputation of the Palladium as the world centre of variety and vaudeville. Most great show-business names from all over the world appeared there from time to time; the televised show, making full use of these great names, was conceived on a scale never before seen on British TV and was deservedly popular. It included an audience-participation feature called *Beat the Clock*, in which members of the audience – often honeymooners – tried their hands at competitive games under the sardonic eye of Tommy Trinder. *Beat the Clock* came intermittently under the same sort of critical fire as *People Are Funny*, but the case against it was demonstrably weakened by the obvious enjoyment of the contestants and the tact of Trinder and his successors.

The ensuing week had its share of novelties from A-R. Two dramatic productions on Monday were both the first in their series and formats new to this country. *The Granville Melodramas* was an entertaining series of nineteenth-century plays from the Granville Theatre, Fulham, whilst *Four Star Theatre* was an elaborately packaged drama series from the United States, featuring the stars of Hollywood and Broadway, usually in 'strong' plays with a good deal of dramatic action. The same evening a still greater

ITV success made its first appearance: *Double Your Money*, with Hughie Green. This was – almost – a straightforward general knowledge quiz, in which correct answers to progressively more difficult questions doubled the prize money the participants had already won, until the most knowledgeable won their way to the 'Treasure Trail' and a possible prize of £1000. At this point the proceedings became earnestly formal. The contestant was ushered into a soundproof glass cabinet with a ceremonious concern on the part of Hughie Green; the questions were intoned with solemn emphasis; failure was greeted with generous compassion; victory with awed ecstasy.

But the 'Treasure Trail' was for the expert, the optimist, or the very lucky; most people failed or gave up before they reached that level. And it was in the preliminaries that most of the fun, and often a touching charm, were found. Green briefly interviewed his contestants, showing real concern for the elderly couple blinking under the unaccustomed bright lights, but at the other extreme overjoyed if some Cockney or Northcountry wag quipped back at him in his own coin. Nor was he unwilling to bend the rules a little so that, for instance, an old age pensioner had a few pounds to take away.

Hughie Green, before the public since his days as a child film actor, was a little larger than life, and frequently ventured into areas where his sincerity might be called in question. But he withstood many years of scrutiny by the cameras without any fracture of his image; indeed, one of the attractions of *Double Your Money* was precisely his flamboyant but tactful exploitation of human interest. Whether he was recoiling in stagey high dudgeon from a contestant's witticism, or whether he was drawing out – almost tenderly – an anecdote from some shy person, he never trangressed accepted limits of good taste in spite of his theatrical manner and persona. Add to human interest a strand of comedy and the excitements of the better sort of quiz, and it is small wonder that *Double Your Money*, like its stable-companion *Take Your Pick*, was never out of the 'Top Twenty'.

On Tuesday another ambitious dramatic production, the first in another series, was screened. The series was called *International Theatre*; the play was Turgenev's *A Month in the Country*, with a star-studded cast. Noel Barber, a distinguished journalist, started a current affairs series under what seemed to be a self-defeating title, *Assignment Unknown*, whilst *Sports Formbook* with Bernard Joy, a well-known football writer who had once been an amateur half-back with Arsenal, and John Rickman, a popular racing correspondent, showed a somewhat tentative approach to its subject. *Cavalcade of Sport*, on Wednesdays, was an hour-long programme promising rather more than it gave; its main feature was the second half of a Rugby League match between Wigan and Huddersfield played in the neutral, not to say foreign, territory of Woolwich. The commentator on this game, and on others in the competition for a Television Trophy presented by A-R, was one Eddie Waring, a fact which did not escape the BBC when they later decided to build up their northern audiences with Rugby League broadcasts.

ITV handled sport rather gingerly; coverage, compared with the BBC's seemed sparse, random, and sometimes amateurish. There were reasons for this, quite apart from a diffidence which often seemed to infect ITV companies when they competed with the BBC in this field. The BBC had long and dearly-bought expertise in covering most sports and games, and had established relations that were usually harmonious with governing bodies, officials, and players. More to the point, the BBC established contractual commitments in respect of many sporting occasions, thus denying them to the new channel. This Wigan–Huddersfield Rugby League match, and the competition for the Television Trophy, was an early example of the tendency for both services to use sport for their own ends, sometimes creating activities rather than merely reporting them.

Other points of interest during this first week of ITV broadcasting were Ralph Reader's *Chance of a Lifetime*, a talent-spotting show run by the man identified with the Boy Scouts and their 'Gang Show'; *Points of View*, chaired by the much respected Leslie Mitchell, an ambitious discussion programme; *The Scarlet Pimpernel* with Marius Goring; the first of the *Hopalong Cassidy* films for children; *Jack Hylton Presents*, a half-hour variety programme soon to be lengthened to one hour, starring on this occasion Flanagan and Allen, with Shirley Bassey as a modest supporting act. Leslie Mitchell chaired another talk programme called *Crossroads* (not the motel saga!) in which guests talked about decisive moments in their lives; among them were Lesley Osmond and Jeremy Thorpe. A play called *The Haven*, with Joan Miller and Robert Harris, appeared on Thursday under the series title *London Playhouse*. From the beginning ITV used single plays extensively, but preferred to screen them as part of a labelled sequence; some of these labels, like Television Playhouse and Armchair Theatre, became landmarks in television history.

There were, of course, many other programmes; there were also various fixed points in the day or the week – news bulletins, programme trails, and so on. As already noted public response from the start was very encouraging, and there were three main reasons. First, novelty in programme content; secondly, novelty in presentation; and thirdly, novelty in programme scheduling. Of innovations in programme content it is enough to say that almost all the programmes mentioned – hackneyed as they may seem to viewers in this third decade of ITV – were novelties at the time.

Novelty in presentation was equally, if not more, important. Newsreaders and announcers were encouraged to 'be themselves', to be informally relaxed, to set up a personal relationship with the viewer. The BBC had traditionally thought of its presentation staff, its newsreaders, and other people who made routine appearances on the screen as mouthpieces of the Corporation; they were expected to be educated, speaking the King's English, decently dressed, but above all unobtrusive and impersonal. Thus the BBC suffered a mild collective syncope when Ron Randell, a panellist on *What's My Line?*, signed himself off at the end of one programme by blowing a kiss at the audience. By contrast, people appearing on ITV were urged to be informal and to speak to the audience as themselves and not as representatives of some august institution. Peter Black tells the story of Christopher Chataway reading a news item about athletics: 'There goes my record!' he exclaimed. 'Tharos beat it by more than nine seconds.'[2]

Thirdly there was novelty in scheduling. The BBC, in the absence of competition, had developed its own methods of providing a varied diet which included many 'one-off' programmes, short series, and similar things which admittedly made a varied schedule but which did not permit regularity in planning. The practice that ITV adopted was as far as possible to place the same programmes in the same slots each week, so that viewers knew where they were and would be encouraged to form viewing habits on a weekly basis. This on the one hand inculcated 'channel loyalty' and on the other enabled advertisers to forecast the size of the audience for weeks ahead. The viewer seemed to approve of this fixed pattern of programmes: audience research revealed a high level of continuity of viewing from episode to episode in a serial or series, and people's habits were often adapted in surprising ways to enable them to see favourite programmes. ITV did not need the potter's wheel and the other time-filling loops used by the BBC.

Even so, by modern standards, the early schedules were bitty: there was a large number of programmes lasting fifteen minutes or even less. It was as though ITV was trying to pack everything in and seeking perhaps too strenuously to be all things to all men. The same tendency was evident within many individual programmes as, for example, the much-praised *Sunday Afternoon*. These signs of a somewhat nervous desire to please were understandable. Schedules, like the hardware, had been put together in haste, and though there was much television experience in the ranks of the ITV companies it had not yet been suffused with certainty of purpose.

(ii) 'RETREAT FROM CULTURE': 1956

In the next few weeks programme schedules remained very much as they were in that first week. The principal category was drama, ranging from the acknowledged theatrical classic to the contemporary thriller. From Friday to Friday in the first week there were no less than ten dramatic productions, of which seven might reasonably be called 'heavyweight'. The second category, in terms of number of shows, was variety, with eight programmes in the week if one includes the short solo acts *Friday's Man* and *Friday's Girl*. The third important genre was the 'quiz' or 'give-away' show (the 'programme with prizes', as the ITA came demurely to name it). General interest programmes, like *Sunday Afternoon* or *Assignment Unknown*, formed another important class, merging with no clear dividing line into special interest features embracing politics, sport, children's programmes, and those addressed to women – some of them serious and some rejoicing in 'silly season' titles like *Are Husbands Really Necessary?* And there were, of course, regular newscasts, some of them short bulletins, others extended with film material.

These schedules were arranged with a good deal of attention to the concept of 'balance' which, like many theological doctrines, was powerful although not precisely definable. Despite the developments recorded in Chapters 24 and 27, the ITA's own attitude was guarded and remained so. It said in its Annual Report for 1955/6:

> The Authority deliberately refrained from committing itself to cut and dried theoretical criteria for deciding, in advance of experience, what constituted high quality and proper balance. . . . The experience of the first six months strengthened into conviction its initial belief that, as a general rule, its responsibilities in relation to programmes would be better exercised by means of frank and continuing consultation with its contractors in private than by the promulgation of any code of standards comparable with those which seemed necessary in the case of advertisements.[3]

The ITA was to be strongly criticised during 1956 and on many occasions afterwards by people who were ignorant of the 'frank and continuing consultation' and expected it to act publicly and perhaps dramatically. An early instance of 'private' consultation happened in respect of the A-R programme *Round the World with Orson Welles*, a travelogue series presented, as the name implies, by Welles. The programme scheduled for 4 November

1955 included material about bullfighting in Spain. The ITA and A-R discussed whether or not it was desirable to show bullfighting on TV, and finally Fraser wrote to Wills saying that in the opinion of the Authority it was 'very undesirable' to show a bullfight as it would be 'offensive to a large body of public feeling in the country'. However, the ITA, the letter went on, understood that there are no absolute standards of judgement in a matter of this kind, and was, moreover, averse to using the powers of censorship conferred upon it by the Television Act. The board of directors of A-R was therefore informed of the Authority's opinion and invited to consider it earnestly.

In reply Wills, who enjoyed such procedural niceties, reported that 'at short notice' he had assembled his fellow-directors and the members of the staff concerned with the programme. They saw it and discussed it; having done so they asked Wills to convey to the Authority their 'firm and united view' that the film was 'completely unobjectionable'. In the light of this opinion, they argued that withdrawal of the film would on one hand damage staff morale, and, on the other, be seen as yielding to pressure groups, some of whom had already made public their objections to the film. The directors and staff of A-R had not seen in the programme 'any affront to public taste' – had they done so they would have agreed to its withdrawal – and correctly prophesied that 'only a small minority of viewers' would object to it.[4]

Relations between the ITA and the programme companies became less formal as time went by, but this episode set the tone of their relationship. Making programmes was the business of the companies; the ITA would only exercise its powers of censorship reluctantly, and if it was obliged to do so, on grounds 'unequivocally related to the provisions of the Act'. Neither the ITA nor the companies should be diverted from what was believed to be a proper course of action by pressure groups, however vocal – or however worthy. And the morale of the people who made the programmes was also important: it might be adversely affected by seemingly captious interference from on high.

This developing relationship was of great importance in the sequence of events which began at about the same time as Fraser and Wills were communicating formally on the subject of bullfighting. By mid-November 1955 it was evident that ITV was attracting an audience which the BBC had barely touched. But it was also becoming clear that, gratifying as public response had been, the audience at that time was just not big enough to secure the level of advertising revenue needed to keep ITV afloat. The necessary expansion of the audience was largely in the hands of the planners and engineers working on the network of transmitters required to extend the coverage into the Midlands and the North; but something could be done by increasing the proportion of programmes demonstrably popular with the new audience. The message was clearly received throughout ITV, but with special force in the boardroom of A-R.

The remedies were obvious: economies where possible – morning TV was off the air by Christmas – and a bigger, faster build-up of the audience in terms of numbers of sets and of time spent in viewing. We noted in Chapter 24 Roland Gillett's remark about giving the public what it wants. He went on to add:

> Let's face it once and for all. The public likes girls, wrestling, bright musicals, quiz shows and real-life drama. We gave them the Hallé Orchestra, Foreign Press Club, floodlit football and visits to the local fire station. Well, we've learned. From now on, what the public wants, it's going to get.[5]

Statements like this were seen, even by critics and others who in general wished ITV well, as evidence of an abdication of cultural responsibility. In its Annual Report for 1955/6, the ITA summed up the situation with a certain detachment:

> During December 1955 and January 1956, however, there was a reduction of the order of one-third in the total amount of transmission time given over to news, news magazines, serious discussion, classical entertainment, and other 'balancing' programmes. It is true that this quantitative result followed much careful appraisal of the comparative merits of individual programmes: the abandonment of some, the fresh arrival of others, pruning, reshaping, re-positioning and all the many processes of which programme planning is comprised. But nevertheless it led to a remarkably fierce controversy over what in headline terms was called independent television's 'retreat from culture'.[6]

This controversy got ITV a bad name. It became established as part of the folklore of the intelligentsia and the middle classes that ITV was selling the cultural pass, that it was crassly commercial, and that it was 'playing down to the lowest common denominator'. And what was worse, the ITA, the appointed watchdog whose duty it was to safeguard the standards of the new channel, was guilty of a new *trahison des clercs*. There was just so much truth in these accusations to make justification difficult.

The assumption underlying the arguments of the intellectuals was that ITV ought to be like the BBC. It was a tribute to the BBC, which had been so long unchallenged and so much admired, that the middle-class viewer took it for granted that any other television service in Great Britain should accept the BBC's standards: thus, where ITV seemed to conform with those standards – the Hallé Orchestra, for instance, or classical drama – it was approved; where it did not conform, even in cases of worthwhile innovation, approval was at best grudgingly given, at worst withheld. But was the BBC the proper yardstick for measuring ITV? The needs and interests of the new audience were quite different from the needs and interests of the audience for which the BBC had been catering.

The experience of the first few weeks of ITV was enough to convince the managements that the new channel could not operate on the same lines as the BBC; it could only exist as a mass medium. Audience measurement and research showed what the audience would tolerate, what it would readily accept, and what it would enthuse about. The public accepted, and took to its collective heart, programmes which many critics said were bad. They were popular, as Fraser put it, not in a *Daily Telegraph* way but in a *Daily Mirror* way.

The choice which led to the retreat from culture was, as Gillett and his colleagues saw it, between extinction and survival. The ITA condoned (if that is the word) the policy because it too was aware of what was at stake, and also because it felt the need to consider very carefully what the implications were of being a mass medium. It recognised its own obligations, but it also recognised several forces inherent in the structure of ITV which would in the longer run lead to better programmes within the context of a mass medium. One was its own influence, which was exercised tactfully and unobtrusively, and thus gained ground with the companies. Another was the natural desire of programme makers to do good work, to excel, and to deserve the esteem of their colleagues. And yet another was the belief, built into ITV with its foundations, though often dismissed with scorn by the BBC, that ITV was a public service with responsibilities other than that of supplying undemanding entertainment. If sights had temporarily to be lowered, in the interests of survival, ITV possessed and retained the will to raise them again. The 'retreat from culture' was halted in a matter of months rather than years, but the damage it did to ITV's reputation amongst the opinion-forming minority was much less speedily repaired. The chickens persisted in coming home to roost.

(iii) NETWORK AT WORK: 1958

By 1958 ITV, its central structure complete and some of its outlying stations either operational or nearing that state, was well on the way to fulfilling Clark's belief that ITV should first find itself an audience. By the end of 1958, ITV was available to 76 per cent of the population of the United Kingdom, and the number of homes within its reach able to receive ITV had risen from less than one-third at the end of 1955 to more than three-quarters by the end of 1958. To see what ITV was doing at this stage in its history we look at a sample week, chosen at random, in May 1958.

We choose the North, at that time served on weekdays by Granada and at weekends by ABC. The Northern Region then extended over both Lancashire and Yorkshire, into North Wales, and into other English counties; it was a heterogeneous region, sometimes called 'Granadaland' in an effort to give it a basic sense of identity. Granada had already established a reputation for trenchant current affairs programmes, whilst ABC was best known for its 'Armchair Theatre' on Sunday evenings which offered competition with the BBC's 'Sunday Play'.

We begin, then, on Sunday 11 May 1958. Religious broadcasting had by this time assumed a pattern – a church service in the morning, *The Sunday Break* at 6 p.m., and a further religious feature at 7 p.m. On Sunday afternoon at 2.50 Simon Kester presented *The Book Man*, which was followed by a film and, at 4.30, a situation comedy with Billie Whitelaw and Diana King. *The New Adventures of Robin Hood*, a serial closely identified with ITV, was shown at 5 p.m., and an ABC advertising magazine, *What's In Store?* with Doris Rogers, at 5.35, with ITN's production *Tell the People* at 5.45, and the News from ITN at 6 p.m.

After the religious programmes and a five-minute news bulletin, evening viewing started with *Martin Kane, Private Investigator*, a bought-in crime series, and *Sunday Night at the London Palladium*, still introduced by Tommy Trinder. *The Sunday Serial* at 9 p.m. was *The Truth About Melandrinos*, an ABC production written by James Parish and starring George Baker. It was a strong mystery serial and dealt with drug smuggling in the oblique and laconic style then fashionable – it was tough and baffling, but literate. The ABC Armchair Theatre play which followed at 9.35, after the final news bulletin, was *Hanging Judge*, a strong play with a strong cast including Raymond Massey and John Robinson; it was one of the plays which gave ABC's drama department its high reputation. The last programme before the Epilogue was *Top Tune Time*, with Anne Shelton, Joan Savage, Ken Morris, and the four Jones Boys – one of the better ITV musical shows.

On Monday Granada took over from ABC, starting at 4.20 p.m. with *Good Afternoon Children*, followed by a programme in Welsh. *Seeing Sport* was a locally-based series for children; on this occasion it was an instructional feature about swimming filmed in a newly-opened pool at a nearby school. Half an hour of *Popeye* on cartoon preceded the news at 5.55; the ITN bulletin was followed by *Northern Newscast*, Granada's own news feature; and at 6.10 *The Adventures of Long John Silver*, a likeable piece of hokum which purported to describe Silver's life before the adventure in *Treasure Island*. It sustained a bravura performance by Robert Newton as Silver which was much imitated by comedians and impersonators. *The Last Word*, a twenty-minute programme which came after 'Long John', was a discussion on the proper use of the English language chaired by Jack Longland with, among others, Professor Ross of 'U' and 'non-U' fame. *Sword of Freedom*, which occupied the next half-hour, was a costume drama starring Edmund Purdom and set in Renaissance Italy; it related what seem in retrospect the endless adventures of one Marco. It was followed by *Shadow Squad*, a police series with Peter Williams and George Moon.

At 8 p.m., *Wagon Train*. This was one of the best of the Westerns: each episode was a self-contained story about a member of a wagon train rolling westwards in the pioneer days. There were regular players – Ward Bond and Robert Horton as the wagon-master and the scout respectively – but the series also enlisted Hollywood stars and bit actors to perform in its weekly episodes. Even on the small screen its pictorial values were very high, and a competent production team, including first-rate scriptwriters, kept the series at an admirable standard. *Wagon Train* was later taken over by the BBC when they decided to fight fire with fire. The evening went on with a fashion show from London in which Noele Gordon was a presenter, a panel game with David Jacobs in the chair, a programme by Daniel Farson about Women's Institutes, a half-hour musical feature produced by Jack Hylton and finally *Alfred Hitchcock Presents*, a series of mystery films one-hour long and introduced by the Master himself.

Tuesday began with *Dewch i Mewn* for Welsh speakers, *Lucky Dip*, a miscellany for children, and the first episode of *Into the Net*, a new children's serial. News and local news were succeeded by a programme about Will Hay and twenty minutes of piano requests by Russ Conway. *The Bob Cummings Show* at 7 p.m. was followed at 7.30 by ATV's *Emergency-Ward Ten*. By May 1958 this twice-weekly serial was in its second year and at the crest of its fame. It was the first major specimen on British TV of the genus soap opera: that is to say, it was a serial with regular and frequent episodes set in a more or less enclosed situation, with a central core of characters and others according to the needs of the plot. Usually several threads of plot are spun side by side over a number of episodes, and the stories are slow-moving for the sake of those who cannot see every instalment. In the case of *Emergency-Ward Ten*, the 'enclosed situation' was Ward Ten in a hospital, the 'central core' of characters was the medical and nursing staff, and the patients and their visitors were the additional characters. It was extremely popular over a long life on ITV screens.

In human and dramatic terms soap operas veer wildly between the competent and the dreadful. *Emergency-Ward Ten* was perhaps not quite in the top class, but it served ITV very well. The successful soap opera assembles a huge audience for its successive episodes; if it is screened at the beginning of peak time, then most of that huge audience may well be available for the rest of the evening on that particular channel. Apart from its audience-gathering function, however, *Emergency-Ward Ten* also discharged a useful social service by familiarising the public with the routine and atmosphere of hospitals.

Granada's *Chelsea at Eight* (or *Nine*) was a show of quality which had soldiered through the retreat from culture. This particular week it was compered by Bernard Braden and featured José Iturbi, the classical pianist, Keith Michell (with others) singing songs from a new musical by Sandy Wilson, the 'famous Negro singers' Gordon Heath and Lee Pavant, Alan King, and Granada's troupe of dancing girls, the Granadiers. Peter Knight and his orchestra supplied the music. It was followed by another Western, *Wyatt Earp*, with Hugh O'Brian in the name part; then Jeremy Hawke presented *Criss Cross Quiz*, based on noughts and crosses. The next programme, *What the Papers Say*, was one of Granada's own bright stars; it began in November 1956 and has continued to the present day. It was supposed to be a review of newspapers during the week before the broadcast, but it has proved almost inexhaustibly various, with many different voices discussing different aspects of the press in many different tones. *Hotel Imperial*, at 10.15 p.m., was a comedy musical written by Alan Melville and starring Vic Oliver, Hugh Sinclair, and Peter Bull; it was followed by the news and *The Late Show*, which this week presented a mystery story of intrigue and crime on the staff of a magazine.

Amser Te, a Welsh magazine programme, began Wednesday's broadcast at 4.20 p.m., to be followed at 5 p.m. by *Junior Criss Cross Quiz* (again with Jeremy Hawke) and *The Adventures of Kit Carson*. After the news came *Melody Ranch*, a programme of Western music, and *We Want an Answer*. This was a series, directed by Granada's own Michael Scott, in which young people interviewed experts on a wide range of contemporary issues; this evening the expert was the Jewish educationalist Rabbi Kopul Rosen. *We Want an Answer* was one of several discussion programmes, all with aggressive titles, with which Granada made a considerable reputation as a company with a hard abrasive edge.

Next came *The New Adventures of Charlie Chan*, a serialised film about the Chinese detective familiar in American fiction. There followed *Boyd QC*, a popular court room series with Michael Denison, and *Spot the Tune*, a musical quiz presented by Alfred Marks and Marion Ryan. 'Play of the Week' was this week made by Granada itself; the play was Arthur Miller's *All My Sons*, with the American actor Albert Dekker, Megs Jenkins, Betta St. John, and Patrick McGoohan. Miller had been very pleased with an earlier Granada production of *Death of a Salesman*, then perhaps his best-known play, and was happy to let the company screen *All My Sons*, the play that established his reputation.

The customary change of mood came with *The Carrol Levis Discoveries*, a talent-spotting show, and *Sports Outlook* with Gerry Loftus, the news at 10.45, *Palais Party* from the Hammersmith Palais de Danse with Lou Preager and his Orchestra, and finally *Mark Saber*, a private eye series with Donald Gray and Diana Decker. In spite of the length of *All My Sons* (95 minutes), the Granada viewer was given no less than fourteen programmes from half-past five.

Children's programmes on Thursday included Granada's *Zoo Time*, Popeye cartoons, and an episode of Sir Walter Scott's *Ivanhoe* with Roger Moore. *Roving Report*, at 6.40 p.m., was networked from ITN; it was a highly-regarded current affairs review, and this edition was an account of Florence with Robert Tyrrell. *I Love Lucy*, which came next, was a product of the Lucille Ball studio in Hollywood. At this time in the long history of 'Lucy' shows, Lucille Ball was supported by Desi Arnaz, Vivian Vance, and William Frawley, arguably the best team she ever assembled. Another episode of *Shadow Squad* gave place to *Double Your Money*, which was succeeded by *Val Parnell's Star Time*, with Jewel and Warris among others; at 9.30 *This Week*, a programme which will receive attention in Chapter 35, was on this occasion presided over by Ludovic Kennedy; it was followed by another staple Western, *Gun Law*, with James Arness, and *The Late Show*, which was Part One of a serial based on the life of George Edwardes of the Gaiety.

Friday's programmes started with racing from Lingfield at 2.15 p.m. and a visit to the Royal Windsor Horse Show. In due course *Dewch i Mewn* and the children's programmes followed, the latter including *Rin-Tin-Tin*. After the news and *Northern Newcast*, *Duke Ellington and His Quartet* discoursed the better kind of popular music with Valerie Masters and the Mudlarks; then came *Sea Hunt* with Lloyd Bridges, another episode of *Emergency – Ward Ten*, Michael Miles with *Take Your Pick*, and *The Army Game*. This last was a long-running programme with spin-offs and sequels; it started in June 1957 and eventually ran for 150 episodes. It was a Granada production dealing with some improbable army recruits, played by Alfie (Excused Boots) Bass, Michael Medwin, Bernard Bresslaw, and others. The Sergeant-Major, without whom no army comedy is complete, was played in the first place by William Hartnell; later Bill Fraser took it on and became so identified with the part of Sergeant-Major Snudge that the audience quite forgot that he was a brilliant, sensitive, and versatile actor.

There was another outside broadcast visit to Windsor and the Horse Show, 'Television Playhouse' presented *Dark Pastures*, a play about the life of a miner with Mervyn Johns, and *Only Yesterday*, a pleasant 'scrapbook' programme, told the story of Amy Johnson. After the news a record programme, *Cool for Cats*, was compered by Kent Walton who went on to become the guide, philosopher, and friend to wrestling fans, and Douglas Fairbanks Junior introduced another in a series of short dramas, *The Enchanted Doll*.

Saturday opened in the early afternoon at Lingfield, and remained out of doors for *The Festival of Stars*, a Variety Club of Great Britain entertainment to mark the beginning of that year's season at the Festival Gardens in Battersea. *The Transfer* at 4 p.m. was a dramatised ghost story; it was followed by an episode of *Robin Hood* and *Let's Go Shopping*, the ABC advertising magazine. This was succeeded by *The Mark of Zorro*, a series based on the old silent Fairbanks film, the sports results, the news, and *The Jack Jackson Show*, now slotted at 6 p.m. *Highway Patrol*, with Broderick Crawford, was another American police series which became popular in this country, its radio procedure providing a ready joke for imitative comedians. *Maverick* was a Western with hour-long episodes about a Western knight-errant starring the durable James Garner; *African Patrol* was an adventure serial set in Africa; *The Saturday Show* was variety with Jacqueline François and Dave Morris. 'Great Movies of Our Time' showed *Dive Bomber* with Fred McMurray, Errol Flynn, and Alexis Smith, and so to the Epilogue and close-down.

Several things have now emerged. The network of major companies was complete, with two 'regionals' – STV and TWW – also on air. The system was working to some effect: Granadaland viewers were receiving many programmes made or bought in by other major companies; they were not dependent solely on production in Manchester nor yet in London. Further, the 'plural' arrangement was encouraging some degree of specialisation; Granada, for example, had already made a name as the pioneer of aggressive current affairs programmes. What was more important was ITV's increasing certainty of touch, born of a greater assurance about what it could do and ought to do. The first programmes had been planned, as it were, in a vacuum; now the companies had learned a good deal about their audience and were more self-confident as a result. Balance had been restored, and the companies had made the discovery that their audiences would now accept material that in earlier days would have meant 'switch-off-or-switch-over'; the public would take from ITV what it wouldn't have taken from the BBC.

Appropriately enough, 1958 was the year when ITV received its first Royal recognition. On 13 November 1958 Her Majesty The Queen and His Royal Highness The Duke of Edinburgh attended a reception at 14 Princes Gate. It was attended by Members of the Authority and its staff, and by the chairmen and senior officers of the programme companies.

(iv) TOWARDS COMPLETION: 1961

We move forward in time to 1961 and southwards to London. By this time the ITV network was nearing completion; Hugh Greene had become Director-General of the BBC in the previous year with the intention of facing the competition of ITV and 'to dissipate the ivory tower stuffiness which still clung to some parts of the BBC';[7] also in 1960 the Pilkington Committee had begun its work. In *The Third Floor Front* Greene charges the heads of ITV with undue complacency: they did not realise to what extent the BBC would marshal middle-class prejudice against them. Greene knew all about 'psychological warfare', and he waged it with consummate skill. But the ground was prepared for him not so much by the 'retreat from culture' itself, but by the reluctance of middle-class opinion to re-examine its assumptions when that retreat had been stemmed.

On Sunday 1 October 1961 the day's broadcast in London began with a church service introduced by Bill Allenby. After a close-down a crime series occupied the half-hour from 2.15 p.m., to be followed by *Sir Francis Drake*, a romanticised account of the navigator with Terence Morgan as Drake and Jean Kent as Queen Elizabeth I. At 3.15 *Call Oxbridge 2000* took over, a hospital drama series of some merit lasting for 45 minutes. The extra quarter of an hour was important, since it allowed the scriptwriter – in this instance Diana Morgan – more elbow room than was customary in this genre. *Plateau of Fear*, an adventure series dealing with a nuclear power station somewhere in South America, followed at 4 p.m., and *Supercar*, one of Gerry Anderson's ingenious puppet productions. *Tempo*, at 5 p.m., was ABC's ambitious and usually successful arts and general interest programme edited by Kenneth Tynan and presented by the Earl of Harewood: this particular edition gave the viewer not only Laurence Olivier but also the 'Beyond the Fringe' team of Jonathan Miller, Peter Cook, Dudley Moore, and Alan Bennett. *Get This*, an ATV advertising magazine, was screened at 5.50; then followed the news, *The Sunday Break*, and a thoughtful and moving 'About Religion' feature from ATV called *Inquest at Golgotha*. It took the form of a coroner's inquest on Jesus Christ, and was both reverent and intelligent.

At 7.30 *Bonanza* was screened – a well-made Western about a family of ranchers whose members were remarkably adventure-prone; like *Wagon Train*, it was eventually taken over by the BBC. *Sunday Night at the London Palladium* was now compered by Bruce Forsyth; the star of this show was Sammy Davis Junior. 'Drama 61' presented *Joke Over*, in which a misfired practical joke revealed deep psychological levels; finally *77 Sunset Strip*, with Efrem Zimbalist Junior, concluded the evening's TV except for the weather forecast and the *Epilogue*.

Monday remained very much as it had been in 1958 with one remarkable exception. *Coronation Street* was now almost one year old and had been fully networked since May 1961. It dealt with people living in a street in 'Weatherfield', adjacent to Manchester. This was Salford in real life, and the fictional Coronation Street was Archie Street, now demolished. It was generically soap opera: each episode advanced several story lines, and the stories progressed with the slow dignity of strip cartoons. The viewer found it easy to pick up *Coronation Street* in any episode, to miss it for weeks or, indeed, months, and then to pick it up again. It has been criticised for its reach-me-down moralities, for the curious absence of children in a neighbourhood otherwise teeming with vitality, and so on. It has often been condemned by intellectuals, social scientists, politicians, and others with axes to grind. Yet enormous numbers of ordinary folk have been 'hooked' by it for months and years at a stretch; it is presented with a high degree of professionalism; it takes full advantage of the gnomic possibilities of its northern speech; its characters are memorable and oddly attractive; it is persistently and intrinsically human. Soap opera it may be, but it is the most successful and the most distinguished of its kind. It may not be 'important' or 'significant', but it has brought pleasure to millions of people and has been a vital element in programme planning and the ratings war. It has sustained its qualities, its essential wholesomeness, over twenty years or more to become part of the national mythology. 'The Street' reached its 2000th episode on 2 June 1980 which happened to be the 27th anniversary of the Coronation. It has rarely been out of the Top Ten programmes; it has been shown in Australia, Belgium, Canada, Denmark, Eire, Finland, Gibraltar, Greece, Hong Kong, New Zealand, Sierra Leone, Singapore, Sweden, Thailand, and the USA. There are many people in this country who have seen well over a thousand episodes; there are some who have never seen one. 'If you think,' wrote Ian Nairn in the *Sunday Times* of 24 August 1980, 'the *Coronation Street* characters are soap opera stereotypes, think again. They're real, alive and well, and walking round Salford.' The emergence, survival and sustained excellence of this unique serial is a fitting memorial to the quiet man of ITV, the late Cecil Bernstein who was the programme's founder and protector.

An event of national interest covered during this week was the Labour Party Conference at Blackpool. The ITV reporters who covered it were Ian Trethowan, now Director-General of the BBC, and George Ffitch, now managing director of LBC Radio. But most of the technical and other coverage was in the hands of Granada – it was another advantage of the 'plural' system that facilities were usually at hand wherever occasions of national interest took place. Regular coverage of Party Conferences had begun in 1960, and of the TUC as far back as 1957.

'Play of the Week', shown on Tuesday, was an A-R production called *Thinking of My Darling* by Raymond Tranfield, with Jacqueline Ellis, Stanley Meadows, and John Ronane; other familiar names in the cast were Reginald Marsh and Dandy Nichols. On Wednesday a favourite programme was *Rawhide*, another Western in which Clint Eastwood first made his presence felt amongst the British public. Thursday brought *Double Your Money*, *Our Kind of Girl*, with Alma Cogan, Gary Miller, and Mike and Bernie Winters, *Family Solicitor*, part fictional and part legal advice, and a popular American series, *My Three Sons*, with Fred McMurray. But pride of place must go to Granada's 'Television Playhouse' production of Harold Pinter's *The Room*, with Catherine Lacey, Daniel Massey, and J. G. Devlin.

An interesting programme on Friday was *Probation Officer*, an ATV series which started in 1959. Its stories were fictional but its backgrounds were thoroughly researched; its leading actors – John Paul and Jessica Spencer – received many letters from the parents of problem children asking for advice. It may not have been the first, but it was among the most distinguished of the programmes dealing with social problems in a 'realistic' way, and incidentally explaining to the public how society worked. As in the case of *Emergency-Ward Ten*, such programmes offered entertainment, but they also gave information and comfort to many an anxious citizen.

Programmes of this kind were instances of ITV leadership. Having gained public confidence and, indeed, public enthusiasm, it was unobtrusively giving information and advice, and also without too much fuss asserting values. There were many other such instances around that time: the lectures of A. J. P. Taylor and Kenneth Clark; the series about life in Camberwell by Michael Ingrams; the series with Daniel Farson: *Farson's Choice* and *The Pursuit of Happiness*; Southern TV's *Sea War* about the Royal Navy; Granada's *On Trial*, dramatised reconstructions of famous trials like those of Admiral Byng, Roger Casement, and Oscar Wilde; and Malcolm Muggeridge's *Appointment With . . .*, in which he talked with Professor Bernal, Jacques Soustelle, Harold Nicolson and others.

Obviously, a single week cannot provide a complete picture of what ITV was now like. It cannot, for example, catch such initiatives as that of Bill Ward of ATV in securing the first television pictures out of Moscow. He took a mobile video tape recorder to the British Trade Fair that year and recorded some material using Russian cameras. He covered the Fair and a performance of the Bolshoi Ballet and then did a documentary on tape about Moscow itself.

ITV screened in 1961 many classical or near-classical plays, including works by Noel Coward, Jean Giraudoux, D. H. Lawrence, Charles Morgan, Sean O'Casey and Somerset Maugham. But drama is not only the classical repertory, and perhaps the most important event in ITV drama – indeed, in TV drama as a whole – was the appointment in 1958 of Sydney Newman to take charge of ABC's '*Armchair Theatre*'. In the Canadian Broadcasting Corporation, Newman had witnessed, and had also contributed to, the remarkable flowering of the dramatic arts on television in North America, in which new writers, new actors, and new directors had all played their parts. He also recognised that television was a mass medium or nothing; that because of cultural inequalities most of the audience had little experience of the theatre but much of the cinema; that TV drama should reflect and comment on the world familiar to the mass audience. The story goes that Michael Barry, then head of BBC drama, took Newman to see Osborne's *Look Back in Anger* at the Royal Court Theatre. That play, with its unusual worm's-eye view of society and its derisive radicalism, seemed to Newman the dazzling light on the road to Damascus; more accurately, it summed up what he had come to believe about the drama. He had developed the notion of 'agitational contemporaneity', and *Look Back in Anger* confirmed his ideas. An outsider in this country, he found both the country and its problems utterly fascinating. He wanted to make plain statements to the mass audience – statements falsified neither by sentiment nor by doctrinaire beliefs. Within a couple of years of his appointment to ABC he had built up a school of British writers and directors in sympathy with his objectives. His directors included many men of wide experience in film as well as television. Happily, one of them was Dennis Vance, his immediate predecessor as ABC's head of drama. Others were Wilfred Eades, Ted Kotcheff, John Moxey, Philip Saville, and Herbert Wise. 'Armchair Theatre' attracted and increased its audience perhaps not because of the impact of individual plays but rather by the cumulative effect of a generalised creative drive. His influence spilled over into other ITV drama series like 'Television Playhouse' and 'Play of the Week' and even into the BBC.

The whirligig of time brings in its revenges. In 1961 Michael Barry resigned from the BBC to join the new Telefis Eireann in Dublin. After a year's delay – time enough, said the cynics, for the BBC to swallow their pride – Newman was appointed head of BBC drama. Many people had travelled the road from BBC to ITV; he was the first, but not the last, significant figure to make the journey in the other direction. His transfer may be seen as a symbolic event, bringing this 'dipstick' review to a close. The BBC had looked somewhat disdainfully at ITV and its new audience, secure in the knowledge that they were, almost by divine appointment, skilled in the mystique of television. In 1960 Hugh Greene abruptly rejected the claims made by Fraser that ITV was also a 'public service' organisation, and made mock of the notion of 'people's television'.[8] Yet the transfer of Newman suggested that the time had come when the two networks were beginning to achieve parity; when ITV had as much to give to the BBC as the BBC to ITV. Competition henceforth would be between equals, and the BBC in their turn would learn the hard lesson that television is, must be, and can only survive as, a mass medium.

In 1961, Burton Paulu, the scholar from the New World, wrote that 'British television has been improved by competition . . . Competition has been an incentive to the BBC at the same time that Independent Television has greatly enriched the country's programme fare.'[9] This view was eventually and convincingly reaffirmed by the Report of the Annan Committee in 1977.

35

PERSPECTIVES ON PROGRAMMES

(i) 'SERIOUS' PROGRAMMES

Fraser's remarks in his 1960 Manchester address about 'people's television' came to be widely quoted in subsequent years. There were those who saw them as almost as great a condemnation of ITV as Gillett's indiscretions or Roy Thomson's naughty phrase. It was, they thought, a characteristically romantic euphemism for the commercially rewarding policy of 'playing down to the lowest common denominator'. It was the sort of attitude which the Workers' Educational Association was to condemn in its evidence to the Pilkington Committee as ignoring 'the kaleidescopic character of each individual'. They were concerned, they said, about the 'assumption that there are two kinds of people, a cultured élite, and the masses, both of whom must be catered for by different types of programme'.[1]

Sir Denis Forman's much more recent references to the 'age of innocence' contained some elements of Fraser's romanticism together with more than a dash of Thomson's genial self-mockery. His recollections are of 'the closing stages of the age of fun, froth and frolic. For in only a year or two Harry Pilkington, the Malvolio of 1962, was to come and snatch away our cakes and ale.'[2] People's television was what Fraser seriously believed ITV to be; but hindsight has tended to exaggerate the aspect of simple vulgarity implicit in the phrase and to discount those features which belonged to the tradition of public service that has never ceased to envelop *all* British broadcasting for nearly sixty years.

We have to turn to the sage Dr Paulu to set the record straight. He published his *British Broadcasting in Transition* in 1961. It was a 'report on the effects of competition on the broadcasting services of a country that introduced commercial television after some thirty years of service from a non-commercial monopoly'.[3] The book sets out with self-evident detachment what Paulu found to be the ingredients of British television, mainly in the years 1958 and 1959.

It might have been expected that views on this subject from an American academic with an established reputation in Britain would receive some notice from the Committee which was at this very time considering it. But in the event its report made no reference to the book, and Dr Paulu's views were not sought on any point. Had he been less modest, Dr Paulu might have laid claim to one characteristic which was not shared by others who were writing and talking about British television at that time. It was detachment. He had observed, not uncritically, the American broadcasting scene, and had previously appraised with genuine appreciation British broadcasting under the monopoly. The uniqueness of his position between 1958 and 1961, unheeded as it seems by the then current committee of enquiry, warrants some mention of his work in a history of ITV.

Paulu examined the television programmes of both services, their impact on radio, press and cinema and how they were received by the audience. The first of his conclusions was quoted at the end of the previous chapter. He went on to say that competition had been good for British broadcasting only because the Television Act of 1954 set up a system of 'controlled commercial television' with conditions favourable to the regulating agency. The separation of programme material from advertisements had eliminated many of the problems inherent in the sponsorship system. He thought the BBC itself had been and remained a superb broadcasting organisation, and that it should be maintained and strengthened on its existing basis. The ITA had on the whole performed well, and Independent Television's programme companies had produced many fine serious as well as light programmes. In fact, the differences between BBC and ITV programmes had been more of emphasis than of quality.

These conclusions were backed by an austere account of the output of both the BBC and ITV services, in which he found much to praise in programmes of news and opinion, of information, education and religion. Of ITV he had this to say:

Coverage of public affairs and controversial issues has shown a degree of freedom and ingenuity never present before – religious programmes, school broadcasts, and regional services have benefited from competition; presentation has improved and timing tightened; and programming generally, to use a British slang phrase, has been 'gingered up'. Furthermore, these improvements have not been accompanied by a general lowering of standards, as the opponents of competition feared in 1954.

Fun, froth and frolic? Cakes and ale? Paulu certainly came across all those elements, but in general he did not find them present in great excess. He seemed to be more struck by ITV's capacity to engage large audiences for news and information.[4]

In November 1961 the ITA provided for the Pilkington Committee, at the latter's request, percentage figures about 'serious' programmes in the London area between 1958 and 1960 (Table 35.1). The ITA entered a strong caveat against drawing conclusions based upon the selection of the period 7–10.30 p.m. This was a period chosen by the BBC and it had come to be widely taken as a definition of 'peak time'. In the ITA's view it was wrong to assume that there was always something specially meritorious and advantageous to viewers in presenting informative programmes during this period. The relevant facts which contradicted this assumption were the size of the audience at other times on ITV. 'The peaks in television viewing . . . rise fairly gently out of extensive uplands, the whole of which were fertile soil for serious programme fare.'[5]

TABLE 35.1 *Serious programmes on Independent Television*

Period	Percentage of hours devoted to serious programmes between 7 and 10.30 p.m.	Percentage of all viewing hours devoted to serious programmes	Percentage of all viewing hours devoted to school programmes
Jan.–June 1958	8.9	17.3	4.6
July–Dec. 1958	12.8	16.8	3.4
Jan.–June 1959	11.6	17.7	5.1
July–Dec. 1959	15.4	18.6	3.9
Jan.–June 1960	9.4	16.5	5.6
July–Dec. 1960	9.3	19.4	3.1

As for the programmes themselves, those of Forman's own company, Granada, may be taken as an example. Overall, Granada were providing some 25 per cent of the programmes which were networked. From autumn 1958 until 1960 there was the regular half-hour news documentary in mid-evening called *Searchlight*, produced by Tim Hewat, specialising in the investigation of social scandals. As 'one-off' documentaries they provided reports on homosexuality (a bold choice of subject for those days), venereal diseases, and the contraceptive pill; and *Saturday in September* about the CND's 'sit-down' in Trafalgar Square. There were also the series of confrontation programmes called *Under Fire*. And in February 1958 there came the breakthrough in political broadcasting with their local coverage of the Rochdale by-election, which alone made possible the extensive national and regional coverage by both ITV and BBC of the 1959 General Election, and which, in turn, included Granada's unique *Marathon* of 229 candidates in the North of England. None of this could be described as fun and frolic.

Other major companies could claim equivalent examples of serious endeavour. Moreover, as has been mentioned, STV, the first of the regionals to be appointed, provided *This wonderful World*, presented by John Grierson, father of the documentary film movement, which for a number of years the network was very glad to have. It was among the 'Top Ten' programmes for the week ended 17 January 1960. Of it Maurice Wiggin wrote in the *Sunday Times*: 'It is here, if anywhere in television, that you are likely to encounter one quiet night without a word of warning, the burning eyes of the proud beast Truth ambling solitary and disdainful through the jungle of the ready-made'.[6]

The ITA's Annual Report for 1961/2 gave figures designed to illustrate the development of 'serious' programmes.[7] It did not limit itself to the periods between 7 and 10.30 p.m. First it pointed out that the classification of television programmes into 'informative' and 'entertaining' or 'serious' and 'light' presented its difficulties. A play was 'entertainment', but it might have a purpose more serious and a value more significant than a poor political discussion. Indeed it might take the form of a political statement in dramatic shape, or seek to illuminate a particular social problem or human dilemma. For statistical purposes, it was best to make a simple separation of news and news magazines, programmes of information, discussion, debate, talks, practical instruction, religious and school programmes, and all programmes of fact as belonging to the serious side of television – and to exclude drama, however fine, as well as opera, ballet and serious music.

TABLE 35.2 *The growth of serious programmes–London, weekly averages*

	Duration (hrs. mins.)			Proportion (%)		
	1956	*1959*	*1962*	*1956*	*1959*	*1962*
News	3.15	3.15	4.13	7	5	7
Talks, discussions, documentaries	3.56	4.32	7.48	8	7	13
Religion	1.05	2.22	2.35	2	4	4
School programmes (inc. repeats)	–	4.35	5.00	–	7	8
Other informative children's programmes	1.08	1.40	2.35	2	3	4
Total	9.24	15.24	22.11	19	26	36

Thus defined, 'serious' programmes on Independent Television represented 36 per cent of the total running time during March 1962. This compared with 26 per cent in October 1959, and 19 per cent in October 1956. The duration of serious programmes was nearly two-and-a-half times as great as in 1956, a weekly average of over 22 hours compared with 9½ hours (Table 35.2).

On ITV's twenty-first anniversary, Forman wrote that the people behind the service when it began 'held a belief, unclouded by any doubt, in the virtues of entertainment'.[8] Indeed they did. But they believed with equal conviction that they could provide informative viewing in a manner which could engage and hold the interest of a significant part of the available audience. Both these beliefs were central to the concept of people's television.

(ii) DRAMA

The predominant aim of early ITV was to present plays which ordinary viewers could understand. Different people put the issue in different ways, but Ted Willis wrote in 1959: 'If I were to boil it all down, I suppose I could say it in two words: simplicity, clarity. Without those two things there will be no communication between you and your audience. And surely television is just that – communication.'[9] But in 1965 a 'consultation' on drama was dominated by much soul-searching about the future of the 'single play', as distinct from drama in series. This word 'consultation' had first been used for a sort of pow-wow amongst people concerned with religious programmes on ITV and it later became an established institution covering all the main areas of programming.[10] For this one on drama AGB Research Ltd had studied how the audience reacted to ten recent plays, selected at random; and the fact had been that only one of the ten had held its audience throughout, the remainder having dropped from 60 per cent to 20 per cent of their audience as they proceeded.[11]

What is of interest in the present context is that Fraser startled the assembled talent – producers, directors, writers, planners, executives and bosses – by stating that he had looked up the audience behaviour for fifteen consecutive plays in an earlier period, chosen at random. It happened to be the spring of 1960. Of these no less than thirteen had held their audience solidly from beginning to end; one had put on about 10 per cent and one had dropped about 20 per cent. 'Something is happening' he said, 'that wasn't happening before.' His own belief was that in 1960 the great majority of plays had been intelligible to the great majority of viewers, but by 1965 many of them were not. Most viewers could not endure obscurity. Whether this was the main reason or whether it was not, the years between 1955 and 1962 were the golden age of the single play. Nice distinctions drawn by professionals between single or 'one-off' plays, series and anthologies or, for that matter, between live or recorded plays and films, were, and still are, of limited significance for many viewers. It was the arrival in 1958 of electronic video recordings and the development soon thereafter of electronic techniques for editing them, which began to raise problems as well as present opportunities for the professionals. Once it was possible to stockpile drama without any loss of technical quality, the attractions of the series form both from the point of view of production logistics and also, it was soon discovered, of sustaining the interest of viewers over weeks at a stretch, began to become more and more apparent. But in the years before 1962 the great debate about the need to preserve the single play for the sake of ensuring the continued creative vitality of television drama had scarcely begun. With a limited supply of cinema films available for television (in a normal week there were not more than two), and with most series drama being produced in film studios, ITV studios were fully occupied with 'live' production, a high proportion of which was plays and serials. A normal week would include one 90 minute, five 60 minute and two or three 30 minute dramas of one sort or another.

Given that light entertainment at weekends was dominated by ATV's *Sunday Night at the London Palladium*, ABC Television decided that Sunday plays should be their particular flagship offering. By a felicitous adaptation of Alfred de Musset's phrase 'Théâtre dans un fauteil' their collective title came to be 'Armchair Theatre'. A book published in 1959 opened with a telling article by Howard Thomas entitled 'The Audience is the Thing'.[12] Whilst agreeing that ITV took the audience with fresh and friendly light entertainment he thought the real battle between the two channels was in drama, in which ITV overtook and outpaced the BBC.

By March 1958, when Dennis Vance relinquished his post as drama supervisor for ABC, 'Armchair Theatre' plays had in the preceding three months reached the Top Ten in audience ratings every single week. Neither the notorious weakness of the BBC's Sunday schedule at that time nor the fact that the Palladium Show immediately preceded these plays can greatly diminish the impressiveness of this record.

Just as BBC play policy reflected, Thomas thought, the solid avuncular attitude of the Corporation itself, so the plays presented by the Big Four became recognisable images of those companies. ATV's close associations with the commercial theatre led them to revive stage plays and to introduce to television for the first time such stars as Gielgud, Olivier and Redgrave Granada, with their accent on social purpose, moved in the direction of plays with a message writ large – by such writers as Miller, Wilder and Osborne. A-R were, as always, the useful all-rounder striving, and with considerable success, to demonstrate their omnicompetence. ABC, with only two days of the week in which to make an impression, sought to be 'different', often commissioning new plays from new writers and putting to work on them sometimes old-hand directors, like George More O'Ferrall, and sometimes young enthusiasts, like Philip Saville.

Within the total universe of what, for want of a better term, might be called ITV's major drama, every kind of play and every kind of talent found a place. They came from five drama 'houses'; the Big Four and Anglia. Pages could be filled by a recital of titles, writers, directors, designers, actors and actresses and producers. And beside the five drama 'houses', there was another much larger 'house' – the drama department of BBC Television.

Peter Black recalls that the policy of Michael Barry, the BBC's Head of Television Drama from 1952 to 1961, had been to advance on all fronts: classic theatre, adaptations of classic novels, original series and serials, and single plays by new authors.[13] ITV inherited the same policy but on a more fragmented scale, and soon began to diverge from the huge centralised drama department of the BBC. ABC's 'Armchair Theatre' as it evolved, first under Dennis Vance who had been trained in the BBC and then (from 1959) under Sydney Newman who had not, led the way. Vance resigned in order to get back to the studio floor and, in particular, into filming drama series for television, and, as we have seen in Chapter 34, it was Newman who took his place. He was an ideal choice to build upon the foundation laid by Vance. Between the autumn of 1959 and the summer of 1960 Armchair Theatre plays were in the top ten programmes for thirty-two weeks out of thirty-seven.

As the golden years of ITV plays moved by during the late fifties and early sixties, there were few living playwrights who did not relish opportunities of having their works performed in Britain before audiences of about 12 million people at a time.

Simplicity and clarity were what Ted Willis had pleaded for, and, by and large, these were what characterised ITV plays during this period. Even when the language used was Greek! For so it was when McMillan persuaded A-R to present a performance of *Electra* by the Piraikon Greek Tragedy Theatre Company on 7 November 1962 under Joan Kemp-Welch's direction. The Press reception was ecstatic. 'Electra leaps the language barrier' ran one headline; 'Was it Greek to you? I loved it' ran another. 'TV's finest hour' and 'Electra rocks the box' – so they went on in one of the greatest choruses of superlatives ITV had ever received. Over the years covered by this volume ITV drama, for whatever reason, flourished bountifully. Paulu said, 'There is no doubt that British viewers are better off for the addition of ITV's drama to that of the BBC.'[14] But while the Pilkington Committee was to report approvingly in 1962 on the BBC's drama policy, it provided no equivalent appraisal for ITV.

(iii) LIGHT ENTERTAINMENT

A salient is a projection of the forward line into enemy-held territory, and it is widely agreed that in the early years of 1955–7 ITV made the projection in the light entertainment sector. But in the event, it was with drama, supported by programmes of information, that ITV advanced all along the line. The light entertainment offensive, with which ITV ensured its survival, had largely spent itself by the early sixties.

At an ITA consultation in 1967[15] a retrospective – and reflective – address was given by Francis Essex, at that time Programme Controller of Scottish Television. He recalled how in the early days of light entertainment on television the BBC had followed a simple and effective policy; producers had unlimited freedom and complete responsibility for what appeared on the screen, and artistes, knowing little about the medium, were content to accept production without question. When ITV came on the scene, the audience smelt for the first time the atmosphere of variety and relished the new pace given to 'situation' comedy by the imported American programmes. New artistes were promoted and new content forms were developed. Television design acquired a new look.

But ITV's initial success contained the seeds of its later decline. There was a tendency to hand to producers a 'package show'. They lost their freedom of expression, and star artistes and their managers began to dictate what they would do in the shows built around them. The package shows tended to confine themselves to a small group of performers whose faces appeared again and again.

The BBC, responding to the challenge, demonstrated their capacity to nurse, build and improve over long periods of time and were eventually able to recapture the Saturday night with *The Black and White Minstrel Show* which built up a following from small beginnings. Another of their shows *Comedy Playhouse* persevered until out of it came such successes as *Steptoe and*

Son and *Till Death Do Us Part*. By contrast ITV companies found themselves less free to nurse a new series through a period of poor ratings.

There was much truth in this assessment. In the very early days quick success in securing the larger share of the audience was vital to the survival of the companies, but when this phase was over they remained intoxicated by the ease with which they had scored it and neglected in this important sector the longer term planning in depth which was necessary for maintaining its momentum.

The history of the quiz programme, or 'give-away shows' as the press tended to call them, strikingly illustrates how ITV found easy success and lingered too long with it for its own eventual well-being. Black has told the story in a sparkling passage in his chapter on 'How they Took the Audience' and Paulu also did so in a cool matter-of-fact account of what for him were 'audience participation programmes'.[16] For Black they were 'a television version of the old fairground sideshow entertainment'.[17]

There was a revealing exchange of letters in the dark days of February 1956 between Fraser and Richard Meyer of ATV. Fraser had said that 'the Authority feels . . . that there is on the whole rather more giving away of money and prizes in programmes than is altogether good for the reputation of the programme companies, the Authority, and Independent Television generally', to which Meyer replied with characteristic honesty:

> We are very conscious of the necessity of putting on programmes which will not give unreasonable people cause to complain. On the other hand, as you well know, the lot of the pioneer programme contractor is not a very happy one financially and we do feel that we must use every possible endeavour to obtain maximum audiences in the initial stages of the development of the medium so that we can be certain of getting worthwhile sales of advertising space.[18]

Doubtless for the reason which Meyer had given, the Authority collectively did not concern itself further with give-away quiz programmes until January 1957, when there were ten such programmes being shown each week, of which two were embedded in other programmes:

Give-away quiz programmes
(London, Midlands and the North)

Programme	Company	Stations	Day and time
Beat the Clock (Tommy Trinder)	ATV	LMN	Sunday 8.00
Make Up Your Mind (David Jacobs)	Granada	LMN	Monday 7.30
Two for the Money (Bernard Braden)	A-R	LMN	Monday 9.30

Do You Trust Your Wife? (Bob Monkhouse)	ATV	LMN	Tuesday 7.30
Double Your Money (Hughie Green)	A-R	LMN	Wednesday 7.30
Spot The Tune	Granada	LMN	Thursday 7.30
Take Your Pick (Michael Miles)	A-R	LMN	Friday 7.30
Lucky Spot Quiz	A-R	LMN	Friday 10.15
$64,000 Question (Jerry Desmond)	ATV	LMN	Saturday 8.30
State Your Case (McDonald Hobley)	ABC	MN	Saturday 9.45

Most of the time the general knowledge element in the programmes was of an elementary character, but there were exceptions.

It was put to the companies that this number of quizzes was 'so great as to lead to a lack of balance' and suggested that at least they might be limited to one a day from Mondays to Saturdays, with *Beat the Clock* remaining on Sundays within the Palladium Show. They were not unwilling to concede this modest request and there thus came into being a loose 'one-a-day' maximum which more than sufficed to allow the genre to flourish and to enjoy what Black calls a 'brief and feverish popularity'.

The conduct of the quizzes and the size of the prizes were found to call for stringent rules which had to be applied with increasing severity as the years went by. The sensitivity of public opinion about such programmes was all too clear from the postbags of the companies and the ITA, but in 1959 allegations in the *Daily Express* that some participants in Granada's *Twenty One* had advance knowledge of the questions provoked a positive furore. With the ITA's agreement, Granada appointed Sir Lionel Heald QC to investigate and report.[19] He acquitted the producer of any serious impropriety but found that he had used 'highly imprudent' methods in order to make the programme more exciting. In his report he said:

> It would perhaps be going too far to compare a television producer with Caesar's wife, but in my opinion it is only natural, if programmes of this kind are to be presented, that the public should expect some positive guarantee from the Network itself that the competition is genuine and the chances even for all.

It was thus established that producing and presenting even the most trivial television programmes was quite a serious business.

The ITA was at pains not only to be serious about the incident but to be seen to be serious about its own role as a custodian of standards over the whole range of its output. On 14 April 1959 it announced that it had completed a review of the arrangements governing programmes with prizes and had agreed with the companies upon the action to be taken. The statement went on to say that in relation to each programme, and according to its nature, a booklet or leaflet would be made available which clearly described the nature of the game or contest and the rules under which, when seen on the screen, it was being played; the way in which members of the public could seek to participate and the procedure of selection of those who would appear; and the exact scope and nature of the other preparations, including the guidance which would be given to all chosen contestants as to how the game or contest was to be conducted. It was also arranged that each company would nominate a supervisory executive whose sole responsibility in relation to each programme was to exercise a close check on the observance of the rules and the instructions.

This statement was something of a landmark for the ITA. 'Frank and continuing consultation with its contractors in private' was not always to be enough.

(iv) INFORMATIVE TELEVISION

In those days, as we have seen in section (i), the talk was, defensively, of 'serious programmes'. Classification and terminology have been subject to confusing variations over the years, but the IBA handbook *Television and Radio 1981* now speaks of 'informative', 'narrative', 'entertainment' and 'sport' as the main categories of programmes.

By March 1957, as we saw in Chapter 31 (i) and again in Chapter 34(ii), the retreat from culture had been halted. The years that followed were ones of sustained advance and they were no less innovatory in informative television than they were in drama. The common element in most developments was the discovery of new ways of attracting and holding very substantial audiences for 'non-fiction' or general knowledge.

Early in 1958 Independent Television acquired its three main master craftsmen in the art of lecturing: Professor Alan Taylor on modern history, Dr Jacob Bronowski on scientific discovery and Sir Kenneth Clark on art. How Clark transferred from the chairmanship of the ITA into being a front-of-camera performer, in which role he was destined to become perhaps the most distinguished television presenter of the visual arts in the world, was described in Chapter 29(i).

The success of John Irwin's production of the Taylor lectures for ATV, delivered without so much as a single visual aid or even a note, lay, thought Norman Swallow, not only in Taylor's personal genius ('if he chose to talk about a blade of grass he could keep his audience spellbound') but in the simple fact that history is interesting.[20] So too are archaeology as it was expounded by Mortimer Wheeler on the BBC, and the wonders of science as first presented by Dr Bronowski in A-R's *New Horizon*. As for Clark, Swallow could say in 1966 that his early series for ATV (much of it produced by Michael Redington) 'is still probably the most effective concentrated attempt by television to treat art seriously and at the same time hold as large an audience as possible'.[21] The task Clark set himself in 1954, when accepting the chairmanship of ITA, of saving ITV from what he believed were the worst features of commercialism (Chapter 9) was completed in a manner he had not foreseen. By the autumn of 1960 his lectures were being watched in some 1,363,000 homes providing an audience of at least 2½ millions. His recruitment to television was not the least of the acts of showmanship performed by Parnell and Grade.

In the field of political television there occurred in February 1958 an event of immense significance, stemming directly from ITV's desire to give its audience what it believed they wanted, undeterred by obstacles that had previously inhibited the medium of broadcasting. This was the coverage by Granada of the Rochdale by-election, which became, as noted in Section (i), the prelude to the first televised General Election in 1959. It was an epic of broadcasting initiative played out by Granada with indispensible support from the ITA and it was described in the company's own publication *Granada Goes to Rochdale* and, briefly, in the ITA's Annual Report for 1957/8. That report records that it was 'the first occasion in the whole history of broadcasting in Britain on which the issues of an election were expounded to audiences other than in party political broadcasts'. Two simple programmes, which had to be fought for every inch of the way, changed for all time the character of the British electoral process. They were first, a programme in which candidates discussed election issues among themselves and secondly, a programme in which the same candidates were interviewed by three journalists. Of equal significance for the future was the fact that the course of this by-election campaign was reported in the bulletins of ITN. Hitherto broadcast news had studiedly ignored all election campaigns of any sort. Since then, the public has become wholly familiar with the role of television and radio in parliamentary elections: the fact that for more than thirty years broadcasting played no role, saving as an agency for disseminating messages from the main political parties, is hard to realise even for those who have lived through that time.

The ITA's Annual Report for 1958/9 had pointed out that between 6 and 7 p.m. and between 10 and 11 p.m., on average four out of ten homes were viewing as compared with an average of five out of ten between 7 and

10 p.m. It was in these early periods and late periods that most of ITV's informative programming for adults was to be seen; although a continuing series of 'feature documentaries' began to be scheduled weekly at 9.35 p.m. in the autumn of 1959.

One of the things which ITV discovered early, when budgets were tight, was that if you could bring people together in a studio and create an event or happening in which these people participated, then you could engage and hold your audience by the sheer drama of what was going on. The acquisition of knowledge, even of understanding, was a by-product of witnessing real-life encounters between people. There was conflict and it was 'as good as a play'. The alternative was to take the cameras outside to the people and this came increasingly to be done, albeit at about fifteen times the cost of what could be contrived in the studio. ATV's *Free Speech* was as much a performance as it was a discussion, and Granada's *Under Fire* in which two prominent public people speaking from London were inter-rogated on controversial subjects by a rumbustious studio audience in Manchester was a deliberately contrived studio event. Both were shown outside the conventional peak time of 7 to 10 p.m. but both had a large and appreciative following. The ultimate refinement in this device was found in *University Challenge* which started with Bamber Gascoigne in 1962 and played at 10.10 p.m. to an audience of some 6,000,000: it became an event (or rather an endless sequence of events) in its own right and is running on as strongly as ever in 1981. Regional companies developed comparable techniques, as, for example, when TWW devised *Challenge* in somewhat the same style as *Under Fire*, except that the audience consisted of university students.

Although ITV was, and had to be, a mass medium, there were factual programmes for which only minority audiences were expected. Even a minority might mean up to 5 million viewers, far larger than the readership of most mass-circulation newspapers. An example was *Tempo*, ABC's Sunday afternoon magazine about the arts; it became the counterpart in its own field of A-R's *This Week* in the field of national and international politics and public affairs. The one played to an audience which could be counted in seven figures and the other to an audience which could be counted in eight. Two programmes of an entirely different kind which were, at any rate at first, also seen as minority programmes both started in 1960: these were Anglia's *Survival* and Southern's *Out of Town* and both were going strong twenty years later. *What the Papers Say* from Granada and *All Our Yesterdays* from the same house had similar roles to play. These latter were the programmes on which Jeremy Isaacs, now chief executive of IBA's Channel Four, started his career.

Isaacs' mentor was Tim Hewat, to whom reference was made in Section (i). It was reported in the *Observer* on 5 October 1980 in a profile on Isaacs:

> His master there was Tim Hewat, a former *Daily Express* man, and one of the first of the Fleet Street 'whizz kids' to make a reputation in the staid and cautious new medium. 'I learned more from him than from anyone else I've worked with in television' says Isaacs. 'He taught me that it is primarily a mass-audience medium and that one must be understood. He wanted TV programmes to say something.'

He could be regarded as the Sydney Newman of ITV Current Affairs. The two men had something in common. They shared a robust disregard for the established order, which endowed them with a certain zest for challenging and putting to the test the ITA's interpretation of the obligations imposed in Section 3(1) of the Act – the famous (some would say notorious) censorship clause.

Insistently during these years Fraser and his colleagues – fully supported by the Authority itself – stressed the unacceptability of 'editorialising' in ITV news and current affairs. Like Geoffrey Cox, Fraser was the product of the Fleet Street of the 1930s when it was still possible to read reports, whether from home or abroad, by a special (unnamed) correspondent which dealt with matters of the deepest controversy without betraying in the slightest degree the opinions of the writer. This was the ideal they sought to establish in ITV's output in so far as it related to political and industrial controversy or 'current public policy' – an ideal which was largely realised by ITN's *Dateline* and *Roving Report*. The objective was often thought of in terms of 'balance' between two or several viewpoints: this was certainly one way of achieving 'due impartiality' and it drew some justification from Section 3(1)(g) of the Act which precluded matter 'designed to serve the interests of a political party unless it was contained in party political broadcasts or included in programmes of properly balanced discussions or debates'. But it was by no means the only way by which impartiality could be attained. A simpler but less safe way was to let facts speak for themselves; it was a style which appealed to Hewat, but only so long as the way in which the facts were selected and put together made the points he wanted.

Searchlight came to an end in 1960 and, after the lapse of two years, was succeeded in 1962 by *World in Action*, a more lavishly produced and wider ranging series. Hewat was its first executive producer and it will engage our attention in Volume II. It must suffice for the present to observe that what distinguished *World in Action* from A-R's *This Week* was that while the latter was relying on the use of 'anchormen' (the best known of whom was Brian Connell), the Granada programme was narrated by off-screen voices and there were never any   interviewers. Statements, skilfully intercut, were made straight to camera, and the questioning intermediary was eliminated. It gave statements the weight and authority of the medium rather than that of an individual person, and, as Norman Swallow put it, 'It suggested, sometimes openly, sometimes obliquely, what the viewer should think about the subject under review. It did not leave him to make up his own mind. It made it up for him.'[22] This was in total contrast to the straight reporting of ITN's *Roving Report* which, from 1957, held the field in the treatment of news outside the context of the bulletins themselves.

Neither in *Searchlight* nor in its more famous successor did Hewat make any bones about the fact that he was editorialising. He did not try to suppress evidence which disagreed with his own conclusions provided the latter emerged with unmistakeable clarity. He had no time for properly balanced discussions or debates and he took the view that it was a sufficient defence against the charge of partiality to say that all the partial statements made were perfectly accurate quotations. The consequential and inevitable clash between Granada and the ITA did not come to a head until 1963 but one of several preliminary skirmishes occurred over a series of four half-hour Granada documentaries entitled *Cuba Si!*, which became in the ITA's view altogether too favourably disposed towards the new Castro regime. 'We can't escape the conclusion' I wrote to Victor Peers on 25 October 1961, 'that the four programmes taken together lacked impartiality and were in places slanted unfairly against the United States.' Eventually the argument led to a meeting between Bernstein and the Authority, over what he described as 'a most pleasant and happy lunch'. But, of course, Hewat's horses had already bolted, and all that remained was for the Authority to spell out in what respects it believed they had breached Section 3(1) of the Act and for the Granada management, with the utmost deference and respect, to beg to differ.[23]

Tongue in cheek, Bernstein was apt to say to Fraser with an air of martyred innocence 'But all we want to do, Bob, is what the newspapers do'. Whether or not they saw their objective clearly, Granada undoubtedly contrived to extend the frontiers of broadcasting about public affairs, and there is a strong connecting line between the Hewat programmes of 1957–62 and the 'investigative' reporting of later years. Other companies, not least the generally circumspect A-R, sometimes stood aghast at what Granada managed to get away with. But A-R's *This Week*, together with ITN's programme extras had acquired over a longer period a reputation which Granada programmes did not as yet match and which gained for ITV much-needed credit at Westminster and also in a wider forum. In ITV's house there were many mansions, and there was room for one called Granada – but only one.

This Week had been born on 6 January 1956 at 9.30 p.m. in the Hungaria Restaurant, Lower Regent Steet, and its midwife was Caryl Doncaster. No trumpets sounded to herald its arrival in the world. It was presented by that seasoned warrior, Leslie Mitchell. It included nearly a dozen items and even more people, ranging from Dr Edith Summerskill to Somerset Plantagenet Fry, the mastermind of the television quizzes. Cheekily it was billed as a window on the world behind the headlines, although it differed from *Panorama* in every other respect. Some 300 items were included in the first fifty programmes under the editorship of Peter Hunt, who, amongst many other contributions to the ultimate distinction of the programme, chose the Karelia march for its title music. Its filmed items were elaborately and expensively shot in 35 mm up to 1963. With Peter Morley to help with its administration, and resolutely supported by McMillan who succeeded Gillett as Controller of Programmes, Caryl Doncaster saw *This Week* through the retreat from culture and stayed with it until 1958.

This lively, sometimes frivolous news magazine did not, however, shy away from serious subjects, and the number of subsequently distinguished producers and reporters who worked on it at one time or another is quite extraordinary. Slowly, over a period of about three years, the programme (like A-R themselves) sobered up and certainly by 1961 it had a steady reputation for serious, factual, lucid reporting. Somewhere along the way, it overtook *Panorama* in many respects, not least its ability to collect and hold a large audience drawn from every section of society. It was tabloid in character without being vulgar or sensational and in its first five years of life not far short of 1000 items had been accommodated, a good quarter of which were on subjects of serious consequence. Public figures from Prime Minister Macmillan downwards readily accepted opportunities to appear in it. One of the first interviews to be recorded on videotape in 1958 was with none other than Harley Drayton who, noting the presence of a full union crew, afterwards remarked to Peter Hunt 'No wonder we almost went broke!'[24] From late 1960 Brian Connell was linkman, interviewer and reporter all in one and conveyed something of the authority which Dimbleby had brought to *Panorama*.

Part of *This Week*'s growing reputation in its first five years derived from its capacity to be light-hearted and even light weight. But in the matters of serious consequence it was usually both impartial and authoritative, and it set a standard which *Searchlight* could not emulate.

Lest it be thought that Granada were merely an awkward cuss, it should be recalled that, when in 1958/9 ITV began to take a serious (and also informative) grip on children's television, Granada came up with *Zoo Time*, *Animal Parade* and *The Living Sea* – all in the field of natural history. A-R provided the magazine *Let's Get Together* and ATV *Seeing Sport*, featuring demonstrations by experts on how to play good football or whatever. *Southern Heritage* came from Southern, dealing with historical, archeological and natural treasures.

Professor Himmelweit's Nuffield Foundation Report on *Television and the Child* had been published in December 1958 and the joint BBC–ITA committee under Miss May O'Conor was set up in 1959.[25] When that committee reported in 1960 it called for an increase in the number of live programmes for children and advocated the introduction of 'more programmes designed to stimulate children into doing things for themselves'. Accordingly in 1960/1 ITV had on Mondays *Seeing Sport*, on Tuesdays *Lucky Dip* (music, sport, art and competitions of skill), on Wednesdays *Zoo Time*, on Thursdays *It's Wizard* involving elementary practical science and general knowledge competitions; and on Fridays various series of which *Crows Nest*, a magazine about ships and the sea was a good example. The Authority believed that a fair balance was being struck in children's television 'between stories and real life items'.

Whatever field of factual television in the late fifties and early sixties is examined it yields a harvest of remembrances of things past. There has been great progress in technique since those days, as brilliantly inventive engineers provided tool after tool to satisfy the hankerings of the creative people. In that respect the changes over the past two decades have been immense. In other respects the story is so often one of cycles repeating themselves in such a way as to convey an illusory sense of innovation. One enterprise started in 1960 and continued for seven or eight years was, however, unique in the annals of ITV. This was 'Intertel', aimed at promoting international understanding through television, formed on the initiative of John McMillan, the second General Manager of A-R and its successor, Rediffusion Television. It was an international consortium of broadcasting organisations which, in addition to McMillan's own company, comprised the National Educational and Radio Centre and the Westinghouse Broadcasting Company of America, the Australian Broadcasting Commission and the Canadian Broadcasting Corporation. They collectively planned a sequence of documentaries to be made by each organisation individually and agreed to show each other's product. Not all were by any means distinguished programmes, although A-R/Rediffusion's own record was a worthy one.

An instance of history repeating itself is the so-called 'personal view' programme which came into fashion in the mid-seventies in ITV. Most of the protagonists appeared to think that they were on to something new, but that was not altogether true. The documentary which expressed a highly subjective view flourished in the early sixties in both television services and especially linked with ITV were producer/directors like Peter Morley, Denis Mitchell and Norman Swallow. But it did not force-feed personal obsessions in the manner of latter day programmes featuring John Pilger. It was Swallow's belief that the objective report and the subjective documentary were essentially complementary. 'A television service which accepted the value of only one of them would be unable to present an adequate picture of the age we live in.' He recognised that there was bias and quoted Peter Morley in his support:

> How can you get at the pure uncontaminated truth when, right at the beginning there is a subjective selection, not only of the scene being filmed, but also in the composition of the shot, let alone the final selection and juxtaposition of the material in the cutting room? The personal attitude of the team concerned is bound to influence the final result.[26]

Where then did this leave 'due impartiality'? It was and it remains an ideal to be striven for, but not to be crucified for. The meaning of the term has never been tested in the courts and seems unlikely to be. What, it might be asked, is 'undue impartiality'? Badly administered, the requisite could easily become the excessive. Daniel Bell, the great American sociologist, once said 'in the wisdom of the Ancients Utopia was a fruitful impossibility, a conception of the desirable which men should always strive to attain but which in the nature of things could not be achieved'.

(v) THE 'SPECIAL CLASSES'

The seemingly bureaucratic insistence of Conservative Governments between 1955 and 1963 on rigidly limiting the 'permitted hours' of television was remarked upon in Chapter 15. Although this was seen by ITV as unreasonable and calculated – if not designed – to serve the purposes of the BBC, the fact was that the new service was regarded both by government and Parliament as on probation until its virtual permanence was confirmed by the fresh legislation of 1963. In the event, the restriction during these years redounded to the advantage of ITV because it provided the opportunity for bringing into existence certain classes of programme which, because there were no advertisements before, during or after them, were allowed off the ration; that is to say, not counted in the tally of permitted hours, which did, of course, contain advertising matter. These were the programmes of formal education and the religious programmes. The ITA called them the 'Special Classes'. (A similar status was conferred on programmes in Welsh.)

It could be argued – and often was – that ITV's motives in providing educational and religious programmes were not disinterested. The permitted amount of advertising was after all a percentage of the total time on the air and this time included the hours occupied by these programmes, which were consequently contributing to ITV companies' earnings. Doubters were frequently reminded that the ITA imposed a maximum of seven minutes' advertising in any one clock hour and that this restriction was continuously and necessarily in operation during peak viewing hours, the times most in demand by advertisers, who were, as all the evidence showed, less interested in off-peak times, when advertising fell well below six minutes per hour. Overall the hourly *average* per day never actually reached that level. However, few of those educationalists and churchmen who had moral scruples about advertising really believed that ITV companies were presenting these programmes at a financial loss rather than a gain. The clergy in general soon ceased to mind whether it was true or not; but many teachers were squeamish, not to say sanctimonious about it, and this had something to do with the fact that BBC programmes were used in many more schools than were those from ITV.

We saw in Chapter 31(iii) how Independent Television for schools got under way and established itself over the years from 1957, but it was to be only after the Pilkington White Papers and the passage of the 1963 Act that the educational service achieved its full development. This was especially true of Adult Education. Initially, the Authority's own interest in televised Adult Education was primarily in the context of a proposed separate ETV channel; but the provision of educational programmes for adults was being advocated by education enthusiasts (e.g. within A-R) from at least as early as 1957. In practical terms the question of incorporating them in the existing general service arose in late 1959, as part and parcel of the companies' efforts to get an increase in the hours of broadcasting. Because the Minister had refused to consider such a possibility in advance of the deliberations of the expected new committee on broadcasting, it was suggested that he might none the less be prepared to contemplate specifically adding adult education to the 'special classes'. Although in early 1960 Howard Thomas of ABC was putting forward plans for a Sunday morning hour of what he called a 'University of the Screen', efforts to persuade the PMG to grant off-the-ration time for programmes 'forming part of a series of instructional programmes on a defined course prepared in association with an educational organisation' met with no success.

The reluctance of Post Office administrators to act in advance of Pilkington was understandable, but, in addition, discreet pressure was certainly being exerted from Broadcasting House to prevent ITV stealing a march on the BBC as they had already done in 1957 with A-R's introduction of broadcasts for schools. It could quite legitimately be argued that any extra time for ITV was potentially revenue-earning whereas it would mean more expenditure for the Corporation. On the other hand, the companies could, equally legitimately, point to Ulster Television's *Midnight Oil* and A-R's even earlier repeats of a French series for schools in evening hours as an earnest of a disinterested concern to provide formal educational material for the general audience. Why, it was asked, should ITV be held back just because the BBC could not, or did not want to, match their effort?

Frustrations were increased by a speech made by the Minister of Education, David Eccles, at a conference of the National Institute of Adult Education in Swansea on 16 September 1960 saying

Radio and TV, those great instruments of universal communication which descend from the skies to minister to the curiosity and pleasure of millions, could help us more in adult education . . . Would it not be a very good thing if television programmes of adult education were put on Saturday mornings? This is a period when millions of people have time to look in say from 9 to 10. I hope we shall see Saturday mornings used for this purpose.

But, when the Post Office's attention was drawn to this statement, their comment was simply 'You may take it that the Minister was expressing his own views with relevance to current considerations . . . '[27]

Not until more than two years later, after the two White Papers of 1962, and the joint elaboration by the BBC and the ITA of an agreed formula defining televised adult education, were ABC's educational ambitions realised. In January 1963, regular transmissions of what came to be known as 'Sunday Session' (including a French language series from ATV) at last began. The further development of adult education on ITV will be examined in Volume II. In the meantime, schools television continued to thrive and to expand in the fields of both secondary and primary education.

A noteworthy fulfilment of the concept of people's television in the years between 1955 and 1962 came in the religious programmes of ITV. Their origin was described in Chapter 16(ii) and their beginnings in Chapter 31(iv) where reference was made in particular to *About Religion* and *The Sunday Break*. Describing the controversy aroused by the latter, the phlegmatic Dr Paulu noted that its audience included many teenagers who did not go to church and might not tune in to ordinary religious programmes. He went on:

> Whatever may be the merits of *The Sunday Break*, ITV must be credited generally with some outstanding religious programming. When Parliament debated the Television Act, Anglican Church leaders strongly opposed commercial television, but by now many of them probably have changed their minds. In fact, ITV has shown more initiative in religious programming than has the BBC, and in addition has led in organising workshops on religious television.[28]

He also noted, however, that, like the BBC, ITV offered little time to non-Christian groups and limited act-of-worship broadcasts to the main-stream churches.

   With the exception of Howard Thomas, well supported in this instance by his Deputy Chairman, Dr Fletcher, the top managements of the companies played little positive part in this 'initiative'. The zealous Methodism of Lord Rank was barely discernible in Southern Television and James Coltart as Deputy Chairman of STV prudently played down his personal sympathies with Moral Rearmament. The managements did, however, appoint dedicated people to their staff; ATV had men like Michael Redington, Bill Allenby, and Gordon Reece, A-R had Guthrie Moir, and Granada had their invaluable Janet Wadsworth. With ABC, of course, there were the immensely resourceful Penry Jones, Tom Singleton and David Southwood. Other companies had Maxwell Deas (Tyne Tees), James Buchan (Grampian), Tony Finigan (Ulster) and the two inseparables Tony Hoyland and Peter Lilley (TWW). This gallery of staff was an impressive one in the context of religious television; but the range and calibre of the advisers from the churches – far too numerous to mention – were equally striking. And yet not one of them would be likely to dispute that in this special area the strongest initiative came from the ITA itself. Clark had charted a course which others followed, led by that brilliant first trio of advisers already mentioned in Chapter 16(ii) who stayed on the Panel for ten years. For once, Fraser himself took a back seat, but the Movement – for such it was – enjoyed his humanitarian support, in all senses of that word.

One of the principal instruments of ITA leadership was – and still is – the 'consultation'. As briefly mentioned in section (ii), the first ever was held in the summer of 1961 at Mansfield College, Oxford. The Secretary of the ITA, E. G. Wedell, who had previously been secretary of the Board for Social Responsibility of the Church of England, produced a published account of the event entitled *Religious Programmes on Independent Television* (ITA 1962). Within this slender volume can be found the evidence to justify describing the progress of religious television in these years as a Movement.

In precisely what direction we were moving or ought to move, and to what useful purpose, were subjects of endless, even agonising debate. For the consultation at Oxford in 1961 part of the preparation had been a specially commissioned survey of the interest in religious programmes among ITV viewers, and it fell to the Reverend Eric Heaton, as he then was, to open proceedings with a keynote address related to the survey and entitled 'The Context in which Religious Television Operates'. It emerged that what the public wanted was 'religion', although the word meant different things to different people. Nine out of ten viewers thought it 'desirable' to have religious programmes, while only 4 per cent specifically disapproved. The vast majority claimed to be 'interested' in religion and only 22 per cent would themselves have no truck with it at all. It was, however, clear that this interest was not of a kind which involved the majority in the life of the Church; only about 30 per cent of the adult population went to church once a month or more. This was how Heaton put it:

Of every 10 people watching our programmes, 7 have little or nothing to do with the Church (but claim this interest in religion), 6 are women, 6 are pretty middle-aged and 8 belong to the working class . . . To risk a rough generalisation, we are no more conspicuously successful than the Church at gaining the hearing of either young people or men. We are, however, distinctive in gaining an audience of semi- and unskilled manual workers in numbers proportionate to their incidence in the population (i.e. about 37 per cent) whereas the Church attracts less than this (about 27 per cent). *But the outstanding feature of our position is that we are probably the only contact with Christianity for a vast number of non-churchgoers of all ages.*[29] [Author's italics]

That was the starting point, that the daunting fact. The problems were easier to discern than the solutions; and those present left the gathering with many reservations in their minds about the efficacy of religious television as a surrogate for the life of the Church. The development of religious television up to then had implied the view that the Word of God could – and should – be proclaimed on television. Dr John Marsh struck a relatively optimistic note:

The eloquent point of some great programmes is that they were communicated not in the words spoken, but in the whole effect of the programme and they may come very near to conveying the Holy Spirit, not a dogma about it. Communication is not merely a matter of words: television shows that words are not so fundamental. Television shows that we can say things through words, but also that words are only part of the field of communication.[30]

Doubtless Dr Marsh had specially in mind the brilliant production by A-R on Good Friday 1961 of *Laudes Evangelii*, the story of the beginning and the end of Our Lord's life set to choreography by Leonide Massine and with the ballet company of La Scala, Milan. (Joan Kemp-Welch directed.) But Monsignor Tomlinson stressed the importance of distinguishing between the proclamation of the truths of the Gospel and the communion of the soul with God: the first could be explained on television, the second could not. Coming down to earth, Penry Jones pointed out that it was at the level of experience that intellectual understanding became meaningful to most people: hence ABC's stress on the discussion of the Christian faith in relation to the contemporary situation.

Jones spoke for most of the programme producers; and, with some exceptions, this was the character, for good or ill, of most of the programmes: *About Religion* and *Eye Level* from ATV, *The Sunday Break* and *Living Your Life* from ABC, the Epilogues and a growing number of regional programmes. Ulster had a good idea when they produced a series called *Seven Whole Days*, illustrating what the Church was doing when it was not Sunday. In July 1960 ABC changed the format of *The Sunday Break*; perhaps mistakenly, the youth club setting was discontinued and the programme became more of a magazine, the centre of interest becoming a film illustrating some aspect of the life of the Churches at work. The accent on Youth with a capital 'Y' was not, however, lost, and it was on 26 March 1961 that viewers, critics and churchmen at all levels were electrified by *A Man Dies*, a play in a modern setting specially written for and produced by teenagers, telling the Passion Story through jive and rock music. For those who like to think in such terms, it could be described as a keynote programme in ITV religion of the early sixties.

Between July 1961 and September 1963, when the next consultation was held in Cambridge, five more companies were to come on the air, completing the network. Michael Ramsey became Archbishop of Canterbury in 1961 and John Robinson's *Honest to God* was to be published in 1963. In the meantime the consultation brought about no immediate change in the character of the religious programmes. There was a tendency on Sunday evenings towards an increasing identity of character between *The Sunday Break* and *About Religion*, a growing proportion of discussion (as opposed to drama or film) and a decrease of inhibition as to subject matter. This last characteristic – which was more marked in *The Sunday Break* – reflected the growing extent to which young people were insistently questioning long-established social and moral standards.

Perhaps the main achievement of the consultation was a collective realisation that *making Christians* was not the prime purpose of religious television. It was much more a question of communicating with what John Robinson subsequently called the 'latent church'. Additionally it underlined the growth during these years of an identity of view between the clergy and programme makers who found themselves, for a variety of reasons, thrown together in the task of supplying useful television out of scant resources. There could be no question of providing caviar to the generals. The call was for people's television which could provide some contact with Christianity for hundreds of thousands, perhaps millions, who would otherwise have no contact at all.

Part VI

ALARUMS AND EXCURSIONS

. . . more control will be needed to prevent a Gadarene descent.

> (Letter of January 1961 from Sir Kenneth Clark to Sir Harry Pilkington quoted in Report of Committee on Broadcasting, vol. II, app. E, paper 232)

36

COMMITTEE OF ENQUIRY: 1960

The 1954 Television Act had given the ITA a life of ten years. During the first five years, both it and the companies had been busy getting the system on to a practical working basis. There had been the planning and building of new stations and the recruitment of additional contractors. There had been the near debacle of the spring and summer of 1956, to say nothing of the following swift leap into exceptionally high profits with all the repercussions, both official and unofficial, to which those gave rise. Little time had been found for longer-term thinking about what was to happen when the ten years came to an end. Yet in the 1953 White Paper and during the Parliamentary debates on the 1954 Bill, it had been emphasised more than once by Government spokesmen that the plan for Independent Television was an experimental one, implying thereby that there might well be found need to modify it in the light of experience.[1]

The PMG had conceded in the Lords that there might be some sense in arranging for both the BBC Charter and the Television Act to expire together, but he was reluctant to commit his successor in eight years' time. When the obvious point was made that this successor could well be a Labour Minister, Earl Jowitt, as Opposition leader in the Lords made his memorable comment: 'This new venture may be the howling success the noble Lord opposite anticipates. If it were, no one would have the courage to touch it or would be very foolish to do so.'[2] As things turned out it was another Conservative administration that in the summer of 1960 appointed the expected committee; and, as will be seen in Volume II, the members of that body showed in the event more than enough courage to risk the charge of folly.

An opportunity for some forward thinking did offer itself to ITV early in 1959. The Television Advisory Committee (a standing committee advising the PMG on technical matters) had put forward the recommendation that British television should change over in due course from the existing 405 lines picture to the internationally more widely used 625 lines standard. This recommendation, made after two years' deliberation, was seized upon by the BBC as an opportunity for putting forward their own ideas about the future of the television services in the United Kingdom. Their management already had their eyes turned towards the expected committee of enquiry. The same could not be said about Independent Television. As early as July 1958, Chapman-Walker, by this time a director of TWW, had told a meeting of the SCC that it seemed likely that a new 'Royal Commission on Broadcasting' would be set up before the end of the year and that the BBC, so he understood, was already setting up 'elaborate machinery to prepare its evidence'. He was told by Fraser that the 'Authority had not yet considered the matter'.[3] The failure of the ITA to initiate in good time adequate preparations for an enquiry on the part of ITV as a whole was understandable in view of the break-neck rush to complete the network, but it was to have serious consequences as will be seen in the next volume.

The ITA responded to the BBC's statement to the TAC in July 1959. Whereas the Corporation had suggested for the future four television services, two BBC and two ITV, with the two new ones 'having the same character as the existing two', the ITA recommended three 'popular' services (of which two would be ITV) and a fourth specialised education one 'aiming at the satisfaction of those interested in the serious side of life'.[4] Both the suggestion for an educational channel and that for a second competitive commercial service were to reappear in the ITA's evidence to the Pilkington Committee.

In the first weeks of 1960, letters were exchanged between the Post Office and the two broadcasting authorities about the terms of reference for the new committee. By 12 January Kirkpatrick was telling Authority Members that he would shortly circulate a staff paper suggesting topics to be covered in evidence, including possible amendments to the Act. At the SCC on 10 February Fraser likewise informed the companies that the committee would probably be set up later in the year, adding that, although both the Authority itself and the companies (either collectively or individually) should be free to give evidence independently, some consultation on matters of fact would be helpful in order to avoid contradictions.[5] But it was not until 13 July that an official announcement was made in the Commons – almost five years since the first ITV programmes took to the air. Reginald Bevins,[6] who had become PMG in October 1959, informed the House that 'the Government have decided to set up a Committee of Enquiry into the future of sound and television broadcasting', and that Sir Harry Pilkington had accepted the invitation to be the Committee's chairman. On the same day

Fraser wrote to Kirkpatrick (who was on holiday in Ireland) telling him of the appointment, adding 'he enjoys the reputation of a progressive industrialist . . . he bicycles'. The *Daily Express* on the following morning described him further as 'a fresh air man' who 'plays tennis before breakfast, keeps bees and grows roses'. Sir Harry did in fact have other qualifications. Apart from the family glass business, he had been president of the Federation of British Industry and had served on official committees dealing respectively with doctors' and dentists' pay and with education for industry, and was a governor of the Bank of England.

After a week a letter from Sir Harry came to the Chairmen of both broadcasting bodies saying that he hoped the Committee would be starting work early in September and would have finished by the end of 1961. 'If you have not already done so, make a start on any submissions you may wish to make . . . I would be grateful if you could let us have a general memorandum within the next two months.' Included with the letter was a statement of the Committee's terms of reference:

To consider the future of the broadcasting services in the United Kingdom, the dissemination by wire of broadcasting and other programmes, and the possibility of television for public showing. To advise on the services which should in future be provided in the United Kingdom by the BBC and the ITA.

To recommend whether additional services should be provided by any other organisation.

To propose what financial and other conditions should apply to the conduct of all these services.

Noteworthy are both the assumption that the BBC and ITV would continue to provide broadcast services and the explicit emphasis on the future, with the present only by implication. It had been the other way round in Beveridge's terms of reference. But, historically speaking, there were two aspects of the job facing this Committee that would distinguish it from all earlier ones. The first of these – obviously – was the mere existence of the competitive television service. On the general question of competition Pilkington was known to have what might be described as a 'balanced' view. He had said in a lecture in 1958: 'Unrestrained duplication is very wasteful and the consumer pays much more for competition than he realises but competitive satisfaction of the consumer is still the best incentive.'[7] The second important difference lay in the fact that this would be the first committee of enquiry into the broadcasting services whose main preoccupation would have to be television. Whereas in January 1951, there had been 11,684,000 sound only licences and 586,000 combined sound and television ones, by December 1961 (when the Committee was in full swing) the number of combined licences had risen nearly twenty-fold to 11,658,000 and sound only ones dropped to 3,659,000. It would be hard to deny that the coming of ITV had had something to do with this change.

Predictably, therefore, the Committee was to direct the main weight of its critical attention on to the operation and organisation of commercial television. In its eventual report, the general appraisal of the BBC Television service occupied 37 paragraphs on 13 pages. General appraisal of the ITV service occupied 60 paragraphs on 17 pages, with an additional 63 paragraphs on 19 pages dealing with television advertising. On the 'constitution and organisation' of the two services, the report had 92 paragraphs on 25 pages about the BBC and 136 paragraphs on 35 pages about ITV. In this respect the Committee was accurately reflecting the attitude of the opinion formers: it was the performance of ITV on which most attention was focussed.

37

THE PREVAILING CLIMATE

When the Pilkington Committee started work in autumn 1960, the programme of Independent Television was being watched on a fairly regular basis by some two-thirds of the British viewing public, and the leader of the Labour Party had gone on public record in the 1959 election campaign with the statement 'commercial television has come to stay'.[1] But the service was not enjoying comparable approval by many of the would-be leaders or spokesmen of public opinion in Parliament, the press, or elsewhere. Far from it. In some sections of the hostile press maybe it would be possible to detect a flavour of sour grapes.[2] For example, the *Daily Express* spoke on 30 April 1960 about a 'dull routine of cowboys, crime, murders, pop singers and half-wit quiz games', and claimed that to discriminate between one programme contractor and another was to 'sort out a rubbish tip'.

Adverse opinion was by no means limited to expressions of 'dismay' at the disturbingly high profits; or to the perverse, but understandable belief that there must be something fundamentally wrong about the products as well as organisational control of a public service that was making so much money.[3] Much of the concern was expressed about the advertisements: there were too many of them, too concentrated in peak viewing hours; they were being inserted in 'unnatural' breaks; and many were, so it was said, blatantly misleading in their claims – even the ones for medical products. True, Lord Hailsham, that most fervently eloquent of the earliest opponents of Independent Television, had, on behalf of the Government of which he was by then a member, asserted during a House of Lords debate on the Television Services in June 1959 that the public were not being misled. The Government had said they would entrust the control of the advertising to the ITA and that control was being exercised. 'If the system is to work at all' it would, he said, 'be wholly inappropriate for Parliament to intervene unless there is a grave breach of the Act, which I do not think has taken place . . . Nor do I think it is likely to take place in the future with the responsible persons who are in charge of the ITA.'[4]

But others were not so sure and some of them would soon be saying as much to Pilkington. The not usually hostile *Financial Times* wrote on the day following the debate that the Act was being interpreted in a 'manner at best evasive'; and that the Authority had undermined public confidence in its willingness to keep the contractors to the terms of the Act by its eagerness to defend them against their critics. 'In fact there is clearly now good reason to review the way in which commercial television is working, and to see where and how it could be improved.'[5] The concept of a servile or pusillanimous Authority was harped on repeatedly. ITA Annual Reports were stigmatised as little more than public relations handouts. To the prejudiced journalist, politician or other 'leader of public opinion', many of whom probably saw very little, if any, television, there seemed to be something ambivalent about the behaviour of an Authority that had said in its Annual Report for 1957/8 that the programme companies were in its judgement 'duly discharging the requirement of the Television Act that there should be a proper balance in subject matter', or about its more recent claim that 'the broad pattern of programmes during the year seemed . . . to be reasonably satisfactory in its balance' (1959/60), when it was in the memory of many that in 1956 that same Authority had been saying that without the promised annual grant of £750,000 it would not be possible to achieve the programme balance required under the Act. In fact little credit was given for the efforts that were being made – and with some success – to achieve improvements in programme balance and standards of advertising, largely by force of moral persuasion. Something of the prevailing mood was perhaps reflected in a *Punch* cartoon of 6 April 1960, which was almost certainly not meant unkindly. It showed the two Directors General, Carleton Greene of the BBC and Fraser of the ITA, dressed as jockeys at a weigh-in respectively labelled 'First' and 'Second'. Fraser also had an additional burden slung from his right shoulder with the label 'Commercials Handicap Weight'.

The year 1959/60, punctuated as it was by reports of even higher soaring profits from the companies[6], was the year in which the 'conspiracy theory' of the origins of Independent Television as a financial ramp was at its height. It was the year which gave birth to the two books *Pressure Group* by the American Professor H. Wilson and *Power behind the Screen* by Clive Jenkins. There was even a curious report in the *Daily Telegraph* on 4 May 1960 by Leonard Marsland Gander that a BBC documentary producer was at work collecting evidence for a programme revealing the link-up between the men of money behind some of the ITV companies and financial interests in the United States.[7]

Such a prevailing climate of published opinion could scarcely fail to exercise considerable influence on the minds and attitudes of the men and women appointed to serve on the Pilkington Committee, to say nothing of the many organisations and individuals who gave evidence to the Committee in such abundance. 'An avalanche of submissions' as Marsland Gander described the 636 memoranda which, with other papers circulated to the Committee members, amounted in total to 852.[8]

The problem for the historian lies principally in the fact that those books, those newspaper articles and those memoranda and 'other papers' are mostly still to be found on the printed, published record. The broadcast service of television programmes and advertisements and the general public's experience of it – which were the things actually being pronounced upon – are all vanished 'snows of yesteryear'. But what was said about ITV by these published items is not necessarily the full historical truth. It is imperative to compare what was said, or written, on a number of salient issues in evidence to Pilkington by the various outside organisations and individuals, what was said on those same matters by the Committee in its report, what the companies and/or the Authority had said on them and, wherever possible and relevant, what the actual ascertainable facts were. Was it true, as more than one of the memoranda of evidence to Pilkington claimed, that the Authority was not doing the job required of it by the Act, so that Philip Purser was right when he wrote on the occasion of the ITV's fifth anniversary: 'Oh, it might have been worse, I suppose. It might also have been a hell of a sight better'?[9] Or was Fraser right when he presented the Authority's Annual Report for 1960/1 with the claim: 'There has been no Gresham's Law. There has been a law of improvement'?[10]

NOTES AND REFERENCES

PREFACE AND ACKNOWLEDGEMENTS

1. *Broadcasting* (HMSO, 1978) (Cmnd. 7294).
2. *Report of the Committee on the Future of Broadcasting* (HMSO, 1977) (Cmnd. 6753) para. 4.3.
3. Ibid. para. 13.46.
4. *Broadcasting*, p. 21.
5. *Report of the Committee on Broadcasting 1960* (HMSO) (Cmnd. 1753) para. 209.
6. Lord Windlesham, *Broadcasting in a Free Society* (Basil Blackwell, 1980) pp. 71–2.
7. B. Paulu, *British Broadcasting in Transition* (Macmillan, 1961).
8. B. Paulu, *British Broadcasting: Radio and Television in the United Kingdom* (University of Minneapolis Press, 1956).
9. P. Black, *The Mirror in the Corner: People's Television* (Hutchinson, 1972).
10. N. Swallow, *Factual Television* (Focal Press, 1966).
11. J. Gable, *The Tuppenny Punch and Judy Show* (Michael Joseph, 1980).

CHAPTER 1: BEVERIDGE

1. H. H. Wilson, *Pressure Group* (Secker and Warburg, 1961) p. 23.
2. *Report of the Broadcasting Committee 1949* (HMSO) (Cmd. 8116).
3. Ibid. pp. 201–10.

CHAPTER 2: BEYOND BEVERIDGE

1. A. Briggs, *History of Broadcasting in the United Kingdom Vol. IV Sound and Vision* (Oxford University Press, 1979) p. 424.

CHAPTER 3: WHITE PAPER: 1952

1. *Broadcasting: Memorandum on the Report of the Broadcasting Committee 1949* (HMSO) (Cmd. 8550) para. 7.
2. Ibid. para. 9.
3. House of Lords, Hansard, (HMSO) 23 and 26 May 1952.
4. House of Commons, Hansard, (HMSO) 11 June 1952.

CHAPTER 4: INTERLUDE 1952/3

1. A. Seldon, *Churchill's Indian Summer* (Hodder and Stoughton, 1981).

CHAPTER 5: WHITE PAPER: 1953

1. (HMSO) Cmd. 9005.

CHAPTER 6: FIELD DAYS IN PARLIAMENT: 1953

1. H of L 25 and 26 November 1953.
2. Lord Simon of Wythenshawe, *The BBC from Within* (Victor Gollancz, 1953) p. 283.
3. H of C 14 and 15 December 1953.

CHAPTER 7: THE TELEVISION BILL

1. Briggs, *History of Broadcasting in the United Kingdom Vol. IV* p. 937 et seq.
2. Letter to the author 22 February 1979. See also P. Black, *The Mirror in the Corner* p. 46.
3. Briggs, *History of Broadcasting in the United Kingdom Vol. IV* p. 933.
4. See A. Smith, *British Broadcasting* (David & Charles, 1974) pp. 19–20.

CHAPTER 8: PASSAGE OF THE BILL: 1954

1. H of C 25 March 1954 Col. 1459.
2. Ibid. Col. 1475.
3. H of C 4 May 1954 Col. 280.
4. H of C 11 May 1954 Col. 1027.
5. Ibid. Col. 1107.
6. H of L 1 July 1954 Col. 318.
7. H of C 29 March 1954 Col. 1736.
8. Ibid. Col. 1747.
9. Ibid. Col. 1748.
10. H of C 20 May 1954 Col. 2424.
11. Ibid. Cols 2399/400.
12. H of C 27 May 1954 Cols 687 *et seq.*
13. H of C 21 June 1954 Cols 39 *et seq.*
14. H of C 27 May 1954 Col. 693.
15. Ibid. Col. 625.
16. Ibid. Cols 713 *et seq.*
17. Ibid. Col. 733.
18. H of C 21 June 1954 Col. 90.
19. H of L 13 July 1954 Col. 967.
20. Ibid. Col. 936.
21. H of C 1 June 1954 Col. 1111.
22. H of L 20 July 1954 Cols 1204–5.
23. H of C 27 July 1954 Col. 291.
24. H of C 27 May 1954 Col. 651.
25. H of L 13 July 1954 Cols 925 and 930.

26. Ibid. Col. 926.
27. H of L 20 July 1954 Col. 1217.
28. H of C 19 May 1954 Cols 2203 *et seq.*
29. H of L 12 July 1954 Col. 811.
30. H of C 27 July 1954 Col. 316.
31. H of C 27 May 1954 Col. 726.
32. Ibid. Col. 713.

CHAPTER 9: THE FIRST AUTHORITY

1. Figure estimated by ITN, taking account of UPITN Daily Satellite Service, Eurovision and Intervision (letter to author from Don Horobin of ITN, 22 December 1980).
2. Lord Clark, *The Other Half* (John Murray, 1977) pp. 137–8.

CHAPTER 10: COMPETITION

1. ITA Annual Report and Accounts 1954/5.
2. *Financial Times* 21 September 1955.
3. ITA Paper 39(55).
4. ITA Minutes 10(54).
5. ITA Paper 11(54).
6. Sir Robert Fraser's papers held by IBA.

CHAPTER 11: THE NETWORK COMPANIES

1. ITA Paper 39(55).
2. Ibid.
3. H of C 3 November 1954 Col. 372.
4. H of C 23 November 1954 Cols 1131–88.
5. *Royal Commission on the Press* (HMSO) (Cmd. 7700) para. 615.
6. H of C 23 November 1954 Col. 1137.
7. Ibid. Col. 1147.
8. Ibid. Col. 1152.
9. Norman Collins' papers.
10. ITA Paper 39(55).
11. Fraser to D. F. S. McClean on 8 November 1954 ITA File 7002/1.
12. H of C 23 March 1954 Col. 1474.
13. Letter dated 5 November 1954 ITA File 7001/1.
14. Ibid. Letter to Fraser.
15. Ibid.
16. But not, it seems, to his Chairman. On page 143 of his book *The Other Half* Clark writes a personal account of Colston's resignation saying that he quite deliberately sought to involve the ITA in fund-raising for the Tory Party and had to be persuaded to resign by Lord De La Warr.
17. ITA Minutes 17(54).
18. Enclosures to letter from Herbert Oppenheimer & Co., the solicitors acting on behalf of the group, dated 14 September 1954 ITA File 7/8.
19. Ibid. Letter dated 5 January 1955.
20. Ibid. Letter dated 10 March 1955.

21. Ibid.
22. Letter to the Chairman of the ITA dated 2 September 1954 ITA File 7005/1.
23. H. Thomas, *With an Independent Air* (Weidenfeld and Nicolson, 1977) p. 143.
24. Ibid. p. 146.

CHAPTER 12: BIRTH OF INDEPENDENT TELEVISION NEWS

1. ITA Minutes 9(54) and ITA Minutes 13(54).
2. ITA/PCL/1st Meeting.
3. H of C 23 November 1954 Col. 1186.
4. ITA File 7000.
5. Ibid.

CHAPTER 13: THE PROGRAMME CONTRACTS

1. ITA Paper 39(55).
2. ITA Annual Report and Accounts 1957/8 pp. 8–10.

CHAPTER 15: TELEVISION HOURS

1. ITA Paper 33(55).

CHAPTER 16: THE STATUTORY COMMITTEES

1. ITA Annual Report and Accounts 1954/5 p. 8.
2. ITA Annual Report and Accounts 1955/6 pp. 20–1.
3. SCC Minutes 6(55).

CHAPTER 17: 'PROPER PROPORTIONS' OF BRITISH MATERIAL

1. The organisations were: the Association of Cinematograph and Allied Technicians, British Actors' Equity Association, Composers' Guild of Great Britain, Concert Artistes' Association, Electrical Trades Union, Film Artistes Association, Musicians' Union, National Association of Theatrical and Kine Employees, Society of Authors, League of Dramatists, Radio Writers' Association, Screen Writers' Association, Songwriters' Guild and the Variety Artistes' Association.

CHAPTER 18: LABOUR RELATIONS

1. *BBC Staff Association Bulletin* Vol. II No. 24 June 1950.
2. P. Seglow, *Trade Unionism in Television* (Saxon House, 1978) p. 30.
3. Ibid. pp. 97–9.

CHAPTER 19: THE AUTHORITY AND THE PROGRAMMES

1. ITA Paper 47(55).
2. Ibid.

3. Ibid.
4. ITA Minutes 26(55).
5. *Pilkington Report Vol. 11* Appendix E (Cmnd. 1819–1) p. 1113.
6. Lord Clark, *The Other Half* p. 147.

CHAPTER 20: GETTING READY

1. 'presented pursuant to Section 15(3) and (4) of the Television Act, 1954' pp. 1–2.
2. Thomas, *With an Independent Air* p. 157.
3. Letter dated 6 December 1954 ITA File 7001/1.
4. *Year One* (Granada) p. 3.
5. Thomas, *With an Independent Air* p. 161.
6. R. Day, *Day by Day* (William Kimber Ltd, 1975) pp. 171–91.

CHAPTER 21: PUBLICATIONS

1. ITA Paper 31(55).
2. Ibid.
3. *Fusion* (A-R's House Magazine) 19 June 1961.

CHAPTER 22: CURTAIN UP

1. ITA Minutes 37(55).
2. A. Briggs, *Governing the BBC* (British Broadcasting Corporation, 1979) p. 104.
3. TPC Minutes X8/55.
4. *History of Broadcasting in the United Kingdom Vol. IV* pp. 1000–8. Briggs seems to have taken the opportunity to register that a History of Broadcasting is not synonymous with a History of the BBC.
5. White Paper on Broadcasting: Further Memorandum on the Report of the Committee on Broadcasting 1960 (Cmnd. 1893) para. 14.

CHAPTER 23: THE LONDON AUDIENCE

1. TCPA/X10/55.
2. A. Sampson, *Anatomy of Britain Today* (Hodder and Stoughton, 1965) p. 657.
3. pp. 138–9.
4. A. Boyle, *Only the Wind Will Listen* (Hutchinson, 1972) p. 229, quoting M. A. Hamilton, *Remembering My Old Friends* (Jonathan Cape, 1944) p. 28.

CHAPTER 24: PROBLEMS OF BALANCE

1. ITA Paper 52(55).
2. Letter dated 12 December 1955 ITA File 580.

CHAPTER 25: CRISIS AT ITN

1. This reference and subsequent references in this chapter are, unless otherwise stated, to be found *passim* in ITA File 7000.

2. ITA Minutes 42(55).
3. ITA Minutes 43(55).
4. A set of ITN Minutes for this period, which had no reference number, is in ITA File 505/2.
5. R. Day, *Day by Day*, pp. 178–82.
6. Ibid. pp. 180–1.
7. The Board of A-R had announced that in their opinion the Authority should assume responsibility for the affairs of ITN. The idea that the Authority itself should be responsible for news had been canvassed during debates on the Bill. One of the most effective speeches against such a proposal had been made by Lord Layton (H of L 12 July 1954 Col. 791).

CHAPTER 26: FINANCIAL AFFAIRS

1. Pilkington Report Vol. 1 Appendix E (Cmnd. 1819) pp. 425–7.
2. ITA Paper 43(56).
3. Sir Edwin Herbert, later Lord Tangley, was a member of the board of A-R and became Deputy Chairman in 1962. He was senior partner in the firm of Sydney Morse, Solicitors, and a member of the Council of the Law Society. He was also Deputy Chairman of Broadcast Relay Service Ltd (Rediffusion Ltd). During the war he had been Director General of the Postal and Telegraph Censorship in which capacity he received his Knighthood.
4. ITA Minutes 63(56).
5. TCPA/9/56 para. 309(3).
6. ITA Minutes 65(56).
7. ITA Paper 30(57) and ITA Minutes 72(57).
8. ITA Paper 68(57).
9. Appendix to ITA Minutes 76(57).

CHAPTER 27: £750,000: THE GIFT HORSE THAT BOLTED

1. H of L 14 July 1954 Cols 1014–5.
2. ITA Annual Report and Accounts 1955/6 p. 15.
3. ITA Minutes 41(55).
4. ITA File 2008(a).
5. Ibid.
6. Lord Hill of Luton, *Both Sides of the Hill* (Heinemann, 1964) p. 171.
7. ITA File 2008(a).
8. Ibid.
9. ITA Minutes 57(56).
10. ITA Minutes 58(56).
11. H of C 11 July 1956 Col. 382.
12. Chairman's personal correspondence held at IBA.
13. ITA Minutes 60(56).
14. Chairman's personal correspondence.
15. ITA File 2008(a).
16. Ibid.
17. Ibid.
18. ITA Minutes 67(56).
19. ITA File 2008(a).
20. Ibid.

CHAPTER 28: MEN AND MONEY

1. R. Fulford, History of BET *The Sixth Decade 1946–56* (British Electric Traction, 1956) produced to mark the Diamond Jubilee of the British Electric Traction Company.
2. *Television Today* 25 September 1980.
3. C. Jenkins, *Power Behind the Screen* (McGibbon and Kee, 1961) p. 88.
4. G. E. Mingay, *Fifteen Years On The BET Group 1956–71* (British Electric Traction, 1973) p. 34.
5. pp. 447–8.
6. Black, *The Mirror in the Corner* p. 97.
7. Jenkins, *Power Behind the Screen* pp. 246–7.
8. Norman Collins' papers.
9. Black, *The Mirror in the Corner* p. 101.
10. ITA File 7003.
11. ITA Minutes 56(56).
12. Black, *The Mirror in the Corner* pp. 104–6.
13. ITA File 7066/2.
14. Black, *The Mirror in the Corner* p. 103.

CHAPTER 29: SCOTLAND, WALES AND THE SOUTH

1. ITA File 7006/1.
2. Ibid.
3. R. Braddon, *Roy Thomson of Fleet Street* (Collins, 1965) p. 230.
4. ITA File 7006/1 Letter dated 17 July 1954.
5. A fascinating and racy account of the relationship between Thomson and Coltart is given by Russell Braddon in *Roy Thomson of Fleet Street, passim*.
6. ITA Paper 44(56).
7. Letter dated 23 April 1956 ITA File 7006/1.
8. Braddon, *Roy Thomson of Fleet Street* pp. 358–9.
9. Letter to Clark dated 2 July 1956 ITA File 7006/1.
10. *Financial Times* 21 January 1957.
11. *Scotsman* 8 January 1957.
12. *Evening Despatch* 4 May 1957.
13. *Scottish Daily Mail* 19 April 1957.
14. ITA File 7006/1.
15. Clark, *The Other Half* p. 205.
16. Earlier that evening I had said to Val and Lew: 'You ought to get hold of K. for he could become a great populariser of the arts'. The idea had stuck in my mind following a conversation with Fraser some weeks previously.
17. Thomas, *With an Independent Air* p. 168.
18. Lord Derby to the author during an interview on 21 November 1979.
19. *Guardian* 11 July 1963.
20. Jack Hylton was born in Bolton and was known before the First World War as 'the singing mill-boy'.
21. Sampson, *Anatomy of Britain Today* p. 662.
22. Letter to Romney Wheeler ITA File 7007/2.
23. TWW Chairman's Statement, Directors' Report 31 December 1958.
24. Letter to Clark dated 5 February 1957 ITA File 7007/1.
25. Ibid. Letter dated 28 May 1957.

26. Ibid. Letter dated 31 May 1957.
27. Ibid. Letter to Chapman-Walker.
28. ITA Minutes 65(56).
29. ITA Minutes 79(57).
30. Taking as a guideline recommendations of an engineers' advisory committee to the PMG in 1954, the ITA planning engineers had adopted in practice three different service area contours representing different grades of service. The 'primary' service area would be the area in which viewers could receive a good or satisfactory signal with a standard aerial and receiver. In the 'secondary' service area the signal would in most cases be adequate for viewing, but no more. To receive adequate signals in the 'fringe' service area would probably require a special aerial.

Maps were produced indicating these three contours and showing the population living within each contour. Initially these maps had to be based on 'predictions' of the planning engineers, but after the transmitters came into service further surveys were carried out and revised maps with 'measured contours' were produced, and the population figures adjusted as necessary.
31. Letter to Pragnell dated 30 August 1957 ITA File 7008/1.
32. Memorandum to Kirkpatrick dated 18 February 1958 ITA File 7008/2.
33. David Wilson to the author during an interview on 30 November 1979.
34. ITA File 7008/2.
35. Ibid.
36. Letter to John Davis dated 4 October 1957 ITA File 7008/1.
37. Clive Jenkins.
38. The circumstances leading to the extension of the Southern area to include the area covered by the new transmitter at Dover will be narrated in Part I Volume II which will describe the completion of the network and the appointment of further regional companies.
39. *Daily Sketch* 1 February 1960.

CHAPTER 30: TWO OBSTACLES REMOVED

1. H of C 23 February 1955 Col. 1277.
2. ITA File 3019/1.
3. Ibid.
4. H of C 20 May 1954 Col. 2405.
5. Letter to Fraser ITA File 3019/1.
6. H of C 8 November 1955 Cols 1653–4.
7. H of C 30 November 1955 Cols 2329–30.
8. Ibid. Col. 2338.
9. *Beveridge Report* Appendix H (HMSO) (Cmd. 8117) pp. 109–10.
10. *History of Broadcasting in the United Kingdom Vol. IV* p. 607.
11. H of C 30 November 1955 Col. 2444.
12. Hill, *Both Sides of the Hill* p. 174.
13. H of C 30 November 1955 Col. 2362.
14. Ibid. Col. 2364.
15. Ibid. Col. 2368. Here, incidentally, was the classic defence of putting out party political broadcasts *simultaneously* on all channels.
16. See *Report from the Select Committee on Broadcasting (Anticipation of Debates)* (HMSO) 17 May 1956 para. 413.

17. Ibid. para. 723.
18. Ibid. Appendix 8 pp. 167–8.
19. Letter to W. A. Wolverson dated 9 November 1956 ITA File 3019/1.
20. pp. 172–4.
21. Lord Hill to the author during an interview on 16 May 1979.
22. H of L Col. 1226.
23. H of C 27 July 1954 Col. 374.
24. Ibid. Col. 378.
25. ITA Paper 70(56).
26. Hill, *Both Sides of the Hill* p. 170.
27. H of L Col. 70.
28. Ibid. Col. 90.

CHAPTER 31: PROGRAMME DEVELOPMENTS

1. *Manchester Guardian* 18 April 1956.
2. SCC Paper 80(56).
3. Special provisions for party broadcasts were eliminated from the Act of 1963.
4. 7 March 1956 ITA File 5012/1.
5. ITA Paper 29(56).
6. Briggs, *Governing the BBC* pp. 209–17.
7. Source: Television Audience Measurement Press Release dated 8 November 1956.
8. ITA File 5012/1.
9. Ibid. Letter to Brownrigg (A-R), Thomas (ABC), Meyer (ATV) and Forman (Granada) dated 6 February 1957.
10. Ibid.
11. This part of the chapter is based substantially upon a monograph by Joseph Weltman entitled *21 Years of Independent Television for Schools* published by the IBA in 1978.
12. At that time Sir John Wolfenden, who had been made Headmaster of Uppingham School at the age of twenty-eight and had had a distinguished career in peace and war, was Vice-Chancellor of Reading University.
13. The Chairman was the Rt. Revd F. A. Cockin, DD, Bishop of Bristol. It was due to his patient diplomacy that regular religious television on ITV got going with remarkable speed and no small success.
14. Now, twenty-three years later, after a distinguished career in religious broadcasting in both ITV and BBC, he is Chief Assistant (Television) at the IBA.
15. Howard Thomas's memory is at fault in his account on pp. 184–5 of *With an Independent Air*. There was no question of his having to persuade the Authority or CRAC. The whole project was approved without difficulty at the level of the Panel of Religious Advisers after I had sought, and readily obtained, approval in principle at the meeting of CRAC on 10 October 1957. The Revd Mervyn Stockwood (as he then was) was reported as saying that 'there was a large section of the younger generation – Teddy Boys and others – which was completely untouched by religious television. The problem was to reach them at all, and, in his experience, there were very few people of any denomination who had succeeded in making any real impact on them.' The Authority itself had readily agreed at its meeting on 8 October that I should seek the approval of CRAC for the project. The Children's Advisory Committee was also consulted and welcomed it. (ITA Minutes 81(57)).
16. R. Day, *A Personal Report* (Hutchinson, 1961) p. 76.

CHAPTER 32: UNACCEPTABLE PROFITABILITY

1. Third Report from the Committee of Public Accounts Session 1958/9 (HMSO) 9 July 1959. paras 105–15.
2. Committee of Public Accounts. Treasury Minute and Abstract of Appropriation Accounts Session 1959/60. (HMSO) 19 December 1959.
3. Second Report from the Committee of Public Accounts Session 1959/60 (HMSO) 12 July 1960. para. 143.
4. ITA File 2013.
5. Ibid.
6. ITA Annual Report and Accounts 1960/1 p. 46.
7. *Financial Times* 19 April 1961.
8. H of C Written Answers 27 April 1961 Col. 54.
9. H of C 6 July 1961 Col. 1681.
10. Pilkington Report Vol. 1 Appendix E Paper No. 99.
11. ITA File 8043.
12. Ibid.
13. ITA Minutes 155(62).

CHAPTER 33: THE NETWORK CARVE-UP

1. H of L 13 July 1954 Col. 912.
2. ITA Minutes 56(56).
3. ITA Minutes 58(56).
4. I am indebted to Les Thornby for these basic facts which he had recorded in 1961. I have been unable to locate the actual minutes for this period.
5. Thomas, *With an Independent Air* p. 165.
6. Ibid. p. 165 and pp. 181–2.
7. Ibid. p. 182.
8. Pilkington Report Vol. 1 Appendix E pp. 415–23.
9. Memorandum by Sir Robert Fraser dated 31 August 1962 ITA File 7066.

CHAPTER 34: THE FIRST SIX YEARS

1. IBA Lecture 29 March 1978 – *Independent Broadcasting* No. 16 p. 2.
2. Black, *The Mirror in the Corner* p. 117.
3. p. 12.
4. ITA Paper 104(55).
5. Black, *The Mirror in the Corner* p. 110.
6. p. 13.
7. H. Greene, *The Third Floor Front* (Bodley Head, 1969) p. 13.
8. Speech to the Manchester Luncheon Club, November 1960 quoted in Greene, *The Third Floor Front* p. 60.
9. B. Paulu, *British Broadcasting in Transition* pp. 219–20.

CHAPTER 35: PERSPECTIVES ON PROGRAMMES

1. *Pilkington Report Vol. 11* Appendix E pp. 851–2.
2. *Edinburgh International Festival 1979 Official Programme* p. 20.

3. Paulu, *British Broadcasting in Transition* p. v (Preface).
4. Ibid. p. 194 and pp. 219–21.
5. *Pilkington Report Vol. 1* Appendix E p. 485.
6. *The Sunday Times* of 15 February 1959. It is quoted in an excellent chapter on *This Wonderful World* in *John Grierson: A Documentary Biography* by Forsyth Hardy (Faber & Faber, 1979).
7. p. 13.
8. *21 Years of ITV: A Personal Retrospect – Independent Broadcasting* No. 9 p. 3.
9. *The Armchair Theatre* (Weidenfeld and Nicolson, 1959, for ABC Television). p. 22.
10. Lord Hill of Luton, *Behind the Screen* (Sidgwick and Jackson, 1974) p. 25.
11. Report of the ITA Consultation on Television Drama 23/24 June 1965 ITA File 225/2.
12. *The Armchair Theatre* pp. 9–15.
13. Black, *The Mirror in the Corner* pp. 142–5.
14. Paulu, *British Broadcasting in Transition* p. 135.
15. Report of the ITA Consultation on Light Entertainment and Comedy 20/1 June 1967 ITA File 225/6.
16. Paulu, *British Broadcasting in Transition* pp. 137–8.
17. Black, *The Mirror in the Corner* pp. 111–15.
18. ITA File 5004.
19. *The Times* 18 February 1959.
20. Swallow, *Factual Television* pp. 135–6.
21. Ibid. p. 158.
22. Ibid. p. 86.
23. ITA File 3049/2.
24. Letter to the author dated 16 May 1980.
25. ITA Annual Report and Accounts 1960/1 pp. 18–21.
26. Swallow, *Factual Television* pp. 187–9.
27. A. Wolstencroft to Fraser on 5 October 1960 ITA File 3006/4.
28. Paulu, *British Broadcasting in Transition* pp. 128–9.
29. *Religious Programmes on Independent Television* (Independent Television Authority, 1962) p. 14.
30. Ibid. p. 17.

CHAPTER 36: COMMITTEE OF ENQUIRY: 1960

1. 'Its methods of working, contracting for programmes and regulating advertisements would be open to revision at any time and *certainly to review* (own italics) before 1962 . . .' White Paper November 1953 (HMSO) (Cmnd. 9005).
2. H of L 12 July 1954 Cols 671–84.
3. SCC Minutes 32(58).
4. ITA Paper 99(59).
5. SCC Minutes 51(60).
6. Reginald Bevins was at the time Member for the Liverpool Toxteth Division. He came himself from a Liverpool working class background and had been for twelve years an active member of the local Labour Party.
7. Fawley Foundation Lecture, Southampton University, 6 November 1958.

CHAPTER 37: THE PREVAILING CLIMATE

1. Hugh Gaitskell reported in *Evening Standard* 1 June 1959.

2. Extract from Oral Evidence to Pilkington Committee on 29 March 1961, p. 32 ITA File 3055/1/4:

> Sir Harry Pilkington: I thought the *Daily Express* was rather critical.
> Sir Ivone Kirkpatrick: I put it in a category of its own.
> Sir Harry Pilkington: Yes, I think we would all do that.

3. Assistant PMG, Mr Kenneth Thompson: 'I can understand the dismay of the honourable gentlemen at coming across a monopoly set up by statute that makes a profit.' H of C 18 March 1959 Col. 378.
4. H of L 3 June 1959 Cols 638–9.
5. *Financial Times* 4 June 1959.
6. *Financial Times* 8 July 1960: Half-year income reported as £37.38 million, an increase of 35 per cent on previous half-year.
7. I have evidence that this investigation had BBC Board of Management approval.
8. *Daily Telegraph* 18 July 1960.
9. *Vogue* October 1960.
10. *Guardian* 2 February 1962.

Appendix 1

THE NATURE OF THE SYSTEM

EXTRACT FROM THE ITA ANNUAL REPORT, 1961/2

The structure of Independent Television created by the Authority's decisions over the years since 1955 came to virtual completion in 1961–62, and so provides an occasion for the following review of its development, and of the purposes and policies which it embodies.

Its characteristic features, and the marked differences in organisation and modes of operation that now distinguish the two television services, find practical expression in the published figures of programme production. Including in both cases acquired films, the total of all programmes supplied by Independent Television in 1961–62 was not far short of two thirds of the national total of television production – about 7,400 hours out of a total of 11,800. Its production of programmes of local interest for local use was about four-fifths of all such programmes – about 3,800 hours out of a total of 4,800. And while the BBC produced outside London about 33 per cent of its total output, Independent Television produced about 60 per cent. These Independent Television programmes came from thirteen independent companies, and will shortly come from fifteen.

In one fundamental sense, every one of these fifteen Independent Television companies is a regional company, the four largest companies no less than the remaining eleven. For each company is appointed by the Authority to provide it with programmes for a particular area, and no company has any contractual rights or duties outside its area. In the three largest areas of London, the North, and the Midlands, but not elsewhere, the programmes are provided by different companies on weekdays and at the weekends. In every area without exception, the great majority of the programmes transmitted are not produced by the local company, but are secured from other companies, and as far as possible arranged by the local company into the pattern that best suits its region, subject always to conformity with the Authority's directions in the matter of balance, quantity and quality.

In London, the Midlands and the North, where two-thirds of the population dwell, up to 75 per cent of the weekday programmes, other than generally available acquired film programmes, are produced not by the local company – that is to say, the company responsible for the supply of programmes to the Authority in that area on those days – but secured by it from other companies. In the five areas next in size (Central Scotland, South Wales and West of England, South East England, North East England and East Anglia) the proportion of outside programmes is very nearly the same. As the areas drop in size, the percentage rises. The eleven smaller companies responsible for providing programmes throughout the week tend to concentrate their own production during the weekdays. Consequently weekend programmes everywhere come very largely from the two weekend companies in London, and the North and Midlands, in roughly equal proportions. But in every area, over the whole week, dependence upon an outside supply of programmes is universal, the degree of dependence being naturally related to the size of the company.

Because of their size, access to talent, and general productive resources, the four companies in London, the Midlands, and the North are the sources of almost all the programmes which the other companies use in addition to their own local programmes. The aggregate amount of programmes produced by the other eleven companies would be amply sufficient to provide seven days of television a week without the use of any London, Midland, or Northern programmes: but since the output consists mainly of programmes of local appeal it cannot be so used.

So it comes about that the average viewer of Independent Television programmes in Scotland, Wales, Northern Ireland and the smaller English regions will in effect for the large majority of viewing hours see programmes from five independent sources – from his own company, from Associated-Rediffusion, from Associated Television, from Granada TV Network, and from ABC Television – as well as the national news bulletins and other programmes from Independent Television News. In much the greater part of the country in terms of population, he will see about as many hours produced by his local company as by any other single company.

The production of television programmes of national appeal demands large resources in the right places. It is no accident that 'networking' – the supply of programmes for national use from some central source – is a common feature of broadcasting systems of all types in all the countries of the world. The distinctive features of Independent Television are not that it has a 'network', but that the supply of the main body of national programmes is provided by four separate companies, each of the four large enough to hold its own with the other, rather than originating with a single organisation; and that outside the most populous areas, programmes are provided by eleven smaller companies rather than by the extension of the geographical responsibilities of the four large companies and the creation of no further companies at all. It could conceivably be said that, by creating the four companies, the Authority overdid things in its attachment to the principles of diversity, independence and variety of source. Effective television requires a high degree of specialisation: drama, light entertainment and variety, documentary programmes, sport, current affairs, children's programmes, religious programmes and school programmes. And specialisation in any of these fields is practicable only when production is large enough to permit it.

The Authority's simplest course would have been to appoint a single seven-day company based in London, or perhaps two companies. In that case there would have been no problem of the working arrangements between the four companies, for there would have not been four companies to make an arrangement. Similarly, if the Authority had not decided to appoint regional companies, no problem of relationship between the eleven regional companies and the four largest companies would have arisen. (In that case, the term 'networking' might never have been used, unless any programme exchange between companies were so regarded.)

However, the appointment of the limited number of companies that might have satisfied the bare requirements of the Act did not appeal. The Authority did not wish to see a company in London with overwhelmingly large resources or to rest content with less than four independent contributors to the supply of national programmes if means of making this number possible could be devised. The solution was the 'mosaic' arrangement. This was based on the expansion of the existing concept of London as the source of supply of national programmes to include Manchester and Birmingham, the division of this large central area into the three separate service areas of London, the Midlands and the North, and the creation of four companies to serve the three areas by dividing their responsibilities between weekdays and the weekend.

All this is not to say that the arrangements for the exchange of programmes which have grown up with the system as it expanded, and have generally served well during the first decade, should be carried into the second decade, since the institutions of Independent Television have become so much more diverse and mature. Indeed, in the Authority's view, they should not. The Authority thinks that new arrangements are required to permit the more flexible supply of programmes of which the system has become capable. But in the first decade the arrangements adopted made practicable the introduction of Independent Television, with less than a year's preparation, at a level of programme output *initially* greater than that reached by the older service. They encouraged the growth of production, and made possible the appointment of regional companies on a scale no one had thought possible, so adding regional television for the first time to the British television system, and creating substantial centres of regional production in Glasgow, Cardiff and Bristol, Southampton, Newcastle and Norwich, where regional companies soon achieved an output practically equal to that of any one of the four largest companies, as well as smaller centres elsewhere. In general, the arrangements formed the basis of the development of a large popular television service, relatively open and plural, consisting of fifteen broadcasting bodies of separate character, without any one of which the system would be the poorer.

It may well be that Independent Television's creation of television centres in so many cities will in due course widen still further the source of national programmes. Certainly, the new arrangements for the next decade should aim at removing all obstacles to the choice of a programme for a national audience on its merits. But it is equally important to ensure that local companies continue to place first the development of those local programmes that reflect and stimulate regional life and encourage local interests.

It was an essential feature of the original 'mosaic' that the production of programmes for the three large areas should be shared between the four companies appointed. This aim would have been frustrated if one or two of the companies had produced all the programmes while the others 'rode the network', being content to be insignificant producers themselves. Hence the Authority provided in its contracts with these companies that each must produce not less than 15 per cent of the total of programmes transmitted in its area. Here, and not, as it is sometimes thought, in the Authority's arrangements with the later companies, lay the origin of the requirements that companies should produce a minimum of 15 per cent of the programmes transmitted in their areas. In fact, the 15 per cent requirement is not always applied to the smaller companies, some of whom would find it beyond their resources.

It was an essential part of the Authority's plan that the four companies should supply one another with programmes, and enter into arrangements to that end, thus giving the viewer in any area the opportunity from the start of seeing programmes from four sources rather than one – and programmes more likely to excel in variety and originality than from any single company. The common sense of 'networking' is that all viewers see the programmes that are most likely to appeal to them; and the common sense of 'plural' networking is that four producing companies, as long as each is large enough to practise an all-round television competence, are likely to produce a better selection of programmes than one. Indeed, this combination of competitive talent is probably a main reason why Independent Television has succeeded in pleasing and interesting its audience.

In assessing any criticism of present arrangements for the supply of programmes, it must be remembered that Independent Television existed in London, the Midlands and the North for nearly two years before the fifth company, Scottish Television, came on the air. During those two years of extreme and, for a while, desperate financial strain, arrangements to maintain the service had to be made between the four companies. These arrangements had to be adequate to provide in the three areas the total number of programme hours required, and to meet the Authority's standards of quality and balance. It was at this time that fairly fixed arrangements between companies were in some cases made for programmes during the weekdays. These arrangements, a mixture of the fixed and flexible, have perhaps not surprisingly endured through the contractual period. Their value has been substantial. The restrictions they have imposed can be exaggerated. At the weekends the arrangements remained flexible. Neither of the two weekend companies was committed to take agreed quantities over long periods from the other, and the arrangements so remain, with the fruitful consequence that the smaller companies have some choice of weekend programmes.

Nevertheless, the general arrangements devised to meet the initial needs, well enough as they may have served in the first decade, are not the best that can be made from the second. Nor is the formula by which the smaller companies have secured their programmes for the main companies. This formula tends . . . to limit the production of local programmes, whether for local use or for exchange with other local companies. And the arrangements between the four main companies, devised at a time when they had to provide a full programme service from their own resources, have left them without much opportunity to test the merits of locally produced programmes on the network. The Authority explained to the Committee on Broadcasting how, in its view, new arrangements might best be devised. Broadly, they contemplate the encouragement of free competition and equal opportunity in the supply of programmes, the more open exchange of programmes of which the system is now capable and the removal of the rigidities in the system. This line of advance commends itself to the Authority, and it has reason to believe that such a development would commend itself to the programme companies.

Appendix 2

SOME CONTEMPORARY
PUBLICATIONS

Apart from transcripts of programmes, marketing reports and miscellaneous booklets published by the ITV companies (a good collection of which is held by the IBA library at 70 Brompton Road), these few years saw the publication of only a few works of substance relevant to the early history of Independent Television. By contrast, as will be evident from the foregoing pages, the progress of ITV was extensively reported and commented upon in the Press, in the proceedings of Parliament and in specialised journals and periodicals.

What follows is a list of some relevant publications of the period. A useful and wider ranging bibliography, covering a longer period, will be found in E. G. Wedell *Broadcasting and Public Policy* (Michael Joseph, 1968), Appendix IV: Notes Towards a Bibliography on Broadcasting.

ITV handbooks published annually by the ITA from 1963 onwards contain bibliographies which include publications about particular ITV programmes and series.

GENERAL

British Broadcasting: Radio and Television in the United Kingdom, Burton Paulu, 457pp. (Oxford University Press, 1956).
British Broadcasting in Transition, Burton Paulu, 250pp. (Macmillan, 1961).
Broadcasting (Sound and Television), Mary Crozier, 236pp. (Oxford University Press, 1958).
The Coming of Independent Television, Sir Robert Fraser, 35pp. (ITA, 1955).
Independent Television Authority: Annual Reports and Accounts 1954–62 (HMSO 1955–62).
Independent Television Programmes: Facts and Figures 20pp. (ITA, 1962).
Independent Television Programmes: More Facts and Figures 16pp. (ITA, 1962).
New Channels. A Report on Radio and Television, Bow Group, 56pp. (Bow Publications, 1962).
Power Behind the Screen, C. Jenkins, (McGibbon and Kee, 1961).
Pressure Group. The Campaign for Commercial Television, H. H. Wilson, 232 pp. (Secker and Warburg, 1961).
Prospects for Television (*Planning* Vol XXIV No. 427) 27pp. (Political and Economic Planning (P.E.P.), 1958).
TV: From Monopoly to Competition – and Back? Wilfred Altman, Denis Thomas and David Sawers (Hobart Paper 15) 120pp. (Institute of Economic Affairs, revised edition, July 1962).
TV, A Personal Report, R. Day, (Hutchinson, 1961).
Television in Britain (*Planning*, Vol. XXIV No. 420) 29pp. (Political and Economic Planning (P.E.P.) 1958).

The Truth About Television, (Howard Thomas, 321pp. (Weidenfeld and Nicolson, 1962).
Two Years of Independent Television, Sir Robert Fraser, 42pp. (ITA, 1957).

PERIODICALS

The following publications were devoted to television topics:

Commercial Television News (later *Audio Visual Selling*) (weekly).
Contrast. The Television Quarterly (quarterly).
International TV Technical Review (monthly).
TV Mirror (weekly).
TV Today (supplement to *The Stage*) (weekly).
Television Mail (weekly).

PROGRAMME JOURNALS

In each region a weekly publication gave details of the available Independent Television programmes together with feature material, as follows:

TV Times (separate editions for London, The Midlands, The North of England, Southern England, East Anglia, The Borders, North-East Scotland).
Channel Viewer (Channel Islands).
Look Westward (South-West England).
TV Guide (Central Scotland).
TV Post (Northern Ireland).
Television Weekly (South Wales and the West of England).
TV World (The Midlands).
The Viewer (North-East England and Central Scotland).
Wales West and North TV and *Teledu Cymru* (West and North Wales).

PROGRAMME COMPANY PUBLICATIONS

ATV: The Midlands 27pp. (Associated Television, 1962).
Anglia Television 28pp. (Anglia Television, 1961).
The Border Discovered 23pp. (Border Television, 1961).
Both Sides of the Camera: souvenir book of television programmes and the people who make them ABC Television 128pp. (Weidenfeld and Nicolson, 1960).
Formation and Management of a Television Company, based on the Seminar on Problems of Industrial Administration at the London School of Economics in December 1959, by Sidney L. Bernstein, Chairman of the Granada Group. Paper 251. 56 pp. (Granada TV Network, revised edition, 1961).
Fusion. The house magazine of Rediffusion Television (Associated-Rediffusion).
Grampian Television – North-East Scotland's own TV station 6pp. (Grampian Television, 1962).
The Local Television Service 22pp. (Anglia Television, 1961).
The New Journalism 40pp. (Independent Television News, 1962).
Southern Success 12pp.(Southern Television, 1960).
Souvenir 32pp. (Associated Television, 1958).
Spotlight on TWW ('Servant of two tongues' a report on TWW, by Mary Crozier, reprinted

from the *Guardian*, 12 October 1960; and 'What Cardiff does Today' by Alfred Francis, reprinted from *Time and Tide*, 24 September 1960).

The Thomson Organisation in Great Britain 33pp. (Scottish Television, 1960).

Visual Journalism 12pp. (Associated-Rediffusion, 1960).

Wales Today and Tomorrow A symposium of the views of members of the Welsh Board of Directors, TWW Ltd, 36pp. (TWW, 1960).

We Cover the South 29pp. (Southern Television, 1961).

ANNUAL REPORT AND ACCOUNTS

The programme companies for each ITV region, e.g. ABC Television for Midlands and North (Saturdays and Sundays), produced their own annual reports and accounts giving a summary of the year's programmes, technical developments and statement of accounts.

AUDIENCE RESEARCH AND ADVERTISING

ATV's Midlands majority 42pp. (Associated Television, 1960).

Advertising in a Free Society Ralph Harris and Arthur Seldon 216pp. (Institute of Economic Affairs, 1959).

The First Year of Commercial Television. A review 63pp. (F. C. Pritchard, Wood and Partners, 1956).

Granada Viewership Survey, January–March 1960 149pp. (Granada TV Network, 1960).

Half Decade: an Inside Story Leonard Smith 134pp. (Associated-Rediffusion, 1961).

The Londoner – explanatory manual: a study in personality and media 158pp. (Associated-Rediffusion, 1962).

The Londoner. A psychological study of the London population. Three volumes. (Associated-Rediffusion, 1962).

Marketing guide to the TWW region 87pp. (TWW, 1961).

Media and Marketing Survey of the Midlands Television Area. No. 5 April–June 1960 195pp. (Associated Television, 1960).

Notes of Guidance on Television Advertising (Initial sections) (Independent Television Companies Association, 1962).

Principles for Television Advertising 16pp. (ITA, 4th Edition, 1961).

A Survey of Londoners' Opinions on Television Advertising Magazines 44pp. (Associated-Rediffusion, 1962).

Television and the Political Image. A study of the impact of television on the 1959 General Election. Joseph Trenaman and Denis McQuail 287pp. (Methuen, 1961).

The United Kingdom: an economic study George Murray 200pp. (Associated-Rediffusion, 1962).

What Children Watch A report on a Granada survey of children's television viewing. 58pp. (Granada TV Network, 1961).

ASPECTS OF PROGRAMME DEVELOPMENT

(i) CHILDREN, SCHOOLS, EDUCATION

Children and Television Programmes The report of a joint committee set up by the BBC and ITA (Committee chairman: Miss May O'Conor) 47pp. (ITA and BBC, 1960).

E.T.V. Conference. Report on a Conference at Glasgow University. (Scottish Television, 1962).

Educational Television. Some suggestions for a fourth service 12pp. (ITA, 1961).
Educational TV: 1962 – and after 14pp. (Television Mail, 1962).
Midnight Oil A survey on a teaching-by-television experiment. 12pp. (Ulster Television, 1962).
Parents, Teachers and Television 48pp. (ITA/HMSO, 1958).
Record of a Conference on Educational Television held at the Royal Hotel, Norwich, on Saturday 6 January 1962 50pp. (ITA, 1962).
School Report: the first four years 112pp. (Associated-Rediffusion, 1961).
Television and the Child, Himmelweit, Oppenheim and Vince (Oxford University Press, 1958).
Television in Education Report of a conference held at Nottinghamshire County Training College on 21 November 1961. 50pp. (Associated Television, 1961).

(ii) POLITICAL PROGRAMMING

A First Report on Constituency Television in a General Election. The Granada 'Election Marathon' 43pp. (Granada TV Network, 1959).
Granada Goes to Rochdale. TV coverage of the Rochdale by-election, 1958 48pp. (Granada TV Network, 1958).

(iii) TELEVISION DRAMA

Anatomy of a Television Play An inquiry by John Russell Taylor into the production of Alun Owen's 'The Rose Affair' and Robert Muller's 'Afternoon of a Nymph' (ABC Armchair Theatre) 223pp. (Weidenfeld and Nicolson, 1962).
The Armchair Theatre. How to write, design, act, direct, enjoy television plays. (ABC Television) 115pp. (Weidenfeld and Nicolson, 1959).
Emergency Ward 10 A descriptive booklet on the occasion of the 500th episode. 16pp. (Associated Television, 1962).
No Hiding Place: a programme planned for success. A research report 29pp. (Associated-Rediffusion, 1962).

(iv) RELIGIOUS TELEVISION

About Religion. Five years of religious broadcasting. 26pp. (Associated Television, 1961).
Laudes Evangelii A miracle play inspired by Byzantine mosaics, the paintings of Giotto and the Canticles of thirteenth and fourteenth century Italy 26pp. (Associated-Rediffusion, 1961).
A Man Dies A dramatisation for our times of the Passion and Crucifixion. Two booklets. 10pp., 41pp., (ABC Television, 1961).
Religious programmes on Independent Television. 64pp. (ITA, 1962).

ENGINEERING AND TECHNICAL

The Authority's stations (Independent Television papers III) 32pp. (ITA, 1962).
Elstree Studio Centre 38pp. (Associated Television, 1961).
405:625 A plan for changing to 625 lines while retaining VHF transmission 19pp. (ITA, 1961).
How TV Works. The technical story for non-technical people. 48pp. (Granada TV Network/ Methuen, 1960).
Studio Five Description of proposed Wembley Rediffusion studio. 16pp. (Associated-Rediffusion, 1960).
What is a TV Centre? Description of the Granada TV centre, Manchester. 28pp. (Granada TV Network, 1960).

INDEX

LIBRARY 44848
HARROW COLLEGE OF
HIGHER EDUCATION
NORTHWICK PARK
HARROW HA1 3TP.